# THE
# TERRORS
# OF
# JUSTICE

# THE TERRORS OF JUSTICE

## The Untold Side of Watergate

## MAURICE H. STANS

Everest House
Publishers    New York

*DEDICATION*

*To Kathleen, my beloved companion for more than forty-five years, who married me for better or for worse, and took both with calm and confidence.*

# ACKNOWLEDGEMENTS

While the research for this book was almost exclusively my own work, and I am accountable for any inaccuracies or lapses in its record, I am indebted to other persons whose help brought the volume to a conclusion:

Bob Smalley, my speechwriter while I was in Commerce, who first encouraged me to write it, as part of a larger autobiography for my family. Arden Chambers Kendall, my Washington secretary, who suffered through numerous drafts, and added insights that had escaped me. Nanci Candelin, my Los Angeles secretary, who carried a heavy burden in the final production of the book.

Five persons who reviewed parts of the manuscript for fairness and accuracy and gave me their unbiased impressions: Jack Gleason, well acquainted with the Washington scene; Dick Griffith, a California hunting friend with a detached viewpoint; Byron Engle, formerly of the State Department, an objective reader; Wess Price, a neighbor and good friend; and Joe Casson, my former aide in Commerce.

Three individuals who advised me regarding difficult topics along the way: Bob Finch, former Secretary of Health, Education and Welfare; Frank Dale, publisher of the *Los Angeles Herald-Examiner*; and Bob Gray, executive vice-president of Hill & Knowlton in Washington.

Very importantly, Robert Barker, my Washington lawyer, who had lived with me through a large part of the experiences, and who painstakingly read my narrative and made suggestions for increasing its accuracy and sharpness.

And Kathleen, who patiently lived through it all and is still married to me, believe it or not.

God bless every one!

# CONTENTS

This is certainly not the last book on Watergate. But it is one of the first to tell another side of that story: the effect that Watergate justice had on the lives of innocent people caught up in the process of investigation, indictment, prosecution, and reporting.

The perpetrators of the Watergate crime, and other offenses which came to be associated with the Watergate burglary, have seen justice done. The nation itself, badly shaken by this great political scandal, has had its retribution. What has been forgotten until now, and should be entered in the record, is the terrible price of justice paid by many others who were falsely accused and often relentlessly pursued.

Richard Nixon's associates, friends, campaign workers, and campaign contributors were often subjected during the Watergate inquiries to a level of public abuse and legal harassment unprecedented in its intensity. So were many others even further removed from him. For them all, Watergate was anything but a routine criminal investigation. It became a nightmare of rumor and innuendo, of gross exaggeration and character assassination. Most painful of all for those who endured them were the persistent misrepresentations of the press, the blatant hostility of the media, the bungled, fumbling work of investigators and prosecutors. Against this background, Watergate was for many a 20th century witch-hunt, where accusation was taken for guilt and association with Richard Nixon's administration or re-election campaign was grounds for accusation.

It will probably always be argued that the cost in ruined reputations, damaged lives, and the anguish of the innocent was unavoidable in the pursuit of justice. But this reasoning cannot excuse the worst excesses of the Watergate purge. We live in a country that is always seeking to improve on its past, and it is to do justice to those who were unfairly harmed, and to prevent similar injustices in the future, that this book is written.

In another vein, I have tried to give the first comprehensive account of the way in which the 1972 Presidential candidates observed or failed to observe laws relating to campaign finance. This is an area where Watergate hatched numerous reforms, for better or worse, and the record should be set straight.

Finally, this is one man's version of the Watergate episode, and it centers necessarily on his own experiences. Undoubtedly, many things happened beyond his vision. Some events will appear different from the same events told in other accounts, or from other viewpoints, and no claim is made that this book is a total history of one of the most complex and momentous political developments of our time. Furthermore, a full account of damages done the innocent will not be known until many who were trampled in the excited atmosphere of 1972-1975 have told their story, too.


Maurice H. Stans

# ONE

## WATERGATE—A BALANCE SHEET

# 1

## A TIME OF JUSTICE, BUT . . .

Charles Dickens, had he been around to write about Watergate, probably would have started his account with: "It was a time of justice, it was a time of injustice."

How did it happen that way?

On June 17, 1972, five burglars were arrested in the premises of the Democratic National Committee in the Watergate office building in Washington. Two years and seven weeks later, on August 9, 1974, the President of the United States abdicated his high position and went into self-imposed exile.

Even Dickens would have had difficulty making a tale of politics and crime out of two such disparate events. Had he chronicled this era, however, he would not have failed to perceive the glaring contrast of justice and injustice that sprang from the relentless and unprecedented search for wrongdoers, as the one event led astonishingly to the other.

The main elements of Watergate were simple: an illegal intrusion into an opposing political party headquarters on a mission still not clearly defined; a coverup to prevent its affecting the results of a Presidential election; payments to the burglars either to sustain them or to influence their explanations; talk of executive clemency; untruths by a President as to his knowledge of events; and tape recordings that condemned the President in his own voice.

When all this became known, the persons guilty of the burglary and the coverup were sent to prison and the President resigned.

It did not end there.

Three former members of the President's Cabinet, a United States Senator, a Lieutenant Governor of a major state, a former Assistant Attorney General, several reputable lawyers, and some businessmen were put through the ordeal of court trials on unrelated matters, which ended by establishing nothing but their innocence. A member of the House of Representatives, a close personal friend of the President, an Attorney General, a Federal judge, a Secretary of Agriculture, two brothers of the President, and large groups of businessmen, contributors, and workers were pursued, maligned, or persecuted on suspicion, hearsay, or trivia, in varying degrees and in a variety of ways that in the end added little or nothing to the cause of justice.

What led to these consequences?

The early stages of Watergate set in motion forces adversary to the Administration—politicians of the opposing party in an election year, long unfriendly elements of the media, and eager public interest organizations—which saw a way to undercut the re-election candidacy of Richard Nixon. They did not succeed in that but, as disclosures grew, there gradually arose a tidal wave of national recrimination that eventually outpaced the significance of the misdeeds. The break-in at the Democratic headquarters was a crime, but a very minor one except for the political repercussions that followed it; in a non-political setting it would have been unnoticed by the American public. The payoffs and lies were more serious, but not so much as to require a modern-day witch-hunt. Yet, because Watergate involved people in high places whose behavior had not fulfilled the public's expectations of high-mindedness, it mushroomed into a national extravaganza and preoccupation reaching in every direction. Eventually, the disturbing fact became known that a President of the United States, in the course of defending his subordinates, had knowledge of and participated in the coverup, and then denied it, and this was repugnant to the American people. Before the end came, Watergate had shocked the world, shaken the nation, greatly weakened a political party, ended a national Administration, deposed a President, and ruined the lives of public servants otherwise creditable.

It did one thing more. It carried along in its riptide many persons whose only fault was being around.

How did matters get so far out of control?

In the pursuit of justice and truth, zeal led to overstatement and overreaction. Eagerness to investigate, eagerness to prosecute, eagerness to get the story to the public, and eagerness to gain advantage by attack, increasingly influenced the actions of the government's investigators, prosecutors, and politicians, and the attentions of public interest organizations and the media. The competition between and among these forces led to excesses, and the excesses led to harm to persons not culpable. In the wide swings at the presumed guilty, innocent victims were brought down. Justice for the culprits became terror for the innocent.

During the chase no one took time to consider the cruel impact of these excesses. A busy public, spoonfed by blaring headlines and terse over-the-air commentators, took their daily Watergate with little time for searching second thoughts, and accepted the gospel from Washington as it was cast into a single formula—Richard Nixon was corrupt and the men around him were corrupt, with no redeeming virtues. The complacent populace, as de Tocqueville once perceived might happen in a democracy, adopted this one tendered formula—of unequivocal corruption in the White House—and thereafter allowed anyone connected even remotely with Richard Nixon to be overwhelmed.

Thus it was that a foolish crime that itself would have been of little real impact on the nation, arrogant though the coverup was, became enlarged into a cause celebre of national politics. Thus it was that the scope expanded to include many transactions and individuals far removed from Watergate. Thus it was that a combination of opportunistic politicians, an aggressive and hostile media, ambitious prosecutors, and organized "public interest" groups was strong enough to bring down Richard Nixon's Presidency. He may have had it coming to him, but his downfall was made absolute, with little recognition that he had ever done anything right. At the same time, the formula did not allow for any doubts about the tactics used by those who brought him down, or how they impinged on other lives or may have encouraged overkill.

Nixon's adversaries perpetrated excesses that destroyed or injured reputations and lives of helpless bystanders, and maligned institutions essential to common security, in a grand sweep of hostility and hypocrisy. The price the nation paid for Watergate thereby grew out of all proportion to the improprieties involved.

Throughout the long drama, the Watergate affair was presented to the public as a simple case of good guys versus bad guys.

That is the way the media pictured it to the American citizen, and the books and stories so far produced have harped on the same theme. Watergate was a crime of large proportions, the guilty were eventually found out, the innocent were cleared, and once again American justice triumphed.

Right?

Bob Haldeman says so in his book, *The Ends of Power*, in which he calls Watergate "the only major political scandal in history in which not one of those who brought it about was personally benefited by it in any way—and no one other that those who brought it about was personally hurt by it in any way."[1] Ray Price, in his *With Nixon*, repeats the same theme: "Watergate is probably unique among major political scandals—no one got hurt except the perpetrators."[2]

Wrong. All wrong.

It's hard to imagine where Haldeman and Price were looking. Sadly, it wasn't that way at all. In the frenzy of the Washington witch-hunt that followed the petty burglary and the clumsy efforts to hide its meaning, a lot of things were awry. Not only were innocent people accused, their credibility ruined, and their lives distorted, but investigators went rampant and news reporters went wild. From rumors, suppositions, and innuendoes came careless swipes at the reputations of reputable persons. News leaks, sometimes true and sometimes false, were common, even from the supposedly secure walls of grand jury rooms, prosecu-

---

1.  H.R. Haldeman, *The Ends of Power*, (New York: New York Times Books, 1978), p. 319.
2.  Raymond Price, *With Nixon*, (New York: Viking Press, 1977), p. 369.

tors' offices, and Congressional committees. Libel and slander were frequently expressed with impunity. Indictments sometimes occurred on meager evidence, with the prosecutors passing the buck to the trial juries. Grand juries became rubber stamps for eager prosecutors. Prosecutions were bungled. Rights were trampled by judges and by investigating committees. And in the end the prosecutors, the politicians, and the media walked away from the destruction, claiming credit for outstanding service to the nation with not even a word of sympathy or consolation for the many they had undeservingly harmed.

The untold story of Watergate is one of mingled tragedy and justice.

Watergate wasn't the first witch-hunt in American history, or the first time that hysteria overcame reason. The famous witch trials in Salem Town in 1692 saw twenty people ultimately killed and two hundred jailed, their only crime being that some citizen "cried out upon them." The judiciary collapsed under public pressure and were swept along with the mob for almost a year until the Governor called a halt to the frenzy, and sense again returned to the community.

Justice in the old West often bypassed formality and began with a rope. Race lynchings, summary punishment, and mob violence have at times been black marks on the nation's record. By the twentieth century, it appeared that the society had outgrown these excesses, until the McCarthy episode of the 1950's presented a spectacle that outraged our sense of fairness and due process.

Watergate was in most respects a vastly greater and more far-reaching inquisition than anything that had gone before. It was another Salem Town, at least in the perception of anyone close to the scene or caught in the line of fire. Motives of accusers varied, from the town criers of the press and the networks who wanted to report what was being said and done, to the politicians who saw an opportunity for partisan advantage, to news hawks who felt a competitive challenge and met it by getting ahead of the news, to prosecutors who envisioned the fame and glory of bringing down big targets, to rumormongers and scavengers who delighted in the discomfiture of others or saw a way to gain something for themselves.

Watergate got to the point where no charge was unbelievable or unrepeatable.

Any suspicion about a person was reiterated with a visible smirk or snide observation or cynical remark. The presumption of innocence was abandoned; accusation was accepted as conviction. Repetition from one media to the other, and back again, made each charge into fact. The eager probers accepted remote assumptions on hearsay or circumstance, and reported these assumptions as proven disclosures from undisclosed sources. In contrast to Salem, hanging and stoning were symbolic, aimed at reputations rather than physical bodies, but they were equally destructive. The accused were not put in the stocks but were subjected to public harassment and derision, leaving them with an uphill fight to clear themselves.

There was one big difference, of course, between Salem and Watergate.

There was guilt and there were crimes in Watergate, notwithstanding that they were exaggerated because of the importance of the people involved. There was formal process of law, with legal indictments, trials by jury, and rules of evidence. There were some verdicts of guilty and some of innocent, and they were publicized so the nation could know the course of justice. But to many of the innocent, those within the circle of suspicion, there was much in common with Salem.

For the hunters, it was an exciting sport.

Somehow, in the enthusiasm of the pursuit, it got out of control, and no one gave much thought to whether the bounds of fairness were being violated by taking too much for granted, or by relying on the premise that public figures were fair game and little people were expendable, or that the ultimate ends of justice would justify the means. The central idea seemed to be that if everyone was swept into the bright spotlight of the coliseum, those who were not guilty might yet escape, and the terrors they had to suffer would be a small price to pay for identifying those who had violated society's code.

The chase was not confined to major White House and campaign figures.

Thousands of others were embroiled. Secretaries, aides, office clerks, campaign workers, money raisers, contributors, even messengers, all were targets of opportunity for the hunters, perhaps to implicate them but, better still, to get them to drop some word that would implicate others higher up. For them, the harassment was endless, and for many it was the worst experience of their lives.

The impact on the hunted was manifest in many ways, some proper, some not so. Interviews by FBI agents in offices and at home. Quizzing by Federal attorneys and Internal Revenue agents. Testimony before grand juries and investigative hearings. Repeated caustic questions in civil suit depositions. Testimony in court trials of one-time friends. Stakeouts of reporters and cameramen on front lawns. Pictures and tales on television, coming and going, morning and night. News accounts daily of the slightest and most irrelevant nature. Inability to talk to friends under investigation. Frequent dealings with lawyers, friend and foe. Subpoenas and depositions, one after another. And from all this activity friends became suspicious. Querulous glances from family members. Social ostracism. Wondering when the next blow would strike, at whom, where it would lead, and how and when the whole thing would come to an end.

The harassment and suspicion and fear continued long after Watergate subsided as an issue.

Innocent employees in the Washington office of the Nixon campaign were cruelly discriminated against when they sought other employment. A number of worthy individuals lost government appointments for which they were highly qualified because news stories at one time or another had inferred improprieties, without substance.

In the Roman circus atmosphere of the time, the violations of principle and fairness were many.

Watergate was so stretched out, so complex, so technical, and so full of legal obscurities, that the ordinary citizen just could not see the forest for the trees. The populace was caught up in the excitement, willing to accept scapegoats, but without the capacity to evaluate all the issues at hand, or to know what was going on. As a result, they were not repelled by the tactics employed, and were not aware of the dangerous implications of many actions, such as the following:

A United States Senator, using a party-written handout and

with no personal knowledge whatever, makes a vitriolic, unfounded speech on the floor of the Senate, where he is protected against suit, accusing a campaign official of "felonious" actions.

A Senate Committee chairman, in hearings designed to improve the laws, becomes prosecutor and judge of witnesses brought before him, denouncing those he considers guilty, without waiting for the evidence to be added up.

In the same hearings, staff attorneys use sharp tactics, interviewing witnesses in depth privately, then putting them under oath on national television and opening with insinuating questions not previously discussed, to cause the victims discomfort and embarrassment as they fumble for quick answers.

Another Senator, so ignorant of the facts that he has to read a statement prepared for him, blocks the appointment of a competent nominee for an ambassadorship by asserting charges of improper conduct that are never proved.

A Congressman running for a seat in the Senate is defeated handily by publicized charges, likewise never proved, that he had a hand in the "sale" of an ambassadorship.

Two investigative reporters for a Washington paper, in collusion with their superiors, illegally attempt to break the sacred privacy of grand jury deliberations to obtain secret testimony.

Editorial writers for newspapers and news magazines assign guilt to individuals on the basis of unverified news reports, forgetting entirely the historic presumption of innocence in our country.

Publishers refuse to retract misinformation even when confronted with the truth.

An attorney for a public interest group entertains a cocktail party by playing for them White House tapes entrusted to him by a Federal court for privileged examination.

Another public interest organization falsely and indiscriminately accuses political contributors of having no motive other than to buy government favors, and parlays its well-publicized accusations into an increase in its dues-paying membership.

An eager state prosecutor in Florida seeks to achieve fame by intervening in the Watergate legal processes and harassing individuals who wander into his jurisdiction.

A federal prosecutor in New York allows his ambitious young assistants to steal a march on Washington by bringing to trial two former Cabinet members on conspiracy and corruption charges, in the expectation that, since they are presumptively guilty in Watergate, the evidence needed for conviction on their charges will be found somewhere, somehow.

Washington prosecutors, fearful of media criticism, bring individuals to judgment in the courts by coercing them into guilty pleas, only to have sympathetic judges suspend sentences.

Federal prosecutors lose convictions by refusing defendants the opportunity of adequate legal counsel or by withholding evidence helpful to their defense.

A Federal judge in Washington imposes a near-lifetime sentence on a person convicted of a petty burglary because he insists on his constitutional right to silence in his own trial and refuses under a grant of limited immunity to testify about others.

The same judge falsely accuses an innocent witness in public of lying in his testimony.

A prosecutor in Washington accuses a former Cabinet officer of having regularly engaged in illegal political activity while in government, on the sole evidence of a witness whose incorrect assumptions could easily have been checked and corrected in advance.

A pliant and gullible Congress enacts a reduction in the period of the statute of limitations for campaign offenses, not being told that the main purpose of its sponsors is to absolve a high Democrat from willful violations that could have sent him to prison.

Serious 1972 infractions of the election financing law by Democratic candidates are ignored, while less significant and unintentional transgressions by Nixon money raisers are brought to court.

There were many more.

Does this summation exaggerate what happened?

I don't believe so. Names, dates, and circumstances are recounted in these pages, but no one can ever know all the travails that Watergate brought to the undeserving. This book capsulizes the experience of many persons. My own are added in depth because they show just how far things could go and how much needless suffering could result. I have tried as honestly as I can to be objective in this introduction and what follows so that the country can know and avoid a recurrence of these terrors of justice.

To bring into perspective the aggregates of guilt and innocence as they developed, it is time to look at a balance sheet of Watergate—the justice and the injustice. The convictions for guilt have been well publicized. What about the other side of the ledger?

The persons ultimately held by the courts to have been responsible for Watergate are well known and need merely be listed for purposes of this accounting. Divided into two groups for the two phases—the break-in of Democratic headquarters and the coverup payments to the burglary team—they were:

> *The burglary:* The four "Cubans" (Bernard L. Barker, Virgilio R. Gonzalez, Eugenio R. Martinez, and Frank S. Sturgis); former CIA agents E. Howard Hunt and James W. McCord, Jr.; and former FBI agent G. Gordon Liddy.
>
> *The coverup:* Former Attorney General John N. Mitchell; former Presidential aides Harry R. Haldeman, John D. Ehrlichman, and John W. Dean III; and campaign staffers Jeb S. Magruder, Fred C. LaRue, and Herbert L. Porter.

The burglars were relatively small fry, and their crime a not very sensible and wholly profitless escapade, with no money or valuables involved, for which their punishment for a first offense normally would have been a suspended sentence and a lecture from the bench. Sensing bigger stakes, Federal Judge John J. Sirica handed out outrageous "provisional" prison terms of thirty-five years to Hunt, twenty years and a huge fine to Liddy, and forty years to the others, promising reductions if they would talk. All were later reduced, with Liddy serving the longest because he kept silent. The coverup, a serious conspiracy to keep the petty venture from being exposed, had an imposing list of participants, unparalleled in the nation's history in their relationship to the center of power. Their sentences were much lighter than those originally received by the burglars.

Every one of these fourteen individuals served out his term until released or paroled. No one except those convicted argues very strongly against the quality of justice dispensed. The Cubans, for example, contend that they engaged trustingly in the project believing, from previous involvement with Hunt and others, that they were working on a matter of national security for the White House.

Overriding what happened to all of them was the fate of Richard Nixon. Charged by a grand jury with being an unindicted co-conspirator in the Watergate coverup, and named for impeachment on three articles by the House Judiciary Committee, Nixon never came to trial on either one. His resignation of the Presidency disposed of the impeachment issue, and his pardon by President Gerald Ford obviated any criminal action. In the absence of full evidentiary proceedings under due process, no one but Richard Nixon knows the total story of his actions, although his own book[3] gives his defense to these charges.

The only fact essential to the present analysis is that a President with a good record until then, on balance, and a high scale of public approval, was forced into an abdication of the world's highest political office, certainly a high price for him and the nation to pay.

That is one side of the Watergate balance sheet.

## Extensions of Watergate

But that is not the whole range of the Watergate justice. Much more was embraced in the hunt as time went on. Had the improprieties all come to light within a few weeks, they would have had little of the explosive and far-reaching qualities they achieved. The gradualness of the disclosures, extending over almost three years, contributed to the frenzy of political and journalistic interest that not only accentuated every new discovery but brought into the orbit of charge and investigation a host of topics that were wholly unrelated to Watergate. Some were sensible, many were not. In the atmosphere of suspicion and distrust that accompanied them, fed by an immense eagerness in some quarters to prove the worst in as many fellow men as possible, the legal orbit expanded to include allegations of (1) a burglary of the office of Dr. Lewis Fielding, psychiatrist to Daniel Ellsberg, (2) fraud in the preparation of Nixon's personal income tax returns, (3) illegal campaign practices, (4) purported impro-

---

3. *RN: The Memoirs of Richard Nixon* (New York: Grosset & Dunlap, 1978).

prieties by ITT and government officials in connection with the settlement of an antitrust suit, (5) dairy industry bribery of government officials, (6) the sale of government favors (including ambassadorships), (7) campaign financing violations, and literally dozens of other founded and unfounded charges. Despite their lack of direct connection to Watergate, their concurrence in timing caused them to be popularly identified as Watergate-related transgressions. Watergate became an umbrella for any and all accusations that could be dreamed up against the Nixon Administration. In the passionate deire to expose Nixon and his organization, the critics expanded both the length and breadth of the attack. In the one dimension, especially in campaign financing, it ranged as far back as 1970 and 1968, and as far forward as 1974. In the other dimension, it embraced matters as far remote as a presidential election in Chile.

Beyond all this, there were some additional dramas in other off-Watergate theaters. In a slightly later time sequence, there opened up two particular avenues of outcry and finger-pointing that occupied headlines for months—the undercover activities of the country's intelligence agencies, and the outlays of "sensitive" payments by American corporations to secure overseas business. Wholly unrelated to Watergate, except by those who wanted to make extra points about the "corruption of business" or the "improprieties of the CIA and the FBI," the pluses and minuses of these topics are not within the compass of the Watergate balance sheet. Considering the heavy price paid and to be paid by the country for these disclosures, a similar analysis might well be worthwhile in time after the bottom line is more clearly visible and measurable.

Now that the storm of words has settled, here is an account of the final legal outcome of the first six of the incidental Watergate-identified concerns; the seventh, being more complex, is dealt with in Chapter 2. The others produced nothing and are not worthy of attention.

## The Fielding Break-in

The burglary of the office of Daniel Ellsberg's psychiatrist in September 1971 became a cause celebre because it had been perpetrated by some of the same persons who later planned the Watergate entry. Ellsberg, an anti-war activist during the Vietnam era, was a former Pentagon employee who had stolen classified (top secret) military and intelligence records in 1971 and released them to the *New York Times* for publication, an act bitterly resented by the White House as a breach of the national security. In its zeal to make an example of Ellsberg, the administration allowed some illicit tactics to be employed, including this unsuccessful encroachment on his medical records, which was an attempt to establish that he was an unstable character. Actual convictions for the planning and burglary were White House aides Charles W. Colson, Egil Krogh, Jr., and John D. Ehrlichman; Cubans Bernard L. Barker and Eugenio R. Martinez; and G. Gordon Liddy. Colson, Krogh, Ehrlichman, and Liddy were given sentences of imprisonment for their part in this illegal entry, and the two Cubans were given suspended sentences. Except for Colson—who had been indicted in the Watergate coverup case but released from that charge when he pleaded guilty to the Fielding break-in—and Krogh, these persons had all been found culpable in and sentenced for Watergate.

Unfortunately, the disclosure of this escapade prevented a conclusion of Ellsberg's trial. It was stopped in mid-course and the case was dismissed for government misconduct, the judge citing the Fielding burglary and the prosecution's failure to produce data on electronic surveillance, just when it appeared that Ellsberg was headed for certain imprisonment for his outrageous transgression against the security of the nation.

## Income Tax Fraud

Three persons were indicted on charges that they had conspired illegally in the preparation of Nixon's Federal income tax return for 1969. The substance was that documents supporting a deduction for the value of his public papers given to the National Archives early in 1969 had actually been prepared in 1970 and back-dated. One defendant, White House aide Edward L. Morgan, pleaded guilty and received a prison sentence; the second, Ralph G. Newman, a reputable Chicago book dealer and appraiser, was found guilty by a jury and was fined $10,000; and the charges against the third, attorney Frank deMarco, Jr., of Los Angeles, were dismissed by the court when it was found that the government had withheld evidence that might have been helpful to his defense.

## Illegal Campaign Practices

Despite allegations of massive corrupt practices in the tactics of the Nixon 1972 Presidential campaign, most turned out to be common political "dirty tricks" of a style well established in earlier years by a Democratic loyalist named Dick Tuck—misdirecting audiences to meetings, blocking traffic en route to rallies, and ordering bundles of unneeded sandwiches to be sent to the opposition, C.O.D.  There were three convictions for somewhat more notable actions:

> Donald Segretti, a young California lawyer: on three counts of
>     distributing illegal campaign literature.
> George A. Hearing, of Florida: on two counts of fabricating
>     and distributing illegal campaign literature.
> Dwight Chapin, a former White House aide: for twice denying
>     under oath to a grand jury that he knew about the Segretti
>     tactics.

Segretti, Hearing, and Chapin all received and served prison sentences.

There was some lesser chicanery on the part of Democratic supporters that went unnoticed.  There were also possibly a few acts of a criminal kind, such as the fire-bombing of a Republican state committee office in Arizona. Other Nixon campaign centers were destroyed by arsonists or burglarized, disfigured by graffiti, or their contents destroyed or damaged.  Even the office of Nixon's personal physician was broken into and the medical files strewn about.  No one was ever apprehended for any of these occurrences.

## The ITT Case

The ITT investigation was a "much ado about little" affair that covered allegations of wrongdoing so wide-ranging and "extraordinarily numerous," originating in a variety of ways, that they almost had the character of a sweeping public "get ITT" campaign. None of them related to Watergate even indirectly. After quite a few man years of diligent effort by the Special Prosecutor's staff, most of them came to naught. Although there were two convictions, one was set aside by the courts on appeal and one resulted in a nominal suspended sentence. The other issues were dropped as not justifying prosecution.

The original charge was that the company had offered in 1971 to pay a large sum (usually named at $400,000), for expenses of the 1972 Republican convention in San Diego, in return for unwarranted government leniency in the settlement of three antitrust cases that had been pending against the company since 1969. As the investigation progressed, it was augmented by inquiries into other topics, including (1) whether any witnesses in the 1972 confirmation hearing of Richard Kleindienst for Attorney General had committed perjury with respect to ITT matters, (2) whether there was obstruction of the Securities and Exchange Commission by failure of ITT to produce certain documents requested by that agency, (3) whether there was criminal action in October 1972 by the SEC in turning over to the Department of Justice certain ITT documents requested by a House subcommittee, (4) whether G. Bradford Cook, former head of the SEC, should be charged with perjury for certain testimony before the Senate Appropriations Committee, (5) whether any government official had improperly been influenced by ITT or had granted favors to ITT, (6) whether certain income tax rulings secured by ITT had been the product of improper influence, (7) whether ITT or its officials were guilty of fraud on the government or perjury by mispresenting the facts regarding a transfer of certain stock to qualify for a tax ruling, (8) whether ITT had improperly influenced the Insurance Commissioner of Connecticut to give a favorable ruling on a merger, (9) whether ITT officers had given perjured testimony about alleged activities in a Presidential election in Chile in 1970-71, and several tangential issues. Widespread attention was paid to these allegations by the media and the Congress, with the result that the company was widely suspected of mass corruption.

Not much resulted.

The contribution in question was never made; it apparently turned out to be not $400,000 but $100,000, and not from ITT but from a subsidiary owning a hotel in San Diego that was willing to join with other business interests in the usual process of subsidizing a national convention. It would not have gone to any Republican hands but to a local tourist and convention bureau, and it had lapsed when the convention was moved to Miami Beach.

The final report of the ITT task force of the Special Prosecutor on August 25, 1975, concluded that, insofar as the settlement of the antitrust cases was concerned, "we never established that any of these actions were criminal," and "none of the documents, either by specific statement or implication, provided evidence tying the settlement to the convention pledge." Furthermore, "none [of the documents] were evidentiary of a fix of the antitrust cases." This after examining carefully the conduct of twenty-two company and government officials.[4]

As for the SEC's action of turning over records to the Department of Justice, the prosecutor's report stated that "we believe that there was no basis to charge anyone with a crime for the transfer of the documents . . . . It seemed unjustified and unwarranted to proceed with a criminal case on the theory that it was illegal not to turn over material in an investigatory file to a Congressional Committee. Such a principle is both wrong legally and, if attempted, would create a dangerous precedent." As for whether ITT improperly influenced the IRS, "there was no evidence that the rulings were in any way influenced by pressure from outside the IRS, or that the individuals responsible for them were subjected to pressure to reach any result." As to the questioned security transaction, "We concluded that there was no criminal case which we could file in this area, either against ITT or any individuals; . . . we did not find a prosecutable case against anyone." As for illegal intervention in Chile, "there seemed insufficient basis for a criminal case to warrant generally investigating ITT's actions in Chile."[5] As for G. Bradford Cook, "we recommend that prosecution in this case be declined." As to other specified government officials, "what was never established is that the efforts of these administration officials [in assisting ITT] were related to any illegal consideration," and "we generally failed to show that there was any illegal consideration given to administration officials for their assistance to ITT." As for the handling of the SEC's actions regarding ITT, "there is no indication that the

---

4. The Senate Judiciary Committee, in the hearings in 1972 on Kleindienst's confirmation, had reached the same result; it concluded that the settlement "was on the merits after arm's length negotiations" and was "not the product of political influence."
5. In 1978, nevertheless, the Department of Justice got indictments against two ITT officials for perjury in this matter.

result was improperly influenced by any force outside the agency."

All of these issues thereby evaporated except two. Edwin Reinecke, Lieutenant Governor of California, was indicted on three counts of perjury allegedly for having misstated his knowledge of the convention matter to a grand jury, and was found guilty on one count, but later won final acquittal upon appeal. Richard Kleindienst, former Attorney General, pleaded guilty to one misdemeanor for not testifying fully on one topic in the course of his 1972 confirmation hearing, and received a suspended sentence.

The other subjects were quietly dropped after the company and its officers had been held hostage for many months. While these various inquisitions might, if successful, have brought deserved discredit to the company and penalties to its officers, it is almost certain that the real target of attack was the Nixon Administration.

## Milk Fund

The "milk fund" investigation was based on suspicions and civil litigation contending that Nixon officials raised support prices to farmers on dairy products in 1971 beyond a proper level, in a direct deal for a promised $2 million in campaign contributions from the dairy industry. The charge was never proved, no one was indicted, and the investigation evaporated. The Watergate Special Prosecutor, after long deliberation, concluded that prosecution should not be undertaken because of "the absence of viable defendants and a lack of clear criminality." The civil suit produced only one notable result—the titillation of guests at a fashionable Washington cocktail party by the wholly improper playing of some White House tapes by William Dobrovir, one of the public interest lawyers pursuing the litigation; the tapes had been entrusted to him by the court for study, but, strangely, there was no prosecution and little criticism for this obvious and inexcusable breach of court propriety.

The milk industry did find itself in considerable trouble in another respect, however, as a result of widespread political contributions over a period of years, some illegal and illegally covered up, by large dairy cooperative organizations. There were some prosecutions of one large cooperative, and its officials and agents; and one prosecution of a campaign official for Hubert Humphrey for willfully concealing the source of its contributions to his 1970 campaign (see page 29).

## Sale of Government Favors

One facet of the contentions of corruption in Nixon's 1972 campaign was that contributions were solicited and received, in one manner or another, as a quid pro quo for government favors or in response to a variety of processes of extortion and coercion. The range of accusations was as broad as the imagination of the accusers, and a long while had to ensue before the dust settled and the real truth emerged. In the excitement of the hunt, it was impossible for campaign finance officials to take the time to answer each aberrant insinuation, and denials that were made did not get the prominence of the original attacks.

The charges did not always imply actions that would have been illegal. Many were designed to insinuate a sleaziness of conduct on the part of the money-raisers. Thus the stories ranged from reports, stated with varying degrees of certainty, that the Nixon campaign had received stratospheric gifts (usually stated in millions of dollars) from the Shah of Iran, or from unnamed Arabs, or from unidentified sources in South America, or from wealthy Frenchmen; that its solicitors had secured lists of companies in trouble with the IRS, the SEC, regulatory commissions, or other government agencies, and by extortion or promises of relief exacted large sums from them; that money was received in return for promised government contracts or favorable rulings on pending contract disputes; that income tax or antitrust or claim settlements were fixed; that government jobs, particularly posts as ambassador to other countries, were sold (one report even presumed to name the specific prices being asked for various countries); that word was passed that contributions should be made in currency to cover up any quid pro quo dealings; that money was illegally accepted from foreign citizens; that improper contributions received were "laundered" by the money-raisers in foreign countries to conceal the identities of the sources; that contributions were solicited improperly by government officials or on government property; and that an "enemy list" was kept of persons refusing to contribute, so that retaliation by the administration could come later; and to accusations that the laws on illicit dealings had been willfully circumvented and violated in a host of other ways.

Every bit of this turned out to be pure fiction, absolute hogwash. The Watergate Special Prosecutor investigated "several hundred" such accusations, through thousands of interviews and subpoenas for thousands of documents, using his own organization, the Internal Revenue Service, the FBI, the computerized records of data gathered by the Senate Watergate Committee, and information from members of Congress. After two years of ferreting out the facts, he announced in his final report that he could not find evidence adequate to take to court a single instance within this entire range of alleged corrupt practices.

Insofar as the Nixon money-raising in 1972 was concerned, there were only a handful of nonwillful technical violations, and these were less significant individually and in the aggregate than similar oversights and violations by a number of other candidates who were not prosecuted.

That was the surviving sum and substance of all of the alleged financial corruption in the 1972 Nixon campaign. Not a single proven case of corrupt action. No favors granted. No contracts awarded. No cases fixed. No ambassadorships sold. No illegal contributions from foreigners. No overseas laundries. No illegal solicitations. No list of companies in trouble with the government. No enemy lists. No fund-raising by government officials. No extortion or coercion. No intentional circumvention of the law in a single instance. That is precisely what the Department of Justice, the Special Prosecutor, and the courts found.[6]

---

6. To avoid possible challenges of inaccuracy in this litany, a few delineations should be made. Herbert Kalmbach pleaded guilty to participating as a conduit in the sale of an ambassadorship, but this occurred in 1970, well before the 1972 campaign was organized and under way; a few corporate officials before the Senate Watergate Committee were intimidated by Chairman Sam Ervin into agreeing defensively that their illegal contributions had been made under a feeling of coercion or to insure access to government officials, but all this was reduced to absurdity when it was disclosed months later that their companies had freely made hundreds of illegal contributions to candidates of both parties over a long period of years; J. Walter Jones in Maryland was found guilty of having induced a $10,000 illegal contribution and deliberately misreporting it to the finance committee in Washington; and a few contributions were received from foreign nationals by the Nixon committee and by committees for other candidates, but the Department of Justice ruled that such receipts were perfectly proper. None of these alters in any way the sweeping disproof of any claims of corruption in the 1972 activities of the Finance Committee to Re-Elect the President.

This recital of negatives may come as a surprise to people who had total faith in printers' ink and the airwaves from 1972 to 1975, and who believed the enthusiastic tales of politicians and public interest organizations about widespread corruption in Nixon's finances. The "net net" of that false impression was that even the Supreme Court was deceived to the point that its judgment about an important civil function was prejudiced. (See Chapter 15)

# 2

## GUILT IS, IF YOU SAY IT IS . . .

Many years ago the superb politician Jim Farley, who master-minded Franklin D. Roosevelt's win of the Presidency in 1932, uttered a remark which, even in the days before paid television became the most expensive ingredient of national elections, aptly described one of the big hurdles in an election: "There are three requirements for a political campaign. The first is money; the second is money; and the third is money."

In those days a run at the Presidency cost a few million dollars. In 1972, the Nixon campaign organization set a high of $56.1 million.

The early revelations of Watergate led the eager investigators of the media and the prosecutors down a myriad of trails looking for "hot money" in the Nixon effort. With that much raised (actually, more than $60.2 million came in to the coffers), it was inevitable that questions abounded as to where it all came from, who gave it, and why. Those questions were all the more intriguing because, until a date seven months before the election, the law protected the anonymity of contributors who gave to a candidate to help him get his party's nomination. From and after that specific date of April 7, 1972, a report of all contributions had to be made to the government's General Accounting Office.

One of the first to see something sinister about the fact that the Nixon finance committee had raised millions of dollars during the period when the contributors were allowed privacy was John Gardner, the founder and head of a public interest organization, Common Cause. Gardner demanded the disclosure of every detail of those "secret" funds, and carried on his fight for almost two years.

The press picked up the cry. Why wouldn't Nixon tell where his money came from? Was it because there were illicit amounts from Lockheed or from ITT? Was there Mafia money? Were there gifts from wealthy foreigners or foreign governments? Eventually, the details were all revealed, all these questions were answered, and such suspicions were laid to rest.

## Corporate Violations

But this was not before some bombshells exploded that took the Nixon finance committee and its officers wholly by surprise. They began when George Spater, chairman of American Airlines, admitted to the Watergate Special Prosecutor that he had delivered $75,000 to the committee—in response to a solicitation by Herbert Kalmbach—which had come in large part from the company's cash funds, an illegal procedure under the Federal Corrupt Practices Act.

Anticipating a huge number of similar violations, the Special Prosecutor announced that he would treat leniently any other companies that came forth and admitted having made illegal gifts. There followed a sequence of confessions from other companies over a period of months, some of which were initially ferreted out by finance committee researches and some of which were volunteered directly to the Special Prosecutor. By the time the books were closed, fourteen large, publicly owned companies and five small, private companies were found guilty:

Large publicly owned corporations:
American Airlines, Goodyear Tire and Rubber Company, Minnesota Mining and Manufacturing Company, Braniff Airways, Ashland Oil, Inc., and a subsidiary (Ashland Petroleum Gabon, Inc.), Gulf Oil Corporation, Phillips Petroleum Company, Carnation Company, American Shipbuilding Company, Diamond International Corporation, Northrop Corporation, Greyhound Corporation, Singer Company, and LBC & W, Inc. (a subsidiary of Combustion Engineering Co.).

**Small private companies:**
Lehigh Valley Cooperative Farmers, National By-Products, Inc.,
Ratree, Robbins & Schweitzer, Inc., HMS Electric Corporation, and
Time Oil Corp.

Each corporate violator was fined, the amounts ranging from
$1,000 (National By-Products, Inc.) to $25,000 (Ashland Oil). In
addition, one officer of each company was fined a nominal
amount of around $1,000, except George Steinbrenner of Ameri-
can Shipbuilding ($15,000), Thomas V. Jones of Northrop ($5,000),
and a few who received suspended sentences or were required to
pay nominal amounts. A second officer of American Shipbuilding
(John H. Melcher, Jr.) was also fined.

There was no indication that any of the Nixon fund-raisers
knew that illegal funds had been given to them. There was no
intimation that the money was from a source other than pooled
contributions of employees, and no reason for recipients to believe that the contributions were in any way improper. Other
candidates also received gifts, though smaller, from some of the
same sources.

The American Airlines case set the pace in context for those
that followed. Spater's first inference was that he gave because his
arm had been twisted by Kalmbach. That did not hold water,
because Kalmbach is known to be a mild-mannered person who
relies on gentle persuasion, and Spater then explained that he
gave because Kalmbach's law firm was doing legal work for
United Airlines and he felt that he needed to neutralize Kalmbach's possible influence in that direction, since he was known to
have ties with the White House. American Airlines had an application then pending to take over Western Airlines that would
require Presidential approval. Spater eventually conceded that
after making the contribution he had gone to the finance committee chairman (the author) to discuss that case, but he got no
assistance or reply and eventually the application was turned
down. For a while, the press had a merry time putting all its
imaginative suppositions together from these circumstances, to
no end. (Curiously, it turned out that $20,000 of the money was
from a legal source, presumably Spater himself, and the other
$55,000 was from the corporate till.)

Goodyear then acknowledged giving $40,000 illegally;

Minnesota Mining and Manufacturing, $30,000; Braniff Airways, $40,000; Ashland Oil, $100,000; Gulf Oil, $100,000; Phillips Petroleum, $100,000; Northrop, $100,000; American Shipbuilding, $25,000; Diamond International, Singer Company, Carnation Company, Greyhound Corporation, and the Combustion Engineering subsidiary, smaller amounts.

It took a long time for the rest of the story of these violations to come out:  that most of these public companies had large set-aside slush funds from which they had been carrying on the practice of political donations for years; that cash contributions had often been given to candidates of both parties; that eight of the companies used devious overseas "laundries" to conceal the origin of the funds, in some cases risking tax evasion charges; that when the facts began to be investigated some employed elaborate paperwork schemes to cover up, or lied to investigators; that every one of the companies testified or wrote that there was no way any of the recipients, including the Nixon committee, could have known that the money was illicit; that some of the companies had provided phony lists of names of individual contributors; and that the Nixon committee had returned the illegal money as soon as each discovery was made.

A deliberate pattern of devious moves had been used by each of the corporations to mask the sources of its political funds. American Airlines laundered money through the Swiss bank account of a Lebanese agent and charged it on the books as a commission on the sale of aircraft; 3-M paid a fee to a Swiss attorney who repaid part of it to the company; Braniff directed a bogus payment through an agent in Panama who recouped by holding out proceeds of unrecorded sales of air tickets; Gulf carried the money by courier from a subsidiary in the Bahamas; Ashland got its contribution money from a subsidiary in Gabon through a Swiss bank account; Phillips diverted cash from Swiss transactions into its secret fund; Northrop paid fees to a consultant in Paris who returned part; Goodyear used a Swiss bank account that received rebates from foreign manufacturers selling supplies to Goodyear; Singer's payment was made by subordinate officers directly from company funds; Diamond bought cashier's checks from a bank, payable to a campaign committee; Greyhound, American Shipbuilding, LBC & W, and Carnation got officials to contribute with their money and reimbursed them in expense accounts or bonuses.

The Nixon finance committee played no part in these she-nanigans; it did not know about any of the laundering. The actions were exclusively those of the corporations.

Their practice had a long history and involved large amounts of currency. Over the recent decade American Airlines had illegally given candidates $275,000;[1] Phillips, $585,000; 3-M, $497,000; Goodyear $242,000; Braniff, $640,000; Ashland, $730,000; Northrop, $1,200,000; and Gulf more than any, probably $2.3 millions. According to SEC files released in 1978, American Airlines was running an unrecorded fund in Mexico in the early 1940s, and Ashland Oil appears to have made an unlawful corporate contribution to the Presidential campaign of John F. Kennedy in 1960. These disclosures made mockery of the earlier accusations that the 1972 contributions had been arm-wrestled by Nixon's solicitors by force or extortion, or that contributors had been asked to give in cash. At the same time, taken as a whole, they also show the absurdity of the impression left by the frequent news stories that all big business is corrupt, when only a baker's dozen out of the 2,700 listed companies on the two New York stock exchanges had violated the law. Far from demonstrating that American business is universally dishonest, this minuscule number of violations ought to be taken as a tribute to its general integrity, and to the Nixon finance committee's precautions to make it known that illegal money was not wanted.

There was one other revelation of illegal campaign contributions, and this involved the nation's largest organization of dairy farmers, Associated Milk Producers, Inc., some of its officials, and several persons connected with campaigns of Democratic candidates. After a previous history of having supported mainly Democratic candidates, including Hubert Humphrey in 1968, AMPI concluded in 1969 to make contributions to members of both parties and to make special efforts to "get to know" members of the Nixon administration. In 1969, it gave $100,000 to a Republican trust fund held by Kalmbach and managed by Presidential

---

1. John Gardner was apparently a director of American Airlines at the time some of these illegal contributions were made, but had resigned before 1972.

aide Haldeman; then, in July 1970, one of its officers apparently pledged $2 million for the re-election of Richard Nixon, although only a small amount of this was ever contributed (and some of it was later rejected when tendered, because it seemed to have strings attached). Also, in 1970, AMPI gave $12,000 to the Senate campaign of Democrat Hubert Humphrey in Minnesota, $5,000 to the Senate effort of Democrat Phil Hoff in Vermont, $20,000 to the Congressional race of Republican Page Belcher of Oklahoma, and $8,400 to the Senate campaign of Democrat Edmund Muskie of Maine. Most or all of these contributions were illegal, covered up by payment of fictitious legal fees to attorneys and an advertising agency.

Later, in 1972, AMPI made a number of illegal contributions to a Minnesota computer mail service firm, Valentine, Sherman & Associates, for services rendered to various candidates in that year. Of these, $7,000 went to support the Senate campaign of Democrat James Abourezk of South Dakota, $50,000 to the Senate race of Democrat Richard Clark of Iowa, $25,000 for the Presidential campaign of Democrat Hubert Humphrey, $60,000 on behalf of Governor David Hall and the Oklahoma Democratic party, and $50,000 on behalf of Governor Robert Docking and the Kansas Democratic party. Included in the arrangements for these payments were a back-dated contract, false invoices, and other spurious documentation, of which the Watergate Special Prosecutor found Valentine and Sherman to be the architects. Almost all of these amounts were paid by illegal corporate checks of AMPI.

Other illegal AMPI contributions were made to the 1972 Presidential campaign of Wilbur Mills, including $5,000 in cash, the full-time services and expenses of two employees, the printing of campaign materials, and the costs of a big farm rally in Iowa; the total of these items was estimated by the Senate Watergate Committee at $75,000.

For these numerous transactions, and presumably others, AMPI was fined $35,000; its former general manager, Harold S. Nelson, received a four-month prison sentence and a fine of $10,000; David L. Parr, its former special counsel, received a four-month prison term and a fine of $5,000; Norman Sherman and John Valentine were each fined $500; Oklahoma lawyer Stuart Russell was found guilty on felony charges and sentenced to prison for two years; and Jake Jacobsen received a one-year suspended sentence. Minnesota lawyer Jack Chestnut, campaign chairman for Hubert Humphrey, was sentenced to four months imprisonment and fined $5,000 for his willfully illegal acts in covering up, through an advertising agency, the contribution to the 1970 Humphrey Senate race.

There were two other individuals who were found guilty of campaign contribution violations: oil executive Armand Hammer, who was given one year's probation and fined $3,000 for creating false procedures to conceal his contribution of $54,000 to the Nixon campaign; and his agent, former Governor Tim Babcock of Montana, convicted of turning in Hammer's contribution under false names, who was fined $1,000.

This sums up the transgressions of law by contributors in 1972—in all, nineteen corporations and their responsible officers, AMPI and its officers and agents, and two individuals—hardly the crime wave which the repeated and overblown accounts by the media, and repeated demands for reform by public interest groups, seemed to portray.[2]

There is no excuse, of course, for these violations, even though it is almost certain that they were less numerous than in the earlier Presidential elections of 1968 or 1964. Non-enforcement of these laws for many years had produced a belief that infractions would go unpunished, and some companies found it easier in that air of laxity to use a "slush fund" to respond to solicitations than to pass the hat among employees.

## Candidates and Committees

The other side of the coin involved the breaches of law by candidates and their finance committees. Anyone who did not follow closely the course of the prosecutions for 1972 campaign

---

2. The issue of payments made by American companies, in one form or another, to get business in foreign countries, arose in this time cycle and got a lot of attention for five years. Several hundred companies acknowledged having made such expenditures, some petty amounts to facilitate clearances of documents and some venal examples of bribery. Unfortunately, the double-barreled effect of these many disclosures, overlaid on the much smaller number of improper political contributions, tended not only to put corporations in a bad light, but also to confuse the public into failing to distinguish between the two kinds of transactions. A few of these companies apparently also made illegal domestic political contributions at one time or another, but there has been no public identification of them as to names, dates, or amounts, and there have been no prosecutions.

violations would not have noted several features of what transpired.

First, out of thousands of "apparent violations" in 1972 at national and Congressional levels cited by the responsible authorities, some of which they described as serious or significant, less than ten persons were brought to court by the separate efforts of the Department of Justice and the Special Watergate Prosecutor.

Second, the only violations charged against candidates or finance committees were for inadequacies in reporting (failure to report accurately or on time or at all), plus three instances of receiving illegal funds (two unknowingly). This was hardly a catalog of high crimes and misdemeanors.

Third, only Nixon committees were selected for prosecution, and large numbers of almost conclusive violations by other candidates were not prosecuted.

True, the Nixon fund-raising effort was found guilty of some technical violations of the law, but none of these was understood to be other than proper until long after the election, when they came under question as a result of the numerous investigations. This was a very distressing development, because an enormous effort had been made to see that its committees conducted as honest and clean a drive for money as was conceivably possible. Their record-keeping and reporting were in fact superior to those of any other candidate. The records and reports had been computerized, and procedures had been set up to exercise surveillance over the state committees doing fund-raising all across the country. The organization had been alerted about the changes in the law in the middle of the campaign, and the necessity of compliance, and the committees had consulted with their lawyers whenever a question arose. Rules were strict about not accepting corporate money, and more than 100 such checks had been refused. All in all, it was designed to be the best system ever used in a Presidential campaign, most of which had been notoriously uncontrolled in the past. With only one exception, which occurred out of reach in Maryland, the offenses were punished with nominal fines, indicating that the courts did not consider these transgressions to be anywhere near the same as the Watergate crimes.

To put this phase of investigation and prosecution into perspective, here are all the charges held against the 1972 Nixon national fund-raising committees, after the government had spent untold thousands of hours and probably more than a million dollars in its screening of their activities:

(1) Eight misdemeanor charges against the Finance Committee to Re-Elect the President, for failure of its treasurer, Hugh Sloan, Jr., to report four payments totaling about $31,000 during a period of transition from one law to another.

These charges were made by the Department of Justice on the basis of a report by the General Accounting Office. The amounts involved included two payments of $12,000 each to G. Gordon Liddy, $2,000 in traveling expenses withheld by Liddy, and payments totaling $5,300 to Herbert Porter, all shortly after April 7, when the law had changed. Sloan, who made the disbursements at the direction of Jeb Magruder of the campaign committee, was the only member of the finance committee organization who knew about them, and even he did not know their purpose, but the indictment named him as the accountable party. Presumably because of his cooperation and testimony in the Watergate trial of Liddy and Hunt, Sloan was not personally charged with these violations. The finance committee pleaded nolo contendere and was fined $8,000.

(2) Three misdemeanor charges against the committee for failure, even though on advice of counsel, to account for and report a contribution from Robert Vesco when received. (This also during the transition period.)

As disclosed in a later chapter, this contribution from Vesco became the subject of a trial in the Federal Court in New York, on the ground that it was made by him to influence the results of a Securities and Exchange Commission investigation in progress. That allegation was not sustained. The misdemeanor charges were made against the finance committee and not individuals because it was shown by affidavits of outside lawyers that the officers had acted on legal advice that a contribution received under the specific timetable of this one did not qualify for reporting under the law in effect. The head of Justice's election fraud division, Walter T. Barnes, on May 3, 1973, said that "we did not believe that there was a prosecutable case against Mr. Stans or other individuals.... This is a hell of a complicated law. There was a question of some mitigating facts." Because counsel for the committee felt that its legal position was correct, and because the GAO regulations were unclear and confusing, the committee contested the indictment.   However, the District Court held against it and the appellate court upheld the decision, so the committee paid a $3,000 fine.

> (3) Five misdemeanor charges against the author personally for minor infractions (two for nonwillful receipt of corporate money and three for late reporting).

The long and painful story of the devolution of these offenses is told in Chapter 14.

> (4) Two other offenses that occurred in the field by employees of the Nixon campaign.

The major one was against J. Walter Jones, a Maryland chairman, for soliciting and receiving the illegal contribution from Singer Company, which was in the amount of $10,000. His case was entangled with prosecutorial animosities in Baltimore arising out of Jones' personal relationships with Spiro Agnew, then the resigned and convicted former Vice President. Jones was indicted on nine counts on this one transaction. Eventually, he pleaded guilty to one count and was sentenced to imprisonment for three months and fined $5,000.

The other violation was a failure on the part of former Congressman Wendell Wyatt, who was Nixon campaign chairman in Oregon, to report the receipt and expenditure of $1,000 received from a contributor; he was fined $750.

For all of these essentially technical infractions on behalf of Nixon, no worse than many violations by others that went unprosecuted, the government recovered $21,750 in fines.

In contrast, no criminal charges were brought against fund-raisers for other Presidential candidates, and only a handful against candidates for House and Senate seats, notwithstanding a long list of apparent infractions reported to the Justice Department or the Special Prosecutor by agencies charged with surveillance of the election laws, or disclosed in other manners and at other times.

McGovern's people had many violations:

The McGovern campaign violated Section 302 (e) of the new law hundreds of times by allowing committees to be formed to raise money for his candidacy without requiring that each such committee be authorized in writing to do so; the permissible alternative would have been to say in all literature and advertisements of such a committee that it was unauthorized, but this was not done, either. Stating that this was an important matter, the General Accounting Office on June 27, 1973, referred these violations to the Attorney General. According to one source, McGovern had 750 committees; the GAO said only 13 of these had been properly qualified in writing. There was no prosecution.

McGovern in 1973 transferred $340,000 of his 1972 Presidential campaign funds to his forthcoming 1973 Senate race, while at the same time settling debts of his 1974 campaign at 50 cents on the dollar. The settlement of campaign debts at a discount raises a question of violation of the law prohibiting corporate contributions, since both the committee and the companies discounting their bills knew fully that they were thereby contributing. Xerox Corporation, for example, wrote off $9,606 in this way. The total of forgiven debts was over $35,000. There was no prosecution of either the companies or the McGovern committees. The Senate Watergate Committee's staff draft of its report called the post-campaign settlements and transfers of money an apparent violation of the law; McGovern objected, and the statement was deleted.

According to a GAO report on October 17, 1973, the Massachusetts McGovern for President Committee failed to report 1972 receipts of $54,000 and an expenditure of $50,000, and failed to itemize receipts of $67,000. Some of the incoming funds, according to the committee treasurer, were in the form of cash contributions that were laundered by personal checks of campaign workers to disguise the true donors. There was no prosecution.

The McGovern Concert Committee lumped together about $200,000 collected for a 1972 concert in Los Angeles, thereby concealing the names of contributors, in violation of the law requiring recording of each individual amount of $10 or more and reporting of each $100 contribution. There was no prosecution.

The (committee of) Business and Professional Men and Women for McGovern failed to disclose in its September 10, 1972, report having received a loan of $50,000 from Scarsdale National Bank, although it did report the repayment of the loan. No one was prosecuted for this violation.

Altogether, the GAO referred to the Justice Department 42 cases involving McGovern committees in apparent violations of the law, *beyond* mere technical violations. His Wisconsin committee, for example, was cited for records that were "virtually incomprehensible," his Connecticut committee for failing to keep complete records and failing to report as required, and his Nebraska committee for failure to document receipts and expenditures. None was prosecuted.

While these violations were in many cases serious and worthy of prosecution, they were not as egregious as those of the committees for Hubert Humphrey:

In 1971 and 1972 (up to April 7) more than a half million dollars was contributed to the Backers for Humphrey Committee in individual donations in excess of $5,000, although contributions of more than $5,000 were illegal at the time, both for contributor and committee. No one was prosecuted.

The GAO found that the Committee for the Nomination of Hubert Humphrey failed to file its required 1972 reports until late in 1973, after GAO had walked in to start an audit. GAO cited four major lapses of the Humphrey committee: failure to report $456,000 in receipts and $420,000 in expenditures, failure to document more than a third of its expenditures, the receipt of corporate contributions, and failure of its contributors to pay gift taxes on large contributions to a single committee. The unreported contributions included one of $35,000, two of $25,000, one of $15,000, and others of lesser size. Among the expenditures, a listed amount of $6,779 to one person turned out to be 68 checks for $99.99 each, which the payee had actually used to hire 68 people for election-day work in Indiana's primary; the use of this tactic was to hide the expenditures, as checks for $100 would have required documentation and reporting. The committee was unable to account for large amounts of other payments, since there were no records to show for them. The GAO in its report of October 12, 1973, termed the failure to disclose the receipts and expenditures "a serious frustration of the prompt disclosure objectives of the law." It called "equally serious" the committee's failure to document "two to three hundred thousand dollars in expenditures." The committee then partially corrected its reports by amendments filed a full year later than the law specified. The illegalities were referred to the Department of Justice but, surprisingly, there were no prosecutions.

In 1976 Humphrey settled $900,000 in leftover 1972 Presidential campaign debts by paying 4 cents on the dollar. The debts were due to 18 persons, most of them wealthy businessmen who had loaned money to finance his unsuccessful attempt for the Democratic nomination. Several individuals among them had loaned him $150,000 each. Involuntarily, they all became large contributors, presumably also subject to potential gift taxes. There were no prosecutions for excessive contributions.

Humphrey received $50,000 from a New York contributor who illegally disguised the gift under 9 other names, and who was found guilty and fined $3,000 for the offense. Of the total contributions, $2,000 was in cash and this was not properly reported by the Humphrey committee. The committee was not prosecuted.

Humphrey was a universally respected person, a decent, warm man, with high political acumen, and a long, unsullied record of public service. As a member of the Senate, he certainly was well aware that in 1972, under a new election financing law, the rules of many generations of political life were changed in the middle of the game. Nevertheless, these transgressions of law by his money people in 1972 (following receipts of more than $150,000 in illegal funds in 1968 and 1970), included also the concealment of improper milk industry contributions by his computer service company,[3] the destruction of records, and the

---

3. Columnist Nick Thimmisch put it bluntly: "There are plenty of milk stains on Humphrey."

public release of incorrect and incomplete lists of early contributors, evidence that he and his people continued to play their politics by the old rules. When confronted with some of these matters, he successfully evaded the Senate Watergate Committee, and then caused its report to be modified to favor him,[4] saying "I can't stand to have that on my record." These machinations outdid those of any other candidate.

The case of Robert Strauss is one of effective intrigue that makes the quiet public acceptance of it seem unbelievable in the era of public indignation that followed Watergate:

> Ashland Oil Company, which had made an illegal contribution of $100,000 to the Nixon committee from a subsidiary's corporate funds, and had pleaded guilty and was fined, later acknowledged in a second court appearance that it had dispensed an additional $170,000 illegally to other candidates from 1970 to 1972, including $100,000 to unidentified candidates for election to the House and Senate, $7,000 to Hubert Humphrey, $10,000 to Louis B. Nunn of Kentucky, $2,500 to John Tower of Texas, and $50,000 to Robert Strauss, then finance chairman for the Democratic National Committee.
>
> Strauss boldly reported the $50,000 received by him as unitemized "miscellaneous" contributions, a presumably illegal treatment since this category is permissible only for gifts of less than $100. Although he conceded that he may have committed what he called a "technical violation," Strauss was not prosecuted, nor were any of the other recipients. Strauss' lame defense was that the money "was reported in keeping, I believe, with the standards prevailing at the time." He said he reported the $50,000 as contributions under $100 because he felt that the Ashland officials did not want the Nixon Administration to know of the transaction.
>
> This was followed by some extraordinary political coordination between members of the Congress and extraordinary leniency by the staff of the Special Prosecutor. His criminal accountability was avoided by the expedient of an amendment to the Federal Elections Campaign Act in 1974, enacted by the Congress, which reduced the statute of limitations for prosecution of offenses like

---

4. For details, see Fred D. Thompson's *At That Point in Time,* (New York: Quadrangle/New York Times Book Co.), 1975. Thompson was chief minority counsel for the Senate Watergate Committee.

Strauss' from five years to three years! The identified promoters of this adroit amendment, quietly steered through the House and Senate, were Democratic Congressmen Wayne Hays of Ohio, then Chairman of the House Administration Committee, and Phillip Burton of California. The change meant that absolution was instantly given for any improper campaign acts in 1970 and 1971, which just happened to cover the time of Strauss' receipt of the illegal money and his illegal reporting of it. According to the *Washington Star* of April 25, 1975, "there is no question" that charges would have been brought against Strauss had the statute of limitations not been shortened in this way.

Even harder to understand was the action of the Special Prosecutor. On December 30, 1974, just before the reduced statute of limitations became law, he brought Ashland to court to plead guilty, among other things, to making the payment of $50,000 to Strauss. But Strauss, who could have been charged on that same day or earlier for his "nonwillful" receipt of the illegal money and his obviously conscious misreporting, was allowed to escape. Not until March 20, 1975, did the Special Prosecutor ask the Department of Justice for an advisory opinion as to whether the three-year statute of limitations applied to this transaction. In June 1975, after a further period of waiting, the Special Prosecutor announced that Strauss would not be prosecuted because the statute of limitations had run out. His public statement said that "we based our decision on problems posed by the statute of limitations, not on the merit of the evidence."[5] As columnist William Safire commented . . . "how come the Special Prosecutor was able to move in time to nail the giver . . . Ashland Oil . . . and not the Democratic receiver?" The dispirited and inarticulate Republican minority in the Congress raised no fuss about this obvious example of a dual standard.

Strauss was later rewarded by President Carter with an appointment to a cabinet-level post as the President's Special Trade Representative. The best that can be said is that, if it is assumed the Special Prosecutor did not deliberately absolve Strauss by failing to charge, he bungled the matter by not doing so in time.

Disclosures of illegal contributions by corporations led to a

---

5. Under a similar situation involving one of the nonwillful counts against the author, the Special Prosecutor had insisted on a waiver of the statute to prevent it from running out while the proceedings were pending.

considerable number of candidates receiving money who had failed to observe reporting requirements:

> Gulf Oil Corporation, which had illegally used corporate money to contribute $100,000 to Nixon's campaign, admitted that it had given millions of dollars over the years out of a continuing fund for political purposes, and in 1972 had contributed $10,000 to the coffers of Senator Henry Jackson's campaign and $15,000 to Congressman Wilbur Mills' effort, plus many smaller amounts to Congressional and Senatorial candidates. There was only one prosecution of a recipient: Congressman James R. Jones of Oklahoma, who had received an indefinite $1,000 to $2,000 *after* his first election in 1972, was fined $200 for not reporting it.

> Minnesota Mining and Manufacturing Company, which had given the Nixon committee $30,000 in illegal funds, revealed that it had made 379 improper political contributions involving close to $500,000 in the years 1968 to 1972, including $1,000 each to Hubert Humphrey and Wilbur Mills in 1972. The company and several of its officers were fined, and the author was fined for receiving the Nixon money without knowing it was illicit, but none of the other recipients was prosecuted.

> Goodyear Tire and Rubber Company acknowledged that its $40,000 illegal contribution to Nixon's committee in 1972 was only a part of a total of $242,000 used for political purposes between 1964 and 1972. The company and an officer were found guilty and fined, and the author was fined even though he received the Nixon money without knowing it was improper, but again, none of the other recipients was charged.

> Phillips Petroleum Company, after pleading guilty and being fined for making an illegal contribution of $100,000 to the Nixon committee in 1972, admitted having made $485,000 in other illegal contributions over the years 1964 to 1972. The contributions included $75,000 to other Presidential campaigns in 1964, 1968, and 1972, $125,000 for Congressional campaigns, $70,000 for political dinners, and $215,000 for state elections. About $50,000 to $60,000 of the Congressional money went to a "substantial number" of Senate and House candidates in 1970 and 1972. None of the recipients was prosecuted.

> John Lindsay, a Democratic candidate for President whose cam-

paign aborted early, received a number of sizable contributions in 1972 in cash, which he kept in a safe deposit box; included were $5,000 each from two contractors doing business with New York City who subsequently received a $1.7 million contract. There was no prosecution.

Senator James O. Eastland, Democrat of Mississippi, received more than $5,000 in illegal corporate contributions in his re-election campaign in 1972, but the Justice Department took no action. The ten companies involved were absolved because their officers agreed to repay the corporate accounts with personal checks, a procedure which the Special Prosecutor had not allowed to excuse some of the companies which contributed to Nixon's campaign.

The GAO early in 1974 charged Senator Wendell Ford, Democrat of Kentucky, with ten apparent violations of the Federal laws in his 1972 Senate campaign, describing them as "among the most serious violations" discovered anywhere. Included were illegal corporate contributions, mysterious transfers of union funds, an unlawful interest-free bank loan, and other transactions. The information was transmitted by GAO to the Department of Justice for possible prosecution but no action resulted.

Associated Milk Producers, Inc., in 1972 made almost $200,000 in illegal contributions to Democratic parties and candidates in Iowa, Kansas, South Dakota, and Oklahoma, and to the Humphrey 1972 campaign, routed through the computer mail service company, Valentine, Sherman & Associates. The candidates named by the Special Prosecutor as beneficiaries of these improper AMPI payments, in addition to Presidential aspirants Hubert Humphrey and Wilbur Mills, were Senators James Abourezk of South Dakota and Richard Clark of Iowa, and Governors David Hall of Oklahoma and Robert Docking of Kansas. None of these ultimate recipients or their committees was prosecuted, although Valentine and Sherman, the conduits, were personally fined.

The Senate Watergate Committee reported that the 1972 Presidential campaign of Wilbur Mills received up to $75,000 from AMPI and $15,000 from corporate assets of Mid-American Dairymen, Inc., all of which was illegal. The Mills campaign also received $15,000 in illegal corporate money from Gulf Oil and $1,000 from 3-M. His campaign manager invoked the Fifth Amendment when called to testify to the Senate Watergate Committee, and Mills declined to appear. No one connected with the Mills organization was prosecuted for receiving these unlawful funds. After marking time until April 1975, the Watergate Special Prosecutor ended the Mills investigation because the new statute of limitations made prosecution no longer possible.

An official of Hertz Corporation testified to the Senate Watergate Committee that he had provided car rentals to the Muskie campaign in the amount of $8,000 or $9,000 prior to May 1972, but billed the campaign for only $4,100; since he was under orders from the president of the company to provide cars without charge, he then arranged with six lawyers to make contributions totaling $4,100 to the Muskie committee so it could pay the bills, and authorized the lawyers to recoup their money through charges to Hertz for services which had not been rendered. No one was prosecuted.

There were a host of other questionable transactions and probable violations that escaped the courts:

In 1972 the Democratic National Committee settled 1968 campaign debts to business corporations at 20 to 30 cents on the dollar. The total debt carried over from 1968 was $9.3 million, and various public reports have shown that more than half of this was settled at large discounts. Since the DNC is a continuing operation and its campaign debts have traditionally been carried over and paid out of future incomes, it seems a proper conclusion that every one of the corporations which accepted less than full payment thereby knowingly made an illegal contribution, and the committee knowingly received one in each case. There was no prosecution.

Several 1972 committees just wrote off or ignored substantial deficits that left them with unpaid bills, thus forcibly converting loans and credits into contributions. Press reports in 1972 showed such unpaid debts for Humphrey ($903,000), Muskie ($116,000), Sanford ($700,000), McGovern ($100,000), and the McGovern California Committee ($118,000), the final accounting for most of which was glossed over. There were no prosecutions for oversize contributions.

A committee for Senator Edward F. Kennedy filed a report two years late on $41,000 raised from 1972 to 1974 to pay debts of his 1970 campaign, after the failure to report was questioned by the

*New York Times*. Although the matter was referred to the Justice Department for possible prosecution, no such action was taken.

Common Cause boasted in its letters to members of having "filed complaints against 286 *violators* from both major parties." There were no identifiable prosecutions, and certainly none in such numbers.

The General Accounting Office found other apparent violations in the reports and records of the Humphrey, Muskie, Wallace, Chisholm, and Sanford campaign committees, the Idaho State Democratic Central Committee, the International Brotherhood of Boilermakers, the Democratic National Convention Committee, Communications Workers of America, the International Brotherhood of Electrical Workers, and dozens of other unions, local committees, state committees, and national committees of the candidates. GAO referred more than 40 such citations to the Attorney General, but they remained inert and dormant for many months, until the running of the statute of limitations buried them entirely. There were no prosecutions.

Candidates for seats in the Senate and House went almost scot-free despite thousands of cases of reported failure to meet the standards of the law:

For example, none of the Congressional candidates or committees who received $120,000 in contributions from illegal company funds of Ashland Oil Company in 1970 and 1972 was prosecuted.

The Secretary of the Senate reported to the Attorney General 1,098 complaints of apparent violations by Senate candidates, and the Clerk of the House similarly reported 6,100 apparent violations by House candidates; 13 of the House cases were designated as major referrals. Justice said that it considered about 20 percent of all the cases to be substantial. Four House candidates were prosecuted and convicted, with the result being, respectively, a $300 fine, a $1,000 fine, one hour in jail, and a one-year suspended sentence (for filing no reports whatever). After this, the Department of Justice announced that it gave up on the rest. On June 8, 1974, Deputy Attorney General Joseph T. Sneed was quoted as saying that "95 percent of those accused of apparent violations (more than 5,000 in the House and 200 in the Senate) complied with the law after receiving registered letters reminding them of the criminal penalties for non-compliance. Even though compliance came late, further action is not planned." The Secretary of the Senate acknowledged on August 8, 1974, that "the referrals result preponderantly from the newness of the legislation, the extreme complexity of its requirements, and the stringent provisions for disclosure. . . ."

Disclosures of apparent illegalities by other candidates were still coming as late as 1978. The investigation files on Tongsun Park, the Korean businessman who distributed his largesse over many members of Congress until he was exposed, disclose that he included Hubert Humphrey as one of the names in his list of personal gifts. *Time* reported that Humphrey received $20,000 from Park in 1972. No such sum appeared in his campaign reports.

Because the investigative nets brought in some violations prior to 1972, both Republican and Democratic, it is worth noting what earlier offenses did and did not get prosecuted (other than the milk industry prosecutions already cited):

Herbert Kalmbach pleaded guilty to a misdemeanor for promising federal employment to a person in return for a contribution in *1970*, and to raising other funds in that year for Republican Senate and House candidates without a proper committee structure. He was confined to prison for six months.

Jack Gleason and Harry Dent, formerly of the White House, pleaded guilty to one misdemeanor each in connection with the *1970* fund-raising activity. They were given thirty days' probation.

The *Wall Street Journal* reported in 1973 that Senator Joseph Montoya, a member of the Senate Watergate Committee, used dummy committees in the District of Columbia to launder the sources of contributions to his *1970* campaign in New Mexico; more than $100,000 from labor groups and other special interest groups was laundered to avoid disclosure. When the charge was aired, Montoya's people reported that the records of the secret committees had been destroyed, and that the signatures on the report filed in New Mexico, which did not include these amounts, were false. There was no prosecution.

Going back further, the Democratic party treasurer in 1969 acknowledged that at least $3 million in Humphrey-Muskie *1968* campaign bills had been paid directly by individuals or non-reporting committees because "some of these people obviously don't want to be known." The Corrupt Practices Act required national political committees to report such transactions as both contributions and expenditures. Some individuals paid money directly to an advertising agency to avoid public disclosure. Even the treasurer wasn't told about some persons who made loans of $250,000 each to the campaign, and these were not reported, as they should have been. There was no prosecution.

Also, in a highly publicized 1974 lawsuit against Howard Hughes, one of his one-time associates testified that in *1968* he gave Hubert Humphrey $50,000 in cash in a limousine parked outside the Century Plaza Hotel in Los Angeles. Humphrey denied this, and the matter was never judicially resolved.

In *1968* AMPI gave an estimated $150,000 in illegal funds to the Humphrey campaign, the disclosure of which apparently came too late for prosecution of the donor or the donee. It also spent $105,000 to produce a booklet of Lyndon Johnson's messages to the Congress entitled *No Retreat from Tomorrow*; this was to be a piece of campaign material for his re-election, but it had to be abandoned when he announced his withdrawal from the race. AMPI, it was later reported, concealed the printing expenditure as a public relations expense, but it was never prosecuted because the IRS "lost" the information in its files.[6]

As a final bit of irony to the Senate Watergate investigation, in 1974, after Senator Daniel K. Inouye of Hawaii had sat throughout the hearings as a member of the Senate Committee, his own campaign organization accepted an illegal contribution of $5,650 from American Ship Building Co. The contribution was returned after the disclosure and sentence was suspended.

It seems strange in retrospect that so many 1972 transgressions went unpunished, especially those that were identified as significant violations. That prosecutorial tolerance, however, was consistent with the early years of general acceptance of such breaches. From 1925 to 1972 there had apparently been only a

---

6. Herbert E. Alexander, et al., *Financing the 1972 Election* (Lexington, Mass.: Lexington Books, D. C. Heath & Co., 1976).

score of prosecutions against *contributors* (all apparently for willful violations), and no convictions of any *committees* or *candidates* for nonwillful acts, for failure to report, or for late reporting.

The only plausible conclusion is that after the 1972 Presidential race the Nixon committees and their officers were singled out for prosecutorial attention, while serious violations by Democratic candidates were tolerated and candidates for seats in the Congress by and large got full clearance by prosecutorial inattention.[7]  Somehow, the sympathetic understanding and toleration by law enforcement officials that forgave or neglected violations by other candidate committees in 1972—because of the complexities and confusions of a new law, introduced while a campaign was under way, or because they were unintentional—were not applicable to unwitting technical violations of a committee that supported Richard Nixon. This is even more cynically evident when the descriptions of some specific charges are spelled out. (See Chapter 14.)

This double standard was never seriously challenged, even by the Republican party or its members in the Congress. Their embarrassment over the White House shenanigans, and very likely some freehanded movements of cash in their own campaigns, stayed their tongues.

---

7. The same attitude by the Senate Watergate Committee was documented in *At That Point in Time* by Fred D. Thompson.

# 3

## THE LAMBS

The other side of the Watergate balance sheet encompasses the undeserving victims. Not all can be known and listed, because no one can know the grief or fear that the frenzy swirling about Washington and reaching throughout the country may have engendered. However innocent a person may be, to be questioned by the FBI about one's self or friends or associates is frightening. To be put under oath for a deposition or in a court or before a grand jury is a fearful experience, wherein one ill-chosen word or one unremembered incident might lead to indictment for a crime. Good faith statements of information recalled from dim recollection of distant past events long out of mind could easily lead to charges of perjury over the smallest detail. To be interviewed by an insinuating pressman, who holds all the cards because he has the last word, and can twist or distort any casual statement to meet his preconceptions, is a lesson in helplessness. The number who suffered from these experiences and others sometimes worse is beyond counting.

There are some major categories that can be listed, however, and these include particularly the persons who were subjected to the public shame of indictment and were eventually found by a court or by a jury of peers to be not guilty; the many whose lives and careers were destroyed or violated by untrue public assertions against them; and the hundreds who were subjected to unreasonable inquisitional methods in the frantic search for culprits. And another part of the balance sheet that should not be ignored comprises the admittedly guilty persons who were given "a pass" for pointing a finger at someone else.

With no claim to completeness, here are some.

### Innocent Victims—Class 1

Among the criminal proceedings which resulted in convictions for Watergate and other offenses, there were a number of actions in the same orbit against persons who, after having been indicted, and at great emotional and financial cost, succeeded in obtaining their freedom in court.

One of the most notable was the trial and acquittal of John Connally. A former Governor of Texas, former Secretary of the Navy, and former Secretary of the Treasury, he was a man of impeccable reputation and acknowledged political savvy, and also had substantial personal means. Among other events in his career was his wounding in the assassination of President John F. Kennedy when, as Governor, he accompanied the President on the fatal ride in the streets of Dallas; Connally was hit in the arm and leg by the second bullet intended for Kennedy.

An eloquent, fast-talking Texan, patrician in manner and always well-dressed, he could be both witty and harshly direct in repartee, to a degree that sometimes disconcerted officials of foreign governments whom he dealt with in his Treasury post. But his effective work drew him into close friendship with Nixon, who had high confidence in his political judgment. In the summer of 1972, Connally became head of Democrats for Nixon in the re-election campaign, and in May 1973, while Watergate was already swirling wildly around the White House, he announced that he was turning Republican. These acts alienated many of his Democratic friends.

Connally watched the mounting frenzy in Washington with serious concern. He described it plainly on November 16, 1973 in a radio broadcast:

> " . . . in the atmosphere and the times in which we live, the inferences, the innuendoes, the rumors are so rampant and so rife and so irresponsible that I think anybody that is close by might well get damaged to some extent."

Connally later found out how right he was.

At the instigation of the Watergate Special Prosecutor, he was indicted on July 29, 1974, on five counts—two of having accepted two illegal payments of $5,000 each from a representative of Associated Milk Producers, Inc., one of conspiracy to obstruct justice, and two of lying to a grand jury. The key witness against him was Jake Jacobsen, a Texas lawyer and former aide to President Johnson, who as legal counsel for AMPI had purportedly paid the money to Connally, but whose reputation had become seriously impaired by reason of an indictment pending against him in Texas for misappropriating $825,000 from a San Antonio savings and loan association.

Jacobsen testified that he had delivered to Connally the two installments of $5,000 on May 14 and September 24, 1971, in payment for Connally's assistance to the dairy industry in urging President Nixon to increase the price supports for milk on March 23 of that year. It never was established that there was impropriety by anyone in the raising of the milk price supports at that time, although a civil suit alleging that to have been the case had been filed by a Ralph Nader organization, and the Special Prosecutor had investigated the matter fully. The principal conclusion from all the testimony on that subject was that the milk price levels had been raised by the President to forestall a similar move by the Democratically controlled Congress that might have been politically damaging to the administration. White House tapes of the March 23 meeting showed that Connally had argued along this line.

Jacobsen's story was that Connally had thereupon asked to be paid personally for this presumed favor to the dairy industry, and the two payments had followed. Connally denied receiving any money from Jacobsen or anyone else, saying that money had been offered to him but he had refused it. The case thereby became a one-on-one confrontation in which a highly respected former government official was accused by a man under indictment for serious felonies, who had made a deal that would relieve him of punishment in return for pointing a finger. Meanwhile, Jacobsen's predicament had worsened by the necessity of his filing a petition in bankruptcy in June 1972.

The legal preliminaries were very involved. On February 21, 1974, Jacobsen was indicted by the Watergate grand jury for perjury, but this charge was dismissed on May 3 by a Federal judge as unsupportable. On July 29 he was indicted on a single charge of making the illegal payments to Connally, at the same time that Connally received his multiple-count indictment. On September 5, the Texas Attorney General asked a district judge in Dallas to refuse a government request to approve a deal in Washington for Jacobsen to testify against Connally in return for the dropping of the Texas indictment against Jacobsen for his misappropriation of the $825,000. When the Texas judge named a special prosecutor of his own there to try Jacobsen on the serious charges, the Watergate Special Prosecutor appealed and got Jacobsen freed so he could be used against Connally. Jacobsen was eventually found guilty in both jurisdictions, but in return for his "cooperation" was sentenced merely to seven years' probation for his Texas crimes (for which he might have received forty years in jail) and two years' probation for his guilty plea in the Connally matter.

In a prosecutive memorandum of June 18, 1974, before the indictment, the staff of the Watergate Special Prosecutor acknowledged the weaknesses in the government's case. The credibility of three witnesses testifying to circumstantial matters "may be in issue," it said, and "the credibility of Jake Jacobsen will be very much in issue." It pointed out the problem of justifying to the jury a prosecutor's deal with a man accused of serious crimes to free him in return for his testimony against another person; it acknowledged that "it is hard to believe that Connally would violate the law for a mere $10,000," or that AMPI, which "was talking in terms of a $2 million contribution to Nixon's re-election campaign in 1972," would "deal in such small sums" with Connally; and it conceded that Jacobsen had actually drawn $15,000 from AMPI purportedly to give to Connally, not $10,000, and could not explain the difference. In reality, the case against Connally depended on "circumstantial support for Jacobsen's version."

Despite all this tenuous background, the indictment against Connally was secured by the Special Prosecutor. Connally was tried before a jury seven months later on the first three counts and won acquittal on all of them, whereupon the prosecution threw in the sponge and dropped the remaining charges the next day.

The publicity attendant on this series of events injured or

delayed Connally's promising political career and probably cost him the appointment to Vice President when Spiro Agnew resigned (which would have brought him to the Presidency when Nixon abdicated) and the nomination for President or Vice President in 1976. His acquittal by the jury of his peers could in no way remedy the injury to his name, the huge costs of the trial, the loss in time, and the tremor of the experience.

Others who faced trial and imprisonment, but were eventually freed, included these individuals, whose cases are described in abbreviated form that cannot convey the agonies they had to live through:

**John Mitchell,**former Attorney General of the United States and previously Nixon campaign director in 1968 and 1972, and **Maurice H. Stans**, the author of this book. Mitchell and Stans were indicted on May 10, 1973, by the United States District Attorney in New York (under the technical jurisdiction of the Watergate Special Prosecutor) on ten counts each of conspiracy, obstruction of justice, and perjury, relating to the acceptance of a $250,000 campaign contribution from Robert Vesco, allegedly in return for promised assistance to Vesco in connection with an investigation by the Securities and Exchange Commission. They were tried and acquitted on all counts a year later. (See Chapters 11, 12, and 13 for an account of the prosecutorial tactics and other circumstances of this "trial of the century.")

This was the first of Mitchell's two trials, and he was later convicted in the Watergate coverup case. A former lawyer specializing in municipal bond matters, he had become acquainted with Nixon in the mid-1960s when he merged his practice with the New York law firm with which Nixon had associated while out of government. Mitchell was a man of few words, decisive, and considered by some to be brusque, but had a brilliant mind and was Nixon's closest political adviser from the time he undertook to manage Nixon's 1968 campaign. He had no personal political ambitions and had accepted the 1969 appointment as Attorney General with great reluctance.

**Edwin Reinecke**, former member of Congress and Lieutenant Governor of California. Reinecke was indicted on three counts of perjury in connection with his testimony regarding the alleged deal of ITT for a contribution of as much as $400,000 to the 1972 Republican convention in San Diego. The principal issue was the date of a conversation between him and John Mitchell. One count was dropped by the prosecution before trial, one count was dismissed by the judge at the conclusion of the government's case, and one was dismissed by an appellate court. This Pyrrhic victory, at a cost of $190,000 in legal fees, probably spelled the end of Reinecke's political career. He had been a candidate for Governor when the criminal issue arose, and not only lost the primary election but had to resign as Lieutenant Governor after the trial; the lengthy publicity was unfavorable to a comeback.

**Robert Mardian**, former Assistant Attorney General of the United States, in 1972 counsel to the Committee for the Re-Election of the President, and a well-known California lawyer. Indicted on one count of conspiracy in the Watergate coverup, Mardian was tried with the other defendants and found guilty, after his strenuous efforts for a separate trial—because of the sudden illness of his lawyer—were denied by Federal Judge John J. Sirica, and he was forced to proceed with new counsel introduced in the course of the trial. Upon appeal the higher court set aside the conviction and said he was entitled to a new trial. The Special Prosecutor gave up and moved for a dismissal. The experience lost Mardian several years' time, affected his reputation and credibility, and cost him almost a half million dollars in legal fees before it was over.

**Kenneth Parkinson**, a highly respected Washington lawyer who had represented the Nixon 1972 campaign committees in civil and criminal litigation. Parkinson was charged and tried on one count of Watergate conspiracy and found not guilty by the jury. The experience marred his reputation, and cost him a year's time and several hundred thousand dollars in the expenses of his defense.

**Frank deMarco, Jr.**, a reputable Los Angeles lawyer, who had assisted in the preparation of Richard Nixon's Federal income tax returns while he was President. DeMarco was indicted on one count of conspiring to defraud the United States in connection with Nixon's tax deduction in 1969 for the value of his personal Vice Presidential papers contributed to the National Archives. The case was dismissed by the judge before submission to the jury on the ground that the prosecutor had failed to provide deMarco with possibly exculpatory material, thus depriving him of a fair trial, and also that the prosecutor had been guilty of misconduct in enlarging the charges in response to deMarco's insistence that the trial be held in California. The government then appealed the judge's ruling and lost. DeMarco won the case but it was very costly in time, money, and anguish. In connection with the same tax matter, **Roger Barth**, a former Assistant Commissioner of Internal Revenue, was terrorized repeatedly by threats from the Special Prosecutor's office of a "sealed indictment" against him. The indictment did not exist.

**Dwayne O. Andreas**, a successful Minneapolis businessman, and a friend of both Hubert Humphrey and Richard Nixon. Andreas received much unfavorable publicity early in the Watergate case because, being a friend of both candidates in 1972, he had made a secret contribution of $25,000 in cash to the Nixon effort; without his participation or knowledge in any way, this money happened to be cleared through the bank account of one of the Watergate burglars before it was deposited in its own bank by the campaign's finance committee. Next, he was made to face unsupported charges that a new bank in which he was an investor got favored treatment because of his contributions. While absorbing the acutely suspicious publicity that followed, he was indicted on October 19, 1973, by the Special Prosecutor, along with one of his corporations, First Oceanic Corporation, for having made illegal contributions of corporate funds to the 1968 campaign of Hubert Humphrey. Both Andreas and his company were acquitted on July 12, 1974, after trial in Federal court in Minneapolis.

**Bert Cross** of St. Paul, retired chairman of 3-M Company. Cross was indicted for income tax fraud and forced to undergo a long period of suspenseful waiting for trial. Ultimately, the Federal judge dismissed the case because the government had agreed not to prosecute Cross further at the time he had paid a $1,000 fine for having participated in the company's illegal contribution. The company's counsel, **Irwin Hansen**, went through the same indictment and also was freed.

**W. F. Martin, W. W. Keeler,** and **Stanley Learned**, officials of Phillips Petroleum Co. These officers were indicted on multiple counts of conspiracy and tax fraud, related to the improper contributions the company had made to the Nixon campaign. The case was dismissed on all counts by a Federal judge because the conspiracy action would have constituted double jeopardy after fines had already been paid; and in the tax matter, the government withheld exculpatory testimony from the grand jury that could have benefited their defense, and also had misused the grand jury.

**Gordon Strachan**, a White House aide. Strachan was indicted on March 1, 1974, on three counts by the Watergate Special Prosecutor for alleged complicity in the Watergate coverup. After he had endured twelve months of suspense, his case was dismissed on motion of the Special Prosecutor, because Strachan had been promised from the beginning that he would go free for having cooperated with the Watergate investigations.

**Edward J. Gurney**, United States Senator from Florida. A hero of World War II, in which he was so badly wounded that he is a prisoner of pain and can sit only with the aid of a special cushion, Gurney was a Republican member of the Senate Watergate Committee. During its hearings, he occasionally scolded his colleagues for pressing unreasonably on witnesses. He is a tall, gray-haired, handsome man with a pleasant manner of expression, a lawyer who had ably served six years in the House before his election to the Senate. A good legislator who did his homework, his political future seemed assured.

In the whiplash of Watergate, he was indicted on June 10, 1974, in Federal Court in Florida on nine counts for allegedly selling favors in return for contributions to his most recent campaign.  He was tried after a long delay and found not guilty on seven of the counts, with the jury disagreeing on the other two; while the normal action by the prosecution would have been to drop the two charges promptly, they were held over Gurney without decision for a year and a half and he was then put through a second trial on one, with another verdict of acquittal.  Meanwhile, he had resigned his Senate seat during the period of the indictment.  It was a tragic injustice that cost Gurney three years of his life and about $400,000 in legal expenses, leaving him broke and severely handicapped in picking up the pieces of his political career.

To those engaged in the hunt, these persons all may have been merely incidental victims, but their anguish was nonetheless bound to be personally traumatic.  They could recover their sense of well-being, but they could never erase the searing scars they inherited.

No one can know positively whether any of these persons was less than innocent, since it is possible that some of them (particularly the cases in which the government withheld evidence) were the beneficiaries of bungled prosecution.  The eagerness for convictions, in any event, shows through, and the price paid by the victims was a high one to placate the incited public demand for as many scalps as possible.

Even the guilty were sometimes exorbitantly punished.  Worst was the case of G. Gordon Liddy, one of the burglary culprits who played no part in the more serious coverup, and who was fined $40,000 and given a sentence of twenty years by the notoriously tough Federal Judge Sirica, because Liddy exercised his constitutional right not to testify against himself and refused under a "use immunity" statute to testify against others.  President Carter recognized the obvious injustice of this in April 1977 and commuted the prison sentence to eight years, still an abnormal term for his offense, leaving the fine standing.  Liddy served a total of fifty-two months in nine different jails before he was freed, and continues to owe the fine.

## Innocent Victims—Class 2

There were many innocent bystanders who were drawn into the web of suspicion and subjected to extraordinary inquisitions and ignominy. Here is a partial list:

Congressman Louis Wyman of New Hampshire. Wyman, a twelve-year member of the House, was a Republican candidate for the United States Senate in 1974, in an election so close that the Senate finally called it a tie and ordered a new statewide balloting.

During the campaign, it was rumored that Wyman was under investigation for his role in obtaining an ambassadorial appointment for a friend, but the then Special Prosecutor Jaworski issued a statement saying his office "had not uncovered evidence that would support charges against Wyman." Nevertheless the publicity probably deprived him of enough votes to make him fail to win.

The new election was slated for September 16, 1975. A few weeks before that date, the rumor resurfaced and Wyman asked the new Special Prosecutor, Henry Ruth, Jr., to again clear him of suspicion. To Wyman's consternation, Ruth released a public statement on August 27 saying that the matter was still alive and Wyman was still under investigation. This time, with this issue clearly before it, the electorate chose his opponent by a wide margin. After the election, the investigation was ended without the Special Prosecutor finding any cause of action against Wyman, but by then his political future was badly shattered, if not destroyed.

Hugh Sloan, Jr., treasurer of the Nixon finance committee in 1972. Sloan was an innocent conduit for funds used to finance the Watergate break-in, having paid out the money on the instructions of campaign official Jeb Magruder without knowledge of the purpose for which it would be used. After he had testified truthfully to that effect in the trial of the burglars, he was harshly chastised in open court and publicly accused of lying by Federal Judge Sirica. The judge's suspicion that the whole truth had not come out in that trial was no justification for a public attack of this kind, and it was clearly an injudicious violation of due process. With this attack on his character, following on previous publicity of suspicion, Sloan found it difficult to get employment and was out of work for over a year.

**Peter Flanigan**, former assistant to the President and a high-ranking Wall Street investment banker. Flanigan was ruthlessly blocked from Senate confirmation for the prestigious post of Ambassador to Spain by irresponsible and unsupported charges; by Senator Thomas Eagleton of Missouri before the Committee on Foreign Relations, to the effect that he had played a part in the sale of an ambassadorship and in other actions inappropriate for a White House official.[1] The Senator was so ill-informed about the matter that he twice read the same material into the hearing record. All the charges evaporated, but the intended and unfair damage to Flanigan had been done by this unwarranted character assassination.

**Robert Allen**, the respected Chairman and President of Gulf Resources and Chemicals, a Texas mining company. Allen had made a $100,000 contribution to the Nixon campaign and, because for his own reasons he had transferred the money through Mexico, became the subject of a long and well-publicized grand jury investigation. In the end the matter came to naught, except for the trauma and expense to Allen and the harm to his public image in the community.

**Vincent deRoulet**, American Ambassador to Jamaica. DeRoulet was publicly smeared with accusations of attempting to purchase an appointment to a higher-ranking post by offering a large contribution to the Nixon campaign. The charge was not proved and, for this sensitive man, the agony of the experience may have contributed to his death shortly thereafter.

---

1. At one point Eagleton went so far as to tell the committee, "It is my opinion that the position of the Special Prosecutor at this time not to lodge a charge against Mr. Flanigan comes out of the fact that at a later time someone even more prestigious than Mr. Flanigan may well be brought before the bar of justice."

Kenneth Dahlberg, head of a Minneapolis corporation and a regional fund-raiser for Nixon. Because he was the one who received the Andreas contribution of $25,000 under the circumstances mentioned earlier, he became the first identifiable target of the investigative horde after the Watergate story broke. Totally innocent of any wrongdoing, he nevertheless took an extraordinary amount of media supposition that hurt him in his community until the full truth came out.[2]

Harry Dent, a top White House aide and a successful South Carolina lawyer. Dent was charged by the Watergate Special Prosecutor with being a participant in technical campaign violations in the 1970 Congressional elections. The prosecutive memorandum of August 20, 1974, by staff members Charles Ruff and Roger Witten contained this conclusion: "Despite the problems that are posed for any prosecution under the [law] by the enforcement history of that statute . . . we believe the bringing of this charge will have a significant salutary effect on the future enforcement of the campaign laws." Dent pleaded guilty because he felt that, once charged, he could not get a fair trial in the Washington atmosphere of 1974. The judge who received the evidence called him "an innocent victim" and let him off with a thirty-day probation. Another White House aide, Jack Gleason, was similarly treated in the same 1970 matter, although he had been assured by the White House and a New York law firm that his activities were legal.

Richard G. Kleindienst, Arizona lawyer and former Attorney General. Because of the apparent implication in Watergate and related cases of persons with whom he had a close personal and professional association, Kleindienst resigned his post as Attorney General on April 30, 1973, feeling he could not wholeheartedly conduct their prosecution for crimes. His own problems arose later, as a result of an incident which had occurred in April 1971, when he was

---

2. As late as September 1, 1974, a *New York Times* article by Joseph P. Albright still erroneously named " . . . Kenneth Dahlberg, whose $25,000 check was used to help finance the Watergate bugging effort."

Deputy Attorney General and was handling the ITT antitrust cases (Mitchell having disqualified himself as Attorney General because he had previously represented ITT as a private lawyer). ITT had secured a favorable ruling in a lower court in one of its cases, and the Department of Justice was planning to appeal. On the last day for filing the appeal Kleindienst was ordered by the President not to go ahead. Angered by this directive, Kleindienst sent word to the White House that if the President persisted in it he would resign. The President changed his mind and the appeal was filed. In 1974, Special Prosecutor Jaworski charged Kleindienst with failing to tell the story of that incident to the Senate Judiciary Committee during his confirmation hearing in 1972, in which Kleindienst had denied that there had been White House interference with Justice's handling of the ITT case. Jaworski acknowledged that this case carried no implication that the President had acted illegally in issuing the instructions about the case. Kleindienst pleaded guilty to a misdemeanor and received a thirty-day sentence and a fine of $100, both of which were suspended by the court. Federal Judge George Hart, Jr., who imposed the sentence, praised Kleindienst for his courage in standing up to the President, saying the violation was a technical one and it "is not the type of violation that reflects a mind bent on deception. . . . Rather it reflects a heart that is too loyal and considerate of the feelings of others."[3]

**Lee Nunn** of Kentucky, long-time Republican fund-raiser and a top assistant in the 1972 Nixon race. In line for an appointment to a regulatory commission, Nunn was forced into a long wait and was finally passed over because the Special Prosecutor was holding over him the threat of charges for illegal campaign activity. The matter was ultimately dropped, but too late.

**Harold Scott** and **Newell Weed**, also top assistants in the

3. It may be evidence of the killer attitude of some members of the Special Prosecutor's staff that they originally proposed that Kleindienst be charged with thirteen felony counts, enough to incarcerate him for life; and that three members resigned when Jaworski agreed to accept one misdemeanor count.

*30*1972 finance committee. Under consideration for important positions in the Administration, they were forced to wait until questions of the committee's practices within their areas of activity had been satisfactorily resolved by the investigating bodies. By that time, the appointments were no longer practicable for either one.

**Felipe DeDiego**, a Cuban indicted in the Fielding burglary. After several months, the indictment was dismissed by a Federal judge because it was based on immunized testimony he had given to a Florida prosecutor. The Special Prosecutor appealed, but then dropped the charges because of doubts about the legal effects of that grant of immunity.

**Rose Mary Woods**, personal secretary to President Nixon. In the Special Prosecutor's efforts to pin down responsibility for an erasure of eighteen and a half minutes on a White House tape, Miss Woods was subjected to intense questioning on several occasions in court, in a carnival atmosphere, and to blatant news reports ridiculing her explanations and implying her guilt. When it was all over, the Special Prosecutor told her attorney that no case had been found for any legal action against her; unfortunately, no public announcement to that effect was ever made, and the presumption of guilt was not removed. Needless to say, because of her relationship to the President, she was constantly followed by the press and questioned about other matters, on many of which she had no information. She was also subjected to a degree of torment when a list of early contributors, used for social invitations to the White House, surfaced in her possession and became playfully but snidely referred to as "Rosemary's Baby."

**Thomas Pappas**, Boston businessman with major investment holdings in Greece. Because his name came up as a fund-raiser in several White House tapes, the media assumed in news stories that he was secretly collecting payoff money for the Watergate burglars. The smearing implications were false.

**Charles Richey**, judge of the Federal District Court in Washington. Richey was accused by John Dean of having cooperated covertly with the Committee for the Re-Election of the President in civil suits against the committee, by improperly discussing the case and even "suggesting to Stans" that he file a countersuit for libel against Lawrence O'Brien, chairman of the Democratic National Committee. Such a suggestion was never made, to my knowledge, but the news stories hurt Richey nonetheless, even though no charges resulted. The false story was that Richey's suggestion occurred in the rose garden of a man who later testified he had no rose garden.

**Richard Moore**, special counsel to the President, who worked on public relations at the White House. Moore was spectacularly mistreated as a witness before the Senate Watergate Committee on national television. After private interviews with committee staff men that reviewed in detail the range of its interest in his knowledge, he was placed on the stand and at once subjected to a series of rapid-fire questions by a young lawyer named Terry Lenzner on entirely different subjects, causing him to grope for answers and be made to appear confused and foolish. It was a contemptible treatment of a decent man. Later, Moore was named in a news story as an unindicted co-conspirator in the Watergate coverup. The story was not correct, but the damage of the announcement was never repaired.

**Ray Kroc**, wealthy Chicago businessman who built the McDonald hamburger chain. Because he contributed $250,000 to the Nixon campaign, he became the target of press insinuations that he thereby had contracted for favors in return from the Administration. One was that his gift had bought a favorable ruling from the government's Price Commission on the price of his company's hamburgers. Another was that his contribution had bought Administration support for a lower minimum wage for teenagers, which would mean big savings to the McDonald company. There was not a germ of truth to either statement.

**W. Clement Stone**, rich head of a Chicago-based insurance company, who was the largest contributor to Nixon's campaign in 1968 and again in 1972. Although he said publicly on many occasions that he had given with no expectation of any reward except the satisfaction of having played a part in the making of history, he was publicly challenged time and again by news commentators with having made a deal to be appointed Ambassador to Great Britain. An impropriety like that would have been completely out of character for Clem Stone, and the news accounts were written on no grounds whatever and solely on supposition. He was an unusually able, sometimes considered eccentric, person with a pencil-line mustache and a loud enthusiastic voice, who had become wealthy by practicing PMA ("Positive Mental Attitude") in his business and personal relationships, and who was dedicated to selling that message of personal success to millions of others through his speeches and publications. A confirmed idealist, Stone had an impeccable record for business integrity.

**Ben Fernandez**, chairman in 1972 of the National Hispanic Finance Committee and a Los Angeles financial consultant. Fernandez was forced to defend himself in public and in private before the Senate Watergate Committee and the Watergate Special Prosecutor on a false allegation that he had offered to assist a Miami builder, who was having legal difficulties in a housing program subsidized by the Federal Housing Administration, to clear up his problems with the agency in return for a $50,000 contribution. The fact was that the builder's contribution, in the amount of $25,000, had been tendered to Fernandez and rejected. The builder was later sentenced for his contract improprieties.

**Harold Geneen**, chairman of ITT and one of the country's most successful business executives. The multiplicity of investigations against his company, exaggerated by frequent leaks in news outlets, dragged him into a limelight of continuing adverse publicity. Although the Special Prosecutor's task force acknowledged that "from the outset Harold Geneen was a principal target," it was forced to acknowledge at the end that "in sum, we did not make a case of perjury or any other case against Geneen."

Numerous government officials, including Secretary of Agriculture **Clifford Hardin**, Securities and Exchange Commission Chairman **William J. Casey**, Director of the Office of Management and Budget **George Shultz**, and others. These persons were the reluctant beneficiaries of numerous news reports linking them in one way or another to a current focus of investigation. Not all the stories inferred wrongdoing, but many did, and in either case there was an obviously harmful and probably emotional stress from the experience, however hardened the individual may have been to life in politics. Hardin was forced to defend his actions in raising milk price supports in March 1971 after he had first publicly announced he would not do so. The inference of the press accounts was that he had been improperly influenced by the White House to reverse his decision. The Special Prosecutor considered charging him with having made false statements, but found that the evidence supported Hardin's account of the course of events and dropped the subject. Hardin's final decision had been made on proper economic grounds. The publicity over the incident unfairly detracted from his excellent record as Agriculture Secretary.

**Dan Hofgren, Arden Chambers,** and **Ken Talmage**, employees of the Finance Committee to Re-Elect the President. Interrogated frequently by assistant district attorneys in New York, they were wheedled, harassed, abused, and threatened with criminal charges for perjury if they did not change their testimony regarding transactions concerning Robert Vesco, a contributor. Hofgren was called in for quizzing a number of times, including once from Europe where he was on a business trip. He was threatened with a perjury indictment if he would not say that Vesco had been asked by the author to give in cash, and was accused of conspiring with him to mesh their stories, which was not the case. In his own words, he was "roughed up" several times, the last shortly before he testified in the trial. Talmage was brought in from the West Coast five or six times for grilling. All three said later that they were told that "you are lying; we have solid evidence that you are lying," when that was not the case at all. Despite such repeated treatment and under great stress, they insisted on holding to the truth in their testimony. Both Hofgren and Chambers were used as government witnesses, but they were questioned in a narrow range.

**Ed Nixon**, brother of the President and a campaign worker. Although he participated in only two conversations relevant to the Vesco transaction, he was brought from his home on the West Coast to New York ten times, at the insistence of the same prosecutors. His attorney protested strenuously the coercion to which he was subjected, and Nixon testified truthfully and courageously for the defense despite the threats that he received. His brother, **Donald Nixon**, was also drawn into the Vesco case and other matters, and heavily investigated, to no avail. Each of them lost considerable time and incurred expenses in excess of $30,000 in these tormenting affairs. Following the unfavorable publicity on this and other matters, Donald Nixon lost his job with a national hotel chain.

**Clark MacGregor**, former White House aide and former Congressman, who succeeded as Nixon's campaign director in July 1972 after John Mitchell resigned. In that position he inherited all the unanswered questions about campaign practices and bore the brunt of much public criticism and attack for things for which he was in no way responsible. His inability to provide details embarrassed him at searching press conferences and made him more suspect in news accounts. He had walked into a hornet's nest, with no knowledge of what had preceded him or what was still going on in payoffs. No semblance of guilt was ever attached to him. One instance of mistreatment to which he was subjected was Congressman Wright Patman's call for him to testify, with others, in an unauthorized public hearing; when none of the invited guests appeared, Patman staged a side show for the media with vacant chairs bearing the names of those invited, including MacGregor, and presented a monologue about their failure to cooperate. The picture covered the country. MacGregor didn't deserve this cynical treatment, or any of the other annoyances which he was accorded by the distrusting media.

**Murray Chotiner**, Washington attorney. Because of his long friendship with Nixon, Chotiner was under frequent suspicion by the media and prosecutors on many matters, none ever proved to be illegal, until his untimely death in an automobile accident in 1974. Worst of his experience was an accusation by the *Manchester Union Leader* that he was guilty of complicity in the Watergate affair through "a secret fund of $350,000 collected from gambling interests in Las Vegas and from the pension fund of the Teamsters' union." This was a fiction and Chotiner sued and won a monetary settlement for libel, but once again the unfavorable early media reports, spread across the nation, were not matched by those following the vindication.

**Paul Barrick** and his assistants, **Judy Hoback** and **Evelyn Hyde**. Barrick was controller for the Nixon finance committee for a time and became treasurer when Sloan resigned in July. He and his staff were forced to attend numerous depositions and inquisitions, many antagonistic, and were pursued by pressmen into their homes in attempts to pry information that they were in no position to give. Common Cause unfairly accused Barrick of having withheld records of contributions and expenditures from its scrutiny and later subjected him to intensive and sometimes sarcastic questioning over the Nixon committee's published report on these matters.

**Henry Buchanan**, an independent certified public accountant who was retained to prepare the public report of early contributions to the Nixon campaign. After he and his staff had prepared the accounting in a thoroughly professional manner, they were subjected to insulting cross-examination by Common Cause lawyers that implied deliberate misrepresentation. No errors were ever found, and the court finally brought the ordeal to an end in which it criticized Common Cause for the unnecessary harassment. Also,

Buchanan was accused by CBS of having used his professional office as a "laundry" to conceal the uses of committee funds. He filed suit against CBS for libel, but the case was dismissed on the specious legal ground that he had become a public figure and therefore could not be libeled by such an accusation.

**Helen Bentley**, Chairman of the Maritime Commission. Bentley was preparing to file as a candidate for Governor of Maryland when it was publicized that she had picked up two contributions totaling $25,000 from shipping interests and delivered them to the Nixon finance committee. Although perhaps slightly indiscreet, since her commission regulated the maritime industry, this action involved no criminal offense. However, the resulting furor in the press and in Maryland political circles forced her to withdraw from the race.

**Buckley Byers**, a Washington business consultant and an important member of the 1972 Nixon fund-raising team. Byers had the responsibility of organizing industry-wide groups of executives to contribute to the campaign, and because of that found himself in the middle of a series of investigations of suspected corporate misdeeds. Questioned at length and repetitiously by investigating bodies in eight sessions, brought before a grand jury as a witness, and publicized with suspicion by the Washington press, he found his time invaded, his composure disturbed by the strains, and his ability to secure and serve clients affected by the unfavorable publicity. The whole affair, characterized by him as a series of fishing expeditions, produced nothing but harassment.

**William Timmons**, assistant to the President for Congressional relations; **Rob Odle**, assistant to Jeb Magruder during the election campaign, and **J. Glenn Sedam**, a lawyer in the campaign office. All three were accused in a **Washington Post** article in October 1972 of having regularly received reports on wiretapped conversations in the Democratic National Committee's Watergate office, thus charging them directly of complicity in the breakin plot. The story had been based entirely on guesswork and rushed to press in an effort to leapfrog the revelations of a competing paper. It was totally incorrect, and the reporters who wrote it, Woodward and Bernstein, eventually conceded in their book that the men named had never seen any papers having to do with the wiretapping. The callous nature of the news account, and the even more callous attitude of the two writers, is shown by their own words of admission almost eighteen months after the fact:

"Three men had been wronged. They had been unfairly accused on the front page of the *Washington Post*, the hometown newspaper of their families, neighbors and friends. Odle complained to the prosecutors. 'He was almost in tears', one of them said later. The stigma of Watergate stayed with him, though not solely because of the story, and he had great difficulty obtaining a job.

"Timmons was dejected about the *Post* allegations, and his wife had wanted him to quit his job on the White House staff. Only after a long conversation with the President had he decided to stay on."[4]

Not a word of sincere apology, even then. The incident is a prime example of the heartless attitude and indiscriminate marksmanship of some of the hunters of the media in the competitive race for headlines, regardless of cost to those named.

**Kenneth Rietz** and **George Gorton**, both of whom worked in the Youth Division of the 1972 Nixon campaign. Gorton was accused by the press of sundry improprieties, none true, and had trouble getting employment after the election. In untrue press stories, Rietz was charged with having created a "kiddie spy corps" to engage in various dirty tricks and of using funds illegally, and those were never corrected.

**Fred Malek**, former White House aide who held an executive job for a time in the Nixon campaign headquarters.

---

4. *All the President's Men*, Simon and Schuster, 1974, at page 110.

Malek received considerable press attention, principally because of his sponsorship of organized efforts to get more White House credit for government grants and expenditures in the election year (a regular quadrennial procedure for incumbents), and also was grossly characterized in unfavorable terms by the Special Prosecutor's office. He felt that the whole experience had caused his "currency to be devalued" for a while until he found employment as a high official in Marriott Corporation.

**Ron Ziegler**, top White House press aide, who unwittingly was forced to ride the line between inaccurate information on Watergate fed him by his associates in the administration and the skeptically biting assaults of the press corps, until he finally learned the truth and had to declare all his previous statements "inoperative." Ziegler took a horrifying amount of abuse from a press corps that had no reason whatever to believe that he was purposely misleading them. He deserved better.

**George Bush**, former member of Congress and former Ambassador to the United Nations. Bush, who proved he was one of the bravest men in Washington in agreeing to head the Republican National Committee during the 1973-1974 phase of Watergate, kept the party organization together and its morale high, despite massive difficulties of press criticism and growing public disaffection with the administration. Totally without information as to what had gone on in Watergate behind the scenes, he was unable to respond knowledgeably to questions and because of that unjustly became the personal target of continuing sarcasm and cynicism from the media.

**Patrick Buchanan**, a top White House aid for speechwriting. Buchanan was abused by leaks and rumors from the staff of the Senate Watergate Committee, which were broadcast across the land, to the effect that he was the "architect of the dirty trick strategy" in the 1972 campaign. This attack extended over a three-day period prior to his testifying before the committee. His denials of the untruths when he appeared were effective and convincing, but could not wholly overcome the effects of the unfair tarring by the committee staff and the media on him and on the public.

A group of victims easy to describe but difficult to quantify was generated in the elections of 1974. Members of the Congress who had, in one way or another, expressed sympathy for Richard Nixon, or defended his administration or his people, found themselves overwhelmed in the elections by the national wave of Watergate indignation.

Mere allegiance to the Republican party became grounds for disfavor across the country, with the result that the purge retired not only Congressmen, but also state governors and legislators. While it is not possible to isolate local factors from national, and to name with certainty which individuals lost because of the overwhelming sentiment of the times, political commentators generally agree that many good men who normally would have been re-elected (or new candidates who might have won) were rejected by the voters solely because of Watergate. These included five members of the House Judiciary Committee who voted against impeachment—**Charles Sandman, Jr.** of New Jersey, **David Dennis** of Indiana, **Wiley Mayne** of Iowa, **Harold Froelich** of Wisconsin and **Joseph Maraziti** of New Jersey; one other,**Henry Smith III**, of New York, avoided facing the voters on the issue by retiring. Without Watergate, Republican strength in Washington and in state capitals after 1974 would have been much greater.

Most extreme of all the instances of suffering imposed on anyone was that of **Charles Gregory "Bebe" Rebozo**, Chairman and President of the Key Biscayne Bank of Florida. For many years a personal friend and confidant of Richard Nixon, with no official position in the government, in the election campaigns, or in fund-raising, he became the most striking illustration of determined pursuit by prosecutors and the press.

The Senate Watergate Committee's hunt for Rebozo was determined and ruthless, from July through October 1973. Its investigators went over the same ground on four different excursions to Miami, questioning him ad infinitum and examining voluminous documents. Examiners of the IRS spent more than three months auditing his records and those of the bank he controlled. He was investigated by the GAO and by the Miami District Attorney, and finally by the Watergate Special Prosecutor in a saga that continued for sixteen more months and produced twenty-five file drawers of collected records.

The original question related to the legality of his receipt, retention, and possible expenditure of $100,000 in cash delivered to him by an agent of Howard Hughes in 1970. Inspired by suppositions and rumors from various sources, this was enlarged gradually to include allegations and inferences that (1) Rebozo controlled a secret fund of $200,000 to $300,000 for Nixon, (2) some of the Hughes $100,000 was diverted to Nixon's secretary and his brothers, (3) government favors were given to Hughes in return for his $100,000, (4) additional funds were received from Hughes in 1968, (5) a contribution of $50,000 received by Rebozo from the Davis brothers of Jacksonville in 1972 was diverted from proper campaign uses, (6) campaign funds received by Rebozo were diverted for a pool at Nixon's home on Key Biscayne ($26,000) and for jewelry for Mrs. Nixon ($5,000), (7) Rebozo received unreported campaign money from Raymond Guest, J. Paul Getty, and others, (8) campaign money was diverted by Rebozo to finance the purchase of Nixon property in San Clemente, and a Bethesda home rented to Julie and David Eisenhower, and (9) the White House obstructed the IRS investigation of Rebozo.

According to the final report of the Special Prosecutor in October 1975, no stone was left unmoved in the effort to run down these and other incidental suspicions:

> During May and June 1974, the Special Prosecutor's office obtained all documents from the files of the Senate Select Committee and the Internal Revenue Service relating to Rebozo's finances. On the basis of these materials, the grand jury inquiry was broadened and nearly 200 subpoenas for documents were issued betwen April 1974 and July 1975. In

addition, 28 witnesses testified before the grand jury, 75 persons were questioned by the Special Prosecutor's office, and 47 persons were interviewed in the field by a team of specially detailed agents of the Internal Revenue Service. In all, 123 different persons were questioned, many of them repeatedly. Included among those questioned were officials and employees of the White House, the Finance Committee to Re-elect the President, Hughes' Summa Corporation, the Key Biscayne Bank, and many others.

The IRS team also assisted the Special Prosecutor's office in evaluating the voluminous financial records obtained. Between April and December 1974, the agents and Assistant Special Prosecutors analyzed thousands of pages of records received from more than 240 sources.

Secondary sources of information also were systematically and exhaustively utilized. This included records from banks, accountants, attorneys, various business partners and associates, business firms, and so forth. Second, voluminous records were reviewed of telephone calls, travel, meetings with Administration officials, and correspondence with various persons. Third, persons suspected of making secret contributions were questioned and their documents reviewed. Fourth, tapes and hundreds of memoranda and other documents from the White House files were studied for any references to relevant financial transactions or any actions involving soliciting or use of funds for President Nixon.

Extensive investigation was undertaken concerning the source and application of all funds which required examination in order to resolve the matters raised in the Senate Select Committee materials. Documents and information were obtained which had not been available to the Committee, and they helped resolve some questions which were raised by the Senate report.

After all investigation was completed, and the evidence had been evaluated by the prosecutors who ran the investigation and by the General Counsel's office of the Internal Revenue Service, it was concluded by the prosecutors that the evidence would not support an indictment.

The investigator's own report was even more precise in the conclusion: "There is plainly no basis for any indictments," he said. Apparently all that was proved was that Rebozo did receive contributions of $100,000 in 1970 from a representative of Howard Hughes, for campaign purposes, and later returned it; that he received a contribution of $50,000 from the Davis brothers in 1972 which he turned over to Fred LaRue, an official of the Nixon campaign; and that he used about $5,000 of leftover campaign funds from 1968, which he said was due him for expenses, to pay for diamond earrings for Mrs. Nixon. None of these actions was criminal.

The cost in pain and time and counsel fees to Rebozo are beyond measure, and they probably represent the highest price ever paid for the pleasure of the personal friendship of a President. It was an undeserved fate for this mild-mannered, unobtrusive small-town banker, who had never demonstrated a desire for financial or political advantage by reason of that relationship. There is no known evidence that Rebozo ever influenced a Presidential decision or received a governmental advantage for himself or for anyone else.

The cost to the government of the far-reaching Rebozo man hunt has been estimated at $2 to $3 million.

This is only a selected list, certainly not complete. And these are bare outlines. Each experience would need to be enlarged in description to unfold its measures of fear, intimidation, heartache and suffering, and only the victims themselves can provide that. A hundred or more other respectable persons are believed to have suffered unsupported media stories, loss of good will and reputation, and sometimes lengthy investigations and financial costs in defending themselves, because they were somewhere within the circle of Watergate interest or because someone "cried out" upon them.

No one can know how many. No one can know the depth of their agonies. Some were very remote from Watergate: *Bob Aplanalp*, a businessman and a personal friend of the President, who was investigated in a myriad of ways, the worst of which was in response to a report, untrue, that government money had been spent to improve his home in the Bahamas where Nixon sometimes went to relax; the fact was that even the security measures taken there to protect the President and the Secret Service were paid out of his own funds. *Henry Kissinger*, whose superlative effectiveness in foreign affairs was dimmed for a time by untrue accusations that he had used the influence of his position in political fund-raising and, most disturbingly to this sensitive person, that he had participated improperly in wiretapping adventures.

Some, for example, were outside Washington, such as William Liedtke and Roy Winchester of Texas, Frank Middleton of Arizona, and Leonard Firestone and Darius Keaton of California, all the targets of news stories and resulting investigations on matters which turned out to be meaningless.

All of them know how wide-ranging the witch-hunt was.

And the aftermath. Employees of the Nixon campaign who were totally ignorant of any skullduggery found themselves marked with scarlet when it came to finding new jobs. Rob Odle was discharged by the Department of Agriculture in 1973 when it was learned that he had been an office manager for the campaign; he had to seek work elsewhere. Arden Chambers, an expert personal secretary in the Department of Commerce and in the election effort, was turned down for employment time after time by the White House personnel office, government agencies, and private companies, and was unemployed for more than two years. Jack Gleason found his 1970 campaign work, his technical conviction, and short probation destructive to his career as a Washington consultant. DeVan Shumway, press relations man for the Nixon campaign, found it difficult for a considerable period to get suitable employment. **Steve Bull** and **Mike Farrell** of the White House staff had to take a long time to find a new job, as did **John Chadwell, Jr.**, who assisted the campaign in California. Tom Houser, who was campaign chairman in Illinois, found that he couldn't even get his other credentials considered; although he had earlier been an FCC Commissioner and the Director of the White House Office of Telecommunications Policy, he was rejected out of hand for the post of President of the Corporation for Public Broadcasting solely because of his association with Nixon. People not even in the campaign sometimes bore the stigma. John Jenkins and Walter Sorg, officials of the Office of Minority Enterprise in the Department of Commerce, who paradoxically got in dutch with the White House in 1972 for not responding quickly enough to its suggestions for the making of money grants to applicants, were red-lined for jobs on the grounds that they were "too political." There were also persons who lost appointments to important offices because they were temporarily fingered for alleged offenses that were not borne out or merely because they were Nixon contributors.

## Innocent Victims—Class 3

In this category are the large groups of other contributors (several hundred), campaign workers (a hundred or so), and White House employees (dozens) who were abraded in the processes of search engaged in by the investigating agencies, grand juries, and media reporters. (In this category, as in the others, no one can properly challenge the necessity of law enforcement through quiet fact finding. What was objectionable throughout was the frequent repetition of the process, and the competitive thrust to bring every person into the limelight of publicity in ways which were bound to be debilitating and usually damaging to good names. This damage was compounded by leaks emanating from the office of the Special Prosecutor, grand juries, the GAO, and Congressional committees, always reported with alacrity by the media, that frequently were based on isolated and unverified material that eventually turned out to be inaccurate or one-sided.)

Contributors especially got a large share of attention. Hundreds were questioned repetitively by mail, telephone, and interview by persons on fishing expeditions to find some untoward action by them or by the fund-raisers they had dealt with. The Senate Watergate Committee sent out seven hundred questionnaires. The Watergate Special Prosecutor wrote fifty contributors for detailed information, and others were telephoned or called to Washington or New York for questioning or grand jury testimony. The FBI interviewed hundreds of financial officers and other employees of corporations and banks. Their names, innocent or guilty, often ended up in the news, with obviously negative connotations.

One reporter surreptitiously acquired a list of persons invited to a party at the Republican convention and incorrectly assumed it to be a list of contributors. His stories reported the names in their home press and in some national media, in articles extending over several days. No crimes were involved, although it was almost made to appear that contributing was one. No sensible journalistic purpose was served in casting doubt on these individuals, but it continued even after the reporter was told that the list was one of guests, only some of whom were coincidentally givers, and some of whom were not contributors at all.

For the first time in history, contributors in 1972 were subjected to gift tax on the amounts they had contributed, even though it was commonly understood by fund-raisers of both major parties that this tax did not apply if the gifts were broken down into separate amounts for various committees. For many years prior to 1972 it was customary for candidates for President and the Congress to organize a number of fund-raising committees so that a contributor wishing to give a substantial amount could distribute his gifts in amounts not to exceed the regularly exempted $3,000 ($6,000 for a husband and wife) to any one committee. This procedure was understood to be in accord with long-standing Internal Revenue regulations, which were confirmed and reinforced by a Treasury ruling in June 1972 setting forth a simple requirement that at least one-third of the officers of each such committee must be different.

The allocation of political contributions to multiple committees, as permitted in these various rulings, had regularly been interpreted by lawyers around the country, Democratic and Republican, as being adequate to qualify for the tax exemption.

There already was a United States District Court decision, affirmed by the Fifth Circuit Court of Appeals, holding that contributions to political campaigns were not subject to gift taxes because they were merely aimed at insuring good government and not at benefiting a recipient. The IRS refused to accept the decision, however, and adopted the absurd position that it would thereafter prevail as law only in the Fifth Circuit, the states from Georgia to Texas.

In December 1974, in an attempt to clear up the "uncertainty" as to whether political contributions were taxable gifts, Congress specifically exempted them. Ironically, the exemption was made effective as of May 7, 1974, leaving the 1972 and earlier contributions still in legal doubt and the contributors still under the gun.

Despite this background of regulation, practice and law, the Internal Revenue then undertook, in a blatantly discriminatory action, to assess the gift tax on the combined amount of all 1972 contributions by one person or couple to each candidate as though it constituted one single gift; in a few cases of large Republican givers, IRS even went back to 1968 and 1970 contributions to impose the tax. The inequity of this procedure was contested by many taxpayers and it is now in the courts for decision. While some Democrats were affected by the assessments, their number was small compared to the number of Nixon contributors who were assessed.

It is generally believed that the stimulus for this surprising treatment came from Mitchell Rogovin, a Washington lawyer and a former chief counsel of IRS, who had publicly challenged Internal Revenue to assess a wide range of dubious taxes against Watergate characters and Republicans in general. His article, "Revenuers vs Republicans," in the *New Republic* for July 7, 1973, was a poisonous mixture of political hatred, misstatements of fact, and distorted conclusions, but it managed to accomplish its purpose of causing the IRS to invoke new readings into the law to harass Nixon's contributors and campaign workers. Only a few of his flights of fancy were credited with sense, but enough were followed by the revenuers to create ad hoc new approaches to tax enforcement that seemed to go far beyond the law and surely were contrary to common legal understanding of what the regulations had long meant. Interestingly, Rogovin later reputedly appeared as counsel for a Democratic contributor in contesting a gift tax assessment, which may present a fascinating ethical question.

The IRS went far in its antics to exterminate as much Republican wealth as possible. For the first known time, it proposed to assess income taxes against political committees, a procedure which brought in the Finance Committee for the Re-Election of the President in two different ways. Reacting to Rogovin's challenge, and stimulated by news reports that the committee had received as much as $20 million in stocks and bonds as contributions, it demanded that a tax be paid on any capital gains the givers had avoided by making the contributions in that form. The law was clear that when such a gift is made, neither the donor nor the donee has taxable income, even if the securities are worth more at the time than they had originally cost, and both Republicans and Democrats had legal opinions to that effect. Nevertheless, IRS advanced the novel idea that the parties' committees would have to pay a capital gains tax on any such presumed profits and said it would enforce such a levy unless the Congress directed otherwise. After some delay, during which time IRS required that reports of such transactions be filed and the tax computed, the Congress did direct otherwise in a 1974 law, and that was the end of that fanciful imposition of IRS power. (Some McGovern committees were also involved in this issue, but to a much smaller degree.)

Then, IRS staff asserted claims against the Nixon finance committee for income taxes in excess of $1.5 million, but this was reduced by an IRS national office technical advice memorandum to $387,000 plus interest. Immediately the Service, by jeopardy assessment, took $472,000 from the committee (another Rogovin idea), even though the trustees of the funds had agreed to preserve them intact until the issues were resolved. The theory of the tax, as it finally evolved, was that money paid out of a White House fund and from other extraneous sources to the Watergate burglars for legal expenses and living costs somehow could be charged as taxable income to the finance committee, even though the committee had nothing to do with the payments; IRS also alleged that a $300,000 contribution from one person could be taxed as quid pro quo income to the committee because the donor had received an appointment as ambassador, even though it acknowledged that criminal investigations of the transaction had not found evidence adequate to support the charge, and that neither the chairman nor the treasurer of the finance committee had played an improper part.

The committee's tax counsel fought the case vehemently, and the committee chairman presented evidence in support of its objections. At the conclusion of one such hearing on June 9, 1977, the IRS appellate official had the audacity to say, "If this case didn't involve Watergate, I could settle it very favorably for you."

In frustration and without conceding the IRS issues, the trustees for the finance committee finally agreed to settle the case upon the refund of about $200,000 of the money that IRS had appropriated. As a final blow, IRS then announced that it would not make the refund or permit any payments out of remaining committee funds until the last of the gift tax cases against Nixon contributors was settled, as it would assert its right to collect from the recipient committee for any gift tax it was unable to collect from a donor.

## Guilty Who Went Free

There is one more side to the story. While all this was going on, tens of persons received immunity for their testimony against others, in the Vesco case, in Senate hearings, in grand jury proceedings, or in criminal trials. In the game of working up the ladder toward bigger targets, the inquisitors and prosecutors forgave many they believed to be guilty, for their help in pointing a finger. Four seriously implicated persons were used as witnesses in the Vesco trial in return for forgiveness or leniency, thirty were provided full "use immunity" by the Watergate Special Prosecutor, and an unknown list were freed of prosecution by the Senate Watergate Committee.

The practice of granting immunity to cooperating witnesses is proper, but it leads to other hazards. A person given immunity acquires a general aura of guilty conduct, even though he might not in fact have been criminally culpable. Also, eighteen persons were named by the Watergate grand jury as unindicted co-conspirators in the coverup case; this procedure allowed none of them an opportunity, if he wished it, to defend himself in a court trial.

All that has been said up to this point leads to the overriding question. Taking into account the relatively small number of guilty who were found guilty, the guilty who were let go for helping to pin down others, the innocent who were subjected to the travail of criminal charges and found innocent, and the many innocent who were made to suffer in the inquisitions and sometimes tarred beyond redemption, how does the balance sheet of the long witch-hunt come out? Was it all worthwhile in the interest of justice, and did it have to be done the way it was carried on? And were the actions of the media, the politicians, and the public interest groups, in their wild chase for news fodder, more destructive to justice and equity than they were helpful?

It is hard to avoid a conclusion that there were several standards of justice at work during these years. Discriminatory prosecution, targeting of individuals, trials on flimsy evidence, withholding of exculpatory information, and other practices, raise questions of how truly and fairly justice was administered. Even granting the right of prosecutorial discretion, the balance sheet of Watergate is one that raises many doubts.

The aggressive media, the desperate politicians, the ambitious prosecutors, an aroused public, and even courts under public pressure played a part in creating this imbalance of justice while the witch-hunt ran its course. It took courage to believe in a suspect's innocence, and more courage to stand against the crying wolves and deal in fairness.

There may even be a deeper meaning for this apparent varying standard of justice, and some ideas are contained in a book by a perceptive reviewer of the prosecution syndrome in the Watergate era:

> The course of human events being what it is, the people [on the Special Prosecutor's staff] who knew how to prosecute, in 1973, were people conditioned ... by the Kennedy Justice methodology. Imperfectly articulated as it was, that methodology was developed upon the premise that law enforcement should not be passive, but aggressive. The governing hypothesis was that there is an ineradicable difference between good guys and bad guys, opponent to and actionable by, the good guys. Out of that came target law enforcement: upon identification as a bad guy, the suspect may resign himself to merciless investigation, reinvestigation, indictment and reindictment, trial and retrial, until at last the Government secures a verdict which ratifies its prosecutor's assessment of the defendant as a bad guy.
> ... the targets—the people—of the ... process are selected on an ad hoc basis. It is terribly personal. It is not monitored by a disinterested custodian of the due process of law.
> Cox, with Ruth's assistance, arranged the Special Prosecution Force on the aggressive model of law enforcement, which evolved from the development of the Organized Crime and Racketeering Section (of the Department of Justice).
> ... mating the investigative and prosecutive functions, it adds to the territorial designation two further letters of marque and reprisal: designation of prospective suspects (no longer does the prosecutor decide whether to prosecute by asking "Can we prove he did it?"; he begins with the decision to prosecute at least half made, and reasons: "We know he did something, and as soon as we can prove it, we indict the bastard.") and designations of likely subjects which, when investigated exhaustively (income tax returns, for example), may prove fruitful of evidence.[4]

4. George V. Higgins, *The Friends of Richard Nixon*, (Boston: Atlantic Monthly Press, Little, Brown & Co., 1974).

The outlook of anyone toward whom the finger was pointed was bleak, even if he had the guts and the money and the time and the nervous system to fight back for an indeterminate period, (also within the control of the determined hunters). The first Watergate Special Prosecutor, Archibald Cox, and two-thirds of his top dozen aides, had been associated in government or in politics with one or the other of the Kennedy brothers, and only one aide was a Republican. Cox and his successor, Henry Ruth, and Tom McBride and James Neal, two major principals, had worked in the Department of Justice under Robert Kennedy. The partisan leanings of these individuals were exceeded by the fervor of many of the junior staff, most of them brassy lawyers intoxicated with the recognition accorded them by the press and the opportunity of hacking away at people of importance.[5]

These circumstances may explain how it is possible that some people were forced, under the political circumstances of the time, to pay an outrageous price for their close association with a President who fell from grace.[6]

The aggressive actions of the media raise many questions of what their proper role should be in criminal investigations, what needs to be done to avoid their trampling on personal rights, when and how corrective remedies are in order for erroneous reporting, and, in particular, how persons unfairly damaged should be rehabilitated.

Even if it were taken for granted that everything ended as it should have—the guilty found guilty and the innocent found innocent—the question still remains whether that result was

---

5. Columnist Richard Wilson had earlier, after the firing of Cox as Special Prosecutor, said very much the same thing:

> No amount of self-abnegation or professed detachment could mask the fact that Prof. Cox, himself a Kennedy partisan and solicitor general, had surrounded himself with avid Kennedy-ite lawyers who fully expected to be gnawing away at the Nixon administration for three and a half years.

6. Evidence of the intensity of feeling of the Special Prosecutor's staff against those they had targeted for guilt and punishment (and the manner in which they tugged at Jaworski to follow them) is provided by an insider, James Doyle, the Special Prosecutor's assistant for public affairs, in *Not Above the Law*, (New York: William Morrow & Company, Inc., 1977).

worth the price of violating the personal reputations of so many, and of the agony and heartbreak which the innocents in the line of fire and on the sidelines were made to bear. Some day an unbiased group of legal researchers should re-examine all that went on, evaluate it in terms of justice done and justice denied, and of basic human rights protected and violated. There are lessons to be learned from the witch-hunt of Watergate, and they should be framed for all to see, because what happened then can happen again in the nation's next period of man-induced hysteria.

These are matters that historians, too, might well ponder in the quiet objectivity that will be permitted by the increasing distance in time from the tragic events.

This is the point now to begin to fill in the record of one man's travail in the Watergate hurricane, and the next chapters do that in detail. The objective is not to plead for sympathy for Maurice Stans, or to condemn broadly any of the forces at work in this era, but to give an in-depth account of how they could and did impact.

With some temerity, but with a conviction based on my observation, the following chapters raise many questions and suggest some answers about the functioning of the media, public interest crusaders, zealous prosecutors, and the grand jury system—all these inspired by the concern that, while another Watergate will certainly not arise, future events could easily lead to similar abuses, impairing the lives of innocent persons. The objective is to see that in another setting, at another time, the same things do not happen to others.

# 4

## HORATIO ALGER NEVER SAID . . .

June 18, 1972, was like any other Sunday.

I slept about an hour later than on working days, did my morning exercises for twenty minutes on the electric bicycle and on the floor, showered, donned a robe, picked up the *Washington Post* at the front door of our Watergate apartment, and went to the kitchen to put together my regular breakfast of dry cereal, toast, and tea.

Everything seemed quite usual in the news, too. Political speculation was normal for that stage in a Presidential election year. The war situation in Vietnam was unchanged. Business was doing well. The nation was quiet.

One item in the *Post*, on the front page, attracted my attention enough to cause me to read it through. "Five Held in Plot to Bug Democratic Party Office," it said, inferring that they were caught while engaging in some kind of spying operation. A few random thoughts went through my mind. Who in the world could have been up to that? What did they hope to get? Could the same thing happen to the Nixon headquarters? I dismissed the questions lightly and went on reading elsewhere.

I did not recognize the names of the five persons arrested. I did not know of any espionage or sabotage activities of the Presidential campaign, on either side. For that matter, I did not even know that the Democratic party headquarters were in the Water gate office building, although my Watergate apartment was only two hundred feet away.

Nevertheless, this day and this event became the watershed of my life. After having enjoyed a career of fulfillment and satisfaction, I was suddenly plunged downward into a horrifying maelstrom of accusations, investigations, harassments, a long court trial, and continuing character assassination for matters of which I was ignorant. It was three years before the public disclosures of what had transpired and how I had been deceived by the guilty, brought the worst of the experience to an end with established evidence that I was innocent of any knowing wrong.

Within those thirty-six months I was to find myself dragged through a chain of events more traumatic and more prevailing than any nightmare I had ever imagined. In that period:

—Because I was chairman of the Finance Committee to Re-Elect the President, I was accused of having knowingly provided the money to finance the illegal break-in, and became the target of daily charges of criminal activity by opposing politicians.

—The Democratic National Committee and its chairman, Lawrence O'Brien, claiming that I was thereby a major conspirator in a wide-ranging plot to disrupt the 1972 election, sued me, among others, for damages of $6.4 million. Later, the Association of State Democratic Chairmen and its director joined in filing additional actions for another $10 million.

—United States Senator Frank Moss, who knew me only casually and had no firsthand knowledge of any of my activities in the campaign, assailed me in a long vitriolic speech on the floor of the Senate for "collecting millions of dollars in illegal campaign contributions, dispensing with [sic] illicit tax guidance, shredding secret documents ... and engaging in a massive and disreputable coverup job," all leading to his suggestion that I be indicted. (In a public press conference an hour later, where he was not protected by Congressional immunity, he used words only slightly less libelous.)

—Taking off from there, investigative reporters for the media, in an almost daily barrage of stories, charged or insinuated that I was guilty of every conceivable political crime. Much of this was printed in the Washington papers, circulated around the nation through the wire services, repeated on radio or television programs, and amplified in editorials. In addition, I was subjected to constant harassment and badgering by reporters and cameramen whenever I appeared in the open. My unwillingness to answer their questions was interpreted by many as certain proof of guilt, even though I tried to make it clear that I was cooperating fully with the authorities and that my public silence was at the direction of counsel to avoid impairing the civil rights of others.

—In public hearings before the Senate Watergate Committee, broadcast across the country, I was insultingly manhandled by the chairman, Senator Sam Ervin, as a certain guilty participant, without evidence and despite my testimony and protestations to the contrary. I was also subjected to the humiliation of false charges on the record by his staff men, with no opportunity allowed for effective rebuttal before the same nationwide audience.

—A Federal grand jury in New York, at the instigation of young assistants on the District Attorney's staff who were inspired by the Watergate implications, indicted me (together with John Mitchell) for conspiracy, obstruction of justice, and perjury, on ten counts carrying potential sentences of fifty years in prison and a fine of $100,000. After a year under indictment, I was subjected to the intense trauma of a seventy-day trial before the case collapsed in a verdict of not guilty on all counts.

—In a civil suit brought by Common Cause, a purported non-partisan public interest organization, against the Finance Committee to Re-Elect the President, I was not only forced to spend interminable hours in depositions, the collection of records, and the preparation of court documents for drawn-out legal proceedings, but was kept under threat of contempt of court for more than a year because my staff people innocently failed to turn in some irrelevant records.

—Because of my position with the finance committee, I was sued, along with the committee and other individuals, in civil actions for a total amount over $95 million, almost a hundred times my personal net worth, for alleged damages attributed directly or indirectly to the Watergate affair.

—I became, next to Richard Nixon, probably the most thoroughly investigated man in Washington. Finance Committee files were screened for weeks by cadres of government agents. My personal bank records were subpoenaed for years back, and my personal telephone and meeting records for five years were taken and combed, and then passed along from one investigating group to another. Hundreds of contributors and fund-raisers were interrogated about my activities. I was questioned for almost 200 hours in formal and informal testimony, all designed by investigators to establish criminal culpability. The legal costs of defending myself were astronomical.

—The Watergate Special Prosecutor and his staff, after two years of running down false accusations and blind alleys, charged me with five petty misdemeanors under the election financing laws on technical and nonwillful offenses of a type never before assessed against anyone, despite the incalculable and unjustified harm already done to me by the government in the New York trial and in disregard of other mitigating circumstances and of the failure to charge others with more serious offenses.

—As a result of my guilty plea to those counts, even though only technical misdemeanors were involved, the Committee on Professional Ethics of the American Institute of Certified Public Accountants brought me before the Institute's Trial Board on charges of conduct discreditable to the accounting profession.

Behind the scenes of all the public activity was the most searching investigation of a campaign finance operation and a finance chairman in history. In the early months following the Watergate disclosure, I was questioned four times by the FBI, at least that often by the GAO, once by the Department of Justice under oath, and once by investigators for Congressman Patman, and gave depositions on five occasions in the Democratic National Committee and Common Cause suits. Later on, I was questioned twice by prosecutors in New York before the Vesco grand jury, twice in Washington before a Watergate grand jury, once in Baltimore before a grand jury investigating a campaign contribution, and once in a civil suit. I was interviewed at length by the Senate Watergate Committee staff before I testified for two days in the limelight of national television before that committee.

While all this was going on, I was accorded a national notoriety that stigmatized me as the master mind of a heinous Watergate crime and, as an extension of that by imaginative reporters, as being a willful dealer in illicit "secret funds," solicitor of illegal contributions, and dispenser of political favors. The constant tension of these events, however innocent I was, was bound to be a strain on the physical health and mental state of my family and me, and especially so on my wife, who was hospitalized and semi-invalided by a serious and rare blood disease in the midst of it all. The overall effect was to destroy a part of our lives, diminish our resources, and leave us unable, for the first time, to plan or to control our futures. Not until three years elapsed did vindication come.

How in the world does a bystander get so deeply drawn into a matter of which he has no knowledge? How can all of these things happen in a country in which judicial equity is a byword, and in which a free press prides itself on its sense of fairness?

The answers to these questions occupy much of the rest of this book. It sets out in considerable detail the story of my associations and activities in the 1972 election campaign, much of which has not heretofore been told, and it amplifies and corrects the public record of the period in a multitude of ways. It also describes the human impact of living through an endless string of unfair and humiliating experiences solely because of being a bystander to a political crisis of unprecedented proportions. It enumerates similar ordeals of many other people.

Nothing in my previous experience had prepared me for this course of events. Until then life had been good, almost ideal, fully in keeping with my early Horatio Alger ambitions. In sixty-four years I had had the satisfaction of moving from a humble background in a small town in Minnesota to the highest honors in my profession, and then to Cabinet-level positions in Washington in the administrations of two presidents. Along the way there had only been a few memorable setbacks and emotional shocks, all short-lived.

My heritage, my early life and background, came to mind repeatedly as I faced the ordeal of Watergate, and from it I drew what strength I could.

Like millions of other Americans, my grandparents on both sides were immigrants, people who had left Europe for the fresh promises of the New World. My grandfathers had never met at home in Belgium; they came more than 4,000 miles to meet in Minnesota, and there my father, who had arrived at age four, and my mother, who was born there, were raised and subsequently met. They were living in Shakopee, Minnesota, when I was born in 1908, and I too grew up and went to school in this town. Shakopee was an excellent example of the American melting pot. It was a community of hard-working pioneer settlers, dedicated to making a new life for themselves and their children. And it was like hundreds of other small towns that sprang up all over America in the second half of the 19th century.

My father was an able and ambitious man, but life never gave him the opportunity to achieve wealth or success. After he finished the eighth grade, he went to work in a local brickyard as a laborer. By the time he was eighteen he had acquired a high skill in music, largely self-taught, and had been elected the director of several community concert bands. After he left the brickyard at about twenty, he learned house painting and decorating. The 25¢ an hour that his account books show as his charge was then the going rate, but it was pretty meager even at the price levels of the early 1900s to support a wife and family, since the winter weather conditions limited his working year to about seven months. And there were not always jobs to be done, since the townsmen were mostly frugal types who did much of their own painting and papering in spare hours.

So it turned out that the combination of part-time painter and part-time musician produced an income barely ample to provide minimal family comforts. And in the times when conditions were poor, the charge account at the corner grocery sometimes sustained the family for periods as long as a year.

Despite our limited circumstances, though, we never were conscious of poverty even though we knew we had to go without a lot of conveniences our neighbors enjoyed. There was always the expectation of better days, the time when "our ship would come in."

Our family's economic situation was made bearable by the fact that both my father and mother came from backgrounds in which frugality was a way of life. Under the relatively simple conditions of the early 1920s, we did without many of the things which the more affluent might have had available. We did not have an automobile. Many of my early possessions were second-hand, including a bicycle that cost $5, and a heavily taped clarinet that Dad bought me for $2.

From the earliest time I can remember, I had a strong streak of independence and a determined desire to excel. Not having an athletic build, I devoted my interest to studies and became a typical bookworm, with the result that schooling came easily. I was highly competitive and quite a perfectionist, so I never had difficulty with any studies and, whatever the subject, I was always at the head of my class, in elementary school and in high school. Undoubtedly I was somewhat of a grind to my classmates.

I became a voracious reader. We had no library at home, but I would read a book a day from the school library, in the time between classes and in the evenings. And occasionally I would get hold of a Nick Carter adventure. The *Saturday Evening Post* stories of primitive Asia and Africa by Roy Chapman Andrews and Carl Akeley entranced me and I read them over and over. *Boys' Life* brought adventure, too, and I dreamed of the African safaris and Asian tiger hunts that I would take when I was older. Somewhere along the line I was introduced to the stories of Horatio Alger and these made a deep impression on my young mind.

I was impelled to leave Shakopee after finishing high school at seventeen. Opportunity elsewhere was unlimited and inertia was an evil to be avoided. Even in those days there was a deadening quality in small-town life; except for the few who became successful merchants or professional men or elected officials, the promise was meager, and too often the hopeless rut of ordinary labors led to middle-age frustration, excessive drinking, and an early death. I could see that by observing people I knew. And my ambitions were extraordinarily strong. It was not that I rebelled against having been deprived of anything; it was more a matter of wanting instinctively to compete and to achieve, somehow to acquire better things and find a better life. I'm not at all embarrassed to admit even now that Horatio Alger played a large role in giving me the conviction that anything was achievable if I worked hard and lived cleanly. Any of his books I could get my hands on I read several times, and somehow I believed them, even though I knew they were fiction.

Such was the environment and way of life that formed me and became the motive force for all the days that followed. I cannot believe I could have been more kindly blessed than I was in having been born to God-fearing, hard-working immigrant parents in a little midwestern town in the early twentieth century; in having received an education in small, quality schools from teachers who could and did take a personal interest in their students; in having had the opportunity to read widely and develop an urge for adventure; and in having experienced rugged living conditions without feeling a sense of deprivation or poverty. From all this I acquired, consciously but without deliberation, a religious morality, a belief in work, faith in idealism, an urge to excel, a trust in people, a powerful ambition, and a confidence in life's rewards.

On an early September day in 1925, I kissed my parents goodbye and set out boldly for Chicago with a saxophone in one hand and a suitcase containing the rest of my worldly possessions in another. I also had $251 in the bank and unlimited confidence, so I had no qualms whatsoever about what might be ahead, and no doubts about the order of events.

When the overnight train arrived in Chicago, I went directly to Northwestern University's downtown campus and registered for evening classes in accounting, commercial law, and business English. By selecting the specific subjects in this way, I would necessarily miss the cultural advantages of the languages, social studies, and liberal arts, but I would get directly to the topics I needed to master in order to write the certified public accountant examination in a few years. The same day I found a rooming house in which to live.

The next morning the Northwestern University employment office evaluated me and decided I should be a bookkeeper or stenographer, whichever came first. In a day or so I came upon Harry Levi & Company, importers of sausage casings, and was hired as a stenographer at $30 a week. I was set. Now all I had to do was hang on to the job and I could cover my expenses in my austere budget and save money, too.

In this work I got an initiation into business standards, and what I learned took me some years to outgrow. Ethics in the sausage casing business were not very high. Goods rejected by a customer were shipped right back in the same tierce with a few sound layers put on top, poor and unusable casings were mixed in with good ones, and workmen in customer plants were bribed to let shoddy stuff pass inspection. This was all done in such an unabashed way that I took it to be common in business generally. When I wondered about it out loud one day, I was solidly told that it was none of a stenographer's business to ask such questions. The owner's philosophy of ethics, as he expressed it, was "What are friends for if you can't screw them once in a while?" I took this all as part of my education, and fortunately learned quickly enough in life that all business was not done in that way.

After seven semesters and twenty-one courses at Northwestern, I had been through all the basic accounting and commercial law subjects, and had learned some cost accounting, income taxes, economics, business English, business mathematics, and related subjects, so I felt I was ready to make a move to public accounting. By answering a newspaper ad, I got to Alexander Grant & Company, a small CPA firm, took a written examination, and was hired. It was a shock to find that the starting rate for junior accountants was only $125 a month, which meant that I had to take a percent drop in income. But that did not deter me from my objective and I knew I had to start at the bottom. Eventually I spent more than twenty-five years with A G & Co., most of them as managing partner.

In 1928, Milo Hopkins, the manager of Grant's small New York office invited me to join him there as his principal assistant and I accepted. The three years in Chicago had fulfilled my hopes. I had lived frugally, worked diligently, and studied hard. I had acquired business experience and a considerable knowledge of human character. I had completed the major part of the education I needed to write the CPA examination, and I had achieved a good background of diversified auditing experience in a very short time. In New York I could continue my part-time education, and I did so for a few more years at Columbia in evening classes.

There were good things that happened in New York and bad things, too. I arrived in January 1929, in time to lose all my savings in that fall's stock market crash and to see the economy enter the horrendous era of the Great Depression. I stayed there until early 1933 and then moved back to Chicago in the very month that the economy hit its lowest point, the nation's banks were closed, and unemployment was at its highest.

I didn't have much to lose in the stock market, but my loss was total. I got over that quickly and took from it a lesson in caution and conservatism. The Depression was a frightening thing. Our accounting business fell apart as clients went under or, if they stayed alive, couldn't pay their bills. There were months in which there was no money to pay our salaries, and we had to scrimp every nickel, in the office and at home.

Even so, we did better than most people. Anyone who did not live through that period can't possibly know the mood of despair and hopelessness that engulfed those who were out of work and helpless. We at least had some clients and some work to do, and it was enough to provide a meager existence.

By 1931, my education was adequate for me to take the examination for the CPA certificate. I was encouraged in this by the head of our firm, who promised me a junior partnership if I qualified to become a member of the American Institute of Accountants. This done, the firm announced at once that I had become a partner. Under the conditions of 1931, this meant merely that my responsibilities had increased but not my income.

The most fortunate event of the four and a half years I lived in New York, and in fact in my whole life, was meeting Kathleen Carmody. She was from an immigrant family, too. Her father and mother had both been born in County Kerry, Ireland.

Whatever the chemistry is that makes romance bloom, it was present from the beginning for us, and we were married in the fall of 1933, after I had moved back to my firm's Chicago office as its manager. Although she had never been west of the Hudson River, Kathleen adjusted easily to married life in Chicago and the Midwest. A city dweller with no experience in the great outdoors, she became an avid fisherman and hunter. She was with me on fishing trips to the bush country of Canada and on safaris into Africa, taking to the rugged camp life like a native. We found our greatest common bonds in those trips and in our other travels to foreign countries in Europe, Asia, and South America. Kathleen loved adventure and the excitement of new places, new people, and new experiences. Like me, she was interested in the primeval and the primitive, wherever we could find it, and took delight in learning about the cultures of other people in other countries.

Always cheerful, she could buoy me up under any period of stress and divert my attention away from the pressures. Our companionship was laced with deep affection and neither of us ever found the need to stray. Even the doctor's conclusion that we would not produce children was something she could take in stride; we adopted four.

She was an ideal mother, imparting the fullest devotion to those four six-week-old babies and their growing bodies and minds. She filled in for me on the home front when my business pursuits took me away a considerable part of the time during their formative years. She coped with their idiosyncrasies and with their growing-up cycles much better than I. She balanced my European ideas of bringing up children under strict rules with a tenderness and moderation that eventually produced four splendid, clean-living young citizens. Mostly as a result of her guidance, they avoided the drug culture and the tug of radical movements. To my pleasure, they grew up to be good solid Republicans.

All of this remarkable woman's character and affection persisted despite an almost catastrophic medical history. While I went along without any physical maladies, she seemed to collect them all. A few years after we were married, she unaccountably had to spend six months in a tuberculosis sanitarium, and after the cure her lungs continued to carry the lesions of the disease. In a subsequent year she encountered a perforated duodenal ulcer and a few years later a hiatal hernia, both of which put limitations on her pleasures of eating and drinking; then cancer of the thyroid and parathyroids, countered with surgery and radiation treatments that forced her to live thereafter on the chemistry of numerous pills to keep her body elements in balance; a spinal deterioration that caused her difficulty in sleeping and at times required her to spend her nights in a chair; cancer of the cervix, which yielded to surgery; abdominal obstructions on several critical occasions resulting from past surgical adhesions, and each calling for new surgery; and finally a serious blood disease that came within a millimeter of taking her life in 1972.

The blessing of a good marriage is getting to be a unique thing in our restless society, with each wedding now having only a 50 percent chance of lasting. I never fail to thank God for giving me the fortune to find the perfect woman and the sense to keep her. With any less, I could not have fulfilled my lifetime dreams or survived the unpleasant ordeals that befell me.

When we were married, my salary was $60 a week but, like the rent, it just accumulated when there was no money in the firm's bank account. These were not exactly ideal conditions in which to get married, with me having less than $1,000 in savings and with current income indefinite. There was one thing to be said for the conditions in 1933, and that was that they couldn't get any worse. Eventually, the national economy began to improve and Alexander Grant & Company joined the pattern of rapid growth set by the eight larger national accounting firms. As head partner after 1940, I traveled heavily for years from one city to another, dealing with client relations and the firm's growth. The time was right for aggressive expansion and, with the infusion of young partners, Alexander Grant & Company continued to grow until it had become the ninth largest accounting firm in the country by the beginning of 1953.

Twice in the early 1940s I had the temerity to testify before the Senate Finance Committee in Washington on tax matters. In 1943, I presented arguments on behalf of several clients for the repeal of what was known as the "second windfall provision" of the income tax law; originally designed to put a confiscatory tax on windfall earnings resulting from the war, it had been written in a way that caused unintended inequities which I was able to demonstrate from actual case histories. The second time was in 1945 when, as an official of a stove manufacturing plant, I appealed for the elimination of the "luxury" excise tax that then applied to stoves and ranges, which I contended were unquestionably home necessities and not luxuries. In both cases my efforts were successful and I was given to believe that my testimony had been a factor in the outcome.

There was something very exhilarating in these two experiences. Although I began them in trepidation and awe, I found courage in the obvious desire of the committee members to learn what the facts were and then deal with them objectively. The first two I met were Senators Walter George of Georgia and Robert Taft of Ohio, and I was smitten by their informality, interest, and knowledge of the subjects and, of course, was pleased to have them endorse the views I presented. These first touches with Washington stimulated me to want more.

From 1941 through 1955 I gave a large amount of time to work in and for the accounting profession, and I served as an officer or committee member in several professional organizations. At various times I presented technical papers or spoke on general subjects to these organizations or to business groups. In 1950 I received the top award of the American Accounting Association for outstanding professional service. In 1954 I was elected and served for a year as President of the American Institute of Accountants (now the American Institute of Certified Public Accountants) and also won its award for outstanding service to the profession.

Beginning in 1945, I acquired a growing conviction that the accounting practices and financial reports of many large companies were not only unresponsive to social needs, but in some cases were downright misleading. The public accounting profession, one of whose major functions was the attesting of the figures reported by these companies, was itself a party to these inadequacies. What started for me as a relatively casual belief that these things could be and had to be corrected by the profession ended up just short of a crusade. Others joined in and the consequences were a historic turn in the accounting and reporting of public corporations, and a new standard of performance for the accountants auditing them.

My part in this took place within the framework of my membership in the American Institute of Accountants. After several years on its committee on accounting procedure, I became dissatisfied with its progress and restless over the failure of the profession to address itself more forcefully to the enunciation of underlying principles of accounting and auditing. Not only did I become enamored with the potentials of accounting as a means of communicating essential facts of free enterprise, thereby strengthening the system, but also I saw it as a way of eventually resolving much social conflict, especially that between business and labor. Before I got through, I had expressed my ideas so strongly that I made some enemies in accounting circles who viewed me as a maverick, especially old-time accountants who believed in relatively free-handed practices, and businessmen who resented the imposition of rules that impaired flexibility of measuring and reporting earnings. I was not in any sense alone in my objectives, and there were a number of professional leaders who were outspoken along the same lines, but for several years I talked and wrote on the subject more than anyone.

It began, as far as I was concerned, in 1947, when I made some speeches on the social responsibility of accounting, with the theme that "those who deal with financial accounting should help to establish strength for the system by permitting no compromise with independent truthfulness and a vocation to serve the public interest." My full text was reprinted in the *Journal of Accountancy* in August 1948 under the editor's headnote summarizing the content as contending that "generally accepted accounting principles will have to improve if financial reporting is to measure up to the social responsibility accounting should assume. Work must be done on form of income statement; on codification of principles; on concepts of income, reserves, disclosure, terminology. By improving these factors, accounting can help resolve social conflict."

I contended that current accounting practices were inadequate to a real public understanding of the facts of business. I alleged that they lacked clarity, completeness, comparability, definition, limitation, and uniformity; and that they had just enough ambiguity, inaccuracy, inconsistency, uncomparability, and extremes of practice, to create a tool of distortion and confusion for those who served their purposes through unrest or distrust. I deplored the economic assumptions by the public that business makes an inordinate profit (usually believed to be close to 30 percent on sales when it is actually about 5 percent), and the public dogfights of "you do—no, we don't" when the subject of profits came up in wage discussions. I argued that "failure of the free enterprise system to sell itself to the public—with the same eloquent fervor that its tangible products are sold—may cause the system's downfall."

The complexities of these matters, difficulties with semantics, and the resistance to change within and without the profession conspired to reduce the process of change at times to a crawl, and in 1977, public accounting and its practitioners came under severe attack, notably from the Congress, for having failed to bring the job more closely to completion. The critics exaggerated the faults and failed to credit the advances since I and others had first taken up the cry for reform. Unfortunately, the slow progress prevented the achievement of the really important goals. Not much has been accomplished in dispelling the economic ignorance about corporate profits, about who pays corporate taxes, or on the necessity of continuing capital formation; and only meager economic understanding seems to have pervaded labor-management negotiations, certainly not to the point where long-term wage understandings are practicable.

Through these years of exploration I was obviously an earnest activist seeking new ways to increase the usefulness of my profession.

All of these professional activities through the years, in addition to my responsibilities with Alexander Grant & Company and to a number of public companies which I served as a director, made life go by at a lightning pace.

In 1953, my itchy feet took me to Washington. What was intended to be a brief stay there ended up as more than ten years, six of them in Cabinet-level positions, under two Presidents.

The Potomac fever hit me first in 1953. Shortly after Eisenhower was elected and just before he took office, I learned that a group of certified public accountants, some from the business world and some from public accounting firms, was going to be formed by John Taber, chairman of the House Appropriations Committee, to assist in the committee's review of the Federal budget for 1954. Along with about seventy-five others, I volunteered my services to Taber and, in the luck of the draw, was assigned to check the budget of the Post Office Department, a chore to be completed within six weeks.

At the end of that time I presented a report of over 100 pages. It was not of much help in budget-cutting for the Appropriations Committee, because it recommended immediate reductions of only $22 million in a proposed budget of $2.8 billion, or less than 1 percent. But my work could be, I thought, of real assistance to the Postmaster General in appraising his problems, and could produce greater benefits in the long run if it produced helpful, constructive suggestions on how to organize and manage his massive department. My fundamental conclusion was that its budgets had too long been nibbled at by marginal reductions that never got to the heart of the enterprise's problem, and these narrow actions had actually prevented progress. For example, salaries of the entire Division of Research were a paltry $108,000 a year, and that was money wasted because the attitude throughout the establishment was one of opposition to change. Tradition was so strong that the only right way to handle the mails was believed to be the way it had been done for two hundred years. How could addresses be read except by the human eye? How could letters be sorted except in pigeonhole cases? How could mail be transported except in heavy sacks? How could parcels be moved within a post office except by clerks pushing hand trucks? And so on. Everywhere I went, I had met a litany of negativism that previous Postmasters General had been unwilling or unable to challenge. That had to be broken, and petty budget cuts were not the answer.

The time had come for business methods to supplant the historic deference to paternalism and politics in the department. There were more than two hundred recommendations in my report, built around a four-year plan of fiscal modernization. The first was to put back into an immediate research program the money that would be saved by the budget cuts I had identified, and to continue thereafter to spend a suitable percentage of mail revenues each year in search of better ways of doing business. I was hopeful that in focusing on the long-range necessities, I would find a receptive ear somewhere in Washington.

I did, sooner than I expected. After submitting the report, I spent two informal days discussing it with the Appropriation Committee members and saying farewell and thanks to those who had worked with me. On the second day, as I was about to return to Chicago, I received a phone call from Postmaster General Arthur Summerfield.

"I've read your report," he began (and I thought I detected an ominous note that may have meant I had given offense), "and I would like to talk to you about it right away."

It was Summerfield's way of commanding action. I saw him in his office a half hour later, and he came right to the point.

"I like your report and I want you to help me put it into operation. Will you come into the Department as Controller?"

Much as I was complimented, and tempting as the offer was, I couldn't do that. I was head of a national firm of CPAs and could not neglect my responsibilities there. Summerfield and I discussed a number of alternatives and settled on a course which satisfied the desires of us both. I would select a qualified certified public accountant to be Controller, and my accounting firm would contract with the department on a professional basis to assist in the development of a modern financial system. I would spend half of my time for a year directing this work. This contract was later extended for a second year.

Then, late in the summer of 1955, the Deputy Postmaster General, the number two man in the department, resigned, and Summerfield asked if I would succeed him. I took several days to reply. Such a move would require severing myself completely from the accounting firm I had been building up for more than twenty years since I took over the office in Chicago in 1933. My extensive absences in the preceding two and a half years, however, satisfied me that the firm was strong and successful enough, now next in size to the "big eight" among the firms in the United States, that it would continue to grow even if I were no longer around, and the idea of beginning a new career at the age of forty-seven was intriguing.

As a result of my business income and some favorable outside investments, particularly in real estate, I considered that I had achieved my early goal of becoming a millionaire. This meant that we could afford to live conservatively well in Washington, although the salary of the Deputy PMG was only $17,500 a year. I also gave up four directorships in important corporations and severed completely my affiliation with Alexander Grant & Company, even to the point of cancelling out the balance of the term of its contract with the department. Since I had been earning well above $100,000, this was a sacrifice of more than 80 percent in income; this statistic more than anything else measured my eagerness to take an important post in the Federal government. I accepted, saying publicly that "my father was an immigrant; my mother's father was an immigrant. The country has been good to us and I believe we owe it a great deal more than merely paying taxes." I meant it.

I served for two years as Deputy Postmaster General, which means that altogether, as financial consultant to the Postmaster General and as Deputy PMG, I had spent almost four and a half years in the department. The postal deficit had been reduced from $727 million in fiscal 1952 to $522 million in fiscal 1957 without postage hikes and with many forced increases in costs. An 18 percent increase of pieces of mail in this five-year span had been handled with an increase of only 8 percent in man-years of paid employment. Documented savings as a result of new financial and accounting methods alone amounted to $20 million, and much more valuable management information was being produced.

The most unusual of my experiences as Deputy Postmaster General was exercising judgment in cases involving charges against postal employees. This period paralleled in part the era of McCarthyism, in which Communists were being sought out in "sensitive" posts all through government and an employee's past membership in a "subversive" organization characterized him as a security risk. The Congress had passed laws requiring such persons to be judged before they could continue to be employed, and the Post Office, which was considered to be a sensitive agency, had an elaborate set of procedures to apply whenever a charge of subversive activity was made against an employee. As Deputy Postmaster General, I exercised the final decision on cases which were appealed by the individuals involved, and these troubled me immensely. It was like playing God with human lives. I felt sure that many persons who were victims of the Depression of the 1930s could easily have toyed with "un-American" concepts for a time without in any way having become dedicated Communists or wanting to overthrow our system.

Unless the facts showed a long commitment of interest and

effort in "subversive" organizations, I took a compassionate view that accepted the innocence of the accused and his or her suitability to hold the job. It was an unpleasant duty and I worried much over the possibility of doing undue harm to people who were unconscious victims of circumstance. There were also a few instances of alleged homosexual behavior that came up on charges, and these were not made any easier when there was conflicting testimony about individuals with otherwise exemplary records. In a few cases I ordered lie detector tests, but even this didn't resolve my doubts about guilt or innocence, or about the justice of stigmatizing a person for life for one unusual act. My sense of compassion in these matters caused me to be lenient in my decisions, sometimes to the irritation of personnel officials who had worked hard to demonstrate the guilt or unacceptability of the persons involved.

Shortly before I had served two years as Deputy Postmaster General, I was approached by Percival Brundage, Director of the Bureau of the Budget, with the idea that he would like to ask President Eisenhower to nominate me to be his successor in that post. Brundage was a certified public accountant, a retired partner of Price Waterhouse & Co., and he believed that the preparation of the budget of the United States could be done best by a person who had an accounting background. Despite this logic, Brundage had been the first CPA to hold that post, and when I succeeded him I became the only other.

When I was appointed and sworn into the office in March, 1958, I issued a statement saying, "I am accepting this new responsibility of Budget Director under no illusions. This is one of the most difficult budgetary times the country has ever had to face short of war. I am convinced, however, that the soundness of the American economy will soon allow our efforts to be directed again toward balanced budgets." It was the keynote of my three years in the position, and it foretold the event most meaningful in my efforts there.

The full impact of the country's 1958 recession and the Soviet leap forward with Sputnik hit the budget for the fiscal year that began July 1, 1958, and ended a year later. Brundage had presented a balanced budget, but, with a drop of $6.1 billion in revenues from original expectations and an increase of $6.8

billion through unbudgeted expenditures, I found that I had acquired a real hot potato; I had presided over the largest peace-time deficit in history up to that time: $12.4 billion.

By the middle of 1958, when it was necessary to gear up for the 1960 budget, I was confident that it could be brought back into more respectable dimensions. I did not have any thought at first, however, that it would be feasible to go in one quantum jump from a huge deficit to a surplus.

The first run of the spending requests of the government agencies added up to $85 billion. With the best revenue estimate from Treasury then at $75 billion, we were headed for a deficit of $10 billion. That could not be accepted. Close scrutiny at the margins found many vulnerable items that could be pruned or deferred or lopped off. But these reductions were not nearly enough to bring about a balance.

I reported this to Eisenhower. He told me that he would be very disappointed to leave office without bringing the budget back into balance. The 1960 fiscal year was the only one left that would begin and end in his term. I replied that it was not impossible to bring about a balance for 1960, but to do so would require me to apply unusual austerity. He asked me to see what I could work out along that line and said I would have his backing. From this point on, I was determined to present a picture with all expenditures met and a surplus, however small.

Eisenhower kept his word and called an executive session of the Cabinet to lay down the law. He wanted a balanced budget and I had assured him that I would produce it, with his backing, he said. He called for drastic reductions and continued, "We're going to take hold of the bush, thorns and all. I'm tired of being liberal with other people's money." He followed up this lecture with a memo to the heads of all departments and agencies that contained even stronger language. He asked each to live within the amount that would be allocated by the Budget Bureau, "appealing to me only when you feel that to keep within such amount will impair the security or welfare of the country." No director of the Federal budget had ever had such a strong mandate.

Finally, the figures came together, leaving a paper-thin surplus of $70 million. It was the best we could do. The budget was austere and severe, but not heartless. We had proved that even with many uncontrollable commitments, there were ways to cut and save, or to generate revenues to make ends meet. Eisenhower was so delighted that he announced the balancing of the budget the minute we had a final figure, on December 22, almost a month before it would normally have been made public. Columnists Roscoe Drummond and Inez Robb included me among their nominations for Vice President.

Getting this done was not without personal strain. Beyond the physical and nervous effort of the constant analyses, meetings, and tough decisions, there was an emotional stress on me that others never saw. There was not a night that I did not go home and brood over the human, the social, and the national security aspects of the decisions that were taking form. I was the last man who would want the safety of the country to be in doubt, whatever the cost. And yet, with every proposal for spending, I had to press for the answers to the question "why?" The "why" followed me to bed, and I found myself wondering whether I was being too hidebound in my political philosophy. Were we overdoing the fiscal-conservative idea? There were moments of doubt, particularly in regard to the military necessities. But in my thinking, I always came back to one conclusion. In fiscal matters there is no tolerable alternative to conservatism. It is a discipline that can be ignored only at the risk of continuing inflation and, if allowed to prevail for a long period, at the peril of the nation's economic and political survival.

Sending a balanced budget to the Congress was only the first step. The second was to make it stick, and that was bound to be tougher. If we were to succeed, we had to make a real fight for it. What followed was 1960's Battle of the Budget, a classic campaign in which Eisenhower and his Cabinet appealed to the public over the heads of the legislators to help him preserve his goal. It was a real team effort, and when it was all over, the bottom line was black; the budget had been held. What we had achieved in one year was to wipe out the budget's worst peacetime deficit and produce a surplus. There had never been a sharper or more significant improvement in the space of one year. It was one of the few times in recent history that expenditures had been reduced from the previous year, except after a war. Eisenhower was tickled, saying, "This reaffirms to the world that the United States intends to run its financial affairs on a sound basis."

Not only that, our budgets for fiscal 1961 and 1962 were in the black. The next President, John F. Kennedy, for his own reasons, decided to ease up and revert to a deficit, through increased spending, but the country nevertheless reaped the benefit of Eisenhower's sound fiscal policy in stable price levels for the next several years, with inflation held below 1.5 percent.

It was a uniquely memorable experience to work so closely with Dwight Eisenhower. Though not an economist, he was nonetheless interested in fostering the principles of a sound economy. Though not a businessman, he respected the contributions of competitive business to the nation's progress. Though not a legislator, he knew that the key to legislation was compromise. Though not a do-gooder, he felt that the government had a responsibility to help the underprivileged. Though not a crusading states-rights-er, he believed that the best place for government was close to the people back home. My feeling is that he was a great human being, and one of our greatest Presidents, even though unexpected events such as the U-2 incident with the Soviet Union prevented him from being the peacemaker that he wanted to be. All in all, he was the President who was right for that particular period in history, which seemed to call more for stability than for innovation. His years as President were good years, among the very best in our history. We had peace and order, with a sense of security at home and abroad. There was a high degree of unity in the nation.

In high government positions in Washington, where opposing politicians and the press more often find it their mission to criticize performance than to praise it, one has to treasure the satisfactions he gets. From my contact with Eisenhower, I found the most gratification from two events. One was Eisenhower's recommendation to Nixon on the day after Nixon's successful election in 1968. Bob Finch was present when Eisenhower, then in his terminal illness in Walter Reed Hospital, told Nixon that he had only two things to ask of him. One was to treat the retiring Lyndon Johnson as considerately as Johnson had treated him after his Presidency. The other was to give an important place in the Cabinet "to that fellow Maury Stans, who is one of the smartest and most honorable men I have known in government."

The other encomium came from the senior Senator Harry

Byrd of Virginia, for many years known across the country as the symbol of fiscal responsibility in the Federal government. The autographed picture which he gave me in 1960 is inscribed: "To the best Budget Director in my time."

The 1960 election brought a temporary end to my government service, when the Democrats defeated Richard Nixon for President and took over the White House. I returned to private life, first as a commercial banker in Los Angeles, then as an investment banker in New York, both of which helped to bolster my financial resources after the low-pay years in Washington. During this period, Kathleen and I indulged annually in our favorite pastime of travel, including five month-long tent safaris in Africa, and a shikar in India, and these experiences renewed our vitality and broadened our outlook. Life was good to us in these years; our children matured and left the home nest, and we were content.

Except for one thing. I never lost the Potomac fever and, being one of the first to believe that Nixon would make a comeback, I worked hard to achieve that end so I could return to government. That story is in the next chapter. When he won and assumed the Presidency on January 20, 1969, I was with him as Secretary of Commerce.

I was delighted with the honor and with the opportunity. Commerce had been so downgraded under recent Presidents that its prestige and responsibility needed rebuilding. As a blueprint for my service, I adopted the report of a 1968 campaign issues group headed by Senator Charles Percy, calling for strengthening the role of the Secretary of Commerce as a policy maker and innovator. It said that he should be "an effective, responsible and responsive leader of the private business sector in this nation"; it specified that he should be a policy-making spokesman for the dynamic qualities of the private enterprise system; it asked him to be a catalyst for inducing greater contributions from the private business sector toward the solutions of general public problems, a stimulator of economic development through domestic business, and a prime promoter of American business abroad. This comprised an excellent charter and offered a real challenge in terms I could endorse and would try to honor. I believed that the Secretary should not be simply a voice of business in Washington, but the advocate and defender of the

American enterprise system.

Nixon agreed. In our first meeting after the election, he encouraged me to speak out for the business viewpoint on public issues and to do all I could to move Commerce from a defensive to a progressive posture. To be able to do that, I selected my subordinates very carefully, without interference or influence from the White House, and was exceptionally fortunate in being able to build a strong team. My Under Secretary was Rocco Siciliano, a former Assistant Secretary of Labor and Assistant to the President in the Eisenhower era.

I found Commerce to be a massive conglomerate of 25,400 people working in sixteen diversified agencies, their relationships to Commerce not all well known because many of them, like the Weather Bureau, the Patent Office, and the Census Bureau, dealt autonomously with the public. Beyond responsibility in the field of domestic business, Commerce also operated in the stimulation and regulation of international trade. The department in 1969 also included the Maritime Administration, the Environmental Science Services Administration (ESSA), an Office of Business Economics, an Office of Foreign Direct Investments, an Office of State Technical Services, the United States Travel Service, the Economic Development Administration, five regional economic development commissions, the National Bureau of Standards, and a Clearing House for Federal Scientific and Technical Information.

During the three years that I was Secretary, there were some additions and changes in these organizations and duties. An Office of Minority Business Enterprise was created, by Executive Order of the President, to help build business ownership among our blacks and the Spanish-descended and Indian minorities. The Office of Business Economics and some parts of the Census Bureau were merged into a single data-gathering and reporting unit known as the Bureau of Economic Analysis. The Clearing House was recast into a National Technical Information Service, with an expanded range of publications and services. Because I could not see meaningful results from the Office of State Technical Services, I agreed with John Rooney, Chairman of the House Appropriations Committee, to its termination, at a budget saving of $5 million a year. An Office of Telecommunications was created to assist in administration of the uses of the electronic spectrum by broadcast users of all types. By a major Presidential reorganization, the Weather Bureau and other units of ESSA were combined with seven other entities from four other government departments into a National Oceanic and Atmospheric Administration, based in Commerce, with responsibilities in the fields of weather, ocean fisheries, marine minerals technology, mapping and charting, oceanography, and marine research.

These revisions and acquisitions increased the size and scope of the department for the first time in many years.

Our major legislative coup was in getting a new maritime law passed by the Congress in 1970 to rebuild our declining and over-age merchant fleet and aid maritime employment. Early in the term, also, we had to fight serious but ill-conceived efforts to emasculate the 1970 population census, which came under ridiculous but powerful attack in that era of unrest as an "invasion of privacy." After a year's struggle, the Congress got tired of the issue and let it quietly sink out of sight, and the census went ahead as planned.

To a regrettable degree, my efforts were diverted into a bitter battle over imports of textiles, which were growing at such an astounding rate from Japan and the Far East that the American industry was suffering and its employment was dropping. I traveled to Europe, Japan, and other countries in 1969 on this matter, with little progress, and continued in one capacity or another as a succession of White House negotiations tried to find the right combination of carrot and stick to cause the aggressive exporting countries to moderate their invasion of our markets. Nixon and Prime Minister Sato of Japan made several aborted efforts to find a solution, and the Congress tried to help by advancing a trade bill with import limitations. But it was not until Nixon decreed in his August 15, 1971, economic program that the United States would impose unilateral restraints on textile imports unless "voluntary" agreements were worked out within sixty days that the exporting nations came to reasonable terms.

American industry and American jobs were greatly benefited by the result. The serious decline in the fortunes of our textile industry was halted. Foreign goods continued to be imported, but in amounts of only slowly increasing size, thereby giving the consumer the continuing benefit of lower prices without disruption of our markets and our economy. What we had sought and achieved was a managed orderly marketing arrangement that preserved a basic American industry.

In retrospect, while I did the right thing in fighting the battle as aggressively as I did, I paid a price for my dedication. There is no doubt that its time demands impeded my efforts on other worthy programs. Without it to deal with, I could have done much more elsewhere. It also ended up with my reputation falsely being that of an unequivocal protectionist, which hurt the image I wanted to present as being, by and large but with justifiable exceptions, a believer in open and unrestricted trade.

A task even more imposing, but with much greater satisfaction in the long run, and one that absorbed a considerable part of my time as Secretary, was the development of a program to stimulate business ownership by the American minorities. In the 1968 campaign Nixon had promised to help "black capitalism," and right after he took office, he named me chairman of a Cabinet committee to develop a plan. Within a month the committee had approved my proposals to create an Office of Minority Business Enterprise (OMBE) in Commerce, and the President thereupon signed an Executive Order on March 6 giving me authority to create the office and give it a program. The term "minority business enterprise" was more embracing than "black capitalism" in recognition that the Spanish-Americans, the American Indians, and the Eskimos were even farther behind the parade of business ownership.

From the outset, I became imbued with the strong vein of justice in the idea, and I gave a large disproportion of my time toward making it work. The statistics were compelling. In this land of presumed equality, 17 percent of the people making up the minorities owned only 4 percent of the business units, and these were so small on the average that they owned considerably less than 1 percent of the nation's business assets. The inequity was clear, and the stark fact was that until then, the government had done absolutely nothing to redress it.

To improve my measures of the problem and the concepts for dealing with it, I made trips to about twenty of the large cities and met with groups of blacks and other minorities in give-and-take sessions. These were very difficult at first, and many times I was insulted and even threatened by persons who doubted the sincerity of Nixon toward the minorities and believed I had no weight to cause anything good to happen. Although this was discouraging, I took it all patiently and listened to the sober voices, especially those of black and Spanish businessmen whose experiences made them worthwhile commentators.

Thus fortified, I gave a lot of thought and hours, in and out of Washington, to making minority opportunity a growing reality. As the months went by, the figures began to show what we were achieving, and in some respects they were more than gratifying. The total of all government grants, loans, and guarantees by program agencies rose from $200 million in 1969 to $472 million in 1972. The dollar value of government set-aside contracts sky-rocketed from the beginning $8 million in 1969 to $242 million in 1972. More than fifty minority enterprise small business invest-ment companies (MESBICs) were formed by 1972, with private capitalization of $18 million, which by borrowed leverage made possible minority financial capital of $254 million. Minority-owned franchises grew steadily. The number of black-owned businesses of all types grew from 163,000 in fiscal 1968 to 195,000 in 1972, and their receipts rose from $4.5 billion to $7.2 billion.

Many other landmarks were passed. The first census of minority-owned ventures was completed in 1971. Eighty-three local business development organizations were given funds to expand their services to new and growing enterprises. SBA got authority from the Congress to guarantee performance bonds for minority construction contractors. The American Bankers Asso-ciation and the life insurance industry raised their goals for participation in minority business. Private foundations were induced to commit millions of dollars to minority loans and investments, including the financing of some MESBICs. Organi-zations of accountants and other professionals were enlisted to volunteer their skills. And a long list of new activities to provide management and technical assistance, business opportunities, and capital was developed and pursued, with gratifying results.

Objective members of the black, brown, and red minorities credit the Office of Minority Business Enterprise program as being the first and only really successful step ever taken by the government to be helpful in a meaningful way to the cause of equality of business opportunity. While that work must go on for decades to produce "an even chance at the starting line," and basic educational equality is an ultimate key ingredient, I am proud of what was accomplished in my three years toward reversing the long course of historical inequity.

The finest moment of my career in Commerce was the evening of February 24, 1972, a week after I had departed, when two thousand members of the minorities from all over the country gave me a testimonial dinner at the Sheraton Park Hotel in Washington and showered me with words of praise and thanks and many mementos in token of their appreciation for what I had done for them. In the course of a five-hour program, Senator Edward Brooke saluted my work, as did many other blacks, Indians, and Spanish-Americans; and Reverend Leon Sullivan, head of Opportunities Industrialization Corporation and a black director of General Motors, said, "Stans has opened doors that have been closed for 100 years."

It was no less a tribute when in November 1972, as Kathleen lay critically ill in Walter Reed Hospital with a serious blood disease and was receiving frequent transfusions, the director and eleven members of the OMBE staff, most of them black, appeared at the hospital and volunteered their blood to help her. These were the kinds of rewards that erased all the frustrations and insults and cynicism in the early days of OMBE.

A vast array of other new and old problems occupied my interest and attention. One embraced our foreign trade balance, the need to expand exports, and our trade relations generally with other countries; to advance these matters, I visited thirty-two countries in the three years I headed the department. An internal study on the metric system concluded that we should adopt metrication in the United States, almost the last country in the world to do so, and I strongly endorsed the proposal. After reviewing the world situation, I terminated the whaling industry in the United States by cutting off further licenses to take whales. At my instigation, the department issued the first report on the cost of crimes against business, made a pioneering study of the cost of feather-bedding in American industry, initiated examinations of multi-national corporations and their contributions to the welfare of other nations, created the post of Ombudsman for business, and advanced a wide range of proposals to help business in general. Not all were successful. Our determined program to improve commercial services in our overseas embassies was blocked by the State Department. Our innovation of getting American businessmen to sit down together to address constructively the basic problems of the environment and consumerism was defeated in the Congress after a year by skeptical public interest groups who complained that this was "putting the fox in charge of the chicken coop."

Unquestionably, the acme of my Commerce experiences came toward the end, in November 1971, when the President sent me to the Soviet Union on an official trip as his representative six months prior to his own detente-building visit there in 1972. My mission, while not itself historic, turned out to be a prelude to history.

There were a thousand other topics, usually pressing, to be dealt with in days that were never enough and hours that moved too fast. Among them were moments of great elation, times of overwhelming fatigue, and occasions of physical danger.

In retrospect, I feel highly pleased with what we were able to accomplish in Commerce in three years. The department had grown in size, in responsibility, and, I felt, in stature. Employee morale and performance were markedly improved. Important new programs had been launched and given a strong footing. Congressional liaison was better. Operating in low key, we met our basic goals for the department and had created higher ones. There was much left undone, and I was saddened that my opportunities to carry on had to be cut short in midstream. But I also knew I was not that important; Secretaries come and go, and exert whatever influence they can during their short tenure, but the department goes on, into changing times and always-new conditions. No one could capture it or mold it for more than a brief moment in history.

As I sat one day contemplating my forthcoming retirement after the 1972 election, I realized that life had been full. I had achieved enough financial success to be able to give more than eight of the best years to the service of my government at pay barely adequate to maintain our standard of living, and still have enough means left to give us a quiet but comfortable time as long as we might live. We had raised a fine family of four and seen them through their schooling and into marriage. I had sat in the close presence of two Presidents as a member of their Cabinets. I had retained excellent health despite the working stresses, and Kathleen was again getting well after her many bouts with surgery. I had been honored by my chosen profession with all its honors, as head for a year of its largest national organization, as the honoree of awards for public service from two national accounting societies, and as elected member of the Accounting Hall of Fame. I had received an honorary degree from my alma mater, Northwestern University, and from ten other colleges and universities.

I had some outside support for the self-evaluation of my work in Commerce. The *New York Times*, one of my most severe critics at times, in a news analysis on the Commerce Department, gracefully said three years after my departure:

> Within the Department, the Secretary most talked about is Maurice H. Stans, who served in the first Nixon Administration. Commerce traditionally has been an institution without political clout . . . . It mattered under Secretary Stans. Mr. Stans gave the Department much more influence at the White House than anyone could remember, and morale perked up . . . . Under [his successors] the department's traditional lassitude took over.

I did not realize it at once, but the day of my departure from Commerce was a turning point in my life. Within a few months I was caught in the Watergate maelstrom, beset on all sides, fighting to see how much I could preserve of what I had achieved in means and reputation.

How in the world did I get into that position?

# TWO

## ONE EXPERIENCE

# 5

## THE RESURRECTION

Before 1953, my interest in politics had been negligible. My parents had always voted the straight Democratic ticket, even though my father had a generally myopic and cynical view of all politicians. Beyond that, there was little serious family discussion about either politics or public issues.

Dad spoke admiringly a few times when I was young about the ideas of Minnesota's Farmer-Labor Congressman Charles A. Lindbergh (the father of the aviator), who was a constant critic of capitalism and Wall Street. But we never saw or heard Lindbergh, since he lived in a different Congressional district. All we knew about him came from the *St. Paul Dispatch*, which did not seem to approve of him. He was a political maverick whose liberalism in those days was so extreme that it would still be deemed liberal in 1984. He was for nationalization of the railroads, state ownership of utilities and grain elevators and flour mills, and abolition of the Federal Reserve System, among other things, and was a violent assailant of the "wolves of Wall Street." Except for occasionally electing wild extremists like Lindbergh, Minnesota was a conservative Republican state in those days, with a string of Republican governors and United States senators. Despite that, my home town of Shakopee was heavily Democratic, mostly because the local weekly papers were Democratic.

This was my political heritage, but it didn't run very deep and held no roots. In 1920, our eighth grade class at St. Mark's debated the relative merits of the two Presidential candidates, Woodrow Wilson and Charles Evans Hughes. I was leader of the Wilson team so I parroted the literature which we had been handed, but nothing much was accomplished except that at the age of twelve I learned that politics is a vigorous difference of opinion by people who usually know very little about it. In 1928, I was passively for Al Smith, but still too young to vote. I had to work late on election night on an audit assignment in Waterloo, Iowa, and when I came back to my hotel and learned over the "raddio" that Smith was far behind, I shrugged my shoulders and went to bed.

My transition from Democrat to Republican took some detours. While I was living in Brooklyn in 1929, I became enamored briefly with Fiorello La Guardia after hearing him make a stump speech, but I was not moved enough to take the trouble to vote for him. In 1933 I was sufficiently disillusioned with both major parties to cast my first vote in protest for Norman Thomas, the Socialist candidate for President; to my young mind, he was an attractive, eloquent speaker and his intellectual presence appealed to me. What he said sounded good, but I didn't have the time or capacity for a real evaluation of his position on the issues. In 1936 I went back to my heritage and voted for Roosevelt, but lost faith in him in the "court-packing" days that followed.

In 1940, there was a flurry of interest for Wendell Willkie among some of my influential clients, so I voted for him, and this caused me to look more carefully at the Republican party. What I saw was a concept that appealed to me, a party that believed in limited national government and more responsibility at the local level, in restraints on national government spending to produce balanced budgets (a promise Roosevelt had made and broken), and in encouraging personal initiative, responsibility, and rewards under a strong system of free enterprise. This seemed to me to elevate the individual in the scheme of things and downgrade the paternalism of a distant government, and it came closer to my own sense of ambition and conservatism than the alternative of a growing welfare state. Not all of this fell into place at one time, but as I gradually honed my thoughts over the years I came to the conclusion that I was a Republican at heart, so I registered as one.

Beyond voting, however, I did little. In 1950, when Robert Taft ran in Ohio for re-election to the United States Senate against strong labor opposition, I voluntarily sent him my first political contribution, exactly $10.

That was all. And it was some time after I moved to Washington in 1955 to become Deputy Postmaster General before I even felt that I was in politics. I thought of myself as a businessman doing a job in the postal service, and I said something like that in a short talk to a group of Congressmen one evening. It was Congressman Jerry Ford who corrected me when I spoke of "you politicians"; he took me aside later and said, "Like it or not, as long as you hold an appointive job in Washington, you're one, too." The thought shook me, because somehow or other I had the idea that I could give my professional skills to the country without becoming part of the group for which my father had always had so little respect.

Since the Post Office was basically a business institution, I could still comfortably shrug off the idea that I was engaging in politics. Our lunchtime shop talk was about research and mail movement and building construction and vehicles, all part of the mail operations, and we spent little time on the social and economic arguments of those days. In the 1956 Presidential campaign, I made a few political speeches, but they were far from momentous in affecting the result. One was at a Republican county dinner in New Jersey, and the only thing I remember about my sterling logic on that occasion is that three men at a table near the front of the room slept all through it. At the time I was convinced that they had imbibed too much of the spiked punch, but in the light of what I have learned since about political rallies, it could well have been my style of delivery. I'm sure I talked to the audience in the same spirit of reason that I had previously used in addressing groups of certified public accountants. It's no surprise to me in retrospect that the results were soporific.

I gave another talk at a party picnic in Indiana. My plane had arrived behind schedule, and by the time the welcoming committee managed to get me to the site, the crowd had eaten and was in that disorganized state when everyone had left the tables and the women were packing the leftovers in their baskets and loading them into the cars. Many people had already gone. The promoters bravely did their best to collect an audience, but it was useless. I was mounted on the stump of a large tree that had been sawed off about four feet above the ground, given a hand microphone, and told to go ahead. A master orator like Everett Dirksen might have rallied that crowd, but I couldn't. I discarded my prepared speech, talked about ten minutes, and gave up. The committee was as embarrassed at the lack of interest of the group as I was at my ineptitude. After that, realizing that I was not of a political stature to command large audiences and ideal speaking conditions, I accepted no more invitations during the campaign and concluded that I had positive evidence that I was *not* a politician.

In the 1960 Presidential race I was mercifully spared by the Hatch Act. By then I was Director of the Bureau of the Budget. Even though it was a post that ranked its occupant as a member of the President's Cabinet, I found that as the result of a quirk of legislation, I could not legally engage in political action. At one time, the Bureau had been within the Treasury Department, at a subordinate level that brought even its top people into the category of civil servants covered by the Hatch Act's prohibitions of political activity; when the Bureau was moved to the Executive Office of the President, the restriction followed because no exemption was specifically enacted. I was content, because Eisenhower's mandate to get the budget in balance and hold it there took all of my hours.

In my weirdest thoughts up to then I had never considered the possibility that I would get into political fund-raising. That happened almost by accident. When I moved to Los Angeles in 1961 and started in the banking business, I had no political ties there of any kind. Richard Nixon and Robert Finch, both of whom I knew from the Eisenhower days, had also moved there, but our paths didn't cross often. My job was to learn banking, meet business people, and participate for the bank in public affairs.

In a short time, however, I did meet some of the Los Angeles people who had an interest in the Republican party, especially Charles Jones, a wealthy oil man, and Ed Valentine, a retired merchant, both of whom seemed to be regarded as leading money men in the local Republican circles.

In the summer of 1961, they buttonholed me at a lavish lunch

put on by Jones in a roof garden at his office and asked me to be
chairman of a county Republican $100-a-plate dinner to be held
late in the year. Had I known then what the circumstances were, I
am sure I would have declined and probably never would have
become a political money-man. They didn't tell me that there
was so much bitter factionalism in the local party at the time that
it had been impossible to agree on a chairman for the event. Being
new in the community and without alliances, I was a compromise candidate. My employers thought it would give me an
exposure in Los Angeles that would be valuable in a business way,
so they consented and I took on the job.

Once in it, I learned that I had to steer a course that would
keep me from being aligned with either faction, which meant that
every detail of the occasion, beginning with the clergyman who
would give the invocation, the program, and even the menu, had
to be cleared all around. Much more importantly, I found that I
had to take control of the ticket-selling organization and whip its
groups into an effective effort. I worked almost full time on this for
about two months. One of the persons who helped me considerably was a young lawyer-businessman named Herbert Kalmbach,
whom I met for the first time and was to see often in later years.
Everything seemed to come out well, the dinner was a financial
success, and, ready or not, I was launched into fund-raising for
politics.

The next one took me statewide. By the end of 1961 I had
come into more frequent contact with Nixon and, through him,
with Finch, and as Nixon pondered the question of whether he
would run for Governor of California, each of them talked with me
several times. After Nixon made the decision to run and the time
came to map out the campaign, I became the choice for finance
chairman, although my credentials for that were limited to the
one successful dinner event. This gave me a long pause, because
it would be a vastly different chore than selling tickets to a dinner,
and besides, I did not want to get the bank for which I worked too
strongly identified with one political party. My employers again
encouraged me to go ahead and, after first getting promises of
assistance from men like Kalmbach, Jones, and Valentine, I did so.

It *was* different, believe me. I had to travel to the cities around
the state, help organize local committees to raise money, fix their

quotas, set up a treasurer's office to handle the incoming and outgoing funds, and at the same time make as many personal sales "pitches" as possible to potential large givers. Bob Haldeman, then a young advertising executive, bright, attractive, fast-thinking, precise, and confident, was the campaign manager, and he came up with a budget of $1,500,000; I was in no position to dispute the amount, so I set out to raise it. However, he and I did work out a system to insure that there would not be an unmanageable deficit when the election was over. We established a minimum level of $800,000 and laid out its components to finance a viable, but weak, campaign. That much would be spent in any event. Then we worked up several separate spending increments of about $200,000 to $250,000 each, which would be released one at a time only if and when we were both satisfied by the collections and prospects as time went on that we could safely do so without ending up with a big debt. It was a very satisfactory mechanism. Haldeman kept his part of the bargain all the way, and when we finished, the expenditures were $1,697,000 and receipts were $1,700,000. Nixon lost the election, but we had a surplus.

The raising of the money was a much tougher experience for me than that sounds. I had to learn firsthand some of the things about the finances of political campaigns that now seem elementary. For one thing, a very large proportion of the public does not contribute at all; the money has to come from a relatively small number, only about one or two out of every hundred persons who will vote for the candidate. That makes appeals by mail very expensive and sometimes almost fruitless, especially in the early months when excitement is low.

Secondly, those who do give tend to hang on to their money until almost the last minute. About 60 percent of the year's funds are given in the last four weeks before an election (or after the election, which happens a great deal, especially if the candidate is a winner; a lot of checks dated before the election arrive in envelopes postmarked a day or two after the votes are counted). That makes budgetary control very hard at best, because the cash flow outward tends to run ahead of the cash flow inward until the last few weeks. Usually, that means borrowing, which in turn involves getting affluent members among the party faithful to endorse notes for bank loans which they hope will ultimately be redeemed from later contributions.

Thirdly, there is the tendency of the campaigners to spend more than is budgeted. Estimates of some costs are too low to begin with. New ideas come along, with strong sponsorship, and each one is "guaranteed" to win the election singlehandedly; this goes from rallies to sheet music, to billboards, to newspaper ads, to television extravaganzas, and back again. The finance manager is hard put to resist them, because often he can't judge their political value and is assumed not to know anyway. If he is soft, he may give in and then be in real trouble to meet the bills; if he is tough and opposes such increases, he draws the ire of the campaigners, who threaten him with responsibility if the election should be lost. His best course is to retreat behind the line that the originally set total of the budget must be held sacred, and if the political management wants to spend more for something, they've got to give up an equal amount somewhere else. It's a tenuous relationship, and sometimes can lead to bitter differences that disrupt the smooth working of both functions.

Fourthly, the finance chairman learns early in the game that it takes more than the small contributions to finance the campaign. They are important and they are appreciated, but they do not add up to large enough amounts. A candidate for Governor or Senator in California cannot run on $10 or $25 gifts. There not only must be many of $100 or $250, but also there must be some of $1,000. In 1962, more than half of the money raised came from one-half of 1 percent of the contributors, those who gave $1,000 or more. Those larger contributors do not send their checks in response to a mass mailing. They have to be met and talked to, one at a time, to be induced to join for a sizable amount. While there are always some persons to assist in this personal "special gifts" solicitation, a heavy part of it eventually settles on the finance chairman. The big givers, as a matter of ego, want to be solicited by the man at the top.

Next, no candidate likes to be involved in fund-raising. It distracts his mind from the issues, it takes time away from appealing to voters, and in many ways it is demeaning. The candidate should not be expected to beg for money, and should not handle any if he wants to avoid special pleading then or later.

So it settled on me to make a lot of personal requests for

money help, and I had to learn fast. Hardest of all to overcome was a natural timidity, especially in approaching people for the first time. I didn't know how to ask for money. It took courage to get around to a direct frontal appeal, and it took practice to avoid settling too cheaply. A timid pitch might produce $100 from a person who had the capability and the inclination to give $500. I learned that almost everyone who is willing to give at all, whether to an election campaign or to a charity, has a range of amounts that he tosses around in his mind before and during the solicitation. Depending on the solicitor and his personality, the extent of acquaintance, the timing, and the efficacy of the appeal, the same person might give only $100, or as much as $1,000 or even more. It is up to the solicitor to develop the technique which for him will produce the most in the least amount of his time.

After a while I came to the conclusion that the answer was not to be found in a prospect's past giving record. While that information might be helpful in establishing the minimums of potential, it took considerably more knowledge to mine the maximums. What was needed was to know the prospect's personal wealth, his social status, and the extent of his dedication to the party and the candidate. With that in hand, an approach could be made, tactfully, in which he would be asked to give a specific amount. It was not harder to say, "Mr. Adams, this is an important election, and I'd like to see you among the 200 people who are giving $3,000 or more," than to say, "Mr. Adams, we'd like your help," and on the average, it would produce three or four times as much. Sometimes Adams would then give $3,000; more often, he would give $1,000 or $2,000 when he had only intended to give his minimum of $500. Of course, the conversations were lengthier than that, but the principle was applied in that general manner. An important corollary of this rule is for the solicitor to name his figure before the prospect names his, so that a psychological barrier is not set up at a low amount that may be hard to enlarge.

Out of the experience I learned one thing: a person is never offended by being asked to give more than he intended to give, if it is done diplomatically. He may be flattered, or he may think it beyond his means and say so, but he does not resent being given a target to consider. Years later, I read a statement by John D. Rockefeller III that he often used this tactic of naming a suggested amount in asking people to give to the many public causes in which he was interested.

In California in 1962, I had some help from a firm of professional fund-raisers headed by Lou Quinn. He would not solicit funds, but he could give me, or would get, much of the material I needed for setting the targets for the solicitations I made. It worked out well. I don't believe I made any enemies in the campaign, and I know I made many new friends. It is, of course, entirely possible that a few of those I talked to might have resented being approached in this manner, or may have disliked being solicited at all. No one gave me any intimation that such was the case.

There were some light moments. One day Bob Finch phoned and asked if I'd meet a person who had offered to make a "large contribution" if I would spend thirty minutes with him listening to some suggestions that he wanted passed on to the candidate. He sounded like a prospect for at least $5,000 as Finch described him. I agreed.

When the man came in, he didn't look the type, but I welcomed him properly. He sat down and asked whether the understanding was correct that he could have thirty minutes of my time. I said yes. Whereupon he reached into his briefcase and pulled out an alarm clock. "I have five subjects," he said, "that's six minutes each." He proceeded to set the alarm and give me the suggestions, the first of which was that Nixon should declare that he was opposed to unemployment insurance. Each time the alarm rang he switched the subject, but none was any more sensible than the first. I sat in amazement and then amusement, tempted not to end the interview by the thought that he might after all be wealthy, even though he was an eccentric, to say the least. I promised to give his ideas to Nixon, without assuring him they would be adopted. He then said he would keep his word about making a sizable contribution, and with a flourish wrote and handed me a check for $25!

The loss of the election upset me, but Nixon's famous "last press conference" on election night disturbed me even more because I was afraid it was something he would never be able to live down. It was an intemperate criticism of the press, an act of despair by a man utterly fatigued after a hard campaign and shattered by defeat in a contest with an opponent he knew was far less competent than he. I told Nixon it would be costly to him;

I was not thinking of politics at that moment, but its effect on his future practice of law, where his indiscretion might cause some to question his judgment under pressure. By this time, I had become acquainted with him to an extent not possible in Washington, where our respective duties had touched very little, and my admiration for him and his thought processes had grown immensely. He had everything it took for a long political life, I felt—especially a broad experience, analytical ability, decisiveness, courage, and stamina—and the country needed men with those qualities. Beneath a surface that sometimes seemed preoccupied, sometimes curt, sometimes ill at ease, was a capacity for warmth, compassion, and consideration that few gave him credit for. Nevertheless, my concerns at the end of 1962 overshadowed my hope that time would give him another opportunity to demonstrate what a competent human being he was.

After the election, I saw little of Nixon in California. In 1963, when he announced his departure for New York to practice law, Kathleen and I gave a farewell party for him and Pat at our home in Flintridge, with about sixty of their close Republican friends present. In his closing remarks, which were eloquent and touching in expressing his goodbye, he resigned all intentions of ever being a candidate again, and made it definite that from then on, all he wanted was to be a successful lawyer. Certainly he could be under no illusion that he could travel as a newcomer into Rockefeller territory in New York and build a new political foundation, and without a strong home base, it was considered impossible for anyone to move into the national arena. Jimmy the Greek, the Nevada bookmaker, would have given odds of 1,000 to 1 at the time against Nixon ever again being a viable candidate, and surely would not have conceded a prayer of his becoming President.

In political work, one success always begets more things to do, and this applied to me. When 1964 came around I was asked to co-chair the money-raising for Barry Goldwater in California, but my business employment by that time had changed and I did not feel free to take on such a wide responsibility. I did agree to be chairman of a massive dinner and public shindig for Goldwater in Los Angeles on October 30, the Friday before the election, which we called the "Ninth Inning Rally." With the polls standing as they did, a national ninth inning rally was certainly needed for Goldwater to win.

There was the customary flak in getting the event off the ground. A group of the most conservative element in the party had been planning a big open-air affair in the Hollywood Bowl for October 22 and they were so furious with the intrusion on their plans that they threatened to boycott my dinner. I tried to make peace, but at the same time had to go ahead with arrangements and ticket-selling, and it was touch and go for a while as to whether we would lose the support of a sizable section of the affluent backers of Goldwater. I set aside a number of good tables for them, feeling that they had nowhere else to go and in time would join in; and eventually they did. They canceled their party and rallied to ours. As the event grew we had to shift the location to a larger place and ended up at the Arena with 4,000 dinner seats at $100 each and about 11,000 spectators in the gallery for the after-dinner speeches at $10 each.

All the party regulars and dedicated conservatives in Los Angeles were there and it was pandemonium. Somehow, the hope still prevailed that Goldwater would miraculously break through the pessimistic public opinion polls and win, and this crowd was determined to push him through. After all the preliminaries, Goldwater arrived thirty minutes late, and the bedlam of cheers almost literally raised the roof of the place. The wild applause lasted for fifteen minutes and then when I attempted to introduce Goldwater, it overwhelmed me and continued for another fifteen. It was more like a national convention than a local dinner. After a half dozen attempts to gavel the audience into order, I simply discarded my words of introduction and put Goldwater at the podium. It took another ten minutes before he could start and then he was interrupted at the end of every sentence. Sitting at his side, I saw him jettison page after page of his prepared text so he could finish within a reasonable time. Never have I seen such hysteria at a political event.

Once again I had worked for a lost cause, and like many others I wondered after the debacle about the fate of the Republican party. To survive, it had to be redirected. Goldwater's campaign had appealed to the right wing of the political spectrum and it demonstrated, as McGovern's did eight years later in appealing to the far left, that the American people could not be led that far from the center. Reform movements cannot be too sweeping, as a matter of reality, since the bulk of the voters do not want to chance the consequences of extreme change. They want, rather, to believe in slow progress—in their favored direction, of course. By that standard, Eisenhower's term in office, even though somewhat in the conservative mood, was deemed successful by a heavy majority in both directions from the center of the spectrum. Without settling at the time on a candidate to follow Goldwater, I knew that the Republican party had to find one who appealed to the center elements. Not once did I believe the dire predictions of the moment that the party would never revive.

Shortly after the Goldwater rally, I was called on again. George Murphy had broken through the Goldwater disaster in November to win the United States Senate seat in California, and a testimonial dinner was planned for December to get enough money to cover his deficit. I became chairman of that event, and to insure success our committee was able to get Eisenhower to come out of his winter home in Palm Desert to be the principal speaker. He was a hero to me and I introduced him in glowing terms, comparing him to some of the greats of history. He responded to this opening praise with, "I've known Maury Stans for some years and this is the first time I've found him to be extravagant." His presence and his friendly, informal talk to the audience made the evening another success.

By this time the conviction was growing on me that soon I'd have to turn down these money-raising responsibilities or I'd be in them for life. Ed Valentine had managed to get out after many years only by inducing me to take his place, and I knew it would not be easy to find another successor. The more one does that sort of thing the more he knows where the money is and how to tap it. It is easy for the party, therefore, to come to depend on the same person as long as he is willing. I didn't want a lifetime career in that game so I began to cement my determination to say "no" the next time I was asked. Fortunately, in a way, I did not have to face that moment in California, because early in 1965 my business location changed to New York and I moved there.

It was entirely coincidental that my business affairs caused me to move to New York from California about a year after Nixon did. It was in no way premeditated that in New York I bought an apartment on Fifth Avenue just two blocks from his, and that my employer had its office on Wall Street just one block from his. Nevertheless, this chain of events definitely played a part in the relationship that built up between us in the years that followed. Had they not happened as they did, quite by accident, I'm certain that none of the fateful happenings in Washington, good and bad, from 1969 to 1975 would have touched me.

With Goldwater effectively out of the leadership role of the Republican party there was a vacuum that had to be filled before the party could rebuild. Like many others, I looked around at the people I knew in public life to see who might be worthy of that role, and had difficulty finding anyone sufficiently outstanding. In my ruminations I kept coming back to Nixon, who had played a loyal and active part in the 1964 election effort in the face of a hopeless situation, while other near-leaders had given the party lip service or sat on their hands.

The ever-looming obstacle with Nixon was his two successive defeats in 1960 and 1962, a downhill slide that he himself had recognized as ending his political career when he announced on the morning following his loss of the California governorship that "you won't have Nixon to kick around any more." It seemed to be an impossible mission for him to recover to the point of being a national candidate again after having been repudiated in his home state and having somewhat ungracefully bowed out of public life. Yet I was still impressed by the man, his mental capacity, his speaking ability, and his political acumen, and believed he stood head and shoulders above anyone else in the country. On merit alone, there was always the possibility of a comeback if he got plenty of good exposure and lit a new spark, even though he had to bear the burden of having been a "two-time loser." The more I thought about it, the more I began to see a hopeful path, and one night very early in 1965 I sat down and did some mathematical appraisals of Nixon and his capabilities. It was merely a mental exercise to pull together all of my impressions of him in Washington and California and note them on a scale of values. Obviously, it had no scientific basis whatever.

I gave the highest rating to his intellectual powers, his analytical ability, his orderly mind, and his power of organized expression. I had never forgotten, for example, his magnificent and orderly report to the Cabinet, without notes, on his return in May 1958 from his danger-filled trip to South America. I had a clear recollection of some of his eloquent major speeches, and of course remembered his brilliant acceptance of the nomination at the 1960 Republican convention. He had conducted himself well and discreetly, as acting head of the government, without appearing either timid or presumptuous, when Eisenhower was incapacitated by serious illness. He had put the interests of the country ahead of his own when, after his hair-thin loss of the 1960 election to Kennedy, he had rejected the advice of many partisans to contest the ballot-counting in several close states notorious for vote frauds; he knew that Kennedy's leadership of the country would be handicapped and Presidential actions would be in legal doubt while the controversy went on in the courts, and he did not want to subject the nation's orderly processes to that turmoil.

Using a scale of ten, I went on to produce this table of positive values:

| | | | |
|---|---|---|---|
| Ability | 10 | Appearance | 8 |
| National experience | 10 | Past associations | 7 |
| Quality of service | 10 | Geographic appeal | 7 |
| Forensics | 10 | Present image | 6 |
| Stamina | 10 | Election history | 6 |
| Personality | 8 | | |

Then I listed seven negatives he had to overcome, these being
the defeat in 1960, the defeat in 1962, his 1962 post-defeat TV appearance, the intangible "don't like him" feeling of people, the impression that he was a poor organizer, press antagonism, and an overhanging shadow of distrust. To overcome these, I considered that he had some "plus" elements that could be capitalized, including the extreme closeness of the 1960 election, his graciousness in not contesting the 1960 results, and his superior knowledge of foreign affairs. Carried by the idea, I went on to list a series of steps that could be taken to "accentuate the positives" and minimize the negatives, all the way to the election. One of such steps was for him to campaign aggressively for Republican candidates in 1966. The whole document was ten pages long.

This appraisal and plan was solely for my own musing, and I did not show it to Nixon until much later. However accurate or inaccurate this amateur evaluation may have turned out to be in the light of subsequent events, it convinced me at the time. I have never applied the same test to any other candidate, but in Nixon's case it led me to one of the most deliberate conclusions of my life. He was qualified to be President and could be elected, and if he made any moves in that direction I would attach myself to his star and do what I could to help. After my years with Eisenhower, nothing would please me more than to go back to Washington in an important capacity and Nixon could be the means by which I could earn the right. While all this seemed almost indecently deliberate, it was probably little different from the process of mind by which many people attach themselves to a political person and tie their fate to his. As for me, I had Potomac fever, and I wanted to go back, so it was all quite simple: Nixon would make a great President and I would be on his team. I didn't tell him or anyone else about this decision.[1]

I knew practically no one in New York state or local politics, except Nelson Rockefeller, the Governor, with whom I had worked in Washington on matters of government reorganization in the Eisenhower days, so I figured I was safe from being drawn into politics at that level. To be certain, I stayed away from party affairs in the first year or so, and declined some invitations to local political dinners. I wanted to keep my eye on the national scene.

At a big lawn affair given by Eisenhower for Republican leaders at his farm in Gettysburg in the summer of 1961, I had met Peter Flanigan, a young, likable New York investment banker who had been active in the 1960 Nixon race. As soon as I settled in New York, he and I began getting together from time to time over lunch to talk politics. His views about Nixon were very much the same as mine, and, at his instigation, we met with Nixon several times for conversations which inevitably ranged over the spectrum of politics. At first, he gave no sign of interest in going back to political life. He was busy practicing law. While he was fully

---

1. There was a fairly prompt confirmation of my evaluation of Nixon's standing in the party. A Gallup poll on March 24 showed him well out in front among Republicans with 36%. Henry Cabot Lodge and George Romney were next with 16% and 14%.

knowledgeable about the goings-on in Washington, he was apparently living out what he had said in his "final" press conference in 1962.

That began to change rather quickly. William Safire, a public relations consultant whom Nixon knew, had joined our circle, and, in response to the discussions, prepared a long, ten-page letter on the problem of Nixon's image and what had to be done to restore it. It was an impressive professional document, optimistic about the possibilities but realistic about the difficulties. Out of it came the program that brought Nixon back actively in 1965 and 1966 on the political trail. How much of his renewed activity was the result of the encouragement given him by us, how much was due to his party loyalty in the face of party need, and how much was accounted for by a revival of his own ambitions, only he could say. In any event, he was eager to go, like the firehorse at the bell, and before long he was in action in full swing.

1966 was not a Presidential election year, but there would be Congressional and Senatorial elections, and uppermost in the plan was to help the Republican delegations in both Houses recover from the serious setbacks that had been sustained in the disaster of 1964. In April 1965, Flanigan and I drafted several papers, after talking with Nixon, to crystallize the joint thoughts as to what might be done. One proposal was for a "Committee for a Republican House" to do what the regular party mechanism couldn't ethically do, which was to raise money to find and finance new young faces with "winability" to run in the Congressional primaries in 100 marginal districts. That one didn't get off the ground.

Two events in the last half of 1965 helped to cement my dedication to the Nixon cause. In September, he paid me a meaningful and generous personal tribute by stopping off in my home town of Shakopee to be the principal speaker at a "community recognition" dinner in my honor. He had just been on a trip to the Far East and was on his way back to New York, and his current views on foreign affairs were of much interest to his audience and to the Twin City media. The dinner and speeches attracted a full house for the local school auditorium of 700 seats, despite a heavy rain that began in late afternoon. It was an imposing moment for me to have this former Vice President honor me as "a man of character" and a "nationally outstanding citizen and public servant" before my boyhood friends and townspeople. My main thought of the evening was one of deep regret that my mother and father could not have survived to be present. By then, they were both at rest in the family plot in the hillside cemetery overlooking the town and the beautiful Minnesota River valley.

Around this same time, Kathleen and I invited the Nixons to spend an evening with us and two other couples at the World's Fair on Long Island. We worked out a careful plan to visit four of the exhibit buildings and then have dinner in the Glass Tower Restaurant, and I had arranged with the exhibit managers to receive our group on this schedule without special notice or fanfare. The first stop was at the Johnson's Wax building where we were escorted to seats and saw the entertainment. When it was over and we started to leave, a deluge of people burst over us, hundreds and hundreds of them, all wanting to greet Nixon. The next show was delayed for the full hour it took to get him out of the building, and when we reached the street, another thousand or so gathered for handshakes or autographs. We never made the other three exhibit buildings; by the time we broke loose from the gathering crowd and arrived at the restaurant, we were more than an hour late. The fact that impressed was not that Nixon had attracted attention, but that the interest was so warm and so universal. It seemed that everyone wanted to be his friend. I'm sure Nixon felt it that way, too.

Organizationally, we first put together in 1965 a "non-political" entity which we called the Issues Research Council. Its purpose was to provide Nixon with a small research staff for assistance in his speaking and writing, all aimed at his comeback. The memorandum that informally chartered the group stipulated that "the objective is to restate and reemphasize the candidate's experience and qualifications for public office, and to counter the negative implications of his two election defeats." The original Council, which held several meetings at the Metropolitan Club with Nixon present, consisted of Hobart Lewis and Al Cole of *Reader's Digest*; Tom Evans and Len Garment of the Nixon law firm; Robert Finch, who was then running for Lieutenant Governor of California; Charles Rhyne, a Washington attorney; Pat Hillings, a former California Congressman; H. Chapman Rose, a Cleveland lawyer; and Charles McWhorter of American Telephone & Telegraph, in addition to Safire, Flanigan, and me. Looking ahead to Nixon's campaign travels for Republican candidates in the summer and fall of 1966, we discussed a budget of $100,000, various fund-raising approaches, the need for liaison with and financial support from the Republican National Committee, and enlargement of the group for future meetings. Within a short time thereafter, Flanigan, Cole, and I raised the first $25,000, and we were in business.

As the weeks went by, others joined in and, with the activities taking on an increasing partisan identification, the Issues Research Council was officially succeeded by a political committee called "Congress '66," with me as chairman. Two other committees were also created for fund-raising purposes; a Committee for the Election of Republican Candidates, of which former Governor John Davis Lodge of Connecticut was chairman; and a Committee for the Loyal Opposition with Robert C. Hill of New Hampshire, a former Ambassador to Mexico, as chairman. Flanigan was treasurer of all three. Others who joined us in this early stage were Donald Kendall, the head of Pepsico; Fred Seaton, former Secretary of the Interior and a Nebraska newspaper publisher; Walter Williams, former Undersecretary of Commerce and a mortgage banker of Seattle; Robert Merriam, a former assistant to President Eisenhower; Linwood Holton, a Virginia lawyer, and a half dozen others. In all, our group in 1966 never exceeded twenty-five persons.

By June 26, when a meeting of the Congress '66 group was held in Chicago at a hotel near the airport, the framework had been created, financing had been arranged from a small number of contributors, Nixon and his staff of assistants were in full motion, and advice was coming from many directions. He was with us at this meeting and outlined his plans for the rest of the year. It was a full-time schedule of speeches and media appearances running right up to Election Day.

There was a brief hassle about this time when Ray Bliss, Chairman of the Republican National Committee, refused to cover any of Nixon's travel expenses on behalf of Republican candidates because he felt that, even though Nixon had been the party standard-bearer in 1960, the National Committee could not pay the expenses of one non-candidate traveling about the country without being subject to criticism and to similar demands from others. (That led to a strained relationship between the two that persisted when Nixon ran for President a few years later.) As we got into the summer, we worked out an alternative arrangement for the Republican Congressional Committee to pay Nixon's travel expenses, with our committee financing his research and secretarial staff. Altogether we raised and spent about $70,000 from about forty contributors.

The conditions for Nixon's venture in 1966 were auspicious, because the off-year Congressional elections usually favor the party out of power. In October, Nixon predicted that the Republicans would gain forty seats in the House, three in the Senate, and six governorships. It came out better than that, with net gains of forty-seven in the House, three in the Senate, and eight governorships. He campaigned hard and effectively, appearing in three-fourths of the states, and party members gave him a large share of the credit for the substantial victory. One analysis made shortly afterward showed that seventy-five of the one hundred and five candidates that Nixon specifically worked for were winners. It was a new beginning and, with Goldwater in limbo, it restored Nixon to the leadership of the party. There was a long way to go, but 1968 and the Presidency were beginning to seem closer for him and Washington was looking closer for me. On election night in 1966, Nixon was in a suite of rooms in the Waldorf-Astoria, getting returns from the districts and states in which he had campaigned and then calls of gratitude from the winners he had worked for. It was a high night, and I was sure he was thinking ahead as the victories added up. I talked to him for only a moment during a brief lull in the activity around midnight.

"Let's go now for 1968," I said. "We'll really show them how to run a campaign this time." He thanked me and smiled. All he said was, "We'll see how it unfolds." I knew he would be a candidate. This time his power base would be the entire country, not just his home state.

With those exhilarating thoughts racing through my mind, I took his wife Pat back to her apartment in a cab and walked the two blocks to mine. Nixon himself stayed at the hotel, getting and making phone calls most of the night.

Flanigan and I were eager for him to give a public sign of candidacy before the end of 1966, but he countered by announcing publicly that he was taking a six months' moratorium from politics. It was a master stroke, because it built up public interest and speculation without any visible exertion on his part.

He did authorize us on November 23 to get the word out to our close group that "there will be a campaign," and discussed various possibilities for campaign manager. In January 1967, he met informally with some of our Congress '66 committee, ostensibly just to thank them and to exchange ideas on current issues, but he was in complete control and the objective was not in any doubt. He also met about this time with several pick-up groups as he groped toward a hard core for an organization, and acquired Ray Price of the New York *Herald Tribune* for speech writer.

The next step was an organizational meeting which I hosted on March 12, 1967, at the Plaza Hotel in New York, attended by McWhorter, Hillings, Garment, Evans, Rhyne, Seaton, Rose, and Flanigan, together with Nixon. New faces also present were Robert Abplanalp, manufacturer of the valve used in aerosol cans; Sumner Whittier, former head of the Veterans Administration; and Patrick Buchanan, by then Nixon's principal research aide.

The other members of Congress '66 had also been invited to the meeting but were unable to attend. With recent additions, the entire Nixon working group still amounted to only thirty persons. The discussions included a full review of plans for 1968, and ended with the conclusion that a Nixon for President Committee would be formed by Lodge, Seaton, Hill, Williams, and Holton, with me as chairman. We considered that Nixon was fully committed to run for the nomination and election, but understood that he would remain publicly aloof until an appropriate time to announce. In the meantime the campaign would move ahead. The meeting was one of high spirit and optimism, and those present had no doubt, after hearing Nixon's careful analysis of the party's prospects, that he could be the next President. Fundraising was to continue informally by the Nixon for President Committee under Flanigan and me, with help from some of the others, until later in the year. The remaining members of the disbanded Congress '66 team would stay in the background until Nixon's announcement.

On May 3, 1977, Fred Seaton and I sent a joint letter to 408 of the major Eisenhower appointees, asking them if they would support Nixon for 1968. The response gave us no cause to jump for joy. As Seaton put it, the enthusiasm was downright diminutive. The "Nixon is a loser" image had its damaging effect even at this level of his presumed friends. We tabulated that 85 percent of those who had been his teammates in key positions in the Eisenhower-Nixon Administration either straddled our question or didn't even reply.  In the 15 percent who did give a definite answer, fifty-two individuals said they would support him without reservation, and nine replied boldly that they were for other candidates, naming Romney, Percy, Rockefeller, or Volpe. Of the twenty or more persons besides Seaton and me who had held Cabinet positions under Eisenhower, the only early commitments to Nixon came from Postmaster General Arthur Summerfield, Commerce Secretaries Sinclair Weeks and Frederick H. Mueller, Commerce nominee Lewis L. Strauss, Attorney General Herbert Brownell, Jr., and Treasury Secretary Robert B. Anderson.

Those of us dedicated to the action for 1968 began to realize how imposing a task it would be for Nixon to live down his past defeats. When I passed this report on to Nixon, he was incensed to learn how few of the Eisenhower team had the confidence and courage to stand up for him. As the campaign moved forward, however, and the bandwagon began to roll, many of the uncommitted did join in one fashion or another. A second letter that Seaton and I sent out on February 20, 1968, brought more favorable responses from many of the hesitant. Despite his general irritation at the Eisenhower people who hedged on early support, Nixon nevertheless later appointed some of them to important jobs in his administration.

Our small group carried on. Don Kendall gave a large party for a group of businessmen at the New York Yacht Club, at which Nixon wowed the audience, especially during a question period that followed his talk. It didn't end until late afternoon, with everyone showing rapt interest in his views, particularly on international matters. At this and other affairs, including some small dinners at the Links Club, Nixon was doing a very effective job in the non-candidate posture that traditionally precedes an open candidacy.

By October, we were ready to set up a formal fund-raising effort, and I began giving it more, but still part-time, attention.

Herb Kalmbach came from California as a volunteer, working full time. We took some office space in a decaying uptown building and I wrote personal letters asking for help. At first the results were meager. The best amounts came as a result of phone calls by Cole, Flanigan, and a few others who tapped a small number of wealthy people that they knew. Nixon also attended two or three cocktail parties at the Links Club, with fifteen or twenty potential contributors at each, but he always left before the subject of money was raised. Flanigan and I did the following up, again with all the help we could get from others in our still small coterie.

Nixon was especially diffident about contacts with contributors, then and later. He did not want to be present when solicitations were made and did not want to handle contributions. He did not like to speak at fund-raising parties on his own behalf. He resented people who would thrust envelopes or checks at him during public or private affairs. During a campaign he did not want to know who had given money to help, and only after it was all over would he briefly peruse and discuss a list of contributors with me. He made it definite that he did not want contributions taken from anyone who felt he was entitled to something in return. Nixon was willing to consider later the appointment of contributors to government service on the basis of qualifications, but not as a matter of commitment.

Despite his reluctance about discussing money, he did occasionally pass on information to me about prospective contributors in memos written to me by "DC," presumably meaning his aide Dwight Chapin, but actually a pseudonym that Nixon used to avoid possible later embarrassment. In one such memo he said positively, "Don't take any money under any circumstances from H. L. Hunt" (the Texas billionaire), but I never learned why. He also told me not to take a proffered contribution of $75,000 from Owen Cheatham, the retired head of a national plywood company. I had no contact with Hunt and received nothing from him, but in Cheatham's case I did accept a contribution, without Nixon's knowledge, after Cheatham assured me in very unequivocal terms that he did not expect favors of any kind.

By January 1, 1968, all signals were "go," although Nixon had decided not to make the formal move of throwing his hat in the ring until the second of February, when he would travel to New

Hampshire, the earliest primary state and one in which he had strong support. Again, it was a fine stroke of timing and performance and it gave him an impressive start.

There were three special incidents in the 1968 fund-raising drive, all related to times when the till was empty and urgent needs were looming. The first was in January, which started with nothing in the bank and the New Hampshire primary only sixty days away, and a lot of funds needed to organize and publicize the campaign there. With Nixon due to make his announcement soon, there had to be money to open store fronts, start mailing, put together committees in all the cities and towns, and generally crank up the action quickly. I was almost helpless in that I had not yet perfected a technique for getting big contributions, and the mail returns were insignificant. The situation was getting gloomier day by day until the sixteenth, when James Crosby, the head then of Mary Carter Paint Company, came up with a contribution of $100,000. Nixon was ecstatic and wrote me a note which said that "at last, we are under way." He was right because public interest began to grow, our appeals began to work, and money came in well enough to get us through a very successful vote in New Hampshire.

In the same note Nixon said, "Also in the good news department, my partners have agreed to give John Mitchell the time to be my personal Chief of Staff." It was the first I had heard of Mitchell. In March 1967, Nixon had selected Gaylord Parkinson of California to be his campaign manager; Parkinson had achieved some notice in Republican circles as the author of the 11th Commandment in the 1966 California elections: "Thou Shalt Not Speak Ill of Another Republican." Unfortunately, his term in the campaign was short-lived as he found it necessary to resign after a few months when his wife was stricken with a terminal illness. He was succeeded for about six months by Henry Bellmon of Oklahoma, until Bellmon resigned to begin his own campaign for the United States Senate. Robert Ellsworth, a former Congressman from Kansas, also had a loosely defined leadership role for a while as executive director and then as national director, but ultimately Mitchell took full charge as campaign manager and carried through the primaries, the convention, and the fall election.

When Nixon won a strong victory in New Hampshire, I

thought it would be an opening that would induce a freer flow of contributions, and it was, but they did not grow as fast as the campaign demands from the next primary states, where the dates were getting closer and needs were getting progressively larger. On March 31, there was not enough in the bank to meet the payroll, and in desperation I loaned $25,000 of my own money to the committee to tide it over. That was the second rescue.

The third was more significant by far. As I sought sources of large contributions, someone suggested that if I would talk to W. Clement Stone in Chicago, he might be induced to give as much as $25,000. Herbert Kalmbach and Bob Ellsworth flew out to Chicago with me to see Stone, and we had lunch together at the Attic Club. I wasn't sure how to phrase the approach to Stone, so in uncertainty, I let him do the opening. Yes, he was strongly for Nixon and felt he would make a fine President; Stone knew him through mutual service on the Board of Directors of the Boys Clubs of America. Yes, he would contribute substantially, but he didn't name a figure. I hesitated to name one, too, because I was beginning to feel that Stone might give more than $25,000; maybe $50,000. So I temporized while we went through the meal, Stone talking more positively about how he wanted to help, and I raising my expectations higher and higher, still unsure what amount to try for, and ready to kick Kalmbach or Ellsworth under the table if either started to suggest one. Finally, after lunch was finished and I had concluded to ask for at least $100,000, Stone broke through bluntly by saying that he believed in "matching gifts" and that he would match anything we could raise in the next sixty days. I gulped and said, "Up to what amount, Mr. Stone?" Without hesitation, he said, "Up to a million dollars!"

By then my courage had mounted and I had the nerve to ask Stone if he would be willing to advance $200,000 on account. He said he would, and he did. Another crisis was over.

That was the turning point. We solicited others right and left, telling them of Stone's offer and suggesting that their contribution would do double duty; a $25,000 gift would thereby be worth $50,000. It worked, and before the deadline date I gave Stone a list of people who had given a total of $1,020,000 in response to his offer. He covered all of it, every cent, and as time went on repeated the proposal until he had given a total of more than two million dollars. In September, I wrote a note to Nixon saying, "When this is all over, I hope you will canonize Clem Stone," and I meant it. Haldeman replied, saying Nixon had already done so in profuse thanks. Nixon and Stone became close friends, but after he won the White House, Nixon hesitated to give Stone the ambassadorship which by all precedent he deserved, for fear it would look as though it had been sold. Stone never received any political reward for his astounding help and he never asked for any.

From the beginning of 1968, I gave full time to the chairmanship of the Nixon Finance Committee and organized within it about 100 leading names around the country, some of whom really became active, some not so. To do this I took a leave of absence from my employer for the entire year of 1968. Kalmbach agreed to be associate chairman. Other staff principals were C. Langhorne Washburn, an experienced fund-raiser borrowed from the Republican National Finance Committee; J. William Middendorf, an investment banker, who became treasurer; Patrick Dugan, a certified public accountant, who was controller; Dan Hofgren, Tom Pappas, and Donald Brewer, business executives; Jack Gleason, who came from a firm of fund-raising specialists; and Jeremiah Milbank, Jr., a wealthy New Yorker. Charles Thomas and Lee Kaiser, California businessmen, each spent several months helping us with organization matters and in contacting important prospects. This was the entire organizing and soliciting squad at national headquarters for the year. Tom Evans, borrowed as needed from the Nixon law firm, was our counsel.

Washburn worked on setting up fund-raising dinners across the country; and Kalmbach, Brewer, Hofgren, Milbank, and Gleason helped me to manage the operation, create fund-raising committees in each state, and solicit major contributions.

From the outset my staff and I became growingly frustrated at the disorganization and lack of discipline among the people directing the political activities of the campaign at headquarters and in the field. There was little coordination and almost no discipline over their spending, and meager communication with those of us who had to raise the money. The conditions got so bad that on February 23 I addressed a letter to Nixon, Ellsworth, Mitchell, Flanigan, Garment, and Evans insisting that a number of steps be taken at once to improve the situation. It contained some strong words: "It is increasingly evident that there is little or no discipline being exercised on the campaign side over commitments and expenditures . . . a more realistic approach could eliminate many of our costs. There seems to be no limit on the number of people who can make commitments or approve bills." Among other things, I demanded that they begin budgetary control over all campaign divisions, and place full responsibility on the head of each division to conform. It was a strong communication, and I was aware that it would bring a lot of wrath upon me, perhaps to the point at which I would be asked to depart, and I was reconciled to that as the only alternative. There was no direct response, but it had its effect, because Mitchell and I gradually worked out satisfactory operating mechanics between his campaign committee and my fund-raising committee. Basically, the campaign group would handle no funds; that would be our responsibility. We would play no part in campaign strategy or tactics; that would be the work of his team. We would raise the money and pay without question any bill approved by designated key men in his committee. To provide a measure of control, a budget would be laid out for each campaign division for each month, and a Budget Committee would exercise general surveillance over the trend of expenditures and would consider proposals for changes in the budgeted amounts.

The Budget Committee met weekly, but it was effective only to a limited degree because it could never exercise restraint over the spending of the hundreds of campaign operatives who had the power to commit money. The "advance men" in particular made my hair curl, with their extravagances when they set up rallies, meetings, and other public events. It was not unusual for them to spend $50,000 to get people out to a public rally in a city like Buffalo; some of them chartered private planes to get around from city to city, or spent $100 a day in lavish hotel suites; their phone and travel bills were astronomical. Their attitude was that failure might result from underdoing, and that their only sure success lay in overdoing.

In the end the budget was greatly overspent. I could see that result coming months ahead and poured on extra effort to keep the funds flowing in as fast as they were needed to go out. We were successful in doing so, and I think we set some kind of a record for Presidential campaigns in not having to borrow one cent from banks, and in having made only one small temporary loan from a contributor.

Another difficulty came to hand when a separate Citizens Committee headed by Charles Rhyne was authorized by Nixon and given the power to raise its own funds. I objected strenuously to having another money-raising structure set up in competition with our efforts, and contended that the combination would raise less money rather than more, because some people who were solicited could use the routine of saying they had given to the other and then give to neither, or at best would give less to the Citizens Committee than they might if approached properly by us. This hassle was finally resolved when Richard Scaife, who was the finance chairman for the Citizens Committee, worked out with me a careful plan to coordinate his efforts with ours to best overall advantage. The Citizens team raised about $2.5 million and ended with a small surplus.

The momentum given us by Clem Stone's generosity carried us through to November, although at no time after the convention in early August did we have enough money in the bank to pay more than the next week's expenses. In September, as insurance, our treasurer made arrangements for a line of credit of a half million dollars, to be backed by twenty individual guarantees for $25,000 each. We had all the papers signed and ready but managed to skin by without making the loan. With 60 percent of the year's money not coming in until after the first week in October, that was a difficult feat. Our gratification at not having created or left any debt was multiplied by the knowledge of the horrible difficulties that Humphrey had in getting contributions and the huge liability of more than $9 million that he and other candidates left the Democratic party when the election was over.

The cost of the Nixon race in the primaries and in lining up delegates in other states for the convention was $9 million. We received considerably more than that, but the surplus up to the time of the nomination was set aside on advice of counsel, for use after the election. Under the law we had to keep pre-nomination funds separate from post-nomination money or we would have to take on a vast load of additional responsibilities for reporting the earlier contributions.

Right after the convention and nomination, Kalmbach, Washburn, and I had met at Mission Bay, near San Diego, to work out with Mitchell's people the spending plans for the rest of the year and then figure out how to find the money. The budget, after some tightening by John Ehrlichman, then a Seattle lawyer who became one of the campaign chiefs, came out at $20 million, but I was already skeptical about it being held to that amount, and mentally expected to have to raise at least 10 percent more. The final cost for the general election alone was $25 million, and the total for the entire race from beginning to end was therefore $34 million, plus the $2.5 million spent by the Citizens Committee. We had raised enough beyond that, principally with the pre-convention surplus, to reserve about $1 million for "transition expenses" and still carry over about $1.6 million for future uses. The "transition" costs were those of the Nixon organizaton at the Pierre Hotel in New York from Election Day to Inaugural Day in recruiting people for Washington, in setting up task forces and studies, and in planning and starting the work of the new Administration before it was sworn in. Although the Federal government provided some money for the transition from one administration to another, the portion of that amount available to Nixon was only $450,000 and it was grossly inadequate.

The Pierre Hotel was a convenient transition headquarters, being just two blocks from Nixon's apartment, but my fiscal conservatism was shocked by the lavish facilities and the extravagant costs that were incurred during this period. The bills ate up not only the government allowance but our entire $1 million reserve from the pre-convention contributions.

The other $1.6 million in cash and bank balances left over was entrusted, with the approval of Mitchell, to Kalmbach, to preserve it for 1972. It was to be under the sole direction of Haldeman, who became White House Chief of Staff. The later uses of these funds afforded some of the intriguing disclosures of White House actions in the pre-Watergate period, but I was given no insight into those transactions when they occurred. While in the President's Cabinet I kept aloof from all political fund matters and Kalmbach did not report to me where he was keeping the left-over campaign money or what he was doing with it.

After Clem Stone, the next largest contributor in 1968 was John Mulcahy, a New York industrialist, who gave $250,000. Altogether, there were 26 persons who qualified for our strictly honorary Century Club by giving $100,000 and over, another 59 who gave in the range of $50,000, and 58 more who gave approximately $25,000.

Contrary to some political folklore, these contributors were not promised favors or government jobs in return. People of large wealth do not need such inducements; they will give to their party because of dedication to the country and to the candidate and what he and his party stand for. A man who is worth $400 or $500 million, as Clem Stone was reputed to be, can give $2 million to a campaign with less sacrifice and no less honest motivation than a man who has $20,000 and gives $50. Their contributions are acts of patriotism, frequently to express appreciation to a country that gave them opportunity for success and to insure that it continues to be managed according to principles in which they believe and which their party exemplifies.

There is ample proof of that statement. Stone and Mulcahy were later invited as friends of the President to some social affairs at the White House, at Camp David, and on the President's yacht *Sequoia*. But that was all the reward they got, and I know of no time at which they sought favors for themselves or anyone else.

The other contributors making up the top 143 received scant recognition as a whole. Ten of them were named ambassadors, but I had identified and recommended more than 30 as having the qualifications and ability for such responsibility and the financial means to undertake it. Some of the others received minor honors like appointments to part-time work on committees or boards, but I was disconcerted later to find so little use was being made of these qualified persons, and I complained to the President about this in a memorandum in 1970. Having in mind the fact that there might be a rerun of the campaign in a few more years, I felt that initial supporters should be given better follow up in the form of assignments, or at least offers of assignments, within their specific fields of interest and ability. My own responsibilities were elsewhere by this time, however, and beyond one or two complaints I did nothing. It was a revelation to me that there was so little meaningful patronage for contributors, which is certainly contrary to popular belief.

The $36.5 million in expenditures in 1968 set a new record for Presidential campaigns. Humphrey's spending was estimated at only $16 to $18 million, of which $12 million was in the general election, largely from borrowed money and unpaid bills. The Goldwater candidacy in 1964, the previous high, apparently had cost approximately $21 million. The acceleration in 1968 set the stage for the still higher level of spending that later developed in 1972. Had we been less successful in fund-raising in 1968, and not covered all the expenses, the 1972 story might have been different. I would probably not even have been asked for a repeat performance and that would have avoided all the unexpected trouble that befell me when Watergate exploded.

Eisenhower's enthusiasm for Nixon was strong in 1968 and he was anxious to avoid the kind of criticism that came after 1960 for his failure to be of more assistance. On March 13 he told me that he was telling his friends quietly that he was "all for Dick." He went on to say, "People ask me if I'll do more than I did in 1960. I guess I should have made more political speeches that time, but Dick and I agreed on what I should do. I don't know what I can do in 1968 but I'll make my position strong after the convention."

He continued: "Rockefeller called me a few days ago for advice. I told him I couldn't tell him what to do; he'd have to make up his own mind. I urged him not to make a personal campaign if he entered but to keep on the issues. I asked him if he would go all out for the Republican nominee, whoever it was, and he said he would. Rockefeller said 'Believe me, General, I don't want it, but the pressure on me to run is very heavy!' " Eisenhower also told me in this conversation that he didn't think Reagan had a chance for the Presidency, in 1968 or at any time in the future; he felt that Reagan didn't want to run but was being thrust forward by his backers.

Nixon was apparently anxious in 1968 to be sure that Eisenhower would really want to be helpful. On February 1, he told me that he considered it most important that I keep Eisenhower advised on how the campaign was going, and asked me to send copies of reports from the campaign staff and other reading items to Eisenhower with a note from time to time. I did so whenever possible through the year.

While the raising of money occupied all my time, I did try

once or twice to inject myself into political issues with memoranda suggesting possible initiatives Nixon might adopt. However, I did not get any indication of interest, so I came to feel that his campaign advisors thought I should tend to my own knitting, which I did.

Nixon himself, however, did refer two subjects to me. One was a request for my suggestions as to the best economic ideas to stress in his talks, and I replied to that in some detail, drawing on reports I had prepared for the Republican Coordinating Committee in previous years. The other was a referral to me of a proposal that he come out strong for government reorganization, which he was being urged to do by David Lawrence, publisher of *U.S. News & World Report*. Nixon sent me a handwritten note through Rose Mary Woods in June saying: "Possibly the germ of a good idea here? A broad reorganization of the government *is* needed. Maybe Arthur Flemming, Milton Eisenhower and Stans could undertake a study? Ask Maury to consider and together recommend a plan." The three of us had worked on government reorganization matters under Eisenhower, so that was a logical direction for the request, but after taking soundings I reported back that there was not enough time to round out any initiatives that would be useful for the election. Nixon agreed, but he hung on to the idea and after he became President worked strenuously but with negligible success to restructure the Cabinet departments and independent agencies along more efficient lines.

At the convention, immediately after he was nominated, Nixon went through a series of late-night sessions to get advice on the selection of his Vice President. He appeared to be genuinely at sea as to whom to select for greatest strength to the ticket, and the two group meetings I was invited to observe ranged all over the possible candidates without coming up with any consensus.

The next morning I learned that he had narrowed the field and was closeted with Finch, Haldeman, Ehrlichman, and one or two others to make the final decision. Having generated some enthusiasm for Governor John Volpe, I asked to join the group for a few minutes but was refused in a blunt manner that left me embarrassed and brimming with resentment for a few days. It was not a treatment I deserved after all my back-breaking work, but I recognized it as the beginning of the staff's protective ring around the soon-to-be President. I could be more understanding than most people because I knew from the Eisenhower days about the unreasonable and limitless demands on a President, and I knew he had to have people around him who would fight to save every possible minute of his time. I could never have imagined that, to a large degree, some of the 1972 and 1973 actions of this inner circle would contribute to his downfall.

I soothed myself with the thought that Nixon himself probably didn't know about my request.

Volpe was one of those who went to the wire in the selection process, but Nixon surprised most of his advisers by choosing Spiro Agnew, Governor of Maryland, as his running mate. I did not know Agnew. No one could have foreseen the unfortunate end of that association that was to come six years later with Agnew's forced resignation on a charge of income tax fraud.

As was customary, when Nixon became the nominee of the convention he acquired the entire party machinery of the Republican National Committee. I became Chairman of the Repubican National Finance Committee and carried on the finance activities of all the national committees as a single operation, moving funds from one to another as they were available and were needed. From this point the bookkeeping and reporting were carried on in Washington by the staff of RNFC, and the money-raising continued out of New York.

It was a clumsy arrangement but it seemed to work well until the windup, when I got a severe jolt. Immediately after the election I put all hands in the finance group to clear the decks so we could close up shop. This meant calling in all unpaid pledges and getting campaign bills in hand and paid. The latter was the more difficult and it took months for all accounts to be submitted. Some of the campaign personnel, again mostly the advance men, continued to use their credit cards and this was a real annoyance. By the time I resigned on January 19, 1969, as Chairman of the Republican National Finance Committee and of the Nixon-Agnew Finance Committee, it looked as though we would end up with a surplus of about $600,000, but after that late date an amazing lot of bills turned up in desk drawers and odd corners in the Washington office that changed it into a final audited deficit of $600,000 for the Republican party. This was a terrible disappointment, and the news came too late for me to do anything about it.

On January 21, 1969, I became Secretary of Commerce, upon

appointment by President Nixon and unanimous confirmation by the Senate. From that day on I cut all ties with fund-raising and for the three years I was in that position did not solicit a dollar of political money. Nor did the fact that anyone who came to my office was or was not a contributor, influence any action I took in that post. Most times I didn't know whether a visitor was Republican or Democrat, a contributor or not. So far as I know, no one ever presumed to contend that I misused the power of the office to favor anyone for political reasons.

After the arduous 1968 campaign, there were others who had worked with me who were entitled to reward for the strenuous and often unpaid work in raising the money to fund the election. It was not only customary but fair that a winner's team be given the opportunity to continue to toil for him and his programs. The White House agreed, and eight of my fund-raising staff were named. Kalmbach, my deputy, was offered an opportunity to be Undersecretary of Commerce, but he turned it down for personal reasons, which I took to mean that his family didn't want to move to Washington. Dugan became Treasurer of the Export-Import Bank; Brewer was named Deputy Administrator of the Small Business Administration and later a member of the Interstate Commerce Commission; Gleason worked for a time as one of my aides in Commerce and then was moved to the White House, where he stayed until mid-1970, when he left to become active in the administration's central campaign to raise and provide money for Republican Congressional and Senatorial candidates; Washburn became head of the United States Travel Service, for which he was admirably suited; Middendorf was named Ambassador to The Netherlands and later Secretary of the Navy; Hofgren became a White House aide and then for a time Vice Chairman of the commission named to negotiate on the Panama Canal, with the rank of Ambassador; Arden Chambers, my efficient secretary, went with me to Commerce. Hugh Sloan, Jr., who had assisted Washburn, was taken over by the White House to help Dwight Chapin in handling the President's calendar. These people were all worthy in experience and ability of the positions they were given, and all did excellent work in them.

At this point in my life, I looked forward to a successful career in the Cabinet, followed by eventual retirement from full-time activity into a role of elder statesman. Fate had other plans.

# " . . . anything of value"

When the Senatorial and Congressional elections came along in 1970, I stayed entirely aloof from fund-raising, but I did make a few sorties into the states for speeches in favor of Republican candidates. None of them won. The only conversations I had with anyone about money were with Kalmbach, who was active again in getting major contributions, and these talks were limited to a few friendly chats in which he told me about some of his successes. Kalmbach did not ask me for help in any way, and I did not offer any, because we both thought that would be improper for someone in my position in the Cabinet.

In the spring of 1971 a skeleton organization for the 1972 election race was set up, but I was not consulted about that. The finance office opened in March, headed by Hugh Sloan, Jr., and Lee Nunn, both experienced fund-raisers in Republican causes. Kalmbach had already been chosen to get early money commitments from the best prospects, and he began to do so in November 1970, again as an unpaid volunteer. Jeb Magruder, a White House staffer whom I barely knew at that time, headed the planning of the campaign operation from the beginning, presumably under the direction of the White House and with guidance from Mitchell. I disavowed any interest in these activities for many months.

Kalmbach visited me two or three times during that summer

and fall, eager to report some of the pledges he had received, but again did not ask me to take any part other than that of a friendly onlooker. In the later months of 1971, he began urging me to take the finance chairmanship for 1972. I resisted strongly because I was enjoying my work in Commerce, had a feeling of substantial progress, and didn't want to interrupt the forward motion of many of the programs I had stimulated. There were activities I particularly wanted to see come closer to fruition—in minority business enterprise, in the nation's energy needs, in trade expansion, in oceanic and atmospheric research, in national minerals policy, in patent policy, and in voluntary action by business in the fields of consumerism and the environment. Furthermore, my visit to the Soviet Union as the President's representative late in 1971, six months ahead of his first summit conference with Soviet leader Leonid Brezhnev, had shown me some of the extraordinary possibilities of commercial and diplomatic detente that I felt could unfold in 1972 and the succeeding years. I wanted to play a role in that.

Kalmbach tried to bait me by suggesting how my future could be made interesting, such as by heading the World Bank or the Export-Import Bank, or being an ambassador to an important country. I was not interested in any full-time assignment. Notwithstanding, word somehow leaked out to the press that I might be named to head the World Bank after the election; this report brought about a flurry of action, presumably with the blessing of the State Department and Henry Kissinger, to forestall such a nomination, with the result that Robert McNamara, the incumbent, was hurriedly re-elected for a new five-year term more than a year ahead of the usual time for such an action. I was amused.

Kalmbach kept increasing the force of his arguments and it became clear that he was speaking for the White House in trying to influence me to accept. He spent quite a few hours over several months trying to break down my resistance, mostly by flattering me with the idea that there was no on else who could do the job as well. As we approached the year-end I knew I had to make a big decision. Since the President wanted me to accept the chore, I either should do so to meet his desire or, if I declined to help out where he felt he needed me the most, I should resign as Secretary of Commerce. I tried to avoid the issue by suggesting other persons for the job, but Kalmbach rejected all of them and insisted that Nixon wanted the successful 1968 team of Mitchell and Stans to head the 1972 effort. Despite my wish to stay for about six consecutive years in Commerce, in the hope of making a real mark there, finally I gave in.

On January 6, 1972, I met with President Nixon at the Western White House in San Clemente to talk about the coming election and to offer my services wherever he thought they would be most valuable. If he wanted me to be finance chairman, I would accept, but only after I had stated some of the conditions that I felt should prevail and the understandings that I wanted to have. I had rehearsed all of this with Kalmbach, whose urgings had brought me to this point. Before seeing the President I also spent a good hour with Haldeman and Ehrlichman, discussing the topics I had in mind.

Drawing on the experiences in the previous election in 1968, I laid down these specifications:

—The fund-raising was to be done only by the finance committee, which was to be exclusively under my jurisdiction and independent of the campaign committee. There were to be no separate "citizens committees" or other groups raising money except with my advance approval, and anything that was raised by anyone was to be delivered intact to the treasurer of my committee to be acknowledged and recorded. I did not want to compete with other fund-raising groups for the same contributors as in 1968; lesser committees tended to "settle too cheaply" with a great many individuals who could have and should have given a lot more. I felt that a single unified fund-raising program across the United States, centrally controlled and with computerized records, would bring in a lot more money with less effort.

—No one was to have power to disburse funds except my committee, whose treasurer would pay all approved bills of the campaign committee, without responsibility to verify them or judge their efficacy. I did not want a policing responsibility, and I did not want finance committee people having to verify campaign payrolls, second-guess the television or radio ads, or judge the appropriate number of balloons to be used at a rally. All that was to be held under control by the campaign committee, whose management would set up means of enforcement of reasonable policies.

—The campaign would be run under a budget approved by a budget committee, half the members of which would be from the campaign committee and half from the finance committee. By this mechanism, I hoped to have some measure of influence on the aggregate amount of spending, within about a dozen major categories, like advertising and travel and literature, that I could compare with 1968.

—Before I became chairman, Kalmbach was to close out and turn over to our finance committee every cent of money left from the 1968 campaign, which had been consigned to him to administer under Haldeman's direction. This he was willing to do. Kalmbach would again be my chief deputy as he had been in 1968.

—I would not be expected to report regularly to the President or the White House and could choose my own proper ways for finding money, but my committee would not have authority to make any promises of favors or jobs to contributors. The President would not be asked to participate at all in fund-raising, except to address one nationwide closed circuit dinner in September.

—I wanted no reward for my work in his behalf. When the campaign was over I would be close to my sixty-fifth birthday and it would be time to begin tapering off. I hoped, however, that the President would find a few occasions to use my services on short assignments or overseas missions during his second term of office. Except for that, I would move into the private sector, probably as a professional director of a limited number of major companies.

—All necessary legal advice would be arranged for me and my committee to assure that we would be fully protected under the pertinent laws. This would be worked out with Mitchell when he became campaign director.

Haldeman and Ehrlichman found no fault with these provisions, although I think they were surprised that I didn't want a greater reward. Before we broke up, Haldeman left for a few minutes to brief the President, then returned and took me into the President's office, leaving me there alone with him.

Nixon was very relaxed, expressed his appreciation, brushed aside my conditions as presenting no problem, and said he certainly would like to call on me occasionally in the future for brief trips to foreign countries in his behalf and might want my help on other things once in a while, too. He then leaned back in his chair, set before a big window that gave me an open view of the Pacific as I faced him, and talked about his goals for a second term. His main objective was international peace, and he reviewed the situation in Vietnam and in the Middle East and also talked about China and the Soviet Union. I had made my eleven-day official visit to the Soviet Union just six weeks earlier as his representative, laying the groundwork for the economic matters that would come up in his forthcoming visit in May, and I took advantage of the opportunity to emphasize my conclusions in the written report of that trip.

He was a poised, confident, alert man, and I was sure I saw in him one of the outstanding Presidents of the twentieth century. I was eager to help him get re-elected.

The visit lasted only about thirty minutes. At the end, I asked if he would agree to defer my departure as Secretary of Commerce until February 15, since there were a few matters I wanted to conclude before taking on the finance job. Especially, I wanted to participate in a White House Conference on "American Business in 1990," which I had promoted and at which Secretary of Labor James Hodgson and I were to officiate. He agreed.

I knew I could not wait longer than that because the Congress was about to pass a new campaign financing law that contained requirements that all campaign contributions thereafter be published. There was considerable tactical value in getting around to major contributors and pointing out that they could make their gifts in privacy if they gave while the old law was still in effect. This was wholly proper and in clear conformity with the intent of the Congress, which had inserted a provision stating that the new law would not go into operation until sixty days after it was signed by the President. I did not expect that it would be difficult to collect what was needed—a sum then estimated at not over $30 million. The President had a good record, the economy was doing well, and he had shucked off the "loser" image that handicapped him so much in 1968. Besides, my experience in that election had overcome my inherent timidity in approaching people for money, and I knew many of the potential contributors from having passed the hat then.

My departure from the Cabinet was announced by Nixon at a White House press conference on January 27. He spoke very graciously of our friendship and of my service as Secretary of Commerce:

> "In his leaving the Cabinet, I, of course, have very deep regrets, because of all the people in our official family, Secretary Stans is one of my closest personal, as well as political, friends. He has served splendidly in the position of Secretary of Commerce. He has initiated a number of new programs which have been covered in the 15,000-word report that I presented to the Congress just a few days ago. And he, I know, in any position that he undertakes, can be expected to do a very, very competent job."

One bizarre incident occurred shortly before I moved to the finance committee offices on February 15. A Washington socialite whom I had met a few times phoned me excitedly to say that she had come across a man who wanted to offer a major contribution. When she said he was talking in millions, I decided to meet with him right away. Although the law prohibited me from "soliciting" political contributions on government property, I reasoned that seeing a volunteer to learn his intentions would not be a violation, and I was intrigued. Was there another Clem Stone?

He came in and introduced himself, a retired Admiral in the United States Navy. His opening remarks confirmed what I had already been told, and then he reviewed his background. It went like this:

"Twenty years ago at a port in the Middle East I met a man who was prospecting for oil. He was down on his luck but had lined up a new concession for drilling and was confident he would strike it rich.

"Although I realized that it was a horribly long shot, I invested a few thousand dollars in his venture. I never heard from him again and I decided I had played patsy to a con game. Then last year, just before I retired from the Navy, I was back in the same port having dinner, when an old man came up to me. It was the prospector.

"He said he had been looking for me for years. He had lost my name and address and wanted to report on my investment. My share of profits up to date was over $100 million, which was being held in a bank account in Europe, and my proportion of the remaining investment was worth even more!

"I don't have need for that kind of money at my age," he continued, "so I want to make a big contribution to get Nixon re-elected."

I gulped and then ventured the question. "How much did you have in mind giving?"

"Thirty or thirty-five million," he said, without hesitating an instant. "That ought to be enough to do the job."

By now I was spinning. Could he be for real? The story sounded like fantasy, but if it just happened to be true I could shunt the financial job over to someone else and stay in Commerce. But it sounded too good to be possible, so I decided I had to test him right away.

"When will the money be available?"

"I have to go through some formalities to get it into the country, but I can have a million dollars for you in a week and the rest in a month."

That was the end of that conversation. Much as I didn't believe in genii, I would be ready for anything when he returned. I had watched the man carefully. He had looked normal and talked normally and had given no sign of living in a dream world. I would wait, without getting too hopeful. Even one million would be a great start!

The second meeting punctured the balloon in a hurry. It would take longer than he thought to get the million dollars, he said. Lots of red tape and he might have to go to Europe and get it. In the meantime, would I arrange for him to see the President right away on a matter of an international crisis? One of his personal couriers, who traveled weekly between Hanoi, Moscow, and Washington to keep him up to date on international affairs, had just uncovered some documents that were of critical value and he would give them only to the President.

"What kind of documents?"

"Detailed plans of a joint Russian-Chinese attack on the United States to take place within thirty days."

I checked him out the next day with the Pentagon. The poor fellow's mind had been in a world of dreams for years. He had offered the same papers to the Navy six months earlier. He was not known to have any resources beyond his monthly pension!

I had time before February 15 to finish up some active matters in Commerce and to hold a few meetings with the finance committee staff already in place to study the provisions of the new law, but I did not do any soliciting of prospects or managing of fund-raising until after I left Commerce. The enactment date of the Federal Elections Campaign Act of 1971 was February 7, 1972, to become operative on April 7, and I knew that there were only fifty remaining days in which to offer contributors the benefit of confidentiality under the old law; so everyone moved fast when I went to work.

Kalmbach continued his swings around the country, meeting with selected prospects with the largest potential. By April 6, he had brought his pledges up to more than $10 million, and about $5 million of that had been received. I made quick trips to Los Angeles, San Francisco, Phoenix, Chicago, St. Louis, Dallas, Houston, and New York, helping to organize state fund-raising committees, meeting with their members, and having personal talks with major prospects. In Washington I sent out 5,000 letters to selected past contributors to the Republican party, asking them to send $1,000 each, and about 400 responded. The persons already in the finance office helped me in reviewing old prospect lists and building new ones, and then in meeting prospects. By telephone we talked to hundreds more. In each case we pointed out the reason for the early appeal. If the individual preferred to keep his contribution unpublicized he could achieve that by giving before April 7. If it made no difference to have his name reported, he could give later. This was exactly as the law specified.

The opportunity of privacy was welcomed by many, rejected by some. The occasion of the change in the law, however, gave us a circumstance that promised a fund-raiser's holiday. Seven months before the election we had a target date that we could focus on for early contributions. If we did our work well, we could break the bugaboo of early money, which is the most urgent and the hardest to get. The rest would be easy.

We were successful beyond our expectations. One reason was that many people that we didn't have time to reach sent in contributions voluntarily before April 7. Another was that our state chairmen in states like California, Texas, New York, Minnesota, and elsewhere got into the spirit of the chore and worked as hard as we did in Washington. The growth of momentum was wonderful to see. In the last four days of the old law an astounding $6 million came in, taxing the abilities of the treasurer's office and making it necessary to keep the bank open until nine o'clock on April 6 to get the deposits made. Bookkeeping went by the boards and a lot of money was put in the bank by the treasurer without a good recording of names and addresses, a circumstance that later cost us many hours in reconstruction.

Altogether, the amount that had been received from all sources, from the starting of the campaign organization in early 1971 until I arrived on February 15, had been about $5 million. In the seven weeks from then to April 6 we acquired another $15 million. That gave us enough to cover all expenses to that date, pay $5 million in advance on selected campaign costs, and still have $10 million in the bank. Unless strong competition came along, we now had enough "early money" to carry us through the primaries and the convention eighteen weeks later.

At about this time the budget committee, after some delay, finally set a figure of $40 million for the entire campaign. This came as something of a shock because late in 1971 the campaign people had talked about $26 million and I had expected then that it would more likely be about $30 million. That would have been enough. On January 30, 1972, I said on *"Face the Nation"* that it should be possible to run a campaign for less than $35 million. Nevertheless, if the total were held strictly to $40 million, we already had half of what we needed and the rest would normally be easy. However, after my experience in 1968, I had a feeling that spending would overrun the $40 million level and that we would have to raise a sizable additional margin. Also, I realized that we had collected the "cream" and that from then on most of the money would have to come from smaller contributions. W. Clement Stone of Chicago had again given $2 million, but there was only one Clem Stone after all.

In my mind I set a goal of raising $50 million, and with my staff worked this down into programs designed to reach all levels of support:

| | | |
|---|---|---|
| (a) | Direct mail solicitations to 30,000,000 homes to produce 400,000 contributions at an average of $25 | $10 million |
| (b) | Local efforts in the states, through store front offices, door-to-door contacts, small parties, and sales of literature and mementos; another 400,000 at an average of $10 | $ 4 million |
| (c) | A nationwide dinner in September in 30 cities connected by closed circuit television, at $1,000 a plate; 8,000 tickets | $ 8 million |
| (d) | A "boiler-room" telephone campaign to solicit past contributors across the country in the $50 to $100 potential | $ 2 million |
| (e) | Group solicitations of employees in corporations and institutions | $ 4 million |
| (f) | Individual solicitations of contributors with a potential of $500 or more | $35 million |

The planned total of $63 million allowed room for slippage in some categories, which was sure to happen. This exercise did establish one thing very clearly, and that was that we could not finance with small contributions the type of campaign that I expected to see. The Democrats found out this fact of life, too, somewhat later, and adjusted to it by soliciting and receiving some large contributions of $100,000 or more.

The Washington structure gradually became fully organized. There were the same two top committees as in 1968, one for finance and one for the campaigning, with of course some changes in the cast of characters. The campaign group (formally the "Committee for the Re-Election of the President," or CRP)[1] was headed by Francis Dale, a Cincinnati newspaper publisher; John Mitchell became its campaign director about March 1 and

---

1. These are the only initials we ever used for the campaign committee, and FCRP was the abbreviation for the finance committee. Later, it became fashionable in cynical circles to refer to them collectively as CREEP, an obviously insolent expression, used regularly by the media and even by the presumably unbiased office of the Watergate Special Prosecutor.

was succeeded by Clark MacGregor of the White House staff on July 1; Jeb Magruder, a young White House public relations man, was deputy campaign director throughout.

The finance committee (the "Finance Committee to Re-Elect the President," or FCRP) was run by Hugh Sloan, Jr., until February 15 when I took over as chairman and he became treasurer; on July 15 he resigned that post and was replaced by Paul Barrick. Sloan was a sophisticated fund-raiser who had served with me in the 1968 Nixon campaign and also had worked for more than three years for various Republican money-raising organizations on Capitol Hill. Barrick was an experienced certified public accountant who started in the 1972 campaign as controller on the same day I began as chairman. Others enlisted were: Lee Nunn, in charge of liaison with our separate fundraising committees in the states; Robert Odell, to assist in the direct mail and telephone solicitations; Washburn back again to handle the $1,000 dinners across the country, and also to be deputy chairman for a time, later to be succeeded by Tom Evans; Newell Weed and Harold Scott in charge of a plan to induce officials or employees of corporations and institutions to conduct employee group solicitations; Buckley Byers to set up a program of industry-to-industry solicitations of employees; and Dan Hofgren and Tom Pappas to help me in major solicitations from Washington.

Almost all of these people were well seasoned. Nunn, Byers, and Odell had been in Republican money-getting on the Hill for years, and knew many party workers and contributors around the country. Evans was still a partner in the former Nixon law firm. Washburn, Hofgren, and Pappas had helped me in 1968. Weed was an official of a national insurance-brokerage firm and Scott had been an Assistant Secretary of Commerce with a previous successful background in private business. They were all very able, and it was an extraordinarily efficient group that never wasted time. I monitored them principally by means of a staff meeting every morning that I was in Washington to compare notes, make assignments, review progress, and resolve problems.

The major assistance in the field came from industrialist Max Fisher of Detroit, entertainment magnate Taft Schreiber of Los Angeles, and investment banker Gus Levy of New York, each of whom was especially effective among the Jewish community and in business circles. In addition, some of our state chairmen were remarkably productive, with the largest amounts being raised in California under industrialist Leonard Firestone and in New York under banker Harold Helm.

In conformity with the plan originally worked out in 1968, the functions of the two committees were entirely distinguishable and neither directed the other. The campaign committee developed the strategy and tactics of influencing the public on the candidates and the issues; it managed the state primary efforts and wooed convention delegates; it developed and executed programs of advertising and public relations, including direct mail, telephoning, radio and television; it set up state and local organizations and store-front offices, and provided them with literature and other propaganda materials; it scheduled the appearances of the candidates for President and Vice President, and their surrogate speakers, and moved them around the country from city to city; and it carried out the hundreds of detailed chores behind the vote-getting function, from renting halls to chartering airplanes to buying balloons and confetti. One thing it was not supposed to do was to handle money. It was not to solicit or receive contributions or pay any bills.

That is where the finance committee came in. Through a national and state structure of independent but cooperating finance committees, it developed prospect lists, solicited contributions, banked the money, and paid without question any bills okayed by the campaign committee. The finance committee had no voice in campaign strategy or tactics, no veto power over spending, and its only interface with the campaign people was through the budget committee made up of representatives of the two groups. The budget committee argued ineffectively about the overall amount to be spent and the categories into which it would be divided, but in the absence of a strong system of controls over commitments it had little restraint on the cost of the campaign. It did not exercise any influence over program activities, and its discussions were a frustration to me and my associates who had to raise the money, rather than a help. Spending plans always increased, never decreased.

The budget meetings were so fruitless in promoting economy that, on one occasion when I was confronted with a situa-

tion where we were asked to ratify a sizable unbudgeted commitment that had already been made, I walked out in protest, leaving
the rest of the members in bewilderment as to what to do next.
There was a deadlock for a while, but the argument had been lost
before it started, and I had no choice but to surrender.

The separation between the campaign and finance committees was intended to be watertight, and this explains why later,
when Watergate broke, we were able to prove that officials of the
finance committee had no knowledge of what some people in the
campaign committee were up to. In effect, the finance committee
found that its job was to try to raise money as fast as it was needed
to pay the bills sent over by the campaign committee. That was
no small chore, as I could see evidence on all sides that the
campaign heads were not going to be able to exercise money
discipline over their troops in the field. Early in the game, Mitchell had decreed that no credit cards were to be employed in
1972, and this had closed one of the loopholes that had cost
an unnecessary fortune in 1968. But national political campaigners, at least those below the top levels, are so imbued with
the idea that overkill is better than underkill, or that fistfuls of
money can conceal gaps in judgment, that almost never can a
budget be held in bounds. From the early day in 1972 when Ed
Nixon, the President's brother, who had worked throughout the
relatively economical 1968 effort, said the planners were running
a "gold-plated" campaign, I had the fear that a lot more than $40
million would be spent.

On May 10, I wrote a memorandum of several pages to
Mitchell, pointing out where I thought millions of dollars could
be saved, but I never got a reply or even an expression of sympathy. The real problem was that the White House and the campaign managers knew that I knew that I could raise more than $40
million if I had to. I quickly reconciled myself to the conclusion
that if Mitchell and Magruder were giving me lip service, or even if
they meant well, there would be a big overrun in expenses. There
was. Before it was all over, the costs of re-electing Nixon and
Agnew, excluding the legal fees to defend innocent employees of
the two committees who were drawn into the Watergate miasma,
but counting the expenses of fund-raising, were $56.1 million.

Sloan and I worked out a clear and obvious division of duties between us the minute I joined the committee. In effect, he became the "inside man" and I became the "outside man," not meaning in location but in responsibilities. He took over the handling of incoming contributions, recording them, sending acknowledgments to the contributors, banking the money, paying bills, and preparing reports. He had very little contact with contributors and made no solicitations. It was my job to organize the fund-raising across the country, state by state and at head-quarters, prepare lists of major prospects and assign names for solicitation, make solicitations to the extent time permitted, supervise the committee activities and deal with problems, see that the committee stayed in conformity with the law, handle the complaints and criticisms, and maintain necessary liaison with the campaign hierarchy. Accompanying all this was a mass of daily mail, telephone calls, dictation, and meetings when in Washington, and a considerable amount of traveling around the country.

With such a workload, I could not and did not take part in Sloan's internal money-handling except when he brought a matter to me for advice. I did not sign checks. I did not approve bills for payment except to resolve a few disputes over individual traveling expenses. I did not have a cash fund, but turned over all receipts of cash and checks to Sloan, with identification of their source. With but one exception, a loan to our Maryland finance committee, I did not direct Sloan to make any payments in cash. He handled his work with a rather full autonomy and kept me posted on incoming contributions through a daily typed report. I had no knowledge of expenditures except through the publicly filed reports, which began after April 7. I did not work with or see the books of accounts.

These facts account for the money being received and payments being made without my knowing, as was generally the case, except as contributions came directly to me or were listed on the daily report. It accounts for my not being aware of, except in one instance, the timing or amounts of payments by Sloan to Liddy, Porter, Magruder, and others, which later became promi-nent in the Watergate disclosures.

I was determined from the start to see that the finances of the campaign would be conducted strictly according to law. Having been through the 1968 election, I was familiar with the old law which remained in force until April 7, and I had carried over a number of written legal opinions and considerable background on that law. Clearest of all was the provision that any money raised for a candidate to secure the nomination for the Presidency, up through the nominating convention, was not required to be reported, but the funds raised and spent for the general election were reportable. With a new law coming in, even though I had not yet joined the committee, I sought to insure future compliance by arranging for key people to be briefed at an all-day meeting in January by John Dean of the White House, Roemer McPhee, counsel for the Republican National Committee, and Glenn Sedam, counsel for the campaign committee. They diagnosed the statute in detail, line by line, noting carefully all differences from the old 1925 law. Later, Dean and I also worked closely in reviewing the regulations before and after their issuance by the Comptroller General. I warned the finance committee officers and staff on several occasions to be wary of lapses. Sloan confirmed this to the Senate Watergate Committee hearing in 1973 in these words:

> "[Stans] indicated to me that he wanted to be sure that every single contribution in the post April 7 period went through a bank account so that there would be a clear audit trail in front of the new law which the General Accounting Office did have the right to inquire into; he wanted to have a very precise accounting within the ground rules of the new law."

To provide day-to-day guidance, I employed a lawyer full time on our staff, beginning in the middle of March. The first was G. Gordon Liddy, who, despite the faults that got him into serious trouble later for campaign espionage unknown to our staff, performed well as committee counsel on all topics assigned to him. When Liddy refused to cooperate with the investigating authorities in June and I discharged him, he was succeeded by Stanley Ebner, a competent lawyer with legislative experience as a Congressional staffer, who remained until well after the election.

On March 2, in a staff meeting, I directed Sloan, Nunn, and the others present to read the new law again so they would be fully informed and would avoid infractions. From the beginning, I established the policy that no corporate contribution would be solicited or knowingly accepted, caused that to appear on all contribution cards and written solicitations, and so advised my staff, contributors, solicitors, and audiences. Any identified corporation contributions were promptly returned.

On July 25, I wrote a memorandum to the staff telling them again that there could be no exceptions to the requirements of the law. I stressed on a number of occasions, some in writing, that no promises of reward of any kind could be made in return for contributions. The records of staff meetings show about fifty requests to counsel for opinions on legal questions involved in the handling of contributions. Matters such as the acceptance of foreign funds from an American national, and many other technical points, were carefully considered by our counsel and their advice was followed. I wrote occasional memoranda to the treasurer calling his attention to less obvious parts of the law, such as the accounting required for sales of campaign jewelry and novelties. Minutes of daily staff meetings were kept to fix responsibilities to be carried out by the various persons present. I was sure that all bases were covered. The organization responded wholeheartedly, and our recordkeeping and other compliances appeared to be excellent.

Lee Nunn set up a finance committee in every state and territory, about fifty-five in all, and followed up on their progress from week to week, prodding those who were behind on their results and complimenting those who did well. With a computer on line at headquarters we were able to give each state a report every week on the money raised from its residents. Weed, who joined the committee on the same day I did, originated the idea of our using a corporate group plan, designed to be similar to the procedures of business concerns for Community Chest and other local charity solicitations. This plan was in complete compliance with the law and permitted each employee to determine which candidates would be helped by his money. It was contemplated that officers of a company would name one person to solicit employees above a certain salary level, collect the results, and send them in. We concluded that it would be tactful for the solicitations to be bipartisan, to remove the hesitation that some companies might have about being publicly partisan, and our literature was prepared on that basis. We knew this would produce some money for the other side, but we were confident that a high percentage of the total would come to us. It worked out that way, with about 95 percent to Nixon and 5 percent to McGovern. We never were thanked by the opposition for that help, although there is no indication that any of it received in this way was refused.

Scott came on board June 1, and he and Weed divided the country to contact officials of the top 2,000 corporations and institutions under this plan. By early October they had made their pitch to about 1,500 companies, and 550 had taken it on. The actual results were hard to tabulate, because some of the proceeds became merged into the general flow of funds, but we estimated that from $2 to $3 million came in through this activity. It would have been broader in participation and bigger in results if there had not been disagreement among corporation lawyers as to just what political activities could or could not be done under the 1971 Act amendments to Sections 610 and 611 of the Corrupt Practices Act relating to corporations. Nonetheless, we were pleased with the program and felt that it could be a forerunner to the use of similar techniques in the future on a much larger scale by the two political parties to induce broader public participation in the financing of national elections. Under the frenzied conditions of Watergate this plan was investigated from end to end and nothing was found wrong about it, but unfortunately the irritation of such investigations to many of the companies tended to slow its expansion for a while. This was regrettable, since the plan offers a democratic alternative to reliance on government financing on the one hand and large contributions on the other. The precise procedure used by us was cleared by the Federal Election Commission in 1976 in the SUN PAC decision as being proper and legal under the latest election laws.

The plan for a $1,000 nationwide dinner connected by closed circuit television had been originated by our committee in 1968 and we revived it again in 1972, with Washburn in charge and General Lucius Clay the national chairman in both years. We avoided most of the earlier confrontations with the regular party machines in the states for taking all the proceeds of the $1,000 dinners for our national budget by abdicating the field of $100 dinners to them. The net proceeds to our committee from the big dinner, after expenses, grew from $4.9 million in 1968 to $7.5

million in 1972. The President participated with enthusiasm, and even allowed the San Francisco and Los Angeles events to be spun off from the one on closed circuit; these two were held the next day, with him in personal attendance at both. I kept my word to him that this was all he had to do in money-raising. It was an advantage his opponent didn't have, as McGovern was forced to give considerable of his time to meeting and talking with prospective givers.

Early in March 1972, I made a decision that stuck my neck way out and could have been disastrous had it not turned out to be successful. Sensing that the pre-April 7 period would give us a good start on the year's money requirements, I told each state finance chairman that I would guarantee to his committee the entire budget of the campaign in his state and see to it that the needed money was sent in advance on the first of each month, provided only that all contributions in excess of $100 received in the state were forwarded directly to us in Washington for handling. The advantage of this was that we could run one unified and centralized treasurership for the whole country, letters of thanks would go out to givers from Washington, most of the records and public reports would be prepared at national headquarters by computer, and the state committees would have only a limited amount of letterwriting, bookkeeping, and reporting. The risk in the idea was that some state finance chairmen would figure that they had it made, and would lie down on the job.

The success we had in accumulating a sizable bank balance by April 7 insured the workability of this plan at our end, and as the months went by, the state campaign organizations had none of the usual problems of fighting for cash resources to pay bills. To some extent our plan also answered the usual complaints that "they're taking all of the money out of our state to go to Washington." No doubt we were, but our people could reply by pointing out precisely how much we were sending back to finance the campaign within their state. While not all of the states met the quotas we had assigned to them to raise, about half of them did, especially the larger ones, and many overran substantially; I had no feeling that any of our state committees had deliberately loafed on the job because we had guaranteed to cover the cost of their campaigns.

We had high expectations about getting massive numbers of contributions by mail from smaller contributors, but this was only partially realized. Our best mailing list was the one of regular contributors to the Republican National Finance Committee and we used that several times, but it had only about 600,000 names. To get broader coverage we tested one commercial mailing list after another, with only marginal success. In all, we sent out 30 million letters and received about $8.5 million in contributions. This was expensive money to get, because in total we spent approximately 50 percent of this in making the mailings. It was a cost which could be justified only in two ways: the mail solicitations also carried a political message and thereby performed a secondary service, and the persons who did respond became additions to the party's mailing list and could be expected to answer similar appeals in future years. Knowing how hard we had to work to get this limited amount, however, I was skeptical about the glowing reports attributed to the Democratic camp about the amounts of their direct mail contributions, some quoting amounts as high as $30 million. Final summaries, however, do show that they outdid us in this program, ending up with $15 million received from direct mail, television, and newspaper solicitations, at a cost of $5 million.[1] In any event, they too had to seek out as many large contributions as possible, because the small contributions couldn't carry the load. Our average contribution in response to direct mail was about $22.50, a bit less than we had expected.

The mass telephoning activity began in the late summer and carried on until October 20. It produced about $2.5 million in identified gifts, at a cost of 20 percent for personnel and phone bills. The fund-raising by local city committees disappointed us, and all we could trace to store fronts, door-to-door solicitation, jewelry sales, tea parties, and similar affairs was about $2 million.

On out-of-town travel I developed a standard one-day stay in each city that included a breakfast meeting with our state finance committee people, separate meetings with three or four major individual prospects at 45-minute intervals in the morning, a

---

1. Herbert E. Alexander, et al., *Financing the 1972 Election*, (Lexington, Mass.: Lexington Books, D.C. Heath & Co., 1976).

luncheon meeting with anywhere from 30 to 200 important prospects, more individual meetings in the afternoon, and then a trip to the next town. Sometimes I did two cities in one day, like Denver and Colorado Springs or Wichita and Kansas City. Usually trips were two days in duration, but on one longer trip of nine days in July, I visited three cities in Georgia, three in Florida, San Francisco, Seattle, Portland, Des Moines, and Dayton, before returning to Washington. After Kathleen went to the hospital in August, I cut my travels so that I would not be away more than one night at a time.

All this travel was strenuous, and it was not without tension. On a day in Florida in a light plane piloted by George Champion, Jr., our state finance chairman, we made stops in Miami, Tampa, and Ft. Lauderdale. The first trip across the state was through rolling black clouds that tossed us about roughly, and Champion did his best to skirt the worst of them by a route twice as long, extending over the Gulf of Mexico. After a late arrival in Tampa, we cut our pitch short in order to get back to Lauderdale before dark, only to discover when we reached the airport that the landing gear would not lock in place. Champion circled the field a dozen times, under futile observation from the tower and from rescue planes, and finally as dusk was approaching decided he had no choice but to risk a landing. We came into the runway, lined with six fire trucks, and made a miraculous touchdown under his skilled hands. Maybe the experience was worth it; we raised about $250,000 as a result of the day's work.

A typical day in Washington was like a madhouse. My staff meeting began at 8:30 A.M. and lasted a half hour. It was followed by a continuous schedule of individual meetings with staff people, or with contributors or fund-raisers from out of town, or with lawyers or public relations people, interspersed with phone calls, dictation, and signing of "thank you" letters. On October 23, for example, my schedule showed a staff meeting, two long meetings with lawyers, six meetings with staff members, a meeting with a large contributor and one with campaign people, in addition to forty-one completed telephone talks around the country, after which I spent three hours visiting Kathleen in the hospital and returned home by 11:00 P.M. To maximize as much as possible the time to see her, I cut out dinner and picked up a McDonald's

"Big Mac" on the way. The next few days almost completely involved legal matters. October 27 began with the daily staff meeting, five meetings with staff members, six meetings with contributors, two meetings with fund-raisers, thirty-two completed telephone calls, handling of mail and replies, and then my daily visit to Kathleen. This time I took along some Marriott fried chicken and ate it in her room.

In all, the efforts in 1972 of our various drives and the solicitations by the national Republican party organization did produce about 1 million contributors from an estimated 900,000 thousand persons. It was the personally sought major contributions, however, that brought the large bulk of the money. After Clem Stone's $2 million came Richard Scaife of Pittsburgh with an even $1 million, and John Mulcahy of New York with $600,000. There were 20 other contributors of $200,000 and over, 71 who gave in the $100,000 range, another 81 who gave approximately $50,000, and 155 who gave $25,000.[2]

When it was all over we had raised $60.2 million. Our expectations had been borne out in each category of effort except the local community programs and the group fund-raising, and had missed slightly in direct-mail returns. The total was enough to take care of the most extravagant plans of the spenders. It needn't have taken this amount of money to elect a President; only the obvious mania of the campaign leaders for a maximum victory dictated such spending.

Nixon was not told the names of his larger contributors until December, well after the campaign was over. Then he held two stag dinners at the White House on March 6 and 7, 1973, each attended by over 100 of the most generous donors. Not unimportantly, at each of the dinners he extolled my skill and integrity as a money-raiser, saying that "no one has ever been more efficient, more honest and more successful in political fund-raising," and

2. McGovern had 6 persons who loaned or contributed $200,000 and up, six around $100,000, 29 at $50,000, and 52 at $25,000 each. In his short run for the nomination, Humphrey reported two contributions over $100,000 and four others over $50,000. He also had a number of loans, several in the half-million-dollar range, that were only partially repaid. His records, however, are not complete enough to assure precise figures in either category.

I was absolutely delighted when those present each time gave me a standing ovation for more than three minutes. It proved that the tactics I had employed had actually made friends, not irritated people, and certainly it denied that any of them had been coerced or misled. Several corporate officials who later were coaxed by Senator Ervin in the Watergate hearings to say that they had been unduly coerced for their contributions were present and joined enthusiastically in the ovation!

7

## "HOW MUCH FOR LUXEMBOURG?"

There was no magic or genius in our ability to break all records in political fund-raising. With Nixon running from the White House and sure of nomination, it was possible to plan our campaign early and to organize it into a smooth machine in which most parts functioned well. McGovern had to fight off his opponents in the Democratic party until early July, and then had to work his way out of the misfortunate choice of Senator Thomas Eagleton as vice presidential candidate, before his people could gear up to get money. It was impressive that they did as well as they did, which by all previous measurements was outstanding, in a cause that was so outmatched. Because McGovern had about 750 different committees, his figures are hard to collect, but best estimates are that he raised and spent about $42 million from beginning to end.[1]

Most helpful to us were McGovern's economic proposals, which were so frightening to people of even modest means and to businessmen at all levels, that it did not require much salesmanship on our part to induce them to give. Had it not been for the

1. Herbert E. Alexander, et al., *Financing the 1972 Election*, (Lexington, Mass.: Lexington Books, D.C. Heath & Co., 1976).

incredible series of handicaps that evolved to distract our efforts, especially Watergate, we could have raised $100 million against McGovern, had we needed it. I honestly believed that his economic ideas threatened to destroy the American system, and said so. They sought to give handouts to everyone ($1,000 a year to every man, woman, and child), prevent inheritances from one generation to another, tax capital gains (much of which are merely a reflection of inflation) as ordinary income, tax capital gains at death, tax municipal bond interest, reduce business deductions and investment credits, and in many other ways impede capital formation, level out the wealth of the country, and remove personal incentives. To my mind then and now such socialistic developments would destroy the ambitions, opportunities, and rewards for all Americans, especially the young. Most of those I addressed shared my fears that his reforms would be a traumatic shock to the economy and would seriously endanger the future of the nation.

One midwestern businessman was quoted in a *Wall Street Journal* article as saying that "if McGovern gets to the White House I'd probably want to go out and commit suicide." The minute I read that, I telephoned him and made an appointment so I could tell him I was working to save his life; I came away with a $250,000 contribution, the first of any size that he had ever given to a political campaign.

I had a sheet printed that summarized McGovern's economic and welfare proposals and their cost, and when I spoke to individuals or an audience, I handed out copies and asked each person to have his tax man tell him how much his taxes would have to be increased to finance them if McGovern were to win.

The conversations in which I solicited funds were not based on a memorized tape-recording of identical words, but they all followed a close pattern . . . a dissertation on the importance of the election, the dangers of the opposing candidate's platform, the cost of the campaign, the need for large contributions to finance it, and the appeal in which I named a hoped-for amount. With wealthy businessmen, I hung a lot on this: "For the first time in forty years you've got a President who understands business and has lived in the business world. You've agreed with most of his policies. Don't you think it's worth something to keep him in the White House for another four years?" Normally, I went on to say: "Some folks in companies your size have raised as much as $100,000 from their employees. Can I count on your people to do as well? If not, what do you think I can expect?" Some said they would try and others said my sights were too high. Except for a few companies like Goodyear, who asked whether their first amounts raised were in line with our expectations, I did not ever try for more. We accepted all amounts with the same gratitude, and when we were turned down we shrugged our shoulders and went on to more hopeful prospects.

As I went from audience to audience, I also evolved the "insurance" concept, in which I suggested that each person give in accordance with his means, and since I could not know what that was I asked each one to calculate what 1 percent of his net worth would be. I urged that this would be a reasonable amount to pay every four years to insure the right kind of management for the country, and especially to defeat the kind of ideas offered by the opposition. I did not ask for that 1 percent, but suggested that with such an amount in mind each person ought to want to give a lot more than he may ever have given in the past. It was a novel approach for many and it helped often to bring their checks into higher brackets. This was a perfectly proper tactic, but it soon became distorted in a variety of ways by the media to imply that I was making assessments, levying a tax on income, or otherwise applying coercion. All that was nonsense.

One distraction, which I suppose was normal politics, was in the form of stories planted by the opposition to cut down on our contributions. The first of these was a circular letter mailed to millions of people by Senator Edmund Muskie in January, when he was confident he would be the Democratic candidate, in which he said, "Richard Nixon is amassing a political war chest of $40 million, with $30 million already in the bank. Most of it has been contributed by powerful special interests." The amount in the bank was 90 percent wrong and the source was more so. We had less than $3 million at the time. This exaggeration was sometimes enlarged to $40 million, and was repeated over and over again in an eighteen-hour Democratic telethon in the early July weekend just before their convention. We denied these gross misstatements at every opportunity, but we never succeeded in catching up with the big lie. This political sabotage by our oppposition was, from where I sat, far more effective as a weapon and far more difficult to counter than all the "dirty tricks" the Nixon campaign agents were later found guilty of doing to the opposition.

Later in the campaign, around October 15, rumors were rampant that we were so wealthy we were turning down contributions and these got us a lot of harmful press publicity, including some stories to that effect planted by fellow Republicans running for Congressional seats. Again we issued denials, because at that time we still needed about $9 million to meet commitments across the country. The surplus we later produced was nowhere in sight then. Adding to the difficulties caused by all this was the fact that from July to November Nixon ran 25 to 35 percentage points ahead of McGovern in the polls. Many prospects decided we didn't need money to win and didn't send any.

A distraction that didn't turn out as badly as I first feared was the creation of the committees of Democrats for the Re-Election of the President. I learned about this operation in July when Charles Colson called me over to lunch with him and John Connally at the White House. As it was conceived, that committee would raise $3 million to finance its activities, and I could see potential conflicts with our own fund-raising. Creating another money organization was contrary to the understanding I had with Nixon in January, so I was not very gracious about the idea, to the irritation of both Connally and Colson. As time went on, however, there were less than a dozen important instances in which money solicited and expected by our committee went to Connally's. In all, his people raised about a million dollars. To simplify matters, they took over some of the television "spot" pieces that had already been prepared and budgeted for by the Committee for the Re-Election of the President. In that manner, we financed all of their costs in excess of the money they raised without straining either budget.

On the spending side, my efforts to get the campaign people to exercise restraint were only minimally successful. The budget of $40 million grew to $43 million, then $46 million; and I could see from simple observation of the trends that it was going to run much higher. I objected strenuously in meetings of the budget committee to the "overkill" represented in the expansive plans to reach voters repeatedly by television, radio, direct mail, telephone, and door-to-door visitation, but was unsuccessful. In retrospect, I can see that the motive was not merely to win the election, or to win it by a good margin, but to win it by the highest possible vote, and this precluded giving much weight to economy or frugality. The campaign people were confident that we in the finance committee could raise any amount that might be spent. At one point Clark MacGregor, who had succeeded John Mitchell as campaign director, tried to placate me by saying that he wouldn't be concerned about a campaign deficit of as much as $3 million. A deficit was anathema to me, and I'm sure he knew that. I continued to argue futilely against what I considered to be extravagance, watching the amounts go up, while MacGregor's people kept the truth from him and from me as to how much was being committed. Perhaps even they didn't know.

My people in the finance committee staff in Washington eagerly met the stresses of the campaign, including the undeserved consequences of Watergate and my own preoccupation with litigation and Kathleen's illness. The only time they complained was when the President spent an hour on a drop-in visit to the campaign personnel at their headquarters and failed to appear at our finance office, which was in the same building. They remonstrated through the grapevine so bitterly that he held a special session for us in the Cabinet room of the White House a week later to remedy the omission. It seemed as though the persons who handled his schedule had little regard for those who pursued the money for the campaign, as the same kind of situation occurred again on election night. We had a party for several hundred of the major money supporters and I had invited the President to attend. When the returns showed him a winner, he paid visits to the campaign workers and to a general public reception, but not to our place. I squawked so much that Vice President Agnew came over and made a short talk of thanks to the contributors. I don't believe Nixon himself made these decisions.

It is a fact, however, that the finance side of a major campaign is little noted when the activity is over. It galled me in both 1968 and 1972 that major books like those of Theodore White, which recounted in 400 pages the events of the candidates and their organizations in planning strategy and corralling votes, summarized in one or two scattered sentences the sweat and strains of the people working furiously to get the money fast enough to pay the accumulating bills. The sacrifices of fund-raisers and givers were wrapped up in one phrase such as White's in 1972:

"Unhappily, Maurice Stans was too successful—there was too much cash around."

At the end of August 1973, when we considered all elements of the campaign wound up and the bills paid, and after refunding more than a million dollars in contributions discovered to be illegal or undesirable, we had a surplus of $4.1 million. The expenses, including those of raising money, had been $56.1 million against the revenues of $60.2 million. This is how the $56.1 million was spent:

|  | *Millions* |
|---|---|
| Advertising—broadcast and print | $7.0 |
| Direct mailings to voters | 5.8 |
| Campaign materials and literature | 4.2 |
| Mass telephoning to voters | 1.3 |
| National headquarters—personnel, rent, press relations, publications, telephone, travel and other expenses | 5.8 |
| Travel of President, Vice President, surrogates, and advance men | 3.9 |
| Special activities of ethnic, women, youth, and other groups | 2.9 |
| Polling | 1.6 |
| Convention and election night expenses | .8 |
| State campaign committees—primary elections, personnel, locations, travel, and voter contact | 15.9 |
| Fund-raising—costs of direct mail appeals and dinners | 5.0 |
| Fund-raising—national and state committees | 1.9 |
| Total | $56.1[2] |

When these figures were voluntarily released in September 1973, it was the first time a public accounting had ever been made for all the expenditures of a Presidential campaign, from beginning to

---

2. This did not include expenditures of the various committees of Democrats for the Re-Election of the President, estimated at $2.4 million.

end, and combining all committees and entities. The total was excessive, beyond all reason and certainly beyond the necessities for winning. But by this time I had come to recognize that there was no precisely right amount to spend in an election, and surely no precisely right way in which to spend it. Jim Farley, when he was the campaign manager for Franklin Roosevelt, was credited with the statement that "half the money that is spent in a political campaign is wasted, but which half?" As I looked at our figures, I wondered, too.

It was our intention to turn our surplus over to the Republican party, but we were unable to do so then because of the pending claims and lawsuits growing out of Watergate. As those matters dragged on I concluded that I did not want the full responsibility for the decisions that had to be taken in disposing of them. With the concurrence of the White House, we wound up our committee on February 11, 1974, by transferring the bank account, then down to $3.6 million, to a 1972 Campaign Liquidation Trust, with a proviso that the amount remaining after settling all valid claims would go to the Republican National Finance Committee. The trustees, in addition to me, were former United States Senator Charles Potter, who was chairman, and former Ambassador to Denmark Guilford Dudley. I resigned as trustee on July 31, 1974, and was replaced by Paul Barrick, the former committee treasurer. The eventual settlement with the Democrats and continuing legal fees and administrative costs kept reducing the surplus until less than a half million dollars was available at the end of 1977.

A problem arose in 1972 when the various Watergate investigations and lawsuits began to proliferate, and that was what to do about the legal expenses of officials and employees of the campaign committee and the finance committee. Realistically, it was appropriate for each person to have his own independent counsel, since there could be conflicts of interest with the committees and with other persons. It is an accepted practice in business companies, and a proper one, to reimburse the legal costs of employees who are required to defend their actions made in good faith on behalf of their employers. We adopted that practice early in 1973 upon formal approval of the budget committee. It did not cover employees of the White House. The trust agreement creating the 1972 Campaign Liquidation Trust specifically carried forward that policy. The total cost of all legal expenses and litigation of the committees and their employees, including settlements with Democratic claimants for Watergate damages, was in excess of $3.5 million, a regrettable consequence of the Watergate crimes. Later in 1978, another million dollars in unpaid claims for legal fees was still pending, awaiting settlement of income tax and gift tax matters and final wind-up of the campaign finances.

The worst impediments to our work were the Watergate affair and its aftermath in the form of investigations, inaccurate press stories, and lawsuits, all of which diverted much of our time. What seemed in January 1972 to be an easy assignment changed after June 17 into a nightmare for me and some of our people. Sloan and I and most of our staff were put through FBI interrogations and grand jury testimony. Civil lawsuits spawned by Watergate took hundreds of hours working with lawyers, planning strategy, and participating in court proceedings and depositions. Overriding all this was Kathleen's bewildering illness in the last half of 1972 and continuing into 1973 and her dejected mental state; the chemotherapy injections left her nauseated and weakened, and her chronic depression was the opposite of her usual cheerful disposition. The press stories that grew more and more imaginative were devastating to morale. The demands in time to meet all these untoward circumstances, and the strain of the personal crises involved, transformed the year from a relaxed confident workout to a period of unbelievable pressure and anguish.

It is a real credit to the personnel of the committee that they worked as well as they did in the face of all the disturbances. They withstood the inquisitions and none of them was charged with any wrongdoing in the handling of the campaign financing (excepting Gordon Liddy, whose illegal acts were directed by Jeb Magruder of the campaign organization, and Liddy's secretary, who presumably had some knowledge of his covert actions). But it was embarrassing to have contributors sitting in the reception room while a steady procession of process servers and FBI agents walked in. It was a constant nuisance to have a number of GAO investigators paging through the records, often making snide remarks to our people. It was not easy to meet the demands, sometimes urgent, of the scouts for the Senate Watergate Committee, who culled out and took copies of thousands of pages of corespondence and reports. It was even more difficult to work while coping with the Internal Revenue agents acting for the Special Prosecutor's office, as many as eight at a time and continuing for weeks, in scrutinizing our files.

Most disagreeable of all for our people was the daily hounding of the press in person and by phone as the revelations broke and any tidbit of news or rumor was pursued for a new break; reporters took to visiting employees at their homes after hours and on weekends. There were also occasional insulting letters, the "nut mail" that some distorted minds enjoy writing to persons in the public eye, with vicious and sometimes obscene statements having no relation to the facts. There were threatening letters and payoff demands, equally insane. While I took the brunt of this, I marveled at the assured way in which the staff ignored most of it and carried on their work.

True to my compact, I made no attempt to play any part in the political side of the campaign. However, some weeks before the convention I was drawn into the White House's romancing of Walter Hickel, who had been discharged by Nixon as Secretary of the Interior in 1970. Wally and I were good friends and had been on the same side in some difficult issues within the Administration, especially on oil imports, so I had kept in touch with him after his departure. Some of my Cabinet colleagues and I had some concern that in his unhappiness at the time he might go over to the Democrats and we wanted to prevent that, even holding the hope that he might support the President in 1972. He assured me that he was not about to leave his party, but that his future support of the President would depend on the "credibility" of the action, who the opponents were, and other factors that could not be anticipated. He was not bitter, and was not averse to taking over a work assignment for the administration if it were an important one within his background and capability, and not artificial. We talked about some possibilities along these lines, but nothing came of them. He was then busy completing and publicizing his book, *Who Owns America*. I reported these conversations to the President.

With all this as background, Bill Timmons of the White House staff called me in July 1972 to say that Nixon would like, as a show of party unity, to have Hickel be one of the seconders of his renomination at the convention, and asked me to talk to Hickel about the idea, which I did. When I put it to him as a matter of party loyalty and urged him to rejoin the team, Hickel agreed. He was a strong advocate of an increased national and international program of Arctic research, and he wanted me to carry to Nixon his urgings that something be done along that line in a second term. This I did. He also wanted assurances, which I was able to get, that he was not going to be used and then discarded, but would be consulted and listened to from time to time. The convention program called for ten persons to make one-minute seconding speeches, and Hickel's only condition was that he not be the last one. I'm sure that it was not easy for him to appear in public and endorse the man who had fired him, but he did it gracefully and well.

Shortly after the election I received a call from Robert Bennett, a Washington lawyer who represented Howard Hughes and had delivered Hughes' contributions of $150,000 to our committee earlier in the year. Bennett said that Hughes expected no reward but did want the President to know that his seventieth birthday was coming up on December 24 and nothing would please him more than a phone call of greeting on that day. I passed the word on to the White House and arrangements were made for the call. Ironically, a massive earthquake hit Managua, the capital of Nicaragua, where Hughes was then living, early on the morning of the 23rd, destroying all communications, and the connection could not be completed. I did not learn whether the call was ever made.

One unfortunate issue that arose late in the campaign and continued after the election was the contention that our vacuum cleaner was so thorough that we took all the money and left none for Republican candidates for the Senate and House, causing some of them to lose their seats. I never answered this charge publicly but did so in a memorandum to the President in December, which included these excerpts:

> As Chairman of the Republican National Finance Committee, I granted subsidies of $300,000 to the Republican Senatorial Campaign Committee, $300,000 to the Republican Congressional Com-

mittee, and $50,000 to the Republican Boosters Club. These grants were received very gratefully by these committees at the time and substantially closed their budget gaps.

Our Finance Committee to Re-Elect the President arranged for direct contributions to Senatorial and Congressional candidates in a total amount of approximately $250,000 plus additional contributions to the Republican Senatorial Committee and the Republican Congressional Committee amounting to about $75,000.

This added up to just about a million dollars that was diverted from our campaign. I do not believe any Congressional candidates lost their seats for lack of money just because we were too successful in gathering ours. Senator Margaret Chase Smith returned a $3,000 check we got for her, saying she didn't need it. Several other candidates who were defeated told us that they had all the money they required. The Chairmen of the House Republican Congressional Committee and the Republican Senatorial Committee both were very appreciative of the funds I turned over to them, and assured me at the time that the amounts were adequate to see them through. Besides all this, I'm sure that our campaign people had in mind in their lavish spending the "coattail" theory that the bigger the Nixon win the more Republican and Senate candidates would pull through. It didn't seem to work this time, however, because Republicans lost seats in the House and gained only a few in the Senate, despite Nixon's 61 percent victory that carried forty-nine states.

In the ambience of Watergate in Washington, and the early revelations, true and untrue, regarding the financing of the break-in, it was inevitable that suspicions would be directed at our finance committee. The political pressure on us to disclose the names of our early contributors, the discovery that some corporations had made illegal contributions, and the disclosures that payoffs had been secretly made by others to the burglars, unleashed a legion of political and media accusations. Some were based on a modicum of truth, greatly enlarged; some on circumstance, rumor, belief or just imagination. We could not possibly keep up with them, much less answer them individually and in detail, although we denied many as we went along. Now that it is all over, it seems best to deal with them in this form, stating the charges and our answers to them as proven by the evidence:

Charge 1. That in its solicitations the finance committee used a list of companies in trouble with the government, pressuring them to contribute under duress or promising favors in return.

Answer   No such list ever existed. The committee never used the circumstances of a corporation's relationship with the government as a basis for soliciting contributions from its officers and employees, and there is no worthy evidence that any corporation or individual having a pending matter with a government agency was ever offered assistance in return for a contribution or was threatened with retaliation if it refused to give.

Charge 2. That the finance committee had an enemy list of persons who refused to contribute.

Answer   The finance committee made no such list of non-contributors and no evidence ever was presented to support this claim.

Charge 3. That I had improperly engaged in fund-raising in 1969, 1970, and 1971.

Answer   Prior to becoming Secretary of Commerce in January 1969, I had addressed a letter to all concerned stating that I would no longer carry on any fund-raising responsibilities, and I adhered to that during the entire period that I was Secretary of Commerce. There is no evidence whatsoever that I solicited any contributions during those three years.

Charge 4. That the finance committee solicited contributions from corporations, knowing they were illegal.

Answer   No contributions were sought from corporations and none was knowingly accepted. All the committee's literature made that clear. Many companies had "good government" funds contributed by their employees, or regularly conducted political fund-raising campaigns among their employees. Both were perfectly proper under the law. The intent and assumption was that the officers we solicited would raise money for our cause either from such collected funds on hand or by passing the hat among their associates. Only a few, and those among the most knowledgeable as to what the law prohibited, gave illegally by using company money; no one connected with the committee solicited such illegal funds or knew they were illegal. When the facts were disclosed, our committee returned the contributions at once; its correspondence files accumulated a record of a hundred or more donations that were sent back. All the major companies that made illegal contributions acknowledged in testimony and letters that no one in our finance committee had any way of knowing the improper source of the funds. A staff report of the Senate Watergate Committee in June 1974 reported that there was "no evidence that any Nixon fund-raiser had directly solicited an illegal corporate contribution."

Before the Senate Watergate hearings began, our committee, on its own initiative, asked the persons who had transmitted cash contributions to us to provide the precise names and addresses of the individual contributors so the records would be complete, even though we and they knew it was not required by law. Some of the companies, unfortunately, sent lists of names that turned out to be false. Finally, a *New York Times* survey of about 100 corporations, which it reported on July 15, 1973, confirmed that our standard request to business leaders was for "individual executive contributions . . . contributions that would be legal."

**Charge 5**. That the finance committee and I made commitments to give government positions to contributors.

**Answer**   No one was "sold" an ambassadorship or any position in the government.[3] I instructed the finance organization a number of times on the record that such deals could not be made. The general policy, specifically worked out in an early meeting with Haldeman, was that if a prospect indicated an interest in serving the government, he was to be told that his desires would be conveyed to the White House after the election, regardless of the amount he contributed and regardless of whether he made a

---

3. Herbert Kalmbach pleaded guilty in 1974 to having promised a post to Fife Symington of Maryland for $100,000, with White House approval, but that happened in 1970, long before our committee came into being.

contribution at all. He was also to be informed that such appointments would be made only by the President, on basis of qualifications, with the concurrence of the State Department, and after full investigation by the FBI. A record was kept by me of all such persons, and the White House was given a list of them in December 1972. It contained the names of fifty-six individuals interested in foreign service posts and seven offering to serve in Washington; more than a third of them had made no contributions or had given minor amounts. There were no commitments to any of them.

**Charge 6.** That the committee employed coercion and extortion in its fund-raising, or made assessments against companies and individuals.

**Answer**    There is no evidence of any kind to justify such a charge. Nothing was done to fix quotas for contributors, or to make assessments or to insist on the size of contributions. It is normal and proper fund-raising to suggest a hoped-for target for a prospective contributor, or to propose a goal for a solicitor to try to reach, and these things we did. Some contributors asked for guidance as to "fair share" amounts. But we applied no pressure of any kind to anyone and amounts of any size were gratefully received. No threats or arm-twisting were ever applied. No prospect or contributor who was approached by anyone from the committee ever objected or complained to me, at the time of solicitation or later, about being pressured, or said he felt compelled to give, or expressed regrets later at having given. Even after all the Watergate disclosures I found no ill will among contributors toward the finance committee or toward me.

The three or four statements implying coercion or extortion that were dragged out of intimidated witnesses by Senator Ervin at the Senate Watergate Committee hearings have been fully discredited by the disclosures that their companies had large political funds over a period of years, and had made sizable contributions to many candidates for Presidential, Congressional, and Senatorial seats, some Democrats as well as Republicans. A *Wall Street Journal* poll of corporate officers in December 1973 found that officers of companies had not been intimidated, but had been willing to give. One said that our pitch was merely that "Nixon deserves another four years"; others said there had been "no hard-sell pressure from Stans or anyone." More positively, the Watergate Special Prosecutor, after intensive investigations of all alleged instances, found no evidence to support charges of coercion or extortion, and said so.

**Charge 7.** That the committee received contributions in return for promises of government assistance or favors.

**Answer**   There is no truth to such a charge. The committee did not promise anyone assistance with the government or favors of any kind. The Watergate Special Prosecutor in his final report said he investigated thirty of such alleged instances and found nothing on which to make a case. Individuals who stated or implied a desire for help were rebuffed and their contributions were rejected. Proffered contributions which were based on conditions were refused, and some contributions which had been received were returned when later information showed that the donors were in trouble. In all, more than $4 million was rejected from or returned to contributors.

**Charge 8.** That the finance committee operated a "laundry" in one or more foreign countries to conceal the sources of contributions; among others, it funneled $750,000 through Mexican banks and $2,000,000 through Bahamanian banks.

**Answer**   All of this is wholly untrue. The committee did not funnel a cent of money through banks in Mexico or any other country. The handful of contributions that came through foreign sources were so routed by the contributors, not the committee, and without the committee's participation. No investigating body found any evidence that the committee had laundered money in other countries.

**Charge 9.** That the committee received illegal contributions from foreigners.

**Answer**   A contribution from a foreign national was not illegal unless it came from an agent of an undisclosed foreign principal. On that assumption, we accepted some foreign contributions until we were told by counsel that there was still a question whether they were legal. We thereafter refused or returned about $50,000 of such gifts, only to learn later from the Department of Justice that it would have been perfectly proper to accept them. The Democratic candidates accepted contributions from foreign nationals.

**Charge 10.** That the finance committee, and particularly I, solicited contributions in cash.

**Answer** No one, to the best of my knowledge, ever solicited a contribution in cash. Our alleged solicitation of cash was one of the issues in the Vesco case and, in trying to prove a pattern of such solicitations, the prosecutors wrote or interviewed about thirty of the cash contributors in 1972 to establish whether they had been asked to give in that form. Not only were they not successful in finding a single instance, but the testimony and the favorable verdict of the jury upheld my denial of having asked Vesco for cash.

**Charge 11.** That the finance committee, at my direction, illegally or improperly destroyed its records of contributions and expenditures.

**Answer** This is a false allegation. We did not destroy any records except some which we were not required to keep in the first place, and finance chairmen for other candidates, notably Humphrey and Mills, did the same thing. Later, when public interest in the campaign led us to conclude that we would nevertheless make a voluntary disclosure of all of our finances, we were able to reconstruct our transactions completely from the data we had retained, whereas some of the other candidates were not able to do so. We made full disclosures to investigating authorities, while the finance chairmen for Humphrey and Mills took the Fifth Amendment to avoid answering questions or producing records.

There were other wild swings that were reported: that the General Accounting Office had found $500,000 in campaign violations; that large campaign contributions were picked up in South America and not reported; that committee funds were stashed away in Swiss banks; that the Shah of Iran contributed $1.5 million in cash; that $2 million in cash was secretly given by a French millionaire named Paul Louis Weiller; that Arab interests covertly contributed large sums, one account of which, published in the Egyptian newspaper *El Ahram*, said that $10 to $12 million had been given; that we had laundered contributions through gambling casinos in the Bahamas; and so on.[4] All of these accounts were said to be from reliable sources, and all were one hundred percent false.[5] Each one required consideration of whether and how to reply, and each left its unfair addition to the aura of suspicion and distrust of our activities. All of these stories about our fund-raising were carefully checked out by the various investigatory bodies. We cooperated to the extent of providing any information we had.

One of the major criticisms of our campaign activities was that we had received a considerable sum of money in currency contributions. While we had never solicited cash as such, we willingly accepted it, as well as stocks or bonds or even wheat or cattle, since the law specifically allowed us to accept "anything of value." So much has been made of these cash transactions as evil and illegal that it is important that they be seen in proper perspective.

---

4. An example of how false charges persisted, to the detriment of innocent persons, appeared in statements by Senator Thomas F. Eagleton on October 2, 1974, in his opposition to the nomination of Peter Flanigan to be Ambassador to Spain, in which he twice used these exact words: "We do know a great deal about the exploits of the Committee to Re-Elect the President and the campaign of 1972. We know that individuals and corporations were asked to pay 'protection' money in return for governmental favors and high-level positions. Nixon fund-raisers, led by Maurice Stans, barnstormed the country in 1971 and 1972, looking for contributions and promising that the red tape in Washington would be cut. The evidence is strong that Peter Flanigan was the key man in Washington. He was the man who, in several known cases, paved the way with the agencies in government.... thus the linkage between money and Flanigan; he was to do the bidding of Maurice Stans, the money hustler. He was to make sure they delivered on the promises that Stans made going around in '71 and '72." Eagleton's coordinated attack, however incorrect and unfair, succeeded in its political assassination of a wholly innocent and able person because such generalizations are impossible to answer except by denial.

5. News stories continued to surface years after the election. As late as September 1976, public assertions appeared that Richard Allen, a deputy assistant to the President for international economic affairs, had asked Grumman Corporation for an illegal contribution of $1 million. Grumman made no contribution and I never heard anything that gave substance to the allegation.
In December 1976 the *Washington Star* carried a story about "unverified reports that South Vietnamese President Thieu and Air Marshall Cao Ky had sent several millions of dollars to the United States for Nixon's political campaign activities." It even said that contributions "may have been received" from organized criminals in the opium trade in Southeast Asia. This too was nonsense.

Not until 1974 was there any law that said that contributions could not be made or received in cash. It was not common for either party or their candidates to receive contributions in that form, and most of the candidates for the Presidency in 1972 did receive and accept amounts in cash; many members of Congress also did so. Humphrey, Mills, Lindsay, Muskie, and Jackson received contributions in currency, some from the same givers as we did. Muskie's finance chairman, Berl Bernhart, acknowledged to the Senate Watergate Committee that he had devised a sealed-envelope procedure to handle such donations, so persons on his staff would not even know the sources, and several hundred thousand dollars had been handled in that manner. He enumerated many bona fide reasons why honest people use cash, including preserving anonymity for protection of family members from blackmail or kidnap threats.

The contributor of cash may have had valid reasons for not wanting his generosity known. He got an added measure of privacy as against issuing checks, in that his banker, his accountant, his secretary, and perhaps even his wife need not know what he had given. This was proper under the old law. There were many cash contributions that we received in 1972 that withstood all investigative scanning. Max Fisher of Detroit, a business executive and member of our finance committee, gave $125,000 in cash; the wealthy Murchison brothers of Texas gave $50,000 in the same way; employees of Standard Oil Company of California combined to give $50,000 in bank cashier's checks; officials of Texas Eastern Transmission Co. pooled $30,000 in cash; James E. Stewart, a Minneapolis executive, gave $50,000; and there were others in the range of $25,000 to $50,000. These contributions in cash were all found to be proper and from legal sources.

Members of the committee who received contributions in cash from wealthy persons had every reason to believe that it was legally acquired, and no reason to suspect that it was not. In the case of contributions in cash from an officer of a company, they could and did understand that it was collected by passing the hat among employees; unfortunately, when investigators pursued these contributions to their sources they found that in most of the nineteen instances the money had come from the corporate till, disguised as to origin. In no such case was the finance committee or any of its people aware of the improper sources of funds, and the companies so stated publicly. There was no way we could distinguish a proper contribution from an improper one, and it is regrettable that a handful of officials of companies were able to cast such a large shadow over an otherwise proper practice.

It is one thing to judge the integrity and legality of the finance committee's actions by considering the evidence and argument in answer to charges of wrongdoing such as these. The replies given should satisfy anyone. There is another way to demonstrate the overall integrity of the finance operation and that is to produce proof of refusals by the money-raisers to be seduced into illegality or impropriety, and there is remarkable evidence on that side of the ledger. Our committee refused many proffered contributions, some in cash and some by check, and returned others, when it felt that either the contributor's circumstances or his motives were in question.

Outstanding among these was a meeting I had in a New York hotel in the last week before election with Michele Sindona, then a wealthy Italian investor with interests in the United States. Among his holdings was a controlling interest in Franklin National Bank of New York, and he was accompanied by the president of the bank. I had been informed in advance that Sindona was willing to support Nixon in a large way so, after an exchange of pleasantries, I came right to the point.

"I understand you are convinced that Nixon's re-election is important and are willing to help us out financially in the campaign."

He was equally direct. "I believe it is important to the United States and the world and for all of us that he continue in office, and I am ready to give a million dollars."

I was no longer abashed by large sums of money, so I was delighted and said so.

"There is only one condition," he went on. "Because I am well known, I do not want any publicity or public recognition. And I am not asking any favors."

With the law then requiring full disclosure of amounts received, there was no way I could comply and I explained the circumstances to him. He expressed regret and the meeting concluded upon his remark that if I found a way to proceed his offer would still be good. I joined one of my associates in the next room with this boast: "I just turned down a million dollars."

Several days later, I wrote Sindona confirming that there was no way in which I could accept his contribution and maintain secrecy. At that date, we still had no assurance that we were going to be able to balance our budget and we certainly would have been more comfortable with his money had we been able to accept it.

There were many similar occasions involving smaller amounts, some of which can be condensed into this recital of amounts rejected or returned:

—$200,000 contributed by C. Arnholt Smith, a San Diego banker, returned in the same month as received, upon reading in the press about possible criminal acts by him in connection with income taxes.

—$100,000 from Robert Allen of Texas, returned because of expenses and embarrassment he suffered on account of his manner of making the contribution through Mexico and because of uncertainty at the time as to the circumstances involved.

—$250,000 contributed by Robert Vesco, returned after disclosure of pending criminal charges against him.

—$150,000 offered on April 4, 1972, by Associated Milk Producers, Inc., refused because it appeared to have strings attached. AMPI was hoping to diffuse an antitrust investigation that was pending. It had actually drawn and signed the checks, and had to cancel them when we turned them down.

—$45,000 rejected from or returned to several foreign nationals because of conflicting legal opinions as to whether it could properly be accepted.

—$25,000 or more rejected from John Priestes, a Florida builder, upon learning that he was in trouble with the Federal Housing Administration.

—$50,000 offered on behalf of A. D. Davis, a Florida merchant, and his brother, rejected because it was not to be reported and was not tendered to the committee within the non-reporting period.

—$100,000 offered by an individual in Nevada, rejected because he was known to be in trouble with the Justice Department.

—$100,000 offered by a woman, now deceased, in return for assurances that she would be named Ambassador to Haiti.

—$305,000 contributed in a promissory note by Walter T. Duncan of Texas, returned to him when it was learned that he did not have the personal wealth to justify his taking on such an obligation.

—$200,000 to $300,000 offered by a businessman if a friend of his were to be named to the President's Cabinet.

—$470,000 returned to eight corporations, immediately upon our discovery in 1973 that the money came from illegal sources.

Our entire organization was geared to recognize and return illegal or unethical money. The offers from C. Arnholt Smith and Associated Milk Producers, Inc., were turned down on his own initiative by Kalmbach. The Nevada proposition was rejected on the spot by our state chairman there.

There were still more tendered contributions of various amounts, and some indefinite in size that were rejected because they were to be contingent upon certain return favors by the government. Included in these were several offered for help on government contracts or negotiations, and others for assistance on resolution of legal or tax problems with government agencies. One contribution was tendered contingent upon government influence in getting the donor a General Motors dealership. Several were dangled in consideration of appointment to a government position.

Early in the fall one of our solicitors brought into my office a Philadelphia businessman who reportedly was prepared to make a major contribution. His approach was as delicate as a Richter-7 earthquake:

"I know you're a busy man, Mr. Stans," he said, "so I'll get right to the point. How much for Luxembourg?"

I was so startled that all I could say was "Could I have that again?"

He came right back with the same bluntness. "I know how these things are done, and I want to be ambassador to Luxembourg. How much do I have to give for it?"

By this time I was ready. "I can't commit an ambassadorship to anyone and I have no way to deal in government jobs. The President makes those appointments, after clearance with the State Department and after an FBI field investigation," I explained patiently. "All I can do is report your interest in a foreign post, and I will do that whether you contribute or not."

Shaking his head in disbelief, the man left my office and I did not hear from him again, but his name appeared on the list I sent to the White House in December of persons who had expressed an interest in an ambassadorial job. The solicitor who brought him in had no advance inkling of what would transpire, and apologized to me a half dozen times afterward.

Not one contingent contribution was accepted by the committee. The fact that more than $4 million was turned down or returned argues well that we were not money-hungry and that we were extremely careful to stay within the spirit of the law. All of our information on these items was given at the appropriate time to the Special Prosecutor.

Without intending to sanction the few technical errors or oversights committed by our committee, I took comfort from the facts that the unusual circumstances of a change in law, the interim period allowed between its enactment date and its effective date, following on a half century of casual neglect and minimal enforcement of the preceding law by the responsible authorities, led other candidates into lapses at least as serious as ours.

The complexity of the law was confirmed in the record of Senate consideration of amendments in 1974. The Senate sponsor of the amendments, Senator Bartlett, remarked in floor debate that . . .

> "because the 1971 . . . Act and the bill now under consideration make so many changes from previous law, and because there has been so little experience in actually operating a campaign under the new provisions, there was considerable confusion about what could or could not be done under different sections of the 1971 Act."[6]

His remarks are echoed in the House report, which points out that "the necessarily complex nature of the legislation may make compliance most difficult even with the most conscientious effort in this regard."[7]

One of the events most distressing to me personally was the fate of Herbert Kalmbach, who pleaded guilty in 1973 to some

---

6. 119 Cong. Rec. S14852, July 27, 1973
7. H. Rep. 1239, 93rd Cong. 2nd Sess. at 9

irregular fund-raising practices in 1970, and served more than six months in Federal prisons. These actions were unknown to me at the time and occurred almost two years before I became active in 1972. He had been my principal assistant in the 1968 campaign and, in all, had worked more than forty-five months as an unpaid volunteer for the Nixon cause in the elections of 1968, 1970, and 1972.

Kalmbach is a tall, dark-haired man, then in his early fifties, always well dressed and always pleasant and outgoing in mien. He is careful and meticulous, sometimes weighing a problem repetitiously, slow in decision and careful to get advice. It was his custom when he met with anyone to prepare in advance a list of topics, on a ruled card, which he checked off as the discussion proceeded. Soft-spoken, he is never forceful or aggressive and his personality belied the characterization of those who claimed he had twisted their arms or used improper approaches for contributions. No matter what his concerns, he was always Pollyanna-ish, always optimistic and confident. A model of integrity, his word was good, and he conducted himself with careful probity at all times. His solicitations for campaign money were in low key, deliberate and slow, without the faintest pressure or threat or promise.

Because he was known to be personal counsel to the President beginning early in 1969, he would not allow his firm to open an office in Washington or handle government relations work. He mentioned this policy to me several times while I was Secretary of Commerce and told me of lucrative clients that he rejected because his ethical sense would not allow him to trade on his relationship with the President in representing them. In the fifteen years that I had known and worked with Kalmbach on a variety of matters, political and otherwise, I had not known him to express an improper, unethical, or dishonest thought. He is a totally moral person. In the Watergate investigations, he never asked for immunity or pleaded his constitutional rights, but told his story carefully as he remembered the facts. While it was disconcerting that on one occasion he testified incorrectly in open court as to two matters relating to me, I attributed it to a normal aberration of offhand memory under the pressures to which he was subject, and was able to set the record straight by documentary proof.

He accepted a felony charge for raising money in 1970 for

Senate and House candidates through a committee set up by the White House, on the technical ground that the committee had not appointed a chairman and a treasurer, as required by law. It was a lapse that could have easily been avoided and can be attributed only to lack of care by someone, since the results would not have differed in the least under a more formal arrangement. He also pleaded guilty to participating in the 1970 promise of an ambassadorship to a contributor, a charge which was valid only, since he had no authority to make such a commitment, because he carried a message of offer and acceptance between the insistent donor and the White House. In his handling of money for the Watergate coverup, for which he was not charged but which entered into the negotiation of his other pleas of guilty, the record shows that he apparently was misled to think that what he was doing was proper by John Dean and John Ehrlichman, two White House lawyers whom he had every reason to trust.

The two successive treasurers of our finance committee, Hugh Sloan, Jr., and Paul Barrick, were not charged with any wrongdoing. Barrick, a very qualified certified public accountant, served as controller for several months before taking over as treasurer when Sloan resigned on July 15, 1972. He acquitted himself with skill and care, his only lapse being an unintentional failure to locate and deliver all pertinent records to the court in the Common Cause case, a lapse easily accounted for by the turmoil and volume of work of the week before election. It was that lapse which had caused Common Cause to charge me and the committee lawyers with contempt of court, a charge that was held open for more than a year before it was finally dismissed.

Sloan's position was more difficult. He held the post from the beginning in March 1971 until he resigned in July 1972. This included the period when no reporting was required, as well as the time of transition from one law to another, a circumstance which caused some confusion because of ambiguities in the new law. Although he handled the actual payments of money to Liddy that financed the break-in, Sloan was without knowledge of their purpose and merely followed directions according to the lines of authority, which he took the pains to verify at the time. Although the General Accounting Office later held him responsible for some reporting lapses, he was given immunity by the Special

Prosecutor because of his valuable testimony against others in the two Watergate trials.

In the ordinary course the 1972 campaign's financial affairs would have been wound up early in 1973, when the last straggling pledges of contributors had been made good and the last campaign bills had been paid. Believing the hangovers of claims and lawsuits were without merit and would soon die an anemic death, I counted on wrapping everything up by that time. But it was not to be. I still had to face other hurdles which would never have arisen except for the Watergate syndrome in Washington.

# 8

## CAME THE DELUGE

The Watergate arrests on June 17 had no impact until a week or so later when I was told that FBI investigators had run into a snag with Gordon Liddy, who had refused to answer their questions. Liddy, a lawyer, had for a while served on the campaign staff and then was farmed out to our finance committee and had been with us for about three months as general counsel.

I did not learn until more than a year later, from public testimony, that his transfer from the campaign organization had not been an act of generosity to fill a vacancy but had been instigated by Jeb Magruder, the number two man there, because of unreconcilable personal differences between them, so bitter that at one time Liddy allegedly had threatened to kill Magruder. On our staff, Liddy was competent as a lawyer and carried a good workload. He gave no inkling that he had been engaging in political espionage before he came with us and was continuing it on a small-time basis under Magruder's secret direction while in our employ. Given my total state of ignorance of these things, he certainly had no such authorization from me.

When Liddy refused to answer the FBI inquiries, I had to discharge him immediately, assuming that his refusal supported the conclusion that he must have had something to do with the Watergate affair. I did not know what the questions were that he did not answer, or what his complicity was, but clearly I could not support his failure to cooperate with the investigative agency.

As the Watergate story developed day by day, and as it became known that a quantity of $100 bills had been found on the arrested culprits, inquiries began to zero in on the sources of these funds. Having no knowledge as to how Watergate had been financed, my suspicions began to enlarge as one revelation after another unfolded. Not for a long time, however, did a clear picture emerge as to who was guilty, and how their actions had victimized innocent persons, including some of our finance committee staff and contributors.

Subsequent events, some several years later, have disclosed how and why I was deceived by the conspiracy and deception that went on around me after June 17. Why was I, so close to the campaign and an associate of all those who were involved, kept in the dark? It could have been that the separation of finance activities from the business of enticing the voters made it inconvenient for the plotters to keep me informed. It could have been that some illegal events that preceded Watergate happened before I took on the finance job and the plotting had a momentum that passed me by. I prefer to think, however, that those who were guiltily involved deliberately kept me uninformed because they feared that I would blow the lid the minute I learned what was going on.[1] Certainly I am grateful to them for never facing me with the dilemma of doing that or going along with them, since my loyalties to the President were so strong that it would have strained me to abandon his cause, even in the face of the misdeeds by others similarly dedicated.

In any event, I did not have to suffer a test of loyalties, because I didn't know about Watergate until it unfolded publicly, and even then I never was told anything ahead of the news stories by those who knew. So I continued to devote my fullest possible efforts in fund-raising all during 1972, although I found them heavily diluted by the demands on my time for investigations, hearings, depositions, and meetings with lawyers as the Watergate criminal and civil cases proliferated. Not until James

---

1. There is testimony by Herbert Kalmbach that "Bebe" Rebozo came to him in the spring of 1973 for legal advice on a problem of what to do about some secret contributed funds from Howard Hughes, with the caution from the President that he should "take it up with Kalmbach but be sure not to discuss it with Stans."

McCord, one of the burglars, sent his famous letter to Judge Sirica on March 23, 1973, revealing the payoff that had been made for their silence and accusing higher-ups in the administration, did the force of the entire drama hit me, as it did millions of Americans, as an incredible action of arrogance, incompetence, and illegality.

Earlier, as Secretary of Commerce, I of course had no occasion to know that there had been a "plumbers" group in the White House charged with seeking out and eliminating leaks of secret government information. I don't believe any Cabinet member was told about them. In time, the plumbers became the source of the personal aggregation that later moved into Watergate, and the fountain of the illegal ideas that led to the downfall of so many.

Even in the fund-raising field, I was not informed of many events that had occurred before I became finance chairman. When White House discussions with representatives of the country's milk producers in 1971 allegedly led to a promise of contributions as large as $2 million to the 1972 race, I was not aware of them. I was not in on the selection of San Diego as the Republican convention site or the alleged negotiations with ITT for a contribution to the convention costs. I was not among those consulted about the subsequent move of the convention from San Diego to Miami Beach, although by that time I had seen a preview of the convention budget and had squawked mightily to the Arrangements Committee about the extraordinary capital costs that were projected for getting the San Diego hall in shape for the ceremonies. I knew very well that if they failed to get enough money through selling ads in the convention program (a matter not under my jurisdiction), they would surely come to my committee to make up their deficit. The convention was going to cost about $3 million in San Diego; this was later cut by more than $1 million when the shift to Miami Beach was made, and it was then safely self-supporting.

My distance from the Watergate action has long since been fully established. The repeated testimony of the principals shows that I was not on hand in January, February, or March for any of the presentations of Liddy's proposals that ultimately led to the break-in. Nor was I ever invited to the daily White House meetings on campaign strategy that were attended by White House and CRP people. I did not receive the secret "Gemstone" reports prepared by Liddy on his espionage or know that they were being prepared. When the Watergate burglary was traced to a CRP connection, I was as surprised as anyone.

After the disclosures of June 17, I was again outside the inner orbit and had no knowledge of the frantic meetings that were taking place. I was not in the group that met to deal with the coverup. I was not consulted about payments to the defendants, was not asked to raise money for them, and did not do so. My views were not solicited as to the testimony to be given at the burglars' trial in January 1973, and I was not called to be a witness. I was not among those who planned the White House defense strategy to cope with the Senate hearings later showboated by Senator Sam Ervin.

The truth is that, once I undertook the money-raising task, I had practically no contact in 1972 with John Ehrlichman and Bob Haldeman, the President's principal aides in the White House, or even with the President. My records show that I had no meetings or phone calls with Ehrlichman, only four short meetings and four phone calls with Haldeman on minor subjects, and one short encounter and one phone conversation with the President up to election day. That was the way I wanted it from the beginning, because I did not want my time divided away from the very demanding finance committee chores, and I did not think the President and his close associates should have their time diverted to money matters. He felt the same way. None of them ever talked to me about the details of Watergate, before or after. In the one brief meeting I had with the President, which was in September, he merely expressed the hope that the adverse publicity that was going on wouldn't weaken my morale or hinder my efforts too much.

In his book *The Making of the President—1972*, Theodore White, after acknowledging that there is no evidence of my playing a part in Watergate, said, "Stans was naive." In retrospect, I should perhaps admit to that, as a natural result of knowing and trusting the people around the President. Some of them, like Kalmbach and Haldeman, I had known for ten years or more. Others such as Ehrlichman and Mitchell, I had first met in 1968 and had dealt with fairly frequently after that. I had implicit faith in them all, and it was almost impossible to conceive that any of them could have deliberately participated in illegal acts. Of these,

Kalmbach was the only one with whom Kathleen and I had close social contacts.

John Dean, the counsel for the President, was the one White House person I saw frequently in 1972. He had consulted me from time to time late in 1971 about the provisions of the legislation pending in the Congress on campaign financing, and, after I agreed to become finance chairman, I in turn began to take counsel from him on legal matters covering the whole range of fund-raising topics. This was not only a natural consequence of the earlier exchanges, but I was encouraged by Kalmbach, Mitchell, and Dean himself to do so. In that relationship I understood Dean to be serving in a dual capacity, as legal adviser to me and the finance committee, and as a watchdog for the President to be sure we conducted our work correctly. This closeness continued until the end of May and then diminished as my staff and I became accustomed to the legal requirements and gained momentum. There followed a period of about sixty days beginning in mid-June in which I had no contact with Dean, and then, as lawsuits and investigations multiplied, I again received frequent counsel from him. Not once did he even intimate that anything was rotten in Watergate.

John Dean was young, in his thirties, his studious, intense nature emphasized by his horn-rimmed glasses. Clearly capable and cool-headed, he had an alert mind, and was quick to understand and quick to reply, the type of person one would expect to see as counsel to the President. He was helpful to me and my committee in interpreting legal matters dealing with the new election law. I trusted him implicitly, and he gave me no reason to doubt him until I learned about some of his deceptions, including one instance, described later, in which he tried to set me up in a Senate confrontation to relieve the Watergate pressures in the White House. There was another incident later on that was potentially more harmful to me. When he was called on in the Vesco trial to corroborate a statement by me regarding a telephone call, he professed not to remember it at all. Considering his prodigious memory on other matters, I could not get over the feeling that he had conveniently forgotten this one so that he could protect his assurances of leniency from the prosecution for testifying as they wanted.

At all times, I was frantically busy. After it was all over, my staff collected some statistics as to how I had applied myself. In the nine months between February 15 and November 15 I had completed 1,850 phone calls; held 500 meetings with members of my staff and 100 more with members of the campaign committee; made 100 speeches to large groups of fund-raisers or prospects; met with 600 individual large prospects or their representatives; dictated and signed thousands of letters; and visited 45 cities in 29 states in travels of 40,000 miles. The staff performed magnificently on the tasks that I assigned to them or I couldn't possibly have carried out such an active program.

Even so, the finance committee was short-handed, especially in personnel able to meet the wealthy prospects, and we never did reach many potential contributors. Kalmbach, who had been invaluable in 1968, was active in getting early pledges in 1971 but withdrew after three months in 1972, and did little thereafter except some follow-up of those commitments. I had counted heavily on his being my deputy all through 1972 and did not understand his unwillingness to spend time in Washington or take on more work in the field, until it came out at the Senate hearings a year later that he had a compact with Haldeman and Ehrlichman all along that they would relieve him of working on the finance chores as soon as I was on board. Ehrlichman told the Senate Watergate hearings that he and Haldeman had "hatched a very elaborate plot to get Kalmbach out of the money-raising business," and "would be his defense when Stans asked him to get back in again." In retrospect, I don't know why this subterfuge was considered necessary when a direct statement could have cleared things up.

The immensity of the workload and the pressures it engendered were multiplied by two factors after the Watergate incident. One was the enormous amount of time I had to spend with investigators on Watergate and with lawyers on various civil suits against the finance committee and its officers, and the other was the serious illness of Kathleen, beginning in August and continuing well into the next three years.

Even before the election, my time was heavily diverted to the Watergate aftermath, by the necessity of answering questions in twenty-four different sessions of investigations, depositions, and hearings. Almost every one of these occasions required advanced preparation and hours of meetings with attorneys. The searching for and producing of documents from committee files was very time-consuming during the months of September and October, when the fund-raising was at its height. Some of the suits were of course calculated to have that effect, in order to divert us from the work at hand. The Democrats were suing us for damages in the Watergate burglary, and Common Cause was suing us to force disclosure of names of contributors that our lawyers told us we weren't required to disclose (those who gave before April 7).

On August 9, which happened to be her sixty-second birthday, Kathleen collapsed at home early in the morning and I took her to Walter Reed Hospital in a very distressed condition. It took several days for the doctors to discover that she had contracted a rare blood disease known as idiopathic thrombocytosis, a condition in which there is an overproduction of platelets, the tiny organisms in the blood which cause clotting. In her case the platelet count was ten times normal, which put her in danger of a serious blood clot anywhere in her body. In fact, shortly after being hospitalized she did have one in her right thigh and it took several days of intense treatment to dislodge it. I sought advice from Dr. Walter Tkach, the President's personal physician, and he confirmed that her condition was one in which the outcome was doubtful. It continued uncertain through a series of ups and downs until well into 1975.

I learned later that this disease had only been identified for about ten years, was better known in England, and that there had been only 100 recognized cases in the United States, of which 35 had been treated in the Mayo Clinic in Minnesota. The doctors at Walter Reed had seen only one previous case, so I urged them to consult with hematologists elsewhere and they did so.

The medications were difficult for her and induced frequent nausea, some vomiting, and an overall inertia. Because the platelets are manufactured in the bone marrow, the treatments repressing that function resulted also in a reduction in the red cell and white cell counts. When the first run of treatments had enough effect on the platelets to bring them down to where they should be, her red cell count was only 40 percent of normal and she was then anemic and very weak. When the treatment was eased up to allow the red cell production to increase, the platelet count went back up. She suffered through four or five cycles of this frustrating up-and-down process without much headway, with the result that she acquired by October what the doctors called a "situational depression," in which she lost much of the will to live.

During August, September, October, and November I spent every evening with her when I was in Washington, and much of Saturdays and Sundays. I recast my travel schedules so that when I felt I had to leave Washington it would be for only two days on a trip, and I would thus miss seeing her for only one night, being back on the next.

Her condition came to a crisis in Thanksgiving week, when the situation suddenly reversed in response to the long continuing treatments, and the excessive platelet count dropped down to a mere 1 percent of normal. It meant that she was now in imminent danger of bleeding to death. She was in fact bleeding internally at a heavy rate and blood was flowing intermittently from her nose and mouth. It was frightening to see her poor emaciated body barely staying alive under this handicap, and gradually I lost all hope. The concern of the doctors was easily visible, and within a period of the four days preceding Thanksgiving she received thirteen transfusions, some of whole blood and some of platelets. No improvement showed in the blood counts during all that and the doctors were mystified.

On Wednesday of Thanksgiving week, I left her bedside convinced that the end was only a few days off. I phoned the children and told them to expect the worst by the weekend. At the suggestion of the doctors, I called two of Kathleen's brothers and asked them to come to Washington at once in the remote hope that the platelets in their blood might be more compatible than those available. They arrived the next morning but were not used.

Prayer was the only recourse remaining, and I gave it my all. With trouble besetting me on so many sides, I needed her more than I ever had in our thirty-nine years of life together, and I pleaded with God to save her. I told the children to pray for a miracle, that without it she wouldn't live, and somehow a miracle did happen. On Thanksgiving Day she was slightly more alive, and on the next morning her blood count showed a tiny improvement. Two days later, at my urging, Dr. Murray Silverstein, the top hematologist from the Mayo Clinic, flew to Washington. He was more familiar with the disease than anyone in the country, and his conclusion was that she had passed the immediate crisis and had a chance to recover. With his counsel added, she did. Within a mere three weeks, her blood elements had all returned to regularity, and though still frail she was able to leave the hospital. This was not a permanent cure because, although the problem had gone into remission, it could recur at any time. And this was not the end of her troubles; three weeks later she was back in the hospital seriously ill with hepatitis, an aftermath of the multiple transfusions.

Through much of this period, my deep concern affected my work. As time went by I was often depressed and without inspiration. While I labored hard, I must have been in a mental fog at times because later I could recall little or nothing of some meetings or conversations. My concentration was elsewhere and I did not retain a clear recollection of events or people or dates, a situation which later gave me unexpected difficulty when I was accused in the Vesco case in 1973 and could not recall accurately the discussions at some meetings in that 1972 time frame.

Without having played any part in Watergate or its coverup, why in the world was I so drawn in and victimized by it? What was the circumstance that caused me to be so vilified by the media and so pursued by investigations, lawsuits, and prosecutions?

There turned out to be several answers to those questions. One was the ready assumption that, as the person in charge of a major task of the re-election effort, I must have known what had occurred; it was a clear-cut case of presumed guilt by association. Another was that in the mystery surrounding the question of how Watergate was financed, a few remarkable coincidences drew some contributors into the scene like red herrings across a trail, under circumstances that seemed to confirm all the suspicions of guilt. A very important factor was that I was regularly advised by counsel for the committee not to talk publicly on the ground that it would prejudice the rights of those accused or interfere with the investigations. On several occasions I drafted press statements to clear the air as far as my finance committee associates and I were concerned, but was advised not to release them. I did not learn until much later that Dean, while acting as one of the lawyers counseling me, was himself the master of the coverup plot; obviously anything done or said to clear myself or my committee would merely have caused the focus of attention to shift to where the guilt really was, and that was inconsistent with his coverup strategy.

So much for the generalities of the situation. When it comes to details, it is hard to sort them out in an orderly manner from the interwoven web of events. A day to day accounting would merely confuse because often the significance of an encounter on one day did not become evident until much later. But some respect for chronology is desirable and this narrative now moves into that pattern for the years 1972 through 1975, but with the principal events recounted in the time frame of their major impact, rather than as they unfolded, in order to make the story as clear as possible.

Almost immediately after I took over, there began a political harangue that gave me a foretaste of some of the bitter infighting that would come later. It was a demand that we disclose voluntarily all the contributions received before April 7. Initiated by Common Cause, yielded to reluctantly but with breast-beating expressions of virtue by one after another of the Democrats running for the Presidency, it was taken up as a moral issue by the press, whose demands for details of these "secret" contributions raged on until long after the election. It mattered not that for fifty years the law had not required the publishing of contributions that were received before the primary elections and the nominating convention; candidates had to report only the amounts received and spent for the final election. It mattered not either that the Congress, in passing the new election financing law signed by the President on February 7, 1972, specifically and purposely allowed sixty more days for it to become effective, during which time the old law prevailed. The new law insisted that beginning April 7 all contributions (in excess of $100) and all expenditures (in excess of $10) had to be reported in filings with the General Accounting Office, an arm of the Congress to which had been delegated responsibility for policing the Act, for the knowledge of the public.

Members of the Congress knew this cut-off well, and many took full advantage themselves of the sixty-day grace period that

they had created. Washington lobbyists and business representatives were treated to a concentrated round of fund-raising
receptions and cocktail parties in that time, sometimes three or
more a night, that well promoted the fact for a hundred or more
candidates, Democrats and Republicans, that money given before
April 7 would have the right of privacy. The campaign coffers of
may of these candidates were filled in this period, and no one
seemed to raise a question of morality about the process.

It is not at all uncommon for a strict new law to allow a period
of time for transition by those affected. A change in a law that
applies a higher standard of compliance than previously existed
presumably reflects a change in public views on the subject, but it
doesn't necessarily imply that the earlier standard was illegal or
unmoral during its time. Yet that was precisely the phantom
issue that was created by our opposition. It gained impetus when
Democratic candidate George McGovern, in a "one-upmanship"
move against his competitors, announced at the end of February
that he was releasing the names of his contributors and dared the
others to do the same. Hubert Humphrey and John Lindsay did
so promptly, Edmund Muskie then reluctantly gave out some of
his names, but Henry Jackson and Wilbur Mills never revealed any
of theirs. Among the Republican candidates, Paul McCloskey
made a disclosure but John Ashbrook did not. Democratic candidate Eugene McCarthy refused to identify his contributors
because, he said, no other candidate had released an honest list.

The attack concentrated on Nixon. Why would he not give
out the sources of his $10 million on hand on April 7? Was it
because there were large amounts from ITT and Lockheed that
had to be kept secret? Was it because more "milk money" had
been received in the face of Ralph Nader's suit charging that
certain amounts known to have been accepted early in 1971 had
illegally influenced a change in milk price supports? Had the
committee solicited illegal money from corporations in return for
favors? Imaginations ran wild.

None of these insinuations was true and there was no evidence to believe they were true. But they made good political
copy and they were regularly repeated by McGovern and by the
press in stories and editorials until they somehow attained a
pseudo-credibility

Those who mouthed these allegations as support for the

alleged "moral" responsibility to disclose contributions completely ignored the moral obligations of candidates *not* to disclose those received before the law required it. As I said publicly at the time: "The contributors have rights which we are not prepared to give away." There were two parties to each contribution, the donor and the recipient. The right of confidentiality before April 7 thus extended to both, and the recipient had no right to violate the donor's intended privacy by publicizing a gift. Many donors wanted that privacy to protect themselves against multitudes of solicitations by other candidates and by "causes" of all kinds, and against the personal risks of robbery or kidnapping, which are often aimed at the obtrusive wealthy.

Despite the barrage of demands, we stood by our guns and protected the anonymity of those who gave under the old law. This was not a one-man decision. I was backed by a meeting on March 14 of representatives of the White House, the campaign committee, and the finance committee, which I called to consider the question. The unanimous conclusion was that the Nixon campaign would continue to take the political heat for non-disclosure, and I accepted that as a mandate to maintain confidentiality despite all criticism. Had the opinion been otherwise, I told the group, I would have felt obligated to offer each past contributor the option of getting his money back, since it had been given in good faith reliance on the right of privacy. The persons present with me at this meeting were Robert Finch, Harry Dent, Gordon Strachan, and Richard Moore of the White House; Jeb Magruder, Fred LaRue, and De Van Shumway of the campaign committee; and Herbert Kalmbach and Hugh Sloan from the finance committee. In a press conference on June 22, the President specifically endorsed this position by saying publicly, "Now, if the Congress wanted this law to apply before the date in April that it said the law should take effect, it could have made it apply. The Congress did not apply it before that date and under the circumstances Mr. Stans has said we will comply with the law as Congress had written it, and I support his decision."

With this policy as a mandate, my committee pursued every possible step to avoid disclosures through leaks or burglary. We stepped up the security of our premises with locked entrance gates, guarded our contributor records in safes overnight, and limited the access to them during the day. As soon as April 7 had come and gone, and a listing of amounts received up to that point had been prepared, I directed Sloan to remove the basic records from the premises and put them in protected storage, and to destroy all nonessential papers and data. He did so. I gave my copy of the contributor list to Rose Mary Woods, the President's secretary in the White House, to use for social invitations. This list attained undeserved notoriety later as "Rosemary's Baby," but it had no special significance as a document because it was hastily prepared and had a number of errors, while the records and data that had been preserved were accurate. Sloan's destruction of the surplus records caused no loss of information needed to provide a full accounting, as we later proved by voluntarily preparing and filing such an accounting.

Common Cause filed suit in the Federal court on September 6 to force disclosure of our pre-April 7 contributions. That began a frustrating and heated battle that convinced us of the anti-Republican bias of Common Cause, since no equivalent efforts were exerted against any of the Democratic candidates on this issue or others at least as valid. After a lot of legal maneuvering, their attorneys managed to get a trial set for the week before the election, presumably in the hope of generating some damaging political smoke out of the moral issue. We concluded that the only hope of avoiding that lay in a compromise with Common Cause and we there upon negotiated one that called for the release of names of those who had contributed before March 9. That took us within one month of the April 7 date, and there were additional and complex legal defenses against going further. Because we had promised privacy to the contributors, and they had that right under the law, I felt that we were obliged to get in touch with as many as possible of the larger ones and get at least their tacit agreement to let us reveal their names. This we did. The lists were filed in the week before the election and had no effect whatever on the outcome. CBS news reporter Daniel Schorr's remark on television that there were "few surprises and no scandals" in the release showed how ridiculous the argument was. Investigative reporter James Polk of the *Washington Star-News*, having in mind early speculation about possible sources of the contributions, conceded that "special-interest money was notably absent." Interestingly enough, the American Civil Liberties Union supported our position that a requirement of disclosure constituted an unreasonable violation of the Fourth Amendment to the Constitution. The continuation and ending of the Common Cause suit, and the tactics of the further pursuit against us, are told later on.

This argument, which was so disruptive and time-consuming during the campaign, had a cynical postlude. We felt all along that it was merely a political ploy to embarrass the President and aid his opponents by creating an issue that should not have existed. While we had our suspicions as to the accuracy and completeness of the disclosures made by other candidates in the spring and summer of 1972, we had no means of disproving them and had to hold our peace. Not until 1973 and 1974 did the truth come out in public hearings and documents. The reports that had been released by the other candidates with announcements of evangelistic fervor, and with breast-beating about their great respect for the public's right to know, turned out to have glaring omissions. McGovern did not report a number of loans ranging from $8,000 to $40,000, although loans are specifically included within the law's definition of a contribution, and also omitted many donations to state and local committees. Muskie's treasurer received $30,000 of "anonymous" contributions before April 7, much of which was in cash; none of this was disclosed. Humphrey's reports, according to Senate Watergate Committee findings, excluded hundreds of thousands of dollars of contributions and loans (one estimate was as high as $700,000), and apparently disclosed less than half of the money raised in this period. Lindsay's committee had at least $10,000 of undisclosed cash receipts. Altogether, there were innumerable errors and exclusions in these virtuous "disclosures" of the opposition. All of them had time gaps except McGovern. It was a bitter surprise to learn the truth eventually, and to find out that Humphrey's finance people had destroyed all his pre-April 7 records in the summer of 1972, at a time when we were being excoriated for failing to make ours public. Of the two who had refused to publish the names of their early contributors, later disclosures showed that Mills got almost half of his money support from the dairy industry, most of it given illegally; and Mills and Jackson both received improper cash contributions from corporations, particularly Gulf Oil Company.

Once the Watergate entry had occurred on June 17 and the culprits had been arrested on the premises with $5,300 in $100 bills, the obvious question was where the money had come from. The attention given to this subject by the investigators and the press was unfortunately diverted to the wrong conclusion because of several remote coincidences. These coincidences centered on two early contributions, one of $25,000 and a second of $100,000 (of which $89,000 was in Mexican bank checks and $11,000 was in cash). All this unfolded in a series of disclosures that came as much of a revelation to me as they did to the public.

Six days after the burglary, the first surprise occurred. Fred LaRue, an assistant to Mitchell on the campaign side, phoned and asked me whether I knew Kenneth Dahlberg. Certainly I knew Ken Dahlberg. He had been Minnesota chairman for our finance committee for a time and now was a regional chairman, responsible for supervising the raising of money in six midwestern states. "Well," LaRue said, "his check for $25,000 has shown up in the bank account of Bernard Barker, one of the fellows arrested in the Watergate." When this news became public a month later it set off some wild conjectures: Dahlberg was the one who had financed the Watergate bugging; Dahlberg represented Cuban interests who wanted the Democratic campaign disrupted; and so on. His explanation that he had purchased the check with a $25,000 campaign contribution in currency from a legitimate but undisclosed giver and then turned the check over to the finance committee wasn't believed; it merely whetted the appetite for speculation. Who was the donor? Why was it secret? Why did it show up in Barker's bank account?

The storm of charge and conjecture ran for weeks until Dahlberg was forced, improperly, by a state's attorney in Florida, Richard Gerstein, who had served a subpoena upon him at the Republican convention, to disclose that the contributor was Dwayne Andreas of Minneapolis. Andreas was a close friend and financial supporter of Hubert Humphrey, and his reason for wanting secrecy was obvious: at the time of his contribution to the President, Humphrey was still a candidate for the Democratic nomination, and Andreas did not want his support of the President to be publicized as a defection from Humphrey, to whom he had earlier given a larger amount. Andreas believed that either man would have made a good President for the country. Later when Humphrey lost out in the Democratic running and Nixon formally received his party's nomination, Andreas increased his contribution to Nixon substantially.

The Dahlberg-Andreas development had a companion that was even more of a surprise. The FBI also had learned and the press next discovered that $89,000 in Mexican bank drafts payable to our committee had similarly been deposited in the Barker bank account. This revelation brought on multiple demands, as in the Dahlberg case, for disclosure of the source, and it increased geometrically the speculations about the financing of the Watergate affair: this was illegal money from a foreign principal; it was illicit corporate money; it was only a small part of a "laundering" operation by which the Nixon committee raised money in the United States, sent it to Mexico to disguise its identity, and then brought it back. The universal assumption then was that these checks, and the one from Dahlberg, had been deliberately given to Barker by my committee to finance the burglary.

The charges were off the mark, but our denials were ignored because we were not allowed at the time to tell publicly the unfolding facts that we were learning as to how the Watergate gang had financed their venture. Counsel for our committee, including John Dean, insisted all along that any premature public disclosures along these lines could prejudice the rights of the Watergate defendants and even result in their acquittal, regardless of the evidence against them. We did, of course, give all the information we had to the FBI.

There were simple and valid explanations for the receipt and handling of the Dahlberg and Mexican checks, but they ran into new coincidences that complicated the stories, and these in turn multiplied the critical publicity. Dahlberg, a wholly innocent conduit for the $25,000 Andreas contribution, was grilled by the FBI, buffeted by reporters, quizzed by the politically ambitious state's attorney in Miami, forced to make a senseless trip down there for several days for a minor trial, and was otherwise embarrassed and annoyed for months. No one could have deserved it less, as the facts plainly showed. But his innocence in the whole matter became obscured by another issue that surfaced—why hadn't the $25,000 been publicly reported by our committee, since Dahlberg's check was dated April 10, three days after the new law went into effect, and had not been delivered by him to the committee until April 11?

The facts given to the General Accounting Office, the official government inquisitor under the new law, by Andreas, Dahlberg, and me and others answered that question, too, and should have cleared all the parties at once. Andreas had promised the contribution to Dahlberg as early as January and had confirmed his commitment in February; he arranged with Dahlberg to give him the money at a meeting of a bank board of directors on March 15; to have it ready, he drew out the funds in cash from a tax-paid account on March 12. When Dahlberg was required at the last minute to miss the March 15 meeting, Andreas placed the money in an envelope in Dahlberg's name and held it for him; on April 5, realizing that the money had still not been delivered, he phoned Dahlberg and asked that it be picked up before the 7th; when Dahlberg said he couldn't get to Florida on time, Andreas took a lock box in his hotel in Dahlberg's name, placed the money in it, and called and told him "the money is the committee's; title has passed"; and when Dahlberg then phoned me and recited the story, I authorized him to accept it over the telephone as of that date, April 5, after checking with our counsel for assurance that this legally completed the transaction.

Dahlberg arrived in Florida on the evening of April 7 and went directly to the hotel to pick up the money, but couldn't do so because the hotel's vault was already closed for the day. The next morning he called Andreas and arranged a golf date with him for the following day at Andreas's country club, at which time, as planned, Andreas handed the money to Dahlberg. Being unwilling to carry that much currency all the way to Washington, Dahlberg purchased a cashier's check the next day, the 10th, payable to himself, and handed it to me at a meeting in Washington on the 11th, endorsed by him. Within a few minutes, I handed it to Sloan, our treasurer, recited the events of April 5, called his attention to the date on the check, and suggested he determine how to handle the contribution in the committee's records.

There was nothing sinister at all to this point. But there were still two persisting questions: why wasn't the contribution reported, and how did the check get into the bank account of Bernard Barker?

Both the election law in effect before April 7 and the law after that date had a similar definition of a political contribution. They said that a "contribution" included not only an outright gift in money or anything of value, but also "a promise, pledge or commitment to make a contribution, whether or not legally enforceable." With the long history of Andreas's commitment, his efforts to make delivery, and the documented evidence of his using the safe deposit box in Dahlberg's name, it was clear to us that his contribution qualified as having legally occurred before April 7, quite apart from the separate point that a constructive delivery had taken place on April 5 when he took several steps to see that "title has passed." Simply, it was his intent to make the gift before April 7, and he had done everything possible to do so, and it was the conclusion of our counsel that in this situation the contribution had occurred before April 7 and was therefore not publicly reportable as a gift after that date. So we did not report it. (Months later, early in 1973, the Department of Justice agreed that our position was valid.)

Because I left Washington on a several-week vacation immediately after April 11, it was not until late in the month that Sloan told me that he had promptly given the Dahlberg check to Liddy, as committee counsel, and asked for his advice as to how to handle it in the committee's accounts. In order that the contribution could be divided into amounts of less than $3,000 each to various committees to avoid causing the contributor to pay a gift tax, Liddy decided to convert the check back to cash, and he thereupon gave Sloan the $25,000 proceeds early in May. Not until after the June 17 episode of the Watergate did anyone learn that Liddy had on his own initiative cashed the check through the bank account of Barker, who apparently was his friend and an earlier associate in FBI activities.

The Mexican checks are a much simpler story. On April 3, I took a phone call from William Liedtke, who was then the Texas chairman for our committee. He said he had a prospective contribution of $100,000 and wanted to know if it was proper to take that amount from an American citizen "who had the money in U.S. funds in Mexico." He did not mention who the individual was. I checked with our counsel and called him back, saying that this was perfectly legal.

The next I heard about this was in the latter part of April, when Sloan told me that he had received the money on April 5 from Liedtke's associate, Roy Winchester, who had delivered it as part of about $700,000 in Texas contributions. There was nothing unusual about that total amount, even though it was large, because Liedtke had accumulated all the Texas gifts from several months of solicitation so they could be delivered at one time.

I learned after June 17, the Watergate date, that $89,000 of the Mexican money had been in bank drafts and $11,000 was in United States currency. I never found out whose idea this division was, nor did I learn the identity of the contributor until December 1972, when we agreed, at his request and on advice of counsel, to return the money. The contributor was Robert Allen, a Texas businessman and a member of our finance team in that state, who confirmed in a letter at that time that "your committee did not participate in that [Mexican] arrangement in any way" and that "I have not until recently informed you that I was the donor." In this instance, there was no contention that the contribution had to be reported because it had been delivered to the committee before the April 7 date that reporting began.

Sloan told me late in April that he had not been sure how to handle Mexican bank drafts and, again properly having in mind the avoidance of gift taxes for the giver, had handed them to Liddy for advice. In any event, Liddy concluded (as he had with the Dahlberg check) that the best course was to convert the checks to currency so it could be divided among committees, and this he did by running them through the bank account of his friend Barker. Sloan later reported to me in mid-May that he had just received the proceeds of the Dahlberg and Mexican checks from Liddy, after some delay and prodding. Shortly thereafter, on May 25, at my direction he included the total of $125,000 from the two contributors in a deposit of $350,000 in cash in the committee's bank account.

That's all there was to the saga of the Dahlberg and Mexican checks. They were valid campaign contributions. Both qualified under the law as contributions completed before the date that required reporting. They had carefully been given by our treasurer to our counsel for advice as to handling, and he in turn had cashed the checks and given the proceeds back to the treasurer who deposited them in the bank. There was nothing at all unwarranted in these actions They had no connection whatever with the plot to break into Democratic offices in the Watergate. That is worth re-emphasis, in view of all the published reports to the contrary. The Dahlberg and Mexican checks played no part in the Watergate burglary, as will be seen when the rest of the story unfolds in this chapter.

That being the case, it is possible to select the most ironic of all the cynical events of Watergate. The final act of Richard Nixon's downfall came when he was forced to release the White House tape of June 23, 1972, the "smoking gun" which in his own words tied him to the coverup, something of which he had denied knowledge all along. The specific act was his attempt to thwart the FBI investigation of the Mexican money by directing the CIA to block the path of the probers. We know now that all the FBI could have done, and did do, about the Mexican money was to trace it back to Robert Allen, who had chosen that circuitous route for his own reasons. Allen withstood a long inquiry and a grand jury investigation. Nixon had euchred himself out of the Presidency by the action of trying to prevent, and then denying, a probe of what turned out to be a wholly innocuous transaction, unrelated to the Watergate crime. He may have gone down in the end anyway, but the notorious "smoking gun" had been aimed at the wrong target.

The investigations of the finance committee staff began about a week after the break-in. One of the first to be interviewed by the FBI was Liddy and, as I have said, when he refused to answer their questions he was discharged. It was done without fanfare. Robert Mardian, a former Assistant Attorney General, who I was told had been named by Mitchell the day after the break-in to look into the Watergate affair, called me into his office on June 28 and read a statement recommending that Liddy be fired for failure to cooperate with the investigators. He asked my approval of the discharge and I signed the paper to that effect. Mardian offered to convey the message to Liddy and I agreed. I saw Liddy for the last time when he stopped in my office to say goodbye, at which time I said nothing except that I was sorry to see him go. He volunteered no information and, on Mardian's advice, I did not ask what it was all about. I sincerely did regret his leaving, because he had been a good lawyer and had worked hard on the legitimate work of the committee, keeping us well advised on the terms of the new law, following its registration requirements, and helping with questions raised by contributors on taxes and other topics.

Almost every one of our staff was interviewed by the FBI, some of them a number of times. The agents met with me on four occasions, the first on July 5, then twice on July 14, and again on July 28. The first interview was brief because the questions related only to James McCord, one of the burglars, who had turned out to be security officer for the campaign committee and whom I did not know. The second meeting went into the Dahlberg transaction and the Mexican checks in detail, and the third was about Sloan's travels and his resignation, which he had tendered on that day "for family reasons." I told all I knew about the Dahlberg check and the source of the funds. I could not account for the various checks showing up in Barker's bank account. Sloan filled that gap later by telling how he happened to give them to Liddy.

My fourth interview was much longer and covered a wide range of topics, including more on the Dahlberg and Mexican checks; the campaign committee; the finance committee organization; the budget committee; Liddy and his discharge; cash disbursements to Liddy, Magruder, and Porter; and Sloan's resignation. To the extent I had knowledge, I answered all the questions. At this interview, as at the earlier ones, Kenneth Parkinson was present as counsel for the committee and took notes. Some time later this procedure was publicly criticized as improper, but I had been told the practice was uniform in the case of all campaign employees, and I had no reason to believe it was unusual. It certainly did not inhibit my answers to the FBI.

At the close of the last interview, as he got up to go, one of the FBI interrogators reached into his pocket and with obvious pleasure handed me a paper. It was a subpoena to appear before the Watergate grand jury on August 2, just five days later. I was incensed, not at being subpoenaed as much as by the attitude and manner of its presentation, and when the agents left I asked Parkinson to find out for me whether I had any alternative to facing the publicity glare that would result from my appearance. He took it from there and talked to Dean, who apparently set in motion an astounding chain of calls that included Ehrlichman, Henry Peterson, who was an Assistant Attorney General, and

Richard Kleindienst, the Attorney General. All of this was unknown to me, and I was merely told a few days later that it had been arranged for me to appear at the Department of Justice and give the government attorneys a deposition under oath, which would then be read to the grand jurors, with the understanding that I would be called back if the grand jury had any further questions. Being without prior experience and not being a lawyer, I took that to be a normal method of procedure, and I learned later that four persons from the White House, including Charles Colson, an assistant to the President, had been treated the same way. For these reasons, I was not prepared for the tremendous furor that Senator Sam Ervin later raised a number of times in the Senate Watergate Committee hearings and subsequently about the "special privilege" I had been accorded.

In my deposition for the grand jury on August 2, I was questioned by Earl Silbert, Seymour Glanzer, and Donald Campbell, the three men who later prosecuted the first Watergate trial in January 1973, at which Howard Hunt and Gordon Liddy were found guilty, the five persons originally arrested in Watergate having already pleaded guilty without trial. I answered all their questions, which went considerably beyond the areas covered earlier with me by the FBI, so I was somewhat unprepared and could not be precisely accurate in details of all names, dates, and other information. At the close, however, I offered to give any further data the grand jury might want, but was not called upon again.

The safe in my secretary's office then became a cause celebre. Whenever I received cash or checks from contributors, it was my practice to give them at the first opportunity to the treasurer, Sloan. Nine out of ten times, this happened on the same day. Once in a while, when I sought to turn over money, he was away from his desk, so I put it in a small safe in her office, adjoining mine, where I sometimes kept valuable papers and files. Almost invariably I handed the funds to Sloan the next day, the only exceptions being when I left town on a trip for a few days, in which event I gave them to him intact upon my return.

Shortly before April 7, I gave Sloan the final cash and checks I had received up to then, with the names of the contributors. At my suggestion, he carried some cash over in his safe as a reserve to meet any obligations created before that date that might pop up, and banked the rest. A few days later $200,000 came in in cash from Robert Vesco as a result of an earlier pledge by him, and this, with the delayed proceeds of the Andreas and Allen contributions and one other of $25,000, was included in a deposit of $350,000 in currency in the bank on May 25. These were all contributions which, as we understood the law, met the statutory requirements as having occurred prior to April 7.

Sloan had the committee's principal safe in his own office, and regularly kept cash funds there, a practice established long before I joined the committee. After April 7, he decided that it would be more secure to keep the carryover currency separate from his financial records, so he placed the funds in the safe in my secretary's office and kept them there until their final disposition. This was done by him without my knowledge, while I was on vacation, and caused me some embarrassment later when I testified in a deposition that this safe had not been used after April 7 and he testified to the contrary. But the important fact is that he handled the cash fund exclusively.

Thus Sloan had access to my safe, but I had no access to his. I used mine as an overnight repository until April 7, and he used it exclusively for about seven weeks after that. Sloan handled all cash and kept a record of it; I did not make any payments from these funds.

In retrospect, Sloan gave me some personal problems on two fronts. First, he did not inform me about some of his cash transactions before and after April 7, and even denied some, leaving me to answer questions of interrogators and investigators without full knowledge of what had gone on. I did not learn of all of his receipts and disbursements until as late as 1974 and 1975, and only with the help of information from the staff of the Special Prosecutor was I able to reconcile the actual figures with my earlier sworn statements as to what I believed had occurred. Second, he allowed the press to pin on me the main onus for his own cash transactions, knowing that news stories referred constantly to "the cash in Stans' safe" when, as a matter of fact, he had sole and full responsibility for the cash funds, and they were exclusively under his control at all times, even when he kept them in the safe in my outer office.

These stories, invariably repeating that precise phrase, appeared first in Woodward and Bernstein articles in the *Washington Post* and the term was adopted generally by the media. The implications were that I held a large amount of cash, stated variously by writers to be from $100,000 to $1,300,000, which was a "slush fund" used for illicit purposes. I couldn't understand how such tales originated, because at no time did I ever have or administer a cash fund.

My secretary, Arden Chambers, knowing that I was unaware of Sloan's use of the safe in her office, queried him one Friday afternoon in May when he opened it and took out a packet of bills. "How is it that you are paying out all this money without Mr. Stans' knowing about it?" she asked.

"It's O.K." he replied. "I keep it in my little black book and never remove any money without authorization."

"Authorization from whom?"

"From Magruder or Mitchell," he answered.

I could not account for the obviously deliberate effort to identify the fund directly and exclusively with me until a year later, when Woodward and Bernstein acknowledged in their book that Sloan had been the secret source of many of their news breaks on the committee's transactions. I did not quite appreciate the cozy arrangement in which they relieved him of all responsibility for the cash funds actually handled by him on his own full authority. It was evident that, as an inducement for his continued cooperation, the two reporters had protected his name by making all of the speculation about improper cash activities focus on me.

To Sloan's credit, however, he made amends by repeatedly telling Woodward and Bernstein that I was ignorant of the facts of Watergate, which they finally acknowledged in their writings.[2]

It is now evident where the money to finance Watergate came from, since it did not come from the Dahlberg or Mexican checks. It came from cash payments made directly by Sloan, out of the cash fund in his possession, to Liddy, at the direction of Magruder. Sloan later testified before the Senate Watergate Com-

---

2. That did not in the least inhibit the producers of the film based on their book, *All the President's Men*, who, despite advance notice from my lawyer, maliciously and deliberately constructed the plot to make it appear that I was guiltily involved.

mittee in 1973 that, in all, he gave Liddy a total of $199,000 in cash. About half of this happened before I joined the committee, without my knowledge, as was the case with some of the later payments. The essential facts are that, according to Sloan, after March 30, the date the Watergate plan was adopted by those responsible, he paid $107,000 to Liddy; and that, of this, $83,000 was turned over on or about April 6, and the balance in two later installments of $12,000 each in May and June. While Liddy has never talked, McCord has testified that he received $65,000 from Liddy on April 12, and spent $58,000 of it promptly on tape recorders, transmitters, antennas, walkie-talkies, and other equipment for use in the bugging of the Democratic headquarters. This was *before* Barker had cashed the Dahlberg and Mexican checks, and *long before* Sloan received the proceeds of those checks back from Liddy. The evidence thus shows that the financing of the break-in occured out of the treasurer's regular cash funds, and not by dedication of these suspected checks to that purpose. There were many reports that the $100 bills found on the Watergate burglars were traced to the bank account in Miami through which Barker had cashed the checks, but FBI chief Patrick Gray told the Senate Watergate Committee that such a connection had never been established.[3]

It can be argued, of course, that whether the Watergate was financed directly from the Dahlberg and Mexican checks or from money paid out by the finance committee treasurer is a distinction without a difference. But that is not so, the significance being in the degree of knowledge, and therefore complicity, that could be attributed to the treasurer or, remotely, even to me. Had contributor checks actually been diverted for the purpose of financing the illegal entry, there would be little point in our claiming ignorance of their end use. With those checks fully

3. Although the full cash proceeds of the Andreas and Mexican checks received by Sloan from Liddy on about May 15 were deposited in the bank on May 25, the possibility is not precluded, since money is fungible, that some of the specific $100 bills received by Sloan for the checks may have been intermixed with other receipts in his hands. In that way, some of them could have been given back to Liddy when Magruder directed he be given money. However, this could have happened only with the payment of $12,000 by Sloan to Liddy in June and could not have occurred with the major amount of $83,000 given to him early in April which bought the bugging equipment.

accounted for and the proceeds deposited, the money to finance Watergate is shown to have moved from the treasurer, as did all campaign expenditures, at the direction of the campaign committee officials, without responsibility on the treasurer, under the arrangements in effect, to inquire into their purpose, and with the right for him to assume that the use was proper.

This is important, because the general public adoption of the conclusion that the finance committee was knowingly involved in the break-in, by reason of the erroneous assumption as to the manner of financing, was the takeoff point for the incredible list of subsequent assumptions as to other improprieties by the committee and by me. If we could be guilty of as crass an action as knowingly financing the Watergate burglary, then we could be guilty of anything else. The accusations thereafter ran rampant, in the media and in political speeches, and we had no practical way at the time to disprove them. Again and again the hopelessness of trying to establish that we did not do something of which we were accused—proving the negative—frustrated us for many months.

I had been told when I joined the finance committee that Liddy had been drawing cash for some special activities in the primary elections, directed by the campaign organization, but since he was a lawyer I assumed he knew what he was doing and that he had proper reasons for maintaining confidentiality, which was then legally proper. Shortly before April 7, when Sloan came to me because he was unsure about paying out the $83,000 requested by Liddy, I asked Mitchell whether Magruder had the right to give such direction, and he confirmed that this was within Magruder's general authority. Mitchell said he did not know what the money was for, since "Magruder is running the campaign." All of this was consistent with our opening understanding that the campaign people were the ones who determined the money needs, and the finance committee provided them without question.

Diversion after diversion of our time occurred as the campaign heated up, all slowing down our ability to raise money. A classic example was the harassment by the eager, publicity-hungry state's attorney, Richard Gerstein, in Miami. He had uncovered the fact that Barker, at the time he cashed the Dahlberg check, had improperly affixed a notarial certification beneath Dahlberg's endorsement. A bank officer stated that Barker had first presented the check for cashing with Dahlberg's signature not witnessed, and later Barker brought in the check with his own notarization under Dahlberg's name.

Gerstein got national publicity by announcing that he would expand this minor case into a full-scale investigation of Watergate, and for weeks he held headlines with his boastful news releases. During the Republican convention in Miami, he subpoenaed Dahlberg and me, and also attempted to subpoena several other persons. In the interrogation of Dahlberg, which was a sealed proceeding, he insisted that Dahlberg tell the name of the contributor of the $25,000, even though it was entirely irrelevant to the notarization case against Barker, and Dahlberg (who appeared without counsel) gave Andreas's name. Within forty-eight hours this "sealed" story was in Jack Anderson's syndicated newspaper column and in the national media.

My subpoena was handed to me in my hotel suite at a highly inopportune time, when I was busy with a myriad of duties in meeting contributors and finance chairmen from all over the country, was increasingly concerned about the health of my wife, who was in the hospital back in Washington and unable to attend the convention, and was in the midst of working with the General Accounting Office about certain items it was investigating. It was no time for me to spend hours being grilled about irrelevant matters, so when I received Gerstein's subpoena, I engaged local counsel to advise me, and they arranged that the questions would be limited to whether the notarization was on the check when Dahlberg gave it to me and I handed it to Sloan. It wasn't, and the whole deposition occupied less than five minutes.

Notwithstanding all that, Gerstein, on October 12, got a judge in Miami to approve an order on the courts in Minnesota and the District of Columbia to cause Dahlberg, Sloan, and me to be extradited to Florida for the Barker notarization trial, which was then scheduled for October 26. The papers served on me asked that I be present in the Florida court from then to November 8, the day after the election. The obvious purpose was to withdraw me from fund-raising during the last twelve days of the campaign and give Gerstein an opportunity for daily political press stories on the Watergate affair.

I resisted the extradition on the ground that my presence was not material, and also presented to the District of Columbia court an affidavit by Kathleen's doctors to the effect that she was in a serious medical condition, complicated by the situational depression, and that my prolonged absence from Washington was not desirable. The court held, on October 20 at the close of the hearing, that my presence in Florida was "not material or necessary to this case." Gerstein appealed to the Court of Appeals and lost again, but managed a flurry of statements about my "evasion of issues" and failure to cooperate. Sloan and Dahlberg were forced to go and waste a lot of their time. The petty payoff of this matter was that when the case did come to trial, it lasted only two hours, and Barker was found guilty and given a sixty-day sentence, which the court suspended upon his agreement to give up his notarial seal. It was this tiny issue that Gerstein managed to annoy us with for several months and build into a headline grabber for himself.

Another convention event received even greater publicity. For several weeks the General Accounting Office had been poring over our records and asking questions. We had done our best to cooperate, the only limit being that GAO's authority extended back to April 7 and not before. This had led to some arguments, but their audit was progressing reasonably well until GAO began receiving inordinate pressures from Democratic politicos to release its report, which they presumed would be critical, while the Republican convention was in session. One batch of data that GAO wanted from us, quite properly, related to the cutoff of the bank records on April 6 and the initiation of a new structure of fund-raising accounts beginning April 7. To meet the GAO request, our treasurer's office and a number of bank employees had spent many overtime hours during the pre-convention weekend sorting, collecting, and photographing hundreds of pages of records. Upon my instructions, the material had been organized in sequence, indexed in several large volumes, and sent to Miami for me to see whether it was responsive to the audit requirements and was in form for delivery to the auditors.

At this point, we ran into crosswinds of hurricane proportions. GAO was demanding the data at once, and I had not been planning to return to Washington with it until the day after the convention, a Friday. In fact, my interim activities had been heavily scheduled, including a meeting of the Republican National Finance Committee on Thursday, at which I was to be elected its chairman. The demand was very untimely. In ordinary conditions, this would have presented no accommodation problem whatever, but my schedule did not satisfy those who were pushing GAO for action to embarrass the convention. I phoned Philip S. Hughes, head of GAO's Office of Federal Elections, on Tuesday and discussed the situation with him, asking for more time. He called back a bit later and said he could not wait for the data, that the pressures were so great that he would have to issue the report without it. This would have done us a lot of potential harm by leaving open some questioned items for which we had validating documents.

I objected to the release of the report under such circumstances, and telephoned Elmer Staats, the Comptroller General who headed the GAO. I proposed that if he would send an auditor to Miami that same afternoon, I would work all night to present the answering information. Hughes then phoned back to say that he himself was coming with one or two other men. I at once arranged for Paul Barrick, who was then our treasurer, to be there also, and we all met from nine o'clock until midnight. At that point I turned the records over to the GAO men and they worked much of the night on them. When we met again the next morning, with Sloan also present at my special request, Hughes indicated that GAO was satisfied with the evidence on the cut-off questions that they had come to inquire into. This left only a few earlier issues which he made clear had not been resolved to his satisfaction, and these were named in their report without change.

Jean Westwood, new Chairman of the Democratic National Committee, who couldn't possibly have been more ignorant of the circumstances, seized on these meetings and claimed we had improperly delayed issuance of the GAO report and influenced its content, saying in a press release that it was a "flagrant violation of the campaign disclosure law and a manipulation of governmental processes by the Nixon administration." She went on:

> The blatant interference of an ex-cabinet officer in influencing the release of the Nixon campaign fund report by the GAO is another example of the scandal in this administration.

Larry O'Brien, the campaign chairman for McGovern, was quoted by the *Washington Star-News* as saying that "every ounce of political muscle available to the White House was being expended to suppress a highly critical government report on campaign financing." He called it part of the "most outrageous conspiracy of suppression that I have witnessed in a generation of political activity." Congressman Wright Patman also got into the act, with equal ignorance, by protesting the sending of a GAO official to Miami Beach before releasing the report.

All of this was wholly irresponsible. The delay of a few days was for the purpose of presenting important evidence needed to satisfy audit inquiries. Neither I nor my associates saw a draft of the report or knew what it contained until after it became public. The GAO officials confirmed that to be the case, and backed up our statement that the meeting had been entirely appropriate. Hughes of GAO, on August 27, told the *Washington Star-News*:

> I was becoming concerned because when I canceled the report and went to meet with Stans, people began to think we sold out to somebody. Actually, it worked out well. We got more information . . . . The report got better.

The GAO report was released a few days after the convention, in substance citing three transactions for a total of eleven counts of "apparent" and "possible" violations. (The law gives no authority or definition for citing "possible" violations, and it is obviously not a valid concept for action under a criminal statute. Some of those points were far-fetched and based on no stated evidence whatsoever.)

The three criticized items related to the failure to report the Andreas money as a contribution *after* April 6, the failure to disclose that Liddy had withheld $2,000 from the proceeds of the Dahlberg and Mexican checks for "expenses" when he turned the money over to Sloan, and the failure to maintain a record accounting for the sources of the $350,000 deposited on May 25.

Despite the clear language of the old and new laws that defined a contribution as including a "promise, commitment or pledge," and despite the long string of steps that Andreas had taken to qualify his contribution as one made before April 7, we were not able to get the GAO to accept this view. Not until January

11, 1973, did we receive a ruling from the Department of Justice to the effect that there was no basis for criminal charges on this item, thereby giving us exoneration.

The $2,000 item was a new one. I did not learn of it myself until I heard Sloan tell about it in the meeting with the GAO men in Miami. I am sure that he considered it *de minimus* and believed that his handling of the proceeds in the net amount was correct, or, if wrong, only inadvertently so. He did disclose the information voluntarily to the GAO. (The fine paid by our committee early in 1973 included $2,000 for this lapse by Sloan.)

Our position on the $350,000 deposit on May 25 was clear and compelling. The deposit was composed of contributions that we considered to have been made before April 7, including the Andreas and Mexican money, plus $200,000 received from Robert Vesco and $25,000 from another contributor. The full amount of $350,000 had been included as cash on hand as of April 7, in the initial report of the subsidiary Media Committee to Re-Elect the President, in accordance with my interpretation, as a professional accountant, of the GAO regulations. With this amount thus unequivocally accounted for on April 7 and deposited on May 25, it was hard for us to see that other records would have been necessary. The regulations of the GAO were quite clear, it seemed to us, in not requiring listing of the individual contributors of that money. The Department of Justice, presumably finding our view legally correct, took no action on this charge.

Nevertheless, Ms. Westwood, with total lack of conscience, charged on August 28 that the GAO report outlined "the largest and possibly the most corrupt set of financial dealings in the history of American presidential politics."

Considering the changes in law in the middle of a campaign, the mass complexities of the new law, and the unprecedented sums of money handled by the committee, it is not surprising that there could have been a few misinterpretations or misunderstandings that could lead to apparent technical violations. The items cited are so defensible that it must be evident that the GAO was more than zealous in its efforts to see that the committee toed the line. It did even more. A month later, in September, the GAO issued another report charging the committee with two more violations—illegally accepting a foreign contribution of $15,000 and illegally accepting some domestic checks from corporations. The foreign contribution was received from an individual who had asked Senator Gordon Allott to pass it on to us, and our clerks promptly deposited it. Ten days later, our committee counsel called my attention to the item and, being of the impression at the time that we could not accept contributions from foreign nationals, I directed at once that it be sent back to the donor. It was so shown in our public report. Despite that exercise of caution, the GAO alleged that the committee was criminally wrong for depositing the ·check in the first place. Ironically enough, the Department of Justice later ruled that it was perfectly proper to take such foreign contributions. Other candidates had accepted them all along.

The charge of illegally accepting corporate checks arose out of a dinner by "Blacks for Nixon" in Washington. The special committee putting on the dinner sold more than a thousand tickets at $100 each and received corporate checks for about a hundred of them, not alert to the fact that these could not legally be accepted. The improper checks were turned over to our committee as part of the dinner receipts. We never deposited them, but held them for a brief time trying to get them replaced with valid personal checks; when that failed, we returned them intact. The GAO contended the handling was illegal, presumably on the ground that we should never have allowed the corporate checks to come into our possession, even though we had clearly not accepted them as contributions.

There was obviously no criminal intent to avoid the law in either of these two cases, and in both of them the questionable funds had been promptly and voluntarily returned. To allege criminal actions in such cases was to me, and to our counsel, an absurdity. The Department of Justice found no basis for action on these charges. Whether the GAO acted as it did through an overexercise of caution on an uncertain law or through the political motives of some of its staff is conjectural, but there is no doubt that some GAO examiners were hostile to our committee. Among other things, they tipped their hand regularly to the press; the GAO organization was like a sieve. Woodward and Bernstein, the investigative reporters for the *Washington Post*, acknowledged later in their Watergate book, *All the President's Men*, that they were in constant and free communication with GAO staff people about our records.

Our relations with the General Accounting Office often troubled me. The GAO had authority under the new law to audit all transactions beginning with April 7, 1972, and to make recommendations to the Department of Justice for prosecution of any improper actions that were uncovered. It had no authority to go into events before April 7, and our counsel insisted on holding them away from such matters because of their propensity for leaking. Anything they learned became public knowledge within hours, and we were committed to assuring our earlier contributors privacy. While Elmer Staats, the Comptroller General, and Philip S. Hughes, Director of the Office of Federal Elections, were fair and impartial persons who had worked under me in the Bureau of the Budget in the 1950s, their staff auditors were young tigers eager to spring at our throats for the mildest suspected infraction. Their working attitudes were so evidently predetermined against us that I complained on several occasions to Staats. While this was going on with us, the same individuals were helping the McGovern committees to correct their books and reports to remove good faith irregularities. They acknowledged openly that our recordkeeping was far superior.

There were some inadvertencies that the trigger-happy GAO sleuths uncovered with obvious excitement that misled them into rash conclusions. One example was the Case of the Cash Cache. Checking the incoming money flow, one auditor discovered that in July several hundred thousand dollars had been deposited by our committee into a bank account that had been closed since April. This had to be a deliberate diversion to create a new secret fund, so he gleefully rushed the news to his superior and taunted our people with it. Told to follow through next to see what pernicious purpose had been pursued with the purloined plunder, he found to his chagrin that all it meant was that (1) a clerk in the treasurer's office had accidentally got hold of a wrong deposit slip, (2) the error had promptly been detected by the bookkeeper, (3) the funds had been moved to a proper bank account and rested there, and (4) the contributions had been publicly reported by the committee within the proper accounting period, all before the auditor arrived on the scene.

A large part of my time in the last fifteen weeks of the campaign was perforce occupied with the civil litigation. Immediately after the burglary, on June 20, the Democratic National Committee and its chairman, Larry O'Brien, filed suit against our campaign committee and the five arrested Watergate burglars for damages of $1,000,000. As a result, there were almost daily meetings with committee counsel, and we received frequent subpoenas for records that had to be collected and depositions that had to be given, in this case and in the Common Cause case which began a bit later.

The Democratic suit was a normal political ploy because it dramatized the affair publicly in a large way, even though there was no substantive evidence of any damage to the party or its candidate, George McGovern. The frequent thrusts of publicity by O'Brien and McGovern convinced us that the suit was designed to hurt Nixon in the campaign rather than to collect damages. The matter dragged along for months, with frequent depositions being taken in the office of the DNC counsel, who conveniently arranged for press and television cameras to be on hand at the entrance, before and after each session, to pose questions designed to embarrass or annoy our witnesses.

On September 11, O'Brien's lawyers filed an amendment to the original suit, bringing me and several others in as defendants for the first time, alleging that we were members of a conspiracy to commit political espionage against the Democrats, and as such had joined in organizing an espionage squad to break into their premises to purloin information. The charges alleged that I was guilty of burglary, larceny, espionage, and violation of the statute relating to electronic surveillance. In other words, I became accused of full complicity in the Watergate crime. At the moment, all I could do was to denounce the allegations as a vicious pack of lies and a contemptible and ruthless maneuver to use the court for political purposes at heavy personal damage to me. So confident were the Democrats of their position that they released the complaint to the media before filing it with the court. To their surprise, the court held that the papers could not properly be received in their existing legal form and they were refiled a few days later. In the amended documents, the defendants were sued for $3.2 million.

The stridency of the campaign accusations against me personally by O'Brien and McGovern grew as the weeks went by. On September 14, over a nationwide television network, O'Brien attacked me broadly for responsibility for the financing of the Watergate burglary, and he and McGovern made similar charges almost daily thereafter.

The campaign was heating up now, and the opponents presumably felt they had to hit hard at someone to score points. I was the obvious target, the one in the campaign closest in standing to the President since Mitchell had resigned on July 1, and they gave me both barrels. In a carefully timed move, Senator Frank Moss of Utah took the floor on September 21 to deliver one of the most scurrilous attacks ever heard in the Senate chamber. It accused me of every possible criminal act, including long-discredited irrelevancies, impugned my character, and cast the whole diatribe in terms that would have been clearly libelous outside the protection of Senate immunity. The tenor and venom of the speech are illustrated in these four excerpts, all of which have since been shown by the record to be without substance or merit:

> "Stans' principle [*sic*] objective was to amass the largest pile of money—to sell the administration for the highest price—before April 7, the date when the new law came into effect.
>
> " . . . to succeed in selling its wares to the highest bidder, Mr. Stans carried the banner of the Republicans throughout his hasty campaign. An avowed disciple of Polly Adler, you say? In her wildest dreams, Polly Adler never imagined taking in as much in her entire lifetime as the Republican Party succeeded in earning in two months—both engaging, of course, in the same profession.
>
> "Maurice Stans would no doubt have succeeded in keeping the public from learning his tactics in this felonious assault on the American people except for his little felony in which his henchmen were caught. I refer here, of course, to the notorious burglary in the early morning hours of June 17, 1972.
>
> "Stans refused to see reporters, because he was 'tightly scheduled' as his aides put it. Indeed he must have been tightly scheduled, running around collecting millions of dollars in illegal campaign contributions, dispensing with illicit tax guidance, and shredding the secret documents at CREEP."

Following his two thousand words of vitriol, Moss (who could not have had any personal knowledge on the matters on which he accused me) appeared before a large press conference. He phrased his attack somewhat differently to avoid direct libel, but in the face of the press handouts of his Senate speech, the distinctions were meaningless. His word "worthy of indictment" went out across the land. And the reality was that I was without any practical way to answer at the time, because John Dean and our committee's lawyers again wouldn't let me tell what little I did know.

The charges by Moss released all restraints on the media and the politicians, and the atmosphere became filled with venom. His language was harsh enough to require no embellishment, but some of the news accounts expanded on his words.

Scant was the mention anywhere that Moss had conceded publicly that he made his diatribe as a result of campaign assignments handed out a week earlier at a meeting in the home of McGovern's campaign manager, Larry O'Brien. No one asked who had actually written the material for him. The Moss charges, according to the orchestration, were immediately picked up and repeated for days with table-pounding emphasis by O'Brien and candidate McGovern in their stump speeches. That naturally got repeated play from the newspapers and on the TV screens.

There was a way I could cope with the O'Brien smears, and I did that by filing a $5 million libel suit against him on September 14.[4] This followed on the heels of a $2.5 million suit filed by the campaign committee and the finance committee against O'Brien for malicious abuse of the Federal court process; in it O'Brien was accused principally of using the court as a forum in which to publicize accusations against innocent persons which would be libelous if published elsewhere.

Filing the libel suit against O'Brien was very much my own idea, but there was strong support from John Dean of the White House and the committee's counsel. The way for it had been opened by O'Brien's failure to observe the proper sequence of steps on September 11 in attempting to bring me into his Watergate suit, thereby losing the immunity from libel that his complaint would have had as a court document. I was bitter about the

---

4. Charles Colson of the White House on September 22 sent me a handwritten note on a news report of the Moss attack saying, "Maury, why not add this S.O.B. to your libel suit?"

wild charges and said so in a press release in my own words that accompanied my suit:

> "I have brought this action not only to defend my reputation against a vicious and wholly unfounded attack, but also to serve notice on Mr. O'Brien and his agents that so long as they persist on the low road of smear and character assassination, they will be held strictly accountable not only to the American people, but also before the law.
>
> "This is a personal action by one who treasures his reputation and who believes in fighting back when falsely attacked. In a broader sense, it is a class action on behalf of all Americans who believe in fair play and in a man's right to protect his good name, even in the political season."

I was astounded by later news stories that a White House tape of September 15 contained an assertion by Dean that the Federal judge in the Democratic National Committee lawsuit, Charles R. Richey, had suggested to a lawyer friend of mine that I should file this libel action. I received no such suggestion from Judge Richey, directly or indirectly.

Kathleen and I were deeply concerned about the effect on our children of all the bad publicity that was developing. They could not know the truth about each charge, and there was no way I could take the time to explain every item to them. Their constant reassurances of faith in me let me know that I need not worry about them, but I did anyway.

The most poignant shock happened to our young granddaughter Sheila in California. She came home from school one day and asked her mother, "Mommy, what's a crook?"

Maureen answered simply, "He's a bad man. Why do you ask?"

"Because Mary said my granddaddy is a crook. Is he really?"

Maureen took the time to explain how people could be misled by false stories and that not everything in the papers or on television was true. She assured her that her granddaddy was a good man and that she should not believe such a thing. The next day Mary's mother called Maureen to complain that Sheila, without saying a word, had met Mary on the steps of the school that morning and punched her in the face.

All this was just the beginning of the troubles.

# 9

## SALT IN THE WOUNDS

Along the way, another political skirmish unfolded in the form of an "investigation" by Congressman Wright Patman and several of his political hatchet men working on the staff of the House Banking and Currency Committee. Without specific authorization by his committee, Patman announced that he was going to investigate the Watergate matter, using as his entry the banking transactions of the Dahlberg and Mexican checks. In the guise of covering that ground, he obviously intended to roam widely, and he almost did, but his own committee, despite its Democratic majority, eventually stopped him.

He started on August 28 with a letter asking me to meet with some of his interrogators, stating that his committee was looking into the subject of campaign finances from the standpoint of the involvement of the banking system. I agreed to see them, but when they appeared at my office two days later, they were officious and insulting, principally because I had arranged for the committee's attorney, Kenneth Parkinson, to be present. When Parkinson asked Curt Prins, the principal investigator, to define the purpose and limits of the questioning, Prins protested his presence, asking me "Why the hell did you have to bring a lawyer into this?" Parkinson tried patiently to explain his right to be present, but then Prins said, "Parkinson, go f--k yourself," and the meeting broke up at that point, after lasting only two or three minutes. I thereupon phoned Patman in Texas and offered to answer any questions put in gentlemanly fashion, provided my counsel and one Republican member of the Patman committee staff were also present, and provided that he would not release any report to the press without giving me an advance copy in time for me to answer it, if I wished, concurrently with his release. He agreed.

With this clear understanding, I appeared on the afternoon of the same day at the hearing room of the Banking and Currency Committee and answered the thirty questions put to me—all except one asking for the name of the contributor of the $100,000 from Mexico. I didn't know at that time. The questions related entirely to the Mexican and Dahlberg checks. I made it clear that our committee had no part in any movement of funds from Texas to Mexico, if any had taken place. We had done no "laundering." If that had occurred, it was the act of the contributor or contributors. I also said that I had played no knowing part in the movement of the checks through Barker's bank account.

The next day Patman wrote a letter asking whether I had any knowledge about how the $89,000 got into Mexico and whether I had participated in the plans for the transfer of the funds in that direction. I replied in the negative, which was the truth.

Patman next announced, without notice to me, that I would appear at a hearing before the full Banking and Currency Committee on September 14. On September 11, our attorney, Parkinson, wrote Patman to the effect that he had advised me not to appear because it might affect the constitutional and civil rights of the individuals involved in the Watergate matter. Upon receipt of this letter, Patman released to his committee a copy of the report of his investigators, but did not send one to me. Although he kept his word in the sense of not himself releasing it to the press, full copies were leaked by his staff at once. I had to ask for a copy to get one, and, of course, it came too late for a timely answer to the insinuating contents.

The report, written by three Patman staffers, was a masterpiece of fantasy. Every fact and circumstance was distorted in an attempt to prove or infer that a regular "laundering" operation had been devised by our committee to collect funds in Texas, send them to Mexico, and then bring them into the United States disguised as to source. It asserted without qualification and erroneously that the proceeds of these checks had been used to finance the Watergate. It alleged transactions "cloaked in mystery," lack of documentation, money from unknown sources, refusal to give names of contributors, shifting positions, failure to disclose information, participation by me in the Mexican transaction, and it took other wild and unfounded swings. In a long, rambling dissertation, these statements were repeated so many times and in so many different ways as to make it appear that a multiplicity of such events had taken place. All I could do was issue a brief denial, characterizing the report as a "mess of garbage," which it was. I called it "a compilation of deliberate falsehoods, misrepresentations, and slanted conclusions, all politically motivated," which it was. But it served its authors' political aim of adding more embellishment to the growing Watergate snowball of publicity.

Patman's authority was then exhausted unless he could get his committee to issue subpoenas compelling witnesses to attend. On October 3, he requested the committee to issue subpoenas to twenty-three persons, including me, notwithstanding his receipt that day of a letter from Henry Petersen, head of the Criminal Division of the Department of Justice, telling him that a committee investigation of the Watergate at that time would jeopardize criminal prosecution of those indicted in the case. By a vote of 20-15, Patman's committee turned him down; six Democrats voted against him.

While this had been going on, the White House, led by John Dean, was, for its own reasons, lobbying hard against Patman. There were meetings and phone talks with Republican members of the Banking and Currency Committee, discussions with minority staff members, and indirect approaches to Democratic members. An all-out campaign was conducted to see that the investigation was killed off, as it successfully was.

In the face of this repudiation, Patman persisted in claiming the spotlight. On October 4, he asked the General Accounting Office to investigate the flow of money to Watergate and report to him by October 26. On October 10, he addressed identical letters to me, Clark MacGregor, John Mitchell, and John Dean, requesting us to appear voluntarily before the full Banking and Currency Committee at noon on October 12 to answer questions concerning the financial activities of the campaign "as they related to the banking system and the expenditure and importation of funds across international borders." This had all the dimensions of a public side-show for political ends. On advice of counsel,[1] all four invitees declined to play that game, citing as a further reason the fact that Patman's committee had not voted on the matter of holding such a hearing. Not daunted, Patman set the stage for the occasion by providing four vacant chairs identified with large signs bearing the names of Mitchell, Stans, MacGregor, and Dean, and invited the press and TV cameramen to photograph the fact that no one had shown up, while he delivered a cynical monologue.

That wasn't the end, either. Patman's hatchet men continued their work and interviewed a number of people in Texas and elsewhere. Whereupon, without any further discussion with me, they wrote and released in the last week of the campaign another and even more garbled version of their report, with increased accusations and insinuations all over the same ground. It was such a poor document and so ineffectively written that the media practically ignored it. It was exactly what I called it in a press release: "A dishonest collection of innuendo and fourth-hand hearsay . . . obviously a fraud drawing false conclusions from misinformation." Patman himself, who had tried to appear above the battle except for occasional press conferences to egg on his people, quietly gave up.

There was a revealing sequel to Patman's efforts to hold a hearing that did not unfold for many months. When Dean confessed in 1973 that he had been the mastermind of the Watergate coverup all along, and when the coverup indictments were handed down in 1974, everything fell into place. The strong resistance to the Patman hearings had been organized and directed by Dean to ensure that neither he nor Mitchell nor others would be forced to appear and testify because that might blow open the lid on the entire Watergate story.[2] MacGregor and I, who knew nothing of a

---

1. Parkinson's letter to Patman said that the Justice Department "had expressed grave concern about holding hearings during the pendency of the criminal case, as it would undoubtedly infringe upon the rights of the individuals indicted, who, under the Constitution, are entitled to a fair trial by an impartial jury."
2. The White House tape of September 15, 1972, when it was revealed in 1973, disclosed that Dean and Haldeman considered these hearings a very great threat that could get out of control and "possibly unravel what was being tied into a tight little ball."

coverup, were led to believe all along that all that was involved was avoiding an undesirable political carnival. Dean admitted all this in his testimony to the Senate Watergate Committee in 1973 when he listed the White House resistance to Patman's probe as one step in the coverup program.

Not until February 2, 1973, did the speciousness of the Patman staff reports become established. On that date Patman belatedly released a letter from Assistant Attorney General Petersen dated January 11, which was summarized in these terms by the UPI press service:

> Patman released a letter from Assistant Attorney General Henry E. Petersen which closed the books on most of the charges the Banking Committee made last year . . . . The Petersen letter, dated January 11, said no Federal law was violated when one of the Watergate defendants, Bernard Barker, deposited $114,000 in Republican campaign contributions in a personal account in Miami. Petersen said the money was converted to cash and returned to the Committee to Re-Elect the President in Washington, and therefore was not an "expenditure" that should have been reported under the Federal Election Campaign Act. Similarly, Petersen said no law was violated when GOP contributions were routed through Mexican banks.

Petersen's letter also concluded that the finance committee had not violated the law by failing to report the receipt of the $25,000 from Andreas. The two Patman staff reports had finally been proven to be political tomahawkery, with no foundation in fact or law.

Another orchestrated Democratic attack on me came through Senator Warren Magnuson of Washington early in October, a month before the election. A press release issued by him made the charge that I had "set up a secret high-level White House meeting to assure the carpet manufacturers that effective regulation [of government flammability standards] would not be forthcoming." The release tied this to campaign contributions by alleging that "having been assured that regulations would continue to be indefinitely postponed, the carpet industry performed its portion of the bargain" by making substantial gifts. It concluded that "this administration is government decision-making on the basis of campaign contributions." By adding the irrelevant statements that household burn injuries cost the national economy a quarter billion dollars a year, and that one million people are burned in the home each year, the release carried economic and emotional dimensions that caused it to be widely reported.

I answered the statement at once by calling it "crass political innuendo to support a charge which he knows full well is contrary to fact. The meeting he described was a constructive discussion of technical industry matters and had no political purpose. It did not deal with political contributions and no favors of any kind were asked or granted." There had been present representatives of the Department of Commerce, the President's Assistant for Consumer Affairs, and two White House staff people, and the discussion consisted entirely of a showing of the growth of the carpet industry and an offer of the industry's technical knowledge in assisting the administration to make regulations to meet statutory requirements. Public statements by those present confirmed that no improper ideas had been presented or discussed, and that nothing had been asked or given. The flurry of public interest seemed certain to last for a while, so on October 11, I telephoned Senator Magnuson, who as Chairman of the Senate Commerce Committee had had frequent occasions in the past to get to know me. His reply was illuminating. "I shouldn't have made it," he said. "They gave it to me to release and said the newspapers already had the information. I should have said 'publish it' without me, or I should have called you first to find out the facts. I promise you I'm not going to follow it up." Magnuson, who is a decent man, was true to his word, and that was the end as far as he was concerned, but the accusation persisted in the campaign.

Needless to say, these events got generous display in the media, sometimes accurately and often not so. There was scarcely a day in the three years that followed the Watergate break-in when I could pick up a newspaper or news magazine, or turn on a television, without finding myself charged, implicated, cited, quoted or misquoted on some aspect of Watergate or campaign financing. Anyone reading or listening to these stories from day to day, without knowing the actual facts, had no choice but to conclude that I was heavily involved and deeply culpable in a large number of crimes. I cringed before the onslaught. It was a trying experience, being on the receiving end of all this attention and not being able to answer it effectively. Mere denials served no purpose and usually were ignored, and proving innocence was impossible in the heat of Washington during this period. The attorneys and advisers to our finance committee insisted all along that I should not attempt to answer each relevant or irrelevant detail, always on the ground that "any public statements might prejudice the investigations under way or might prejudice the rights of other parties." It was not a position I was qualified to debate with them.

The mental pain of these daily reports, over the air and in print, was excruciating. I tried to tell myself that it was only a matter of time before it would all be over and I would be cleared. But I knew the damage would never be undone. The truthful reply never gets the play of the untruthful accusation. I tried to keep the daily newspapers away from Kathleen, or keep her mind off television, so she wouldn't be troubled by all these fantasies. It didn't work, because she habitually went to sleep with her radio turned on and heard it all. She never questioned me about any of it, or showed any sign of doubt, but I knew that the barrage was affecting her composure and her health.

The critical publicity had begun to focus on me six weeks after Watergate, when news of the Dahlberg check broke out and he acknowledged that he had given it to me on April 11. The first story, on August 4, came from the United Press International wire service, quoting Philip S. Hughes, director of the Office of Federal Elections, as saying:

> In my opinion, failure to report either the receipt or the expenditure of the $25,000 constitutes a violation of the [new campaign contributions act].

This was a legal conclusion by Hughes which turned out to be wrong, but the opinion of the Department of Justice to that effect was not available until many months later. In the meantime, the alleged illegality of our action became accepted fact in subsequent stories.

The *Washington Post*, erroneously convinced that the

$25,000 check was at the heart of the Watergate crime, began a series of strident demands for immediate confession of wrongdoing in an editorial on the same day:

> . . . it turns out that a $25,000 check which was given to Maurice Stans . . . as a campaign contribution had ended up in the bank account of one of the arrested men along with $89,000 from Mexican sources. It was this same bank account from which the 53 $100 bills [found on the Watergate burglars] were drawn.
>
> And so there we are—just about nowhere—because Mr. Stans has such a busy travel schedule that he can't find time to talk about this whole affair . . .

The *Post* followed with this on August 9:

> Explanations which are rarely forthright—as the one now seeping out from Maurice Stans about how a $25,000 check slipped through his fingers—have not been reassuring, to put it mildly.

On August 12, the *Post* found support in this quoted remark by Senator William Proxmire of Wisconsin:

> "Even now key facts have been suppressed, high officials including Mr. Stans have failed to make any public statement or explanation . . . ."

By August 17 the *Post* could stand it no longer, and fired a long editorial entitled "Mr. Stans and the Sounds of Silence," which included these excerpts:

> As that silence continues, however, things just seem to get worse for Mr. Stans, a fact that is hardly surprising. For one thing he and John Mitchell . . . have now forfeited the opportunity of coming forward in the posture of men who have nothing to hide.
>
> The explanation Mr. Stans is said already to have given to Federal agents is not what you would call a model of logic. As we understand it, he told them that Kenneth Dahlberg, the veteran GOP fund raiser, did indeed give him a cashier's check in the amount of $25,000 for the campaign and that he—Mr. Stans— gave it to Mr. Sloan, former treasurer of the committee (who has since quit), and that Mr. Sloan gave it to Mr. G. Gordon Liddy,

former financial counsel to the committee (who has since been fired), and that Mr. Liddy gave it to Mr. Barker, the suspect, in exchange for cash and then deposited the cash in the committee's account. Mr. Stans is said not to know why the exchange was made and Clark MacGregor, head of the re-election committee, says he doesn't know either. The committee is said not to be out any money. Got it? We're not sure we do. If anything, the narrative makes things more, not less, obscure and only adds to the importance of the questions concerning this affair which the principals refuse to acknowledge, much less answer publicly."

This series of statements, which was followed by many others, set a tone for the *Post's* attitude that continued for a long time. The presumption of guilt was clear, and the *Post* was determined to find the facts which would prove it. It mattered not that I told the government investigators all I knew and that the facts recited in the August 17 editorial, which the *Post* had extracted from government sources that should have been secure, were entirely correct, as subsequent public evidence showed. Liddy, the only man who knew why the check was deposited as it was, was not talking to anyone, including me. Having established its cynical disbelief, the *Post* continued to maintain its demand for public answers that conformed to its conclusion that there was massive irregularity on my part. Meanwhile, silence was not golden; it was presumed to be incriminating.

As these statements appeared, they distressed me greatly and I sought some kind of relief that would take me out of the line of fire. I talked to Dean and Parkinson about the advisability of issuing a public white paper proving exactly what the course of the $25,000 check and the $89,000 checks and their proceeds had been and thereby disconnecting them from Watergate. There was nothing to fear from such disclosure and it would have cleared the air for Dahlberg, for the contributor of the money, and for me. I showed them a draft statement that I had prepared. They both advised against releasing it, saying that telling the truth to the investigators fulfilled my responsibility, and continuing media stories could prejudice the investigations or any future trials. They saw no right of the press to public disclosure until the investigating agencies wanted the facts released.

I fumed to MacGregor in his office. He was sympathetic and urged me to go ahead with such a statement. I revised my draft somewhat and went back to Dean with it. He knew how strongly I felt, but again he told me not to issue it and urged me to be patient for a while. Still having confidence in Dean and believing that following advice from objective counsel is wise policy, I waited.

The *Washington Star* got wind of these developments and noted them on August 21 and August 26 in articles by James Polk:

> Stans is reported to be eager to issue a public defense of his role in the financial transaction. He plans to make a statement within the coming week, according to MacGregor.
>
> Stans reportedly had statements ready on several occasions only to be overruled by campaign aides close to Mitchell.

A few days later, at a meeting in Mitchell's office attended by Dean, Mitchell, Parkinson, MacGregor, and others, I raised the subject again and it was agreed in response to my pleas that Dean would draft a statement to be released by our finance committee that would clear everything up. Dean drafted one and presented it to me and MacGregor, but it was so anemic and useless that we both asked him to try again. He agreed, but did not deliver, and that was the last we heard from him on the subject.

It was at this point that, growing increasingly restless, I thought perhaps my position would be improved if I employed my own personal counsel to advise me, separate from the committee's lawyers. I broached the idea to Mitchell and Dean early in September and got the same answer from each: "There is no present conflict of interest between you and the two committees, which are represented by Ken Parkinson and Paul O'Brien. If a conflict should develop it will be obvious and you should then get your own lawyer." Parkinson and Mardian felt the same way. I asked Roemer McPhee, a good friend who was counsel for the Republican National Finance Committee, and he confirmed what the others had said. A month later I asked the same questions of the same people and got the same answers. I trusted their judgment and did nothing more on the subject.

It is ironic that Dean later pleaded guilty, Mitchell was found guilty after trial, O'Brien was named an unindicted co-conspirator, Mardian was found guilty but freed after an appeal, and Parkinson was tried for conspiracy and acquitted. How in the world could anyone have anticipated such a turn of events?

On August 22, in the early stage of the Republican convention, the *Washington Post* announced new "revelations" in a news report:

> The General Accounting Office has discovered violations in the handling of nearly $500,000 of campaign contributions and expenditures by President Nixon's re-election committee, according to several reliable sources.
> The $500,000 in question, according to our sources, represents the following: about $200,000 in unreported contributions; another $200,000 in unreported expenditures . . . ; a $100,000 campaign security fund (from which $25,000 was deposited in the bank account of one of the suspects in the Watergate break-in); some errors, apparently in reporting a $50,000 itemization; and an undisclosed amount—probably small—of loose cash.

In an accompanying editorial, the *Post* called these revelations "more than a little troubling." They were more than a little troubling to me, too, since they bore no relationship to any facts in my possession. Nor did they bear any identifiable relation to the GAO report when it was released a week later.

As the events of the Republican convention began to usurp the news columns, the press devoted considerable attention to my Miami meeting with officials of the General Accounting Office regarding their report. UPI on August 24 had reported it fairly:

> The General Accounting Office (GAO), Congressional watchdog agency, withheld a report on the handling of Republican campaign funds after conferring with the party's chief fund raiser, Maurice H. Stans, it was learned today. Washington sources said Elmer B. Staats, Comptroller General of the United States and head of the GAO, felt that he needed more answers to questions about the use of campaign funds before he could approve the report.

The *Washington Star-News*, however, in an editorial on the same day, saw it as much more sinister:

We cannot take kindly to the spectacle of GAO officials sitting down with campaign leaders in Miami Beach to edit, check, delete from or add to a report that should be based only on documents the committee is bound by law to have submitted long since.

Notwithstanding the fact that on August 25 Senator Howard Cannon, Democratic Chairman of the Senate Committee on Elections and Privileges, confirmed that there was sufficient reason for the delay in releasing the GAO report and said, "The GAO is upgrading [it]", the *Washington Post* continued its attack on August 26 in an editorial entitled "A Glimpse of Mr. Stans." In this it referred to my phone calls and meetings with GAO, and a television interview with Mike Wallace during the convention, and questioned "the susceptibility of GAO to political pressure," which it said was hard to swallow, since it was inspired by "as much as $500,000 in questionable campaign financing." So it concluded that "the result of Mr. Stans' two characteristic breaches of his recent silence is to create further uneasiness."

On August 27 the *Post* had no doubt about how "as much as" $750,000 had been "laundered" in Mexico by our committee:

Meanwhile, the *Washington Post* learned yesterday that the $89,000 cited in the GAO report is only part of as much as $750,000 that was collected by the Republicans . . . and then moved through a Mexico City bank to insure the donors' anonymity . . . . Investigators said the donors were assured that their contribution would be "laundered"—made untraceable—by the complicated Mexican transaction.

The *Post* was wrong again.

On August 28, in response to the GAO report, I finally got clearance from my legal advisers to issue a carefully edited four-page statement labeled "Here are the Facts," spelling out precisely the story of the Dahlberg and Mexican checks. Even though the GAO document had failed to bear out the *Post's* advance "revelations," and my answer should have resolved its doubts, the paper was unsatisfied and kept up the warfare. On August 29 it said in a long editorial that "Maurice Stans has talked again" but that he "has contributed nothing but smog." It contended that "there is the matter of several hundred thousand dollars—perhaps as much as $750,000, which was at least in part generated by a fund raising trip in which Mr. Stans participated and which was 'laundered' in Mexico." After stating that my explanation of the $114,000 "stretches credulity" and making assorted references to "the money in Mr. Stans' safe," the editorial repeated its demand that "Mr. Stans speak out to clear this matter up." The problem was that my lawyers would not let me go further, and I felt sure the *Post* was determined not to believe me if I did.

All of these sensational and misleading stories about our funds were of course transmitted across the country to other papers and magazines and reprinted in whole or in part. Radio and TV commentators repeated them with gusto. Some of the accounts went to the ultimate conclusion about how the Watergate was financed. The *New York Times* on August 24 said:

> ... the source of the funds found in the possession of the men accused in the break-in has now become largely clear in the last several days. It is now apparent that the money originated in two packages .... One package originated in Texas. It consisted of $89,000 which was taken to Mexico City and converted into four bank drafts ... Mr. Dahlberg has said that more or less simultaneously he came to Florida and picked up a $25,000 cash donation on April 9.

Columnist Jack Anderson was more direct in his column of August 25:

> The mysterious $25,000 that apparently helped finance the bugging incident ... has now been traced to ... Dwayne Andreas.

The *Miami Herald* on the same day had no uncertainty whatever:

> A $25,000 contribution that helped finance the attempted bugging ... has been traced to [Dwayne Andreas].

The intended coup de grace was administered by Frank Mankiewicz, McGovern's campaign coordinator, on the national TV program *Face the Nation*, on August 28:

> "Former Secretary of Commerce (Mr. Stans) now stands accused, and the evidence seems quite clear, of collecting secret

funds and spending them contrary to law, and indeed, hiring burglars with them."

The idea of secret slush funds excited the commentators and editorial writers. The *Milwaukee Journal*, in an editorial on September 1, asked "why Maurice Stans, the financial chief of the Nixon re-election committee, is unable to clarify his role in all this." Other stories reported that "Stans provided no explanation why the check was not deposited into the campaign account," and "Republican sources are dismayed at Stans' silence." Carl Rowan wrote in the *Washington Post* on September 4 that "Stans . . . funneled [this money] through Mexico so as not to reveal the names of the donors. . . . Imagine Stans having no knowledge of how $114,000 from his slush fund is spent. It is more than any sane American can swallow."

Press and over-the-air stories multiplied with each new development, as the election drew nearer. The amending of the DNC suit to bring me in as a major culprit-defendant, the release of the Patman staff report, and the Senate attack by Moss followed in a close, organized sequence, and the news writers, commentators, and politicians crawled all over me. There was no longer any doubt in their minds that I was in the middle of the whole conspiracy.

It was now a total nightmare. Every day papers and broadcasts tore at me with full conviction that I was a heinous criminal. Stories began to appear with no fear that they might be libelous if untrue, without the usual protective reservations. Thus the *Washington Star-News* could headline "Panel Links Stans to 'Bug' Funds" in quoting the Patman staff report, and the *Milwaukee Journal* could scream "Maurice Stans Implicated," the *Raleigh News and Observer* could say in an editorial that the Patman report "further implicates Mr. Stans in the growing Watergate scandal," and a *New York Times* editorial could announce "Mr. Stans' involvement on the financial side [of the Watergate affair] is increasingly clear." The *Virginia-Pilot* editorialized that "he is not telling the truth, the whole truth and nothing but the truth about the bugging of the Watergate, the $114,000 in campaign funds paid to the suspects, the mysterious $350,000 in cash kept in his safe, and the apparently illegal Mexican transfers."

I agonized over my predicament, day after day, as the clippings came to my attention. My reputation was now hopelessly ensnarled in the inaccuracies of the charges. My legal advisers continued to tell me not to reply, that it was only a matter of time before the election would be over, the guilty persons tried, and my innocence established. When I filed the libel suit against O'Brien and called a press conference to announce it, Dean insisted that I merely read my statement and not answer any questions. Still relying on his counsel, I did it that way, but the reporters present interpreted their frustration as further proof that I was guilty of almost everything.

Only one kind word of understanding appeared anywhere; the *Washington Star-News* in an article on September 29 said this:

> Stans feels the silence imposed on him by Magruder and other campaign bosses has unjustly exposed him and other finance committeemen to severe criticism over the bugging incident.

I withheld my feelings from Kathleen, who was becoming increasingly depressed about her own helplessness in Walter Reed Hospital under chemotherapy treatments. I couldn't see how my world would ever straighten out again. All she ever said was "When will it end?" There was no respite.

On September 17, UPI concluded that I was accountable for Watergate:

> John N. Mitchell and Maurice H. Stans keep cropping up as principals in the tangled [Watergate] affair, leaked to reporters by very reliable sources close to some of the half-dozen investigations triggered by it.

This was followed a month later by a string of stories about "the cash in Stans' safe." The *Washington Post* on October 22 in a rundown of the cast of Watergate characters said, "The secret cash funds for 'sensitive' political purposes were kept in a safe in Stans' office." On October 25 it added that "expenditures of hundreds of thousands of dollars—all approved by either Stans, Haldeman, Mitchell, Magruder or Kalmbach—were made from the secret fund to pay for an extensive undercover campaign." *Time* on October 30 made it "a secret fund of possibly $700,000 in cash kept in the office of Maurice Stans . . . ." It went on to say that " . . . [Donald] Segretti had received from Herbert Kalmbach more than $35,000 for his [dirty tricks] services. Kalmbach in turn got the money from the secret fund in Stans' safe." That one about Segretti was the most farfetched of all; Kalmbach had not paid Segretti from our committee's funds but out of the money he had held since 1968, without committee knowledge of the payment. *Time* later raised its estimate of the cash in Stans' safe to "up to $1 million" and *Newsweek* outbid everyone by saying it went "up to $1.3 million."

At my request, the committee's press office about this time issued a statement that I had cooperated in giving the facts to all investigating agencies and that when they became public it would be seen that I had a "logical explanation" for all the things of which I was aware. Not content with that, on September 25 the *Washington Post* in its editorial asked the impatient question:

> What is Mr. Stans' "logical explanation" of the hundreds of thousands of dollars of money laundered in Mexico?

How does one explain an event that never happened?

On October 6, Woodward and Bernstein of the *Washington Post* changed course, quoting a "knowledgeable Republican source" as saying that the Mexican cashier's checks "had nothing to do with the financing of the Watergate." Their source presumably was Sloan, and the information was right; but an editorial in the same paper two days later refused to agree, saying of the Mexican money:

> Because of the tortured and secret trail it took from corporate coffers to Nixon committee headquarters in a suitcase, it is hard to tell whether it was a contribution by a corporation or by a foreign national. It doesn't much matter, though. Both are illegal.

Again, the *Post*'s surmises, written as fact, proved to be wrong in every respect.

On October 18 the *Post*, in a self-conscious remark, said editorially, "The *Post* has printed nothing which it is not prepared to back." Interestingly, it thereafter made no further charges about my silence, but it did continue to use the phrase "the cash in the safe in Stans' office" as a kind of litany. On October 22, after repeating it, the *Post* nonetheless made an important concession of my Watergate innocence for the first time in a broad wrap-up of the situation:

> Stans has said, and sources confirm, that he had no prior knowledge of the Watergate bugging.

Nevertheless, on the same date it reported on another page that "federal investigators in the Watergate case have revealed that at least several hundred thousand dollars of the undisclosed contributions was delivered in cash to Stans' safe just before April 7 and some of these funds were used in alleged espionage activities against the Democrats." Other publications took up the refrain, as *Time* incorrectly did on October 23:

> Kalmbach gave Segretti more than $35,000, including one payment of $25,000 in cash. The money came from a C.R.P. fund that was kept in the office of Maurice Stans . . . .

When there was no news, some papers imagined it. On November 6, in an editorial, the *Washington Post* stated that Stans had "solicited and collected [secret campaign contributions] from executives he had previously placed on the National Industrial Pollution Control Council and the National Business Council on Consumer Affairs [while Secretary of Commerce] . . . . As if there weren't enough doubts already about special deals, favors and arrangements, Mr. Stans' private operations among the businessmen now raise even more." That this is imaginary is proved by the failure of all the subsequent investigations to uncover a single such instance of improper dealing. Since the members of those advisory boards were important business people, it was just normally coincidental that some of them would have been solicited in the ordinary course for contributions.

The favorable result of the election on November 7 by no means brought an end to the investigations, the lawsuits, or the personal pressures. When Mitchell and I reviewed the situation on November 15, a week after the voting, we believed that the affairs of the finance committee could be brought to an end by about April 1, 1973. That would have been a normal timetable. We assumed that the Democrats would not push their suit against us, now that the election was past, because there was no real evidence of damage to anyone at Watergate. We believed that Common Cause would give up its litigation against the finance committee, because once the voters had expressed themselves, there would be little significance to the publication of a list of our early contributors. We were wrong on both expectations. The Democrats wanted money damages and Common Cause wanted more publicity.

These suits all continued and enlarged, especially since the unraveling facts of Watergate gave political value to the plaintiffs with every deposition they could take and publicize, and every court hearing they could pursue. On February 21, 1973, O'Brien filed a countersuit for $11 million against me and Francis Dale; on February 28, the DNC amended its suit against our committees and various individuals, including me, by raising the alleged damages to $6.4 million; and on June 15, 1973, the Association of State Democratic Chairmen and its director, R. Spencer Oliver, filed another action against me and others for $10 million.

Other civil suits were initiated too. A contributor in Missouri filed a class action case against our committees and a long list of individuals, including me, for various claims, including a million dollars in damages and the right to all contributors to get their money back. Another in Ohio did the same but kindly left me out as a defendant. Several individuals, members of the McCarthy for President Committee of California, filed an action against me and others for more than a half million dollars in damages; it alleged that Donald Segretti, while a campaign worker, had forged and sent out letters to about a thousand McCarthy supporters on McCarthy letterheads in 1972, stating that their candidate had no chance in the California primary and they should throw their support to Humphrey. McCord filed a cross-action in the DNC suit for damages he claimed he had incurred by being misled into crime, alleging among other things that his criminal actions had my advance knowledge and approval. The four Cubans who were in the original Watergate arrest filed cross claims against the CRP for damages on the ground that they were led to believe they were performing legal acts for a government investigating agency in making the Watergate entry. One of the lawyers for the convicted burglars, Henry Rothblatt, filed a suit for $113,500 in legal fees and $10 million damages, also including me as a defendant. Had I been guiltily implicated in Watergate, I might have been held for judgments amounting to $95 million or more in these matters. The legal work in fighting them cost the committee hundreds of thousands of dollars, and the demands on my time were enormous. Not until 1974 did the cases, one by one, begin to come to an end, and not until 1978 was the last one disposed of. Not one cent of damages was found payable by me on a single case, but the loss in time and stress was incalculable.

The Common Cause case dragged on for twenty months, through many depositions, court appearances, press releases, and wrangles among the attorneys. As a show of force, boastfully described later by its counsel as an example of the "countervailing pressure theory of litigation," and without regard to the ethical question involved, Common Cause, presumably to force us to abandon our defenses, asked the court to hold me and two of our committee's lawyers in contempt of court because some records had inadvertently been mislaid for a time by one of the committee staff. Finally, in July 1973, with the Watergate disclosures having created unreasonable suspicions of what might be contained in our contributor records, we concluded that the remaining issues at stake were no longer worth the cost of carrying on the case and sought a way out. After again taking soundings of contributors, we offered to the court to report to the Clerk of the House every one of our contributions and expenditures prior to April 7, 1972, but without an admission by us or a finding by the court that we were obligated to do so.[3] The report was prepared by independent certified public accountants and filed September 28. It was all anti-climax by then and the data released had no exciting disclosures and attracted only momentary attention.

Even so, Common Cause refused to desist after our report

---

3. Very few of the news reports on the court order mentioned the fact that there was no finding against our committee, and that our offer to disclose was voluntary. To the contrary, many asserted that the failure to produce the information earlier was a violation of law, repeating an unsupportable statement by John Gardner to that effect. For example, the *New York Times* reported that "Common Cause won its suit to disclose" and the *Washington Post* stated that the judge had agreed with Common Cause that the law required the disclosure. *Time* asserted that the Federal Court in Washington had ruled that anonymity of contributors before April 7 was illegal. Not so, at all.

was public, and carried on numerous further depositions of our employees and independent accountants, trying to prove that the information in it was inaccurate; meanwhile, it made public statements asserting that we had deliberately omitted millions of dollars. On December 7, 1973, a Common Cause attorney said that several million dollars in Nixon contributions "may be unaccounted for." On February 20, 1974, columnist Jack Anderson said that "secret documents ... show new discrepancies and unreported contributions of at least $1 million, turned up by Common Cause" whose "sleuths believe many millions more remain unreported." On April 14, the *Washington Post* noted that "Common Cause lawyers contend that millions of dollars in contributions may still be unreported." On June 29, a *Washington Post* article said that our final filing had "excluded contributions estimated by Common Cause at $1,825,000 and expenditures of $1,175,000." These allegations were all hogwash, and not a single error or omission was established. On June 28, 1974, almost two years after the election, Judge Joseph Waddy on our motion finally dismissed the case, including the contempt issue, after twice criticizing Common Cause for harassment of our witnesses, saying in one instance " ... every time that the Court authorized one type of discovery, it continued to progress and string itself out to the point wherein in the opinion of this Court it became harassment."

It was a senseless litigation throughout, expensive to both parties, and it served no purpose other than the self-aggrandizement of Common Cause through its repeated press releases and public statements. The continuing reckless publicity no doubt helped Common Cause in its fund-raising. The new law in effect that began April 7 did require full disclosure of campaign finances thereafter and we complied with it, and no beneficial result was obtained by prosecuting for almost two years after the election a determination to make us reveal the names of contributors of an earlier period who believed they had a right of confidentiality at the time they made their gifts. The late revelation could not at all provide useful information for the voters long after they had voted.[4] The filings disclosed no violations of the law by the

---

4. The court, in dismissing the case, said that there was no longer a legal nexus between the injury and the relief sought; the nexus had ended on election day in 1972.

committee. Although it was later revealed that about twenty of the contributions had been illegally made, and Common Cause claimed credit for uncovering them, there is every reason to believe that their illegality would have been discovered in any event by the investigations of the Special Prosecutor, considering the data we compiled early in 1973 and furnished to him in compliance with his requests.

The Missouri contributor's class-action suit was withdrawn, and the Ohio case died of its own anemia. The California case fell from lack of prosecution. The Rothblatt suit was dismissed, appealed by him, and ruled against him in the appellate court. The only cases which resulted in money settlements were those of the Democrats. In early 1973, we paid $775,000 to settle the damage claims brought by the Democratic National Committee, Larry O'Brien and the Association of State Democratic Chairmen. This was an amount far greater than I was willing to approve because I did not believe any provable damages existed. The break-in had not resulted in any discernible handicap to the Democrats in the election, there was no physical destruction, no personal reputations had been injured, and the statutory penalties for wire-tapping were a nominal $100 a day. The only risk I could see was that an emotion-charged jury in the District of Columbia might award punitive damages as a political lesson. There was of course, as almost always with litigation, a nuisance value in the case but I did not consider that important enough to justify paying a huge sum. However, the "suggestion" came from lawyers at the White House that we should close out this embarrassing litigation and the committee counsel feared the expenses and risks of a trial, so I gave up arguing about the amount.[5]

At the time of the settlement with the DNC I found myself in a conflict of interest position because of my libel suit against O'Brien. Dean had said in 1973 that he thought I had a good chance to collect. I wanted to continue it, but the Democrats would not settle unless it was withdrawn. Under the circumstances, I felt I could not be a dog in the manger by holding out,

---

5. In 1976, the trustees then administering our finance committee's leftover money settled separately with R. Spencer Oliver, whose phone had been tapped in the break-in, for $215,000. In 1977, they settled with the four Cubans by paying $200,000.

and I issued this statement:

> I am abandoning my libel suit against Larry O'Brien for three reasons. First, I believe it is desirable that this entire package of lawsuits between Democrats and Republicans be closed out, and to continue the libel suit would impede that purpose. Second, O'Brien has satisfied me that the statements on which the suit was premised were not intended to be personally malicious. Third, it should be clear now, from the reports of the Senate Watergate Committee and the House Judiciary Committee and depositions in this litigation, that I had no involvement in the Watergate break-in or coverup, and this is what I wanted to establish when the suit was filed.

As part of the settlement, O'Brien gave me a weakly worded letter stating that he had not acted out of malice in filing his suit and "any public statements relating thereto were not conceived to malign Mr. Stans' personal reputation." He also had agreed to make an exonerating statement publicly, but did not do so. It was hardly the apology I had asked for and thought I deserved, and hardly an adequate gesture from one who had coldly misused another person's reputation to try to sustain a lost political campaign. A bigger man would have done it better and more graciously.

My attention from the media tapered off for a while after the election. Some of the papers, particularly the *Christian Science Monitor*, mentioned me in retrospective analyses of Watergate, but there was little of the harshness exhibited toward me before the election. The expectancy of the commentators and writers centered on the forthcoming trial of the Watergate burglars, which began on January 8 and ended January 30, 1973, when the five originally arrested had pleaded guilty and Liddy and McCord were found guilty after a trial.

When the trial was held, I was not deemed by the prosecutors to know enough to be a witness. Sloan testified, and did his best to dispel the silly assumptions that had prevailed about the Dahlberg check of $25,000 and the Mexican checks for $89,000. He testified that the proceeds of these checks had come back to him in May; he had originally given the checks to Liddy to cash so he could divide the contributions into smaller units to avoid gift tax for the contributors and also conform to the law limiting contributions to $5,000 to any one committee. In return for assurances of immunity for himself from prosecution, he told all he knew about the Watergate affair. In particular, he recited that he had paid a total of $199,000 to Liddy, of which $107,000 was after April 1, at the direction of Magruder, but he did not know what Liddy was to do with it.

My name came up only once during the trial. Sloan testified that when Liddy came to him around April 1, showed him an unexplained budget for $250,000 and asked for $83,000, all on the authority of Magruder, he came to me and asked whether Magruder had such authority; that I told him I would check with Mitchell; that I reported shortly thereafter that I had checked with Mitchell, who had said that Sloan should pay Liddy any amounts that Magruder directed. Although Judge Sirica in open court accused Sloan of not telling the entire truth, there was no ambiguity in Sloan's testimony and he stated the facts correctly; he said that he did not ask me to verify "the specific amount, but Mr. Magruder, his authorization, was authorization enough to turn over the sums in question." In other words, I had merely reconfirmed with Mitchell Magruder's broad authority to direct payments to Liddy or to anyone else.

Yet the media had a field day in twisting this into evidence of my complicity. The AP announced immediately that Mitchell and Stans "approved payments to the man charged with a political-espionage conspiracy against the Democrats." The *New York Times* headlined erroneously on January 24 that "Watergate witness says Mitchell and Stans approved $199,000 given to Liddy" and reported: "A witness said today that $199,000 in cash payments to a defendant in the Watergate trial had been approved by former Attorney General John N. Mitchell and former Commerce Secretary Maurice H. Stans." The *Washington Post* on the same day said that "Sloan testified that Stans and Mitchell approved disbursements of about $199,000 to Liddy."

A follow-on AP story by Harry F. Rosenthal garbled it this way:

> *Sloan said that former Attorney General John Mitchell and former Commerce Secretary Maurice Stans authorized Magruder to pay the sum to Liddy although not the specific amount.*

An AP story by Don McLeod put it, equally wrongly, like this:

> Judge John J. Sirica, presiding at the Watergate trial, saying some
> important information had been kept from the jury, today read the
> panel testimony that former Attorney General John Mitchell and
> former Commerce Secretary Maurice Stans approved payments
> the government says went to political espionage against Demo-
> crats.

UPI messed it up still more:

> Sloan said during the interrogation that he turned over $199,000
> to Liddy for unspecified political espionage with the approval of
> former cabinet members Maurice Stans and John Mitchell and of
> Jeb S. Magruder.

Totally irate, I had our press office issue a release on January 26 to
clarify what Sloan actually had said, interpreting it as follows:

> Mr. Sloan stated that he inquired of Mr. Maurice Stans whether
> authority of Mr. Jeb S. Magruder extended to authorization of
> substantial campaign funds to Mr. Liddy. He was told by Mr. Stans,
> after consultation with Mr. John Mitchell, that Mr. Magruder had
> continuing and general authority with regard to all campaign
> expenditures.

Despite this correction of the unequivocal errors, the AP continued to say on January 31:

> Sloan told Sirica that his payments of about $200,000 to Liddy
> were approved by John N. Mitchell . . . and Maurice Stans. Neither
> was called to testify.

The *New York Times* on January 29 insisted on saying:

> Judge Sirica . . . extracted from Mr. Sloan the information that
> the payments to Mr. Liddy had been approved by Mr. Stans and
> through Mr. Stans by John N. Mitchell . . . .

On January 31, the *Washington Star* even brushed aside our
objections to its inaccuracy:

> Both former Atty. Gen. John N. Mitchell . . . and former
> Commerce Secretary Maurice Stans . . . have vigorously denied
> knowledge of any illegal activity. But Sloan testified at the trial
> that both men had approved disbursement of large sums of
> money by the committee's deputy director, Jeb S. Magruder,
> some of which the government showed went to Liddy.

The next day the *Washington Post* held to its improper conclusion in an editorial:

> Two of Mr. Nixon's closest advisors, a former Attorney General
> and a former Secretary of Commerce, authorized the payments.

On February 1, in an editorial the *New York Times* continued to insist on its distorted version:

> . . . the public now has on record sworn testimony that former
> Attorney General John N. Mitchell, the President's campaign manager,
> and former Secretary of Commerce Maurice H. Stans, his
> chief money raiser, personally approved the disbursement of
> $199,000 to one of the convicted defendants to carry out this
> espionage.

We repeated at once our press release of January 26, addressed to the *New York Times* editorials, saying:

> To say, as the *Times* did, that Mr. Mitchell and Mr. Stans
> "personally approved" the disbursement of $199,000 to carry out
> "political espionage" is an absolute perversion of Mr. Sloan's testimony
> and of the facts in this matter.

On February 3, the paper recanted. "The *Times* regrets the erroneous statement," it said, but it also noted that the judge had expressed "grave doubts that Sloan told us the entire truth." As late as March 11, nationally circulated *Parade* magazine repeated the untruth that "Mitchell and Stans are on record as having personally approved the disbursement of $199,000 to one of the convicted defendants."

From then on my name was linked with that of Mitchell in

the media's Watergate speculation[6] until March 1974, when he was indicted for the Watergate coverup and I was not.

At the end of February 1973, Dean made a suggestion which at first startled me and then, as I thought about it, became quite appealing. I had on a few occasions discussed with him my desire to wind up the finance committee as soon as possible and look for another part-time career. As I had told the President a year earlier, I had planned on a partial retirement when the election had passed, with the probability that I would associate as a director/consultant with four or five large corporations, several of which had made such offers. But I had become increasingly concerned about the damaging effect on my reputation of the smears that I had quietly endured all during 1972, and was waiting for the right opportunity to tell my full story so that I could establish to the public my innocence of the break-in and the coverup. Dean suggested that I consider accepting a nomination by the President to a post in government that would require a hearing and confirmation by the Senate. He proposed an ambassadorship, such as the one at Geneva, which bears the incredibly long title of "United States Representative to the European Office of the United Nations and Other International Organizations." That particular post didn't intrigue me but the idea of an appointment did. The confirmation hearing would give me a forum in which I could answer any and all charges, and the expected confirmation by the Senate would be my public vindication. I told him that I would consider it and he pressed me for an answer within a week.

I was seriously tempted to accept if a somewhat more challenging post were to be offered, and I so told Dean. Before he could come up with an alternative, I sought advice of a few friends and one of them, Bryce Harlow, who had served in the White House in both the Eisenhower and Nixon administrations as the man who took the pulse of the Congress on issues that came along, advised me strongly against it: "You won't have a fair play with the Watergate hearings pending in the Senate. They'll either try to kill you in the confirmation hearings or raise a lot of doubts

---

6. This linkage was emphasized especially after he and I were indicted in New York in the so-called Vesco case (see Chapter 11). Much of it carried the presumption that indictment equated with guilt.

and then announce postponement of a decision until the Water-gate inquisition is over. You can't possibly win. They would use you to get at Nixon." I told Dean to drop the subject and I heard nothing more at the time, except that he urged me to reconsider and I refused. It was not until about four months later that I learned from Dean's testimony before the Senate Watergate Com-mittee that this had been a setup, planned by him and cleared with Haldeman and Ehrlichman, to get me to a confirmation hearing in March to take the brunt of the Watergate inquiry and thus dull the force of the forthcoming Senate hearings scheduled to begin in May. I was to be the fall guy.

I do not believe this was a deliberate attempt to do me harm, but rather that it was based on Dean's knowledge that I was innocent of Watergate and his confidence that I could handle a sticky hearing. This is confirmed by Dean's agenda for his meet-ing with Nixon on February 28, which contained this topic for discussion:

> (2) **Sending Stans up for Confirmation:**
> —We don't know if Stans wants to do this, but we do know he wants to be rehabilitated and isn't afraid to tell his story publicly.
> —Confirmation hearings would help defuse Watergate hear-ings, and the more of this we get to the public, the less impact the Watergate hearings per se will have.
> —This should be resolved quickly, because it will only be helpful if it occurs prior to Watergate hearings.

The White House tape of the actual meeting with Nixon shows that this conversation ensued:

Dean:   I understand that you and Bob have talked about running Stans out as sort of a stalking horse on it, on another post.
President:   It is not my idea. I guess Moore or somebody men-tioned it.
Dean:   I think it was my idea, in fact. I think it could defuse, be one defusing factor in the hearings. Stans would like to get his side of the story out. He is not in any serious problem ultimately. It could be rough and tumble, but Maury is ready to take it. It would be a mini-hearing, there is no doubt about it, but this further detracts from the other committee.

President:　So you sort of lean to having Stans starting out
　　there?

Dean:　I think it would take a lot of the teeth out of it—you
　　know—the stardom the people are trying to build up to. If
　　Stans has already gone to a hearing in another committee,
　　obviously they will use everything they have at that time and
　　it won't be a hell of a lot. It confuses the public. The public is
　　bored with this thing already.

President:　Stans is very clean. Unless I make a mistake on this
　　thing, the way I analyze it, and I have stayed deliberately
　　away from it, but I think I can sense what it is. The way I
　　analyze the thing, Stans would have been horrified at any
　　such thing. And, what happened was he honestly is
　　outraged. . . .

Dean:　He does and he is a victim of circumstances, of innuendo,
　　of false charges. He has a darn good chance of winning that
　　libel suit against Larry O'Brien.

Dean acknowledged even more specifically to the Senate Watergate Committee in his testimony that the idea of getting an
ambassadorial appointment for me was merely a step in the
Watergate coverup. It is a prime example of the "cute" manner in
which I was not only kept in the dark throughout but was used
when it served the interests of the guilty.

McCord's letter of March 23, 1973, told the world for the first
time there had been a payoff of the Watergate burglars to insure
their silence so that the higher-ups would not be exposed. This
led to the gradual disclosure of the various amounts of money
that had been disbursed for legal fees and for support of the
burglars and their families. None of this came from committee
funds. When the information had finally unfolded, it encompassed four major sources:

　　—Approximately $70,000 received by Kalmbach from LaRue out
　　of a fund of that amount which LaRue had received from the
　　finance committee to hold until after the election.
　　—$75,000 secured by Kalmbach from me on June 29, 1972, on
　　the plea that he needed it urgently for a White House project that
　　he could not describe to me.

—$75,000 secured but not reported by Kalmbach in early August 1972 from a contributor.

—$328,000 or $350,000 secured by LaRue from the White House in December 1972 and April 1973 from a so-called "polling fund" which the White House had held since early April 1972.

LaRue also received and handled in October 1972 an additional $50,000 that came from an early 1972 contribution made through "Bebe" Rebozo; he used half for the payoff fund and gave half to a Senatorial candidate.

The specific disposition of these amounts as "hush money" by
LaRue and Kalmbach is irrelevant here because neither I nor anyone connected with the finance committee had any information as to what was done with it, or was ever accused of having such
knowledge by any investigating authority. The *source* of it is of interest, however, especially the $75,000 that Kalmbach got from me.

On June 29, 1972, he phoned me from a Washington hotel, saying he had an urgent need for all the cash I could put my hands on, specifically mentioned $50,000 to $100,000. He told me it was for a secret White House project that he could not tell me about, and that I would have to trust him and take his word as to the importance of the need. I understood that it had no relationship to the campaign, and since the White House earlier had non-campaign projects I was not concerned. Relying on his word, our friendship, and his relationship to the White House, I did my best to comply. I had that morning received $30,000 from a foreign contributor and was holding it intact until I checked out whether such a contribution from a foreign national could be legally accepted. Knowing full well that I would have to account for it in one manner or another, either by reporting it as a contribution or returning an equivalent amount to the source, I gave this $30,000 to Kalmbach. I also held in a safe deposit box an amount of $45,000 which Kalmbach had advanced to me from funds carried over from 1968 just before I became finance chairman to be used for travel and other expenses, but which I had concluded I would not need, so I gave that to him, too. Since the $75,000 I turned over to him was not to be used for campaign purposes, this was not a transaction that the law required to be reported. (Less than a month later I arranged to return the

$30,000 to the foreign contributor from other funds.)

The $75,000 that Kalmbach got from a California contributor, without reporting it to anyone in the finance committee, turned out to have originated illegally from a corporation. The other $350,000 making up the coverup fund had been given to the White House for polling purposes at the request of Haldeman, on about April 6, 1972, out of surplus funds left over from the 1968 campaign, which Kalmbach had held as trustee; the transfer to the White House was a proper transaction when it took place, and certainly no one in our committee could have contemplated then that the money would be used for an unlawful purpose almost a year later.

Thus, neither I nor anyone in the finance committee was a knowing party to any of the payoffs, whatever their purpose; Kalmbach confirmed totally and unequivocally in his testimony that the circumstances surrounding his request to me on June 29 for cash funds were exactly as I have related them, and absolved me from responsibility for the action, which he had undertaken at the request of Dean.

The *Washington Post* and its reporters Woodward and Bernstein headed a parade of incorrect reports stated as fact from March until June 1973 that frustrated me beyond tolerance. These and other Watergate stories elsewhere took it for granted that I was one of the guilty pack. Accounts of campaign finances roamed all over the imagination, trying to hit a truth now and then. I was hopelessly sensitive to all that was said about my committee and me, but there was no way of proving the opposite, so I knew I had to sit out the storm. Some instances will demonstrate how hard that could be.

I was dragged into suspicions about the administration's handling of the antitrust case against ITT. No one had ever told me about any expected contribution from ITT or its employees or subsidiaries and I had not lifted a finger to help the antitrust results. Yet on March 19 the *Wall Street Journal* ran an article under the heading "Agnew, Connally, Stans Linked to ITT Effort in the Hartford Case." On the same day, UPI had a similar report to the effect that I and others "had a hand in the case, either by letter or meetings with company officials."

The next day the *New York Times* headlined "6 High Nixon

Aides Linked to Accord by U.S. with ITT; Agnew, Connally and Stans mentioned in SEC Data Issued by House Panel." Other articles followed along the same line, in the *National Observer*, the *Washington Star-News*, the news magazines, the wire services, and the networks, each more accusatory than the one before. Finally the story, insofar as it referred to me, settled on an alleged statement by the SEC in a staff document that, after a meeting which I had held as Secretary of Commerce with John Ryan, a Washington lawyer, Ryan had written a memo on August 24, 1970, to a vice president of ITT describing the session and then saying: "This may be the break we are looking for, if Kleindienst will follow through." After that revelation had had its damning effect, it was followed by a quiet announcement that the report was in error in attributing to this conversation with me the quoted portion about a "break" and hoped-for action by Kleindienst, which had instead originated in a meeting between an ITT official and Vice President Agnew. The truth was that Ryan's conversation with me was merely a discussion of the government controls on foreign investments, having no relationship to the antitrust case.

Continuing comments on the Watergate just assumed that I was criminally involved. On April 19, the *New York Daily News* named seven persons as the focus of Watergate and added that "other present and former associates and aides to Nixon have been mentioned, [including] Stans, Kalmbach and Mardian." On the same day the *New York Times* said that " . . . among those figuring in the speculation" as to who would be accused were Mitchell, Dean, Stans, Magruder and Strachan." The next morning the *Times* had it even more ominously: "Along with Mr. Mitchell, Mr. Magruder and Mr. Dean, three other names have been prominently mentioned in Congressional and press speculation as facing possible indictment. They are Maurice H. Stans, Gordon C. Strachan and Herbert Kalmbach."

On April 20, after McCord filed a damage suit against the committees, alleging that all this actions "were undertaken with the foreknowledge and approval of Stans and Sloan," John Chancellor on NBC News narrowed it down to " . . . one of those caught at the Watergate now says Stans knew and approved in advance." Fortified by McCord's action, the *Washington Post* in a news analysis on April 22 concluded that " . . . the case leapfrogged the third echelon campaign operatives with those unfamiliar names and came to focus on four men who have been political intimates and close governmental associates of Nixon—Mitchell, Stans, Haldeman and Dean." The *Washington Star-News*, marshaling all its sources, incredibly said on April 25 that "everyone knows the names of those most frequently mentioned in leaked grand jury testimony, hearsay statements before the Ervin committee and attributed news stories: Mitchell, Stans, Magruder, Dean, Chapin, Kalmbach, LaRue, Colson, Strachan and Haldeman."

At about this time the loud-talking right-wing *Manchester Union Leader* accused Murray Chotiner, a Washington attorney, of being guilty of complicity in the "Watergate caper" through a secret fund of $350,000 "collected by the White House inner circle from certain gambling interests in Las Vegas and from money donated from the pension fund of the international teamsters union . . . . Other members of the White House staff, Maurice Stans, H. R. Haldeman, Herbert Kalmbach, and John Dean III, had knowledge of the operation and had given their approval to the project." This one was so far off base that Chotiner sued the paper and won a money settlement. I was too busy to take part in the suit, even though the statements as to the sources of money and as to my involvement were nonsensical.

On May 21 *Time* magazine stated unequivocally that "both Mitchell and Stans have been deeply implicated in the Watergate scandal itself." The following day, a UPI story naming Mitchell, Stans, Colson, and Ehrlichman went further by saying that "in addition to their involvement in the Watergate case, they were all involved in the ITT matter." On June 8, as the Senate hearings began to gain momentum, an AP roundup on Watergate said emphatically that "those reportedly facing [Watergate] indictment include Haldeman, Ehrlichman, Dean, Mitchell, Stans, Magruder, LaRue and Mardian."

This last excerpt is a classic illustration of the "guilt by association" by which I was publicly condemned. Every one of those named except me was in fact indicted for the Watergate break-in or coverup. This nationwide article and the hundreds that preceded it set the atmosphere into which I would walk when I entered the Senate Watergate Committee hearings. While all that was going on, there was a limitless rash of stories on campaign finances, either centered on "the cash in Stans' safe," which by now had become a household phrase, or alleging illegal fund-raising tactics. There were daily news articles during this period, of which hundreds could be cited, that bore down on me, some fictitious, some exaggerated, some cynical, some suggesting of evil without saying so, some that parroted others, some trying to outdo others.[7] All presumed guilt. Practically none stopped to suggest that maybe it would be a good idea to wait until all the facts were in before reaching judgments. Practically none spoke of a presumption of innocence, although a careful reading might find in the lower text of news accounts an occasional exculpatory remark or denial.

I savored the few kind or comforting words that came along. On May 1, Victor Gold on the *Today* show commented, "I think we have to go a little slowly on the business of Mr. Stans or anyone else. There comes a time when the speculation itself . . . we're entitled to speculate but there's a narrow line here. These things are going to come out through the judicial process." But a remark like that was overshadowed by James Reston writing in his *New York Times* column about the "money corruption of Maurice Stans," or Russell Baker in the same paper telling of "the Arab bazaar in ambassadorships" or the *Times* editorializing about my "pressuring shady businessmen and organized pressure groups for large sums of money, preferably in cash," or Tom Dowling in the *Washington Star-News* talking about "a chilling network of corruption and bribery of unprecedented scope," or Jack Anderson telling about money whispered to be in a secret Swiss bank account, or the *New York Times* reporting that a public interest law firm had accused us of granting favors, bribery and fraud, or

---

7. Typical of the spirit of the times, a New York architectural firm as late as December 1973 contended to the press that it had lost a $500,000 government contract in 1972 because one of its partners refused to make a contribution to the Nixon campaign. Senator Proxmire instantly demanded an investigation. All that had happened was that the partner had been telephoned by a part-time college student engaged with others in a large-scale telephone operation asking for small gifts all over the country (the average was $50). He had contributed $15 and was asked to give again, but refused. It was absurd to suggest that we could coordinate that phone operation with pending contract bids across the government, as all that the callers knew were phone numbers, and they had no idea of business affiliations. Nor did it make sense to presume there could be any system of following up on any declinations. This is a good example of the mob effect when anyone, whatever the motive or the circumstances, can join in an outcry and point a finger.

Woodward and Bernstein writing in the *Washington Post* that "at least $500,000 to $650,000 more was spent on clandestine activities," or *Time* saying that up to $1 million in a safe in my office was earmarked for security or intelligence purposes, with "some of it sent through Mexico to conceal the identity of the sources," or UPI reporting that "there have been charges of government favors to the carpet industry after funds were contributed," or Eileen Shanahan averring in the *New York Times* that "Mr. Stans and Mr. Kalmbach were selling 'protection' . . . what happened wasn't bribery but extortion . . . Enforcers for the mob could not be more insistent in demanding protection payoffs than were the President's fund raisers in 1972," or a *Times* editorial speaking of "the buying of government favors with campaign contributions or their extortion on pain of disfavor," or the *Washington Post* pontificating about "assorted governmental favors—ambassadorships, tax breaks, subsidies, benevolent anti-trust rulings," or the *New York Times* quoting Senator Mondale about "shakedown tactics," "government up for sale to the highest bidder," and "simple extortion, the collection of protection money," or UPI and the *Washington Post* mentioning a report that we laundered $2 million through banks and gambling casinos in the Bahamas, or *Newsweek* estimating that "the total cash allotments for CRP espionage purposes run as high as $900,000, and the donations that may have violated Federal election or influence-peddling laws" amount to $1,616,500. Whatever the sources to which these stories were attributed, or whether a source was indicated, the effect was the same, on the reader and on me. It may have been the greatest catalog of crimes ever pointed at a single person, and it was all false. I wondered if justice was still possible, whether a free press had the right to go this far, whether anyone could live through such an irresponsible and unjustified beating.

To all this were added biting satirizations on national radio and television shows—Merv Griffin,*The Sonny and Cher Comedy Hour*, Murray Kempton, and who knows how many others, assassinations by the bitter cartoons of Herblock, and pillory in a snide pamphlet called the "Watergate Coloring Book."

By the end of May, all these stories merged into a blur as they were reported over and over again, enhanced by the new accounts before and after the Vesco indictment, stories of civil suits being filed, new revelations about Watergate. Watergate-related news held the headlines every day, with other critical stories in between. Elliot Richardson became Attorney General after delayed hearings and named Archibald Cox as special prosecutor; John Loeb pleaded guilty to improper use of names on contributions to Democratic hopeful Humphrey; Kalmbach admitted handling money that was paid to the burglars; the Nebraska finance committee lost a $10,000 check; the SEC filed charges against Nixon contributor C. Arnholt Smith (his money had been returned); the FBI began investigating a $50,000 Nixon contribution by Lehigh Valley Cooperative Farmers; the Maryland committee admitted borrowing $50,000 from the Nixon campaign to pad the receipts of an Agnew testimonial affair; an elevator fire occurred on the same floor as the finance committee; the Ervin hearings began; Congressman Mills of Maryland committed suicide, apparently over a $25,000 campaign loan; Nixon was accused of using campaign funds to fix up San Clemente; on and on. Arm-twisting—secret funds—extortion—government favors—corporate contributions—milk—ITT—Segretti—GAO investigations—Vesco—. All I could think was, "Good God! What next?"

The maelstrom held me tightly, motionless, except as its deadly force drew me downward. There were now columns of stories daily, hours of radio and TV comment, and I felt it all pressing on me. How could I ever prove that I was just a bystander, innocent of willful culpability?

# 10

## COUNTRY LAWYER

I prayed for strength to endure the long night. I took counsel from churchmen I respected, including Dr. Norman Vincent Peale of Marble Collegiate Church in New York, and Dr. George Stone of Unity Center of Christianity in Washington. I took time for meditation, searching for the insight that would show me a way out. Gradually there came an inner solace that grew into a confidence that somehow it would still end well. I gathered my facts to meet the onslaught that I knew was still ahead, preparing an opening statement for the Senate Watergate hearings, gathering pages and volumes of data, looking forward to my first opportunity to tell a full, connected, clear story as to how I had conducted myself in the fund-raising of 1972. On June 12, 1973, I was ready and confident as I walked into the packed Senate Caucus room and faced the seven-man Senate Watergate Committee (officially the Select Committee on Presidential Campaign Activities) headed by Democratic Senator Sam Ervin, in an open hearing before national television cameras.[1]

Insofar as I was concerned, this was the big event of the year.

---

1. The Committee consisted of seven Senators, of whom four were Democrats (Sam Ervin of North Carolina, Daniel K. Inouye of Hawaii, Joseph Montoya of New Mexico, and Herman E. Talmadge of Georgia) and three were Republicans (Howard Baker of Tennessee, Edward J. Gurney of Florida, and Lowell Weicker of Connecticut).

I was the seventeenth witness, and I had listened to or read the narrations of those who appeared before me. That was enough to tell me what to expect. The committee was slow and repetitious, the questions of both counsel and committee members were usually inept, and there was no followup in the questioning to develop points or to bring out both sides. The atmosphere was so bitter that Republican members were hesitant to show sympathy or understanding for a witness, or to help to develop his story. Counsel for witnesses were not permitted to ask questions. It was up to a witness to find openings in which to explain or justify his actions as best he could or he might find himself creating a negative record on the basis of the biased questions of the committee's lawyers and members.

Ervin himself played a rough game designed to emphasize the importance of his contribution to the hearings, while at the same time piously asserting that he was only a country lawyer and hamming up his act like a medieval clown. If a witness pleaded guilty to a crime with suitable penitence to satisfy Ervin, he was extolled as a virtuous boon to society. If he sought instead to deny guilt, he was brutally attacked as a master criminal. There was no place in Ervin's categories for an innocent person who protested his innocence. A protestation of innocence was ipso facto evidence of guilt, and Ervin made the most of that conclusion by savage insinuating questioning that was designed to convince the television audience that he was the ringmaster whipping into line a troop of dangerous criminals.

There was a great amount of consideration by my lawyers about my legal plight in testifying. At the time of my scheduled appearance before the Committee, I was under indictment in New York in the Vesco case, and they felt that any public appearance by me would create publicity that would be harmful to my defense there.

Instead of letting Ervin take the entire lead, my chief counsel, Robert Barker, decided to alter the pace by putting the Committee in a defensive posture for the first time. Relying on Supreme Court cases involving prejudicial publicity, he made a ten-minute legal presentation of valid reasons why I should not be required to testify in Washington at the time, to spare me "the inevitable kleig light of publicity," since "inevitably, directly or indirectly, this hearing will influence any jury which might be called to hear the case in New York." Recognizing the validity of his argument, Ervin commended him on it, but remained adamant that he wanted my story.

However, the Committee did agree to exclude from its hearing any references to the Vesco case. Since it was clear that a refusal to go ahead would have made the public think I had guilty knowledge to conceal and also probably would have brought down on me a citation of contempt by the Senate, I testified fully and responsively, but with a deep concern that it would be impossible ever to overcome the harmful effects of the nationwide exposure to the Ervin tactics. Nevertheless, our efforts placed my appearance in a different perspective from those who preceded me.

Just before the questioning began, an amusing event occurred. Senator Lowell Weicker announced that, since I had campaigned in Connecticut for his opponent in 1970 he would not ask me any questions, as doing so might be construed that he was trying to get even. My memory bank didn't respond quickly enough for me to argue that point on the spot, but the Senator was wrong. I had not campaigned for his opponent. My only appearance in Connecticut in 1970 was at a fund-raising affair of a Republican party organization in Hartford in July, at which no specific candidates were endorsed by anyone because it was before the primary election when the party's nominee would be selected. Both Weicker and his opponent were invited to the affair, but Weicker didn't come. His opponent did, and I was introduced to him and photographed shaking hands with him. That was all. However, I did appreciate Weicker's chivalry and was not ungrateful that I would be questioned by only six Senators instead of seven, especially since Weicker turned out to have a sharp tongue.

In order that there would be no doubt on the part of the Committee as to my exact position on the subject of its hearings, I took full advantage of its policy of allowing witnesses to present an opening statement. At the beginning, I said unequivocally and confidently:

"I had no knowledge of the Watergate break-in or any other espionage efforts, before I read about them in the press, or of the efforts to cover up after the event.

"I had no knowledge of any sabotage program to disrupt the campaign by Segretti or anyone else.

"To the best of my knowledge there were no intentional violations of the laws relating to campaign financing by the finance committees for which I had the responsibility. Because of the complexity of the new law that became effective in the course of the campaign, and the vast amount of work that had to be done, there may have been some unintended technical violations by the committee."

One thing that troubled me in advance of my appearance was that no one had laid a foundation for the financial side of the questioning. The testimony had proceeded directly to isolated details without any background as to how the finance committee worked or what the duties and responsibilities of its principals were. This allowed our committee to be judged in the same context and setting as the campaign committee, where the full responsibility actually lay. I saw the necessity, for the record at least, of making some distinctions, which I described in my statement as follows:

"The campaign committee had all of the responsibility for the planning of the campaign, the development of its strategy and the execution of its tactics. The questions of how many people to employ, the efforts to be expended in each state, the determination of the relative use of direct mail, personal solicitations and media advertising, the kinds of appeals to voters, and the entire gamut of the political effort was developed, organized, managed and conducted by the campaign committee. In effect, their decisions fixed the amount the campaign would cost.

"The finance committee had no part in any of these basic decisions. The role of the finance committee was directed toward a single objective—to raise enough money to pay the bills. The finance committee had nothing to say about which bills to incur. Under the arrangements in effect, the finance committee paid any bill or made any payment which bore the approval of an appropriate official of the campaign committee."

After thus pointing out the separate missions of the two

committees as being in "watertight" compartments, I went on to elaborate upon other important distinctions, such as that the responsibilities for accounting and reporting were fixed by law in the treasurer and not the chairman, the differences in requirements between the old and new laws especially with regard to the right of privacy to contributors, and the scope of activities before and after I joined the committee. If the Senators and the public would come to understand those differences, I felt they would see how the finance committee would readily be absolved from Watergate responsibility, except of course for Liddy who had been pawned off to it by Magruder and had been directed by Magruder in his illegal actions at Watergate.

Beyond the fact that Senator Baker called me a "strong witness," I never learned how much of my message got through. However, my answers seemed to be taken as satisfactory until the order of questioning came around to Ervin, whose interrogation was biased, insinuating, argumentative, at times irrelevant, and certainly designed more to prove his tough stance than to develop information. I was taken aback at first when he began his grandstanding attack, wondering whether to respond in kind or to sit calmly and take it, doing my best to meet irrational questions with rational answers. I decided that he had the drop on me in any debate in his style, and that my best course was to keep cool and calm. I did so.

The net effect of my answers to all the other Senators' questions seemed to be satisfactory. I felt that I had clearly demonstrated that there had been no complicity in Watergate on my part. This obviously did not fit Ervin's two-category classification of witnesses being either "guilty with penitence" or "guilty without penitence," because he eventually found one issue which he kept drumming in subsequent sessions with other witnesses, especially Henry Petersen and Richard Kleindienst. It was that they had been guilty of improper conduct in allowing me to testify by deposition on August 2, 1972, rather than making me appear before the grand jury; his contention was that the jurors might have asked me more questions which could have produced information that would have disclosed that a coverup was going on. He went out of his way almost a year later to reassert this in another Senate committee hearing on the nomination of Earl Silbert to be United States District Attorney, even though it was clearly established in the record of the Watergate hearings that the procedure was wholly legal and was backed by precedent.[2] I had no opportunity on either occasion to answer the charge or to point out that the same proposition could be advanced much more logically with respect to other witnesses. What I had learned about Watergate by June 1973, and could tell the Committee then, was a lot more than I knew in August 1972 when I testified for the grand jury.

The prejudice against me in the hearings was evident from the beginning. I had no more than given my name when Rufus Edmisten, Deputy Counsel to the Committee, who had long been personally associated with Ervin, began the questioning by bringing out a memorandum addressed by Magruder to Mitchell stating that, while Secretary of Commerce, I had accumulated a political fund of $1 million in the department to use for the 1972 election. In the previous weeks I had spent about four hours with Edmisten and his staff in preparation for testimony, reviewing my knowledge on all possible subjects; also my lawyers had met on several occasions with Edmisten, whom Barker had known for some years, and he had assured them of his desire to be completely fair and to spring no surprises. Despite this, the memorandum had never surfaced. Using it in the hearing was obviously a ploy to get headlines, to disconcert me at the outset, and perhaps break down my composure for the remainder of the day. I had no recollection of such a memorandum and had no such fund, but all I could do was to plead surprise and deny knowledge.[3] The damage was nevertheless done, and the news stories carried banner headlines about my $1 million "slush fund." The *New York Daily News*, the paper with the largest circulation in the United States, gave six inches of its front page to this heading:

REPORT SECRET
$1M NIXON FUND

---

2. Before the Senate hearings concluded, Baker apologized in an open session for having said that the taking of my deposition had been improper procedure, as he had learned there were precedents for it. Ervin, however, obstinately said he still regarded it as an irregular procedure.

3. Edmisten, who thus pitched the first curves against me in the hearing, was elected Attorney General of the state of North Carolina in 1974, and shortly after was found guilty of "willful and unlawful" failure to file state income tax returns for 1972 and 1973.

The article cited the Magruder memorandum and my denial. It went on to say that this would represent "misuse of government funds," a violation of Federal law. In its net effect, I felt that it was a devastating story, even though untrue, as I soon established. Within a short time my attorney secured affidavits from three former officials of the Department of Commerce disproving the whole tale, and submitted them to Ervin with the request that they be read in the televised hearings before the same national audience. Despite frequent prodding by my attorney, Ervin did not do anything until July 29, almost seven weeks later, when, after being pushed by Senator Baker and Fred Thompson, minority counsel, he allowed the affidavits to be placed into the record, without a reading, but accompanied by a slurring remark. The news reports of this correction appeared, if they appeared at all, at the tail-end of articles on the highlighted testimony then being given by John Ehrlichman.

Another evidence of the Committee staff's mental predestination was in the summoning of John Priestes several months later to testify before the Committee that one of our fund-raisers, Ben Fernandez of our Hispanic Finance Committee, had arranged a meeting for him with me to determine whether I could help him in problems before the Department of Housing and Urban Development. The consideration was an alleged contribution to be in the amount of $50,000. At the time Priestes testified, the Senate Committee staff knew that Priestes had been convicted of fraud in his HUD dealings, and that Fernandez had convincingly disproved every charge made by Priestes. What had really happened was that Fernandez had brought Priestes to me as a potential contributor, that Priestes had tendered a $25,000 check, that I was suspicious about his story of being harassed by the Miami press, that I refused on the spot to accept the money, that I checked with HUD immediately after the meeting and found that Priestes was in serious trouble, and that I at once directed Fernandez to return the check which he was holding and terminate the discussions. Fernandez so testified the next day, as the Committee's staff well knew he would, and his recital of these facts cleared me completely. Yet the testimony was unfairly allowed to proceed, despite prior advice to them of these circumstances, and damaging first-day news stories were a natural consequence which

Fernandez' later testimony could not counterbalance, even though Priestes himself agreed that my account of the meeting was "basically true."

In an attempt to prove impropriety on my part in making solicitations, Ervin pushed one witness, Orin Atkins of Ashland Oil Company, to get him to say he was unduly pressured. This colloquy took place:

**Sen. Ervin:** Mr. Atkins, it looks to me as if Mr. Stans had made an assessment.

**Mr. Atkins:** I think that is a correct assessment.

**Sen. Ervin:** In other words, he told you in effect that he would let you off with a contribution of $100,000 . . . ?

**Mr. Atkins:** I believe you are right.

**Sen. Ervin:** He never left you much option in the matter, did he?

**Mr. Atkins:** I don't believe so. It is true that I didn't have much of an option.

**Sen. Ervin:** And so departing from the realm of politics into the spiritual, the method of raising campaign contributions now borders on extortion, does it not?

**Mr. Atkins:** Very much so.

Ervin might have asked more objective and less leading questions that would have cast the Atkins contribution in an entirely different light, and Atkins could have been more forthright. Neither took the pains to say that Atkins had given the same amount through another person in 1968 for the Nixon campaign, which might have implied that he was willingly "extortable." Since our committee certainly had no base from which to apply pressure in 1968, it belied any assertion of extortion. What I had asked him in my solicitation in 1972 was whether he would try to raise as much for our committee from his people as the $100,000 that he had raised the last time. Nor did Atkins acknowledge until 1974 that he had made a number of similar contributions in cash, including $50,000 in 1970 to Robert Strauss, the Democratic National Finance Chairman. He didn't say whether this had been extorted.[4]

---

4. By January 1975, Atkins had softened his remarks to the point of saying that "these contributions were made with the genuine belief that they were necessary and in the best interest of the company, given the political environment which existed."

The most cynical aspect of Ervin's intimidating interrogation of Atkins, and Atkins' weak and conciliatory replies, was that the Watergate Special Prosecutor had already found to the contrary and this should have been known to Ervin or his staff:

> . . . we have no evidence that Ashland sought or was offered any particular quid pro quo or favor in consideration of its contribution. Rather, as Atkins stated, Ashland contributed because it was 'expected . . . generally done—[and] accepted' . . . We have no evidence that Stans or anyone else exerted intense, improper or 'extortive' pressure on Atkins.
>
> The evidence of prior acts and attitudes [by Atkins] indicates purposeful, wholesale, 'hard core' violations.[5]

Similarly, in his questioning of Claude Wild, an official of Gulf Oil Company, Ervin implied that we had used coercion to induce a contribution. Gulf's contribution, which we likewise understood to be from its employees but turned out to be from illegal corporate funds, was $100,000. The implication of coercion stuck at the time but became absurdity when it was disclosed in 1975 that Gulf had distributed $2.3 million in hundreds of political gifts to many candidates of both parties over a period of ten years, as part of a secret slush fund of many millions.

I was less than pleased by Ervin's practice of asking these leading questions in his efforts to incriminate me, and even less so by the willingness of three or four thoroughly cowed witnesses to go along with him under the pressure. Not all did so, and I was delighted when Russell DeYoung, chairman of Goodyear, responded right back to Ervin that the contribution "was made solely because we thought the reelection of the President was in the best interest of the country. It was not made with a view to obtaining government favors. Nor was I pressured in any way into making it." That was a far more honest answer. No contributor gave under coercion or extortion or for any other reason known to me than a desire to help in the reelection of Richard Nixon.

Ervin had a way, too, of making statements not supported by

---

5. Watergate prosecutive memorandum of September 4, 1973, by Thomas F. McBride and Roger M. Witten.

the record. He repeated several times the contention that some $100 bills found on the persons of the Watergate burglars had been traced to the proceeds of the Dahlberg and Mexican checks, despite the unequivocal testimony of Patrick Gray, head of the FBI, that such a connection had never been established. He zeroed in on me a few times for not having required our treasurer to keep records of the committee's payments in cash, notwithstanding his undoubted knowledge that it was not customary to do so, that under the law no records of such transactions were required to be kept before April 7, 1972, and that at least two Democratic candidates had not retained their cash records for the same period.

When it got to noon of the second day of my testimony, I went alone to a nearby hotel room rather than back to the office so that I could relax a bit and think over the situation at that point. As I lay on the bed looking at the ceiling, I realized that nothing had been said in the record on behalf of the innocent people who had been victimized by Watergate, including many of the contributors. I also wanted to express a plea for my own exoneration, so I made a few notes on the back of an envelope and returned to the hearing room. Barker encouraged me to go ahead, in the interest of fairness and, hopefully, as a change in the direction of the hearings. Just before stepping down from the witness stand, I delivered these final remarks in essentially extemporaneous form:

> "Mr. Chairman, I want to thank the Committee for your consideration and for the opportunity to me to present my story for the first time. I hope that it creates a picture of a very difficult undertaking, a frenzied activity on my part and on the part of the finance committee in trying to meet the obligations of the campaign. I have done my best to recall from all the records I have everything to answer the Committee's questions but I am only human and I can only tell what I know.
> "Now, I do want to say something about three elements: First, I would like to talk about the people in the finance committee . . . under the conditions of separateness between the two committees, I am confident that no one in the

finance committee, except of course Gordon Liddy, had any knowledge of or participation in the Watergate affair or any other espionage or sabotage activities.

"When all the testimony is in in the course of your hearings, I am confident that you will find everyone connected with the finance committee has cooperated fully, and that all of them are innocent of any involvement. I want to say so particularly with respect to our two treasurers, Hugh Sloan and Paul Barrick.

"The second thing I would like to talk about briefly concerns the contributors. Among all of our committees in this campaign there were about a million contributions received for the President and the Republican Party. Some of them came from wealthy people, some of them came from people in the middle economic strata and some from poor people. We received amounts from one dollar or less up to a very large amount of a million or more. I have always urged people in the course of my travels and solicitation to contribute according to their means, according to their ability to give, just as they pay taxes.

"So it is true there were some large contributions, some very large contributions. But the idea is being purveyed in some circles that no one gives a substantial amount of money to a campaign without buying something in return, without the expectation of a favor.

"I think most of the members of the Committee would agree with me that this is vicious, that it is a lie, and it is belittling to our self-respect as a people.

"I would like to give a couple of examples. Clement Stone of Chicago, pretty well known now, gave $2 million to elect the President. He gave a lot in 1968. He is a very wealthy man and he can afford it. He believes in the President and knows him as a friend. Clement Stone has never asked for anything from his government or the administration in return. He has done it because he believes it is a public service from a man of wealth.

"I would like to give you another case: Ray Kroc is a man in Chicago who is responsible for the development of the McDonald hamburger chain. I visited with him in Chicago in September for about 45 minutes. I had never met him before.

I talked about the campaign and we discussed his success story. Mr. Kroc said, 'On October 3rd, I am going to have my 70th birthday, and in appreciation for what I have been able to achieve I am going to give millions of dollars of my money to charity.'

"I said, 'Mr. Kroc, you are a beneficiary of the great American system and I am sure you believe in it. I have reason to believe that you think the President will help to preserve that system and I would like to make a suggestion. When you get to October 3 and make those distributions to charity, why don't you at the same time give $250,000 to help reelect the President.' He did. There was no discussion in that meeting of anything else.

"Now, what happened after his contribution became known? First the press accused him of making the contribution so that he could influence the Price Commission on matters affecting his company.

"Secondly, he was accused of making the contribution so that he could get a lower minimum wage for the young people who work for his company. He was insulted by these insinuations and falsehoods, they were vicious and unfair, completely conjectural without any fact whatever.

"My point is, there are many people like Mr. Kroc who believe in the country, who believe in the Party, who believe in its principles, and who may believe at a given time in a candidate. There are very few people who want to collect in return for their contribution, and they don't get very far under either Party that is in power, Democrats or Republicans.

"I think the time has come to express more confidence in the honor and integrity of our fellowmen, whether they are rich or poor, and stop manufacturing reasons to attack people who merely exercise their right of citizenship by making a political contribution.

"I want to say one thing more about innocent people and I will be finished. In the course of all the things that have happened since June 17, a lot of innocent people have been drawn through the mire of unrelenting publicity, insinuations, accusations, charges. To name a few, Kenneth Dahlberg, Dwayne Andreas, Robert Allen, and there are a considerable number of others, who paid a horrible price merely because they participated in a campaign as a contributor or as a worker, a price in time and in expenses and even in their reputations. There have been very damaging effects on their businesses and on their personal lives. It is very unfair. Somebody has got to speak up for those people. So when the Committee concludes its work and writes its report, I hope it will make it clear that such people, and by name, are innocent victims of this tragedy. I hope that people like Hugh Sloan and others in the limelight of adverse publicity will be directly cleared.

"I put myself in that category. I volunteered or was drafted, whatever the case may be, because I believed in my President. You know by now from what you have heard, but I know you cannot feel, the abuse to which I have been subjected because of the associations I fell into. All I ask, Mr. Chairman and Members of the Committee, is that when you write your report you give me back my good name."

It seemed to me that someone had to speak for these people and I was the only one who did throughout all the days of hearings. My pleas were ignored in the Committee's final report. I did, however, receive hundreds and hundreds of letters from understanding strangers, who felt I had exhibited commendable restraint in not responding more toughly to Ervin's calculated baiting. The only acknowledgment I received from the Committee for my testimony came two months later: For my two days of testimony, I was sent a check for $25 by the Senate for *one* day's witness fee.

Even after my testimony, staff members of the Ervin Committee continued to leak prejudicial remarks. For example, on September 10, 1973, the *Washington Star-News* quoted an "official" of the Committee as saying that David Dorsen, its assistant Democratic counsel in charge of the campaign finance inquiry, had assembled information that would "show a pattern of use of government instrumentalities to pressure people and companies into making campaign contributions." No such pattern was ever proved, because it did not exist.

Press, radio, and television reports about my testimony were generally fair and objective. The stories centered mostly on the charge that I had accumulated a political fund of $1 million in the Department of Commerce (which was later proved to be false); that I had destroyed some records of the finance committee after the burglary (which we were not required to keep, and which in any event we were able to reconstruct fully from data that we retained); and that there was skepticism among members of the Ervin panel that I could be so close to the center of the campaign and not know about Watergate (which some commentators repeated on their own). The sharp grilling by Ervin was frequently mentioned, as was my unshaken insistence of innocence. Almost all mentioned my closing plea to the Committee to "give me back my good name," and Senator Baker's remark in a subsequent interview that "only the verdict of time will tell. I hope it turns out that way." I was content with that. I had long wanted the opportunity to tell my story in full, rather than in pieces, and that had now been done. What I had said to the Ervin Committee and the American public was truthful in every detail, and no single sentence of my testimony was ever shown to be wrong. No evidence to the contrary was ever forthcoming, despite the testimony of a parade of witnesses, the full unfolding of the events of Watergate in the trials of those found guilty, and the years of the churning publicity about the event.

I was pleased to note that others felt the same as I did about Ervin's treatment. The only one who objected in the course of his questioning of me during the hearing was Committee member Edward J. Gurney, who interrupted to say that he "did not appreciate the harassment of this witness." That had not deterred Ervin. On July 3, 1973, Bernard Levin, a columnist for the *Times* of London, and presumably without bias in American politics, characterized his tactics in this language:

> . . . the conduct of the chairman, Senator Sam Ervin, is so deplorable that the lack of any serious protest against his behavior is itself a measure of the loss of nerve on the part of so many distinguished Americans.
>
> Worse than Senator Ervin's yokum-hokum is the way in which he has clearly decided that some of those appearing before him under suspicion of various malpractices are heroes, and some

villains. Mr. Maurice Stans, for instance, was a villain, his interrogation was relentless, entirely hostile, and plainly based on an assumption that Stans was guilty of everything of which he was accused and a good deal more besides.

The technique was exactly the one used by Senator Joseph McCarthy. Those who stood up to him, denied his accusations, and refused to implicate anyone else were torn to pieces; those who agreed with everything he said and hastened to add the names of others were given an easy passage and congratulated at the end of their session.

The method of senatorial inquisition . . . is unable to determine the question of guilt or innocence in respect of any individual . . . . What it will quite certainly do, however, is to ruin a number of men, some of whom will not deserve ruin . . . .

The *Chicago Tribune* made similar observations about Ervin's manner of treatment:

Sam Ervin did a disservice to his image as an impartial fact-finder when he slammed shut the locks of a pillory this week about the head of former Commerce Secretary Maurice H. Stans . . . . What ticked us off was the manner in which Ervin conducted his interrogation, an event that took on the form more of a terribly argumentative inquisition rather than a calm, reasoned effort to arrive at the facts. Overnight, the 76-year-old senator's style suddenly became that of a bully playing to the gallery in an outburst of showmanship seemingly designed to solicit applause. Ervin could have asked his questions of Stans in a calm manner devoid of the almost bludgeoning, harassing manner with which he handled the exchange.

Others seemed to feel I had nevertheless come out well. The *New York Times* said that "the interrogation, toughest in the ten days of hearings, failed to shake the testimony." The *Chicago Sun-Times* said that the "hard questioning" had "failed to establish any direct contradiction in his testimony." I was proud to read what *Newsweek* had to say about Ervin's long and punishing cross-examination: "Stans took all this with an ineffable calm, the product of breeding, success, and practice before a hundred Congressional hearings; it was the Committee whose temper showed through.

Needless to say, I followed the Ervin Committee hearings closely, both before and after my own appearance, to learn what other witnesses were saying. As the whole story unfolded, my name was not mentioned often by other witnesses. I had a deep concern, however, that a casual or careless remark by someone, motivated by his own defense or merely given in ignorance, would put me in an undeserved bad light, so I followed closely every sentence in which my name appeared. There were three or four such incidents, in fact, but none of any lasting significance. McCord made an unknowing misstatement about sending some illicit intelligence reports to me through Sloan, but this was wrong and was corrected in the record. Magruder at one point used careless language that seemed to imply that I had been told fully about the Watergate affair at a meeting with him and Mitchell on June 24, a week after the burglary, and some members of the Ervin Committee leaped to the eager conclusion that I may have thereby become implicated. However, he cleared this up later, upon questioning, by saying in effect that I had not been clued in at all to the story of the break-in or intended coverup; that the only things I was told on that date were that "an operation we had knowledge of got fouled up; that Liddy was involved and probably would have to be fired; that Sloan was not discussing with us in any legitimate terms how much money had been given to Liddy and it was important for us to know." Mitchell later confirmed this account of the meeting.

John Dean, on one occasion, misspoke himself by saying that in the early days of his involvement in the coverup he was carrying messages between several persons, naming me as one of them, about how it was being handled. This was absolutely untrue insofar as I was concerned, and my records showed that from June 17 to August 9, the period Dean was referring to, I had no meetings with him and only two unrelated phone calls. Nothing in the accounts at the hearings bore out his statement and it dropped out of sight. On another day, when he was asked to identify the persons involved in the Watergate crimes, he gave the names of his accomplices and then, apparently as an afterthought, listed mine followed by a question mark. Later in his testimony he explained this by saying he had no direct dealings with me that would indicate complicity on my part, and just mentioned me as a precaution since I might have been involved without his knowledge.

Sloan caused me some embarrassment by saying in his testimony that on the day I had verified Magruder's authority to direct him to make payments to Liddy, I had said, "I don't know and you don't want to know." Upon questioning, he put this remark into its proper context of the continuing differences between the campaign committee and the finance committee about the level of spending, and indicated that I was unhappy and had "essentially thrown up my hands about the loss of control over the funds." He said he had the impression that this was just a runaway situation and I had lost the argument. He was right. I so testified myself a few days later, indicating that my recollection of the import of my words was more along the lines of a disgusted, "I don't know what's going on in this campaign, and I don't think you ought to try to know."

Such matters sound petty now in retrospect, but I thought seriously of them at the time they occurred because the media pounced on them in headline stories. Each one, until corrected, gave me the fright that such statements would remain unchallenged in the record and would continually haunt me because I could not prove otherwise and would be reduced to mere general denials. The clarification of each of these untoward remarks by their makers gave me the relief and release I had to have to be positioned in the clear. The amplifications, however, did not come until after the headline writers had used the harmful statements, and the later correction, as usual, got little or no play. All of these examples merely added to the terror, day by day, that Watergate continued to inflict.

When various intimations of improper practices or corruption in the 1972 finance efforts surfaced in the hearings, my attorney, Robert Barker, wrote Chairman Ervin on February 7, 1974, denying their accuracy, presenting data in substantiation, and asking that his letter be placed in the record of the hearings. Ervin refused to do so on the ground that counsel had no first-hand knowledge of the facts and could not properly testify. This did not seem fair treatment, in view of the latitude he had allowed for secondhand and hearsay testimony throughout the hearings, and Barker continued to press, but Ervin was adamant in his refusal. It would have done his Committee no disservice, and would have cleared the air in justice to me, had he entered the letter in the record.

The Senate hearings lasted for many weeks through a long string of witnesses to fix the responsibility for Watergate, and then moved into campaign "dirty tricks," with election financing matters to follow. When Ervin and his staff began to discover that some of the Democratic candidates may have been liable for violations, their ardor cooled. Fred Thompson, the chief Republican counsel for the Committee, confirmed this later in his book,[6] saying that "improper Democratic campaign activities were not being looked into with anything like the gusto or detail that was being used in examining the Republicans," and " . . . some of the Democrats on the Committee were trying to suppress some of the essences of Democratic wrongdoing." He also related how the Committee's report was altered at the insistence of Humphrey, to soften its criticisms. His indictment of these practices, containing many details, is very convincing.

Herbert Alexander[7], who made an intensive inquiry into the financial accounts of the 1972 election, reached the same conclusions: " . . . the accounts of Chestnut (Humphrey's campaign manager) have not been investigated with the same detail given to the (Nixon) financing. It was not until late in its investigation that the Watergate Committee publicized information about Humphrey and other Democrats, and then the disclosures came from Republican minority members. None of the investigations of Special Prosecutor Leon Jaworski, the GAO, or the Justice Department seemed to have dealt extensively with some of the questions raised."

In a way, it is too bad that the Senate Watergate hearings did not go further into campaign financing matters. If they had, they would have disclosed in advance the answers to many of the questions later pressed on me by the Special Prosecutor; and they would have uncovered the many more serious instances of violations by other candidates than by us. It would have become gen-

6. Fred Thompson, *At That Point in Time*, (New York: Quadrangle/New York Times Book Co., 1975), pp. 195-202.
7. Herbert Alexander, *Financing the 1972 Election*, supra.

erally evident that the amounts unknowingly received by us from
some of the companies were minor parts of large cash funds they
dispersed for political causes, thus shattering the idea that we
had induced or somehow contrived the illegal system.

In particular, the Humphrey finances were never seriously
probed in the hearings, although the GAO found that his committee had a considerable string of serious violations. McGovern's
people were not publicly questioned by the Ervin Committee,
and Sam Ervin graciously wrote a letter on July 26, 1974, to
McGovern, saying: "We found no activities whatsoever which
could be called illegal, unethical or improper in the conduct of
your campaign." Yet the reports of the GAO showed that McGovern committees had many violations, none of which was prosecuted, and some of which were allowed to be corrected without
charges being filed.

Congressman Wilbur Mills, who later was found to have
received substantial amounts of illegal dairy industry funds,
ducked an appearance before Ervin by just not responding to the
Committee's invitation.

My award for the outstanding finesse of the year, however,
went to Hubert Humphrey. Ervin wrote Humphrey on January
24, 1974, asking him to meet with the Committee staff regarding
some milk industry contributions to his campaign. He followed
up with a second letter on February 5, saying that such a meeting
would be designed "to provide certain specifics regarding the
inquiries the committee wishes to make . . . [and] we feel it necessary for a committee member to speak with you regarding these
circumstances. There are also certain records in your files that
the committee wishes to examine . . . ." Humphrey replied to
both letters on February 20, saying, "Because I know nothing
about the transaction and have no records in my files relating to
it, I see no point in inconveniencing any member of the committee to meet with me." This was several months *after* the GAO had
found massive lapses in financial reporting by Humphrey's committee. Yet nothing more happened. Humphrey's chairman then
invoked the Fifth Amendment and refused to testify. This set of
circumstances caused the *Washington Star-News* to wonder in
an editorial:

It is passing strange that so little has been made of Democratic misdeeds. Imagine how the blood, subpoenas and leaks would have flowed had a Nixon official invoked the Fifth Amendment to keep from testifying or had sent a letter to the committee saying he wouldn't show up because he didn't want to inconvenience the committee.

In view of my experience, it is hard for me to be wholly objective about the value of the hearings of the Ervin Committee. They certainly interfered with the administration of justice by the Watergate Special Prosecutor, as he made clear. Their avowed purpose of gathering information in order to determine what new legislation was desirable, a normal function of a Congressional committee, could have been accomplished more calmly and objectively after the Watergate criminal cases had been closed. They could have been conducted more like a hearing than a trial. The televised insights gratified public curiosity, but they also helped to whip up the frenzy of freehand journalism that inflated the Watergate chase to some of its destructive dimensions.

It cannot be denied that the hearings were politically inspired by the majority party in the Congress, and the record shows that in many ways they were politically directed and manipulated. Democratic members knew what they were after—the embarrassment of Richard Nixon—and Republicans were too intimidated and disorganized by the growing revelations to be willing to face the television cameras and insist on a cool, balanced investigation.

What the public did not know was the blatant hypocrisy of the four Democratic members of the Committee, all of whom sanctimoniously interrogated witnesses, they said, to "get the facts on the record." In 1964, when Bobby Baker, a protege of Senators Lyndon Johnson and Robert Kerr, was charged with running an influence-peddling operation in Washington for high stakes, the Democrats controlling the Senate had blocked an investigation; Ervin, Talmadge, and Inouye voted time after time to prevent the facts from coming out.

Three of them had campaign finance problems, too. In 1970, as pointed out in Chapter 2, Montoya and his campaigners had used nonreporting committees in the District of Columbia to launder the sources of more than $100,000 of funds for his Senate race, and then destroyed the records, to circumvent disclosure laws; and Inouye's organization was found guilty of accepting an illegal corporate contribution in 1974, which was after the Committee's work had been substantially completed.  In 1978, Talmage was in the headlines for a variety of unorthodox and possibly illegal financial transactions over a period of years, including being reimbursed for campaign expenditures in 1973 and 1974 that he never reported making, and receiving many thousands of dollars in gifts from constituents.  The discrepancies were explained by his staff as due to "clear oversight" and "careless bookkeeping."

# 11

## THE TRIAL OF THE CENTURY?

It is a screenplay for a Hollywood epic. The setting is more than common—a President in impeachment trouble, two of his Cabinet members accused of obstruction of justice, an alleged multimillionaire accomplice in flight across the border, an ambitious young prosecutor eager to create history, and enough visible money to leaven a good plot. The witnesses are unusual too: two of the President's brothers, his White House counsel, his personal secretary, two other Cabinet members, two successive heads of a top government regulatory agency, a one-time director of a national political party, and several ordinary folks who are said to have been in on the nefarious scheme.

The courtroom scene is dramatic and the tension builds up: one witness after another for the prosecution tells a story that splashes guilt over the two accused, only to have his tale demolished by a pinpointed cross-examination that brings out the untold truth to the contrary; bystanders change the odds daily on guilt or innocence; the press and TV cameras swarm over everyone to report the century's most heralded trial, with most of the stories assuming guilt.

The action then moves to the jury room and more drama: the jurors begin their deliberations, confused, uncertain, and noisily argumentative, getting nowhere until someone says: "Let's just decide who's telling the truth," and everyone calms down, and the verdict is agreed, and the courtroom hears it and breaks out in a bedlam of cheers for the two freed defendants, who smile through their tears in the final scene.

It's a sensational film. But Hollywood couldn't have made it because Hollywood deals in fiction and its writers couldn't have dreamed up such a scenario.

On May 10, 1973, John Mitchell, a former Attorney General of the United States, and I, a former Secretary of Commerce, were indicted together in Federal court in New York on ten counts of conspiracy, obstruction of justice, and perjury. The alleged criminal actions related to the months in 1972 when Mitchell was director of Richard Nixon's Committee for the Re-election of the President, and I was chairman of its finance committee. The trial began on February 20, 1974, and ended on April 28. The period of fifty weeks from the beginning to end of this experience took us through a bewildering wonderland of juridical process and media attention. The consequence was a continuing level of high suspense and emotion until the very last dramatic moment, when the verdict of our peers brought an end to the uncertainty.

"Not guilty! Not guilty! Not guilty!..."
The two words resounded through the dark New York courtroom eighteen times, answering the clerk's calls for a verdict on nine surviving counts against Mitchell and nine against me,[1] and the political trial of the century was over. We were free!
The timid voice of the twenty-one-year-old forelady of the jury was amplified by the breathless interest of the two hundred spectators and reporters in the room. When she finished the eighteenth recitation, there was a suppressed hush from the audience, straining to express emotions that had to be held back while the judge thanked the jury, and the nine men and three women filed out into the hall and back into the oblivion from which they had come ten weeks earlier. Then the judge left his

---

1. One count against each had been dismissed by the trial judge.

bench, and even before the door closed behind him, a pandemonium broke loose in the courtroom.

Reporters rushed to nearby telephones, the lines having been held open by associates, to pass the message to the world. Defense lawyers boisterously congratulated each other and their clients. Family members and friends gathered happily around Mitchell and me. Newsmen and newswomen thrust microphones in all directions, wanting immediate reactions from defendants, counsel, and bystanders. An atmosphere of ultimate joy overwhelmed me, and the only natural thing I could think of saying to them in the most emotional moment of my life was "I feel reborn," over and over again. The prosecution's four lawyers left the room with downcast eyes, pushing before them a large-wheeled cart containing voluminous documents now useless.

My older son, Steve, who had been with me in court during the last five days, sat in the audience with my loyal secretary, Arden Chambers, clutching each other's hands tightly in the tension of the moment as the jurors had filed in to give their verdict. When the first "not guilty" came forth, followed by the others, one by one, tears came to his eyes and he began to cry. The moment the proceedings were over, he rushed past the railing to where I sat at the counsel table and overwhelmed me with a big bear hug, sobbing and muttering incoherent words. I knew what he meant, and in that moment there was a feeling of mutual devotion that had never before been expressed so warmly between us.

I said a quiet "Thank God" to myself, and turned to greet my lawyers and congratulate Mitchell and his attorneys. That finished, I thought of Kathleen, sitting invalided in the uptown apartment loaned us by a friend for the duration of the trial. "Call Mother right away," I said to Steve, "and give her the news." He left, still sobbing uncontrollably, and that night Kathleen told me about the call.

"The phone rang and I picked up my cane and hobbled over to it," she reported. "I wasn't expecting a verdict at that time of day. When I put the receiver to my ear, all I could hear was someone weeping loudly, and between sobs I recognized Steve trying to say something. My spirits dropped and I summoned my courage to say, 'Give it to me straight, Steve. I can take it,' fearing the worst. It was almost a minute, and it seemed much longer, before he mastered control of himself and managed to yell into the phone, 'We won, Mom! We won!' and then resumed his sobbing. I walked proudly back to my chair and said a prayer of thanksgiving for a verdict that I had expected all along."

There were more interviews in the courtroom, a jammed press conference in the shabby waiting room that Mitchell and I had shared for endless days, a television interview on the steps of the courthouse, and more talk with reporters in my lawyers' suite at Essex House. This was my extemporaneous statement to the TV cameras:

> "When the indictment was handed down a year ago, I said I was innocent and was certain I would be found innocent when it was all over. That promise has been vindicated by this jury.
> "We got into this because we had great faith in a man, the President, and wanted to see him reelected. Everything I did in that connection was proper and right. The verdict of the jury establishes the fact that the type of exaggeration that has taken place in the last eighteen months is not only unfair, but it does not sell itself to the kind of people who were on the jury."

I talked briefly to Kathleen over the phone to explain the delay, and, when the proceedings were over, rushed to greet her in the apartment, where our arms and lips met with the accumulated love of the forty-one years since we had promised to sustain each other "for better or for worse." This was one of the better moments, but it had been long in coming.

Later in the afternoon, she accompanied me back to my lawyers' suite in their hotel, and we talked informally with still more reporters from the newspapers and television. But that was anticlimax, and I cut it short so we could return to our apartment and be alone. Freed from our oppressive burden, we sat and talked for a while, the sense of relief now overwhelming us both. It was a time for celebration, but the fatigue and strain that had been building up for so long would not leave at once, and we went to bed early, in a state of exhaustion. A long night of sleep finally freed us and we woke the next morning to the full realization that our lives were our own again. The crowning evidence of reality was the *New York Times* banner headline, "Mitchell and Stans Acquitted on All Counts." That above all seemed to close the ghastly chapter.

The trial had covered a time period of exactly seventy days, from beginning to end. The record of the proceedings embraced 10,000 pages. By the time the ordeal was over fourteen months had elapsed since I had first appeared before the Vesco grand jury and precisely eleven months and eighteen days had gone by since the *Times* headlined in blaring, front-page letters, "Mitchell and Stans Indicted." Its end was the end of my longest nightmare.

The next evening, at a party in our apartment for New York friends who had given us their thoughts and support, I took my first drink in fifteen years—six of them in fact, all champagne. I was light-headed when I went to bed, and light-hearted when Kathleen and I woke up the next morning to pick up the pieces of our interrupted lives and resume living as free persons. In the ensuing days, thousands of messages came from friends and strangers all around the country and all around the world. Only then did I recognize the intensity of interest the case had held and the importance it had been given. Foreign Minister Andrei Gromyko of the Soviet Union sent a telegram of congratulations through Henry Kissinger to President Nixon on the outcome.

The media had helped to make it so. "The first trial of a Cabinet officer since Teapot Dome," the Associated Press had earlier reported. "If found guilty, Mitchell and Stans could each be sentenced to forty-five years in prison and fined $85,000," the *New York Times* heralded, adding that it "is one of the most extraordinary criminal cases in the nation's history," and calling it "a criminal trial of high drama and historic impact." "The first time in American history that two Cabinet members were tried jointly on criminal charges," the *New York Daily News* asserted. It was, the AP contended, "a courtroom drama unparalleled in the last half century of American history." In the presumed but incorrect association of this case with the concurrent Watergate disclosures, the media saw the political trial of all time. The AP analyzed that we were only the third and fourth Cabinet members in United States history to be charged "in connection with their official political duties," inferring also that the trials of the other two were obviously less meaningful.

In the AP analysis and elsewhere, the Teapot Dome scandal of the 1920s was regularly reviewed and compared with our case. It had ended with a Secretary of the Interior, Albert B. Fall, found guilty of accepting a $100,000 bribe in return for granting drilling concessions on a major oil field owned by the government. Attorney General Harry Daugherty, although suspected and seemingly implicated, was never brought to court on Teapot Dome, but was later tried and acquitted on charges of conspiracy and taking bribes on other matters. In other articles, even the ghost of Aaron Burr and his treason trial was trotted out to find a scale against which to measure our transgressions.

How could all this happen? What trick of fate or deed of man had caused us to be put through the ordeal of defending our lives for the simple act, in this case, of receiving what I had every reason to believe was a legal and proper political contribution? What convolutions of the law wrought that into a cause celebre of criminal justice? Was the trial an act of justice or injustice?

There were two separate chains of events in the story of the Vesco case, one relating to me and the other to John Mitchell, and they did not touch each other except for one brief routine conversation between us. With that exception, Mitchell was not even aware of the events in which I participated, and I did not know of those in which he participated. It was the prosecution's strained attempt to merge the two scenarios into a conspiracy that created the issues that were the subjects of the trial.

My story began on February 13, 1972, a few days before I became finance chairman for Nixon's reelection race. Daniel Hofgren, a part-time volunteer in the fund-raising, buttonholed me to say that he had crossed the ocean by commercial plane on the day before, and had happened to sit next to a man named Gilbert Straub. After they had exchanged pleasantries and discussed various general topics, Hofgren learned that Straub was an associate of Robert Vesco, an international financier who headed International Controls Corporation in the United States and through that company controlled a group of large mutual investment funds. Hofgren remembered that Vesco had been a contributor to the Nixon 1968 campaign and recognized Straub as a door through which he could approach Vesco for support in 1972, so he broached the subject to Straub. Yes, Straub indicated, he was sure that Vesco would contribute again, perhaps substantially; he would talk to Vesco and get back to Hofgren.

Hofgren told me this with enthusiasm and I suggested that

he follow up and let me know the results. Later the same day he wrote a note telling me that "Gilbert Straub, Vesco's director, agreed on the amount of one hundred and will arrange for Vesco to confer with MS next week to deliver." In our shorthand lingo, "one hundred" meant $100,000, so this was to be a sizable contribution and I took a definite interest and told Hofgren to set up a meeting with Vesco at his convenience in my office.

I knew very little about Robert Vesco, and had never met him. However, he had a reputation generally as an up-from-poverty success story, who had acquired business fame by taking over International Controls when it was a small company and building it up to much larger proportions through a series of acquisitions, some bold and a bit tempestuous. By 1969 his company's sales had mushroomed to more than $100 million and its annual earnings close to $5 million, and his stock in it was worth about $50 million. Under normal criteria, Vesco was of a stature that made him a logical prospect for a major contribution. In 1968 he had given the national Nixon-Agnew finance committee $25,000, and apparently had also contributed to one or more of the state committees for the ticket.

In early 1970, by another series of bold strokes, Vesco had negotiated the acquisition by ICC of control of the worldwide empire of mutual investment funds headed by Investors Overseas Services, a creation of a flamboyant international character named Bernard Cornfeld. The IOS funds held several billion dollars in assets. Apparently the only fly in Vesco's ointment of success at this point was that Cornfeld had been in frequent dispute with the Securities and Exchange Commission over certain activities of IOS and, even though those matters had been resolved by agreements providing that IOS companies would do no business in the United States, the SEC had moved its inquisitive eye to ICC and Vesco. The Commission wanted to know whether ICC's acquisition of control of IOS ran afoul of the Commission's agreement with Cornfeld.

With a show of bluster, Vesco had filed suit against the SEC in 1970 to try to resolve the question in favor of ICC, but the court would not agree to limit the SEC's jurisdiction. Apparently, the investigation had continued thereafter in low key, with little public attention, and that was the situation in February 1972. At issue was not a criminal action but an administrative procedure to determine whether IOS should be prevented in any way from exercising its control over ICC. I had seen glimpses of these news stories as they unfolded, but they were very remote in my mind at the time Hofgren reported to me, and their nature did not suggest any illegality on Vesco's part, or any breach that could not be resolved, at the worst by ICC being required to divest the stock.

About two weeks after Hofgren's encounter with Straub, around March 1, I had a drop-in visit from Harry Sears, who introduced himself as a former state senator in New Jersey, a former candidate for governor there, a good friend of John Mitchell, and probably to be the campaign chairman for Nixon in New Jersey. He said he wanted to talk about a contribution from Robert Vesco but did not specify his relationship with Vesco and I did not pursue the point. (I learned later that Sears was then counsel for ICC.) He reported that Vesco wanted to be a "big" contributor and had talked about giving $500,000, but that he, Sears, had suggested that $250,000 would be more in line with Vesco's 1968 contribution, taking into account his increase in wealth since then. I would have been pleased to get either amount for the campaign, and either amount would have been legal, and I said so. Sears asked if I would see Vesco and again I agreed to do so. Before leaving, Sears volunteered that Vesco had a little matter pending before the Securities and Exchange Commission, but that it was winding down and he was sure it would be worked out satisfactorily. From his description, I did not take it to be very significant.

The meeting with Vesco, which was apparently then arranged by Hofgren, took place on March 8 in my office. To my momentary surprise, Vesco was not accompanied by Sears, but by Laurence Richardson, the president of ICC. Hofgren was also present, but took no part in the conversation. Robert Vesco was the archtype of the successful business tycoon. Well-clothed, natty, with a small moustache, tall, gentlemanly and smooth-spoken, he was impressive in appearance and manner. He was the confident picture of the wealthy entrepreneur who had built a corporate empire by his own wits and energy. I had seen the species many times during my business and government career. From his reputation and his demeanor, I had no reason whatever to distrust him.

I thanked Vesco for coming and said I was pleased that he

wanted to support the President, but that I wanted him to know more about the campaign plans before he decided on the size of his contribution. I reviewed the political situation, outlined the campaign budget, and explained how I expected to raise the $40 million or so that was needed. I told him, as I told many others, that my calculations were that I had to find twenty dedicated people in the United States who were willing and able to give $250,000 each, forty more who could and would give $100,000 each, and eighty additional who would give $50,000, in addition to many smaller amounts. I reviewed the expected dimensions of the campaign spending, and the importance of our winning the election. After this monologue, which must have taken eight or ten minutes, I invited him to be a member of the top bracket, knowing he intended to give that much, but feeling also that I had provided him with good reasons for his doing so. He responded as I expected, saying he had once thought of giving more, but had settled on $250,000 and was prepared to make arrangements to contribute that amount.

I pointed out to him, just as I had been doing with many other prospective contributors, that the law would change on April 7 to require that contributions be publicly reported thereafter, and that if he wanted he could take advantage of the right of privacy by giving before that date. He said that that was what he wanted to do, and asked what form the gift could take. I was not surprised by his question, because some businessmen had elected to give in corporate stock rather than by check, and I suspected that this was what he intended. I told him that we would take his contribution in any form he chose, since the law allowed us to take "anything of value." He seemed to be more interested in the idea of giving in cash, and asked a few more questions about that procedure. I told him that while most people gave by check or stock, some did give in cash and it was perfectly acceptable. He indicated that this would be what he preferred and that I could count on getting it before April 7.

Before the meeting broke up, I thought it desirable to ask him to tell me about his SEC matter. I said that I had read in the papers in the past that the SEC had raised some questions about the acquisition of control of IOS by ICC, but had not seen anything lately and was curious as to the status. Vesco replied that he had not been able to end it because of extreme harassment by the staff of the SEC, who seemed to have a fixation about IOS ever since Cornfeld had controlled it. He said that the matter could readily be worked out satisfactorily and fairly if and when he could get to talk to some of the top people in the SEC. I merely replied that he should not find that difficult if he requested it directly; I had always been willing as Secretary of Commerce to talk to people who felt aggrieved, and I believed it was the right of every citizen to be fully heard. That was the end of the discussion except that, as he shook hands to leave, he said he was working on an idea that could be expected to dispose of the SEC problem quite soon.

In an exercise of caution, I thought I ought to check a bit further on the SEC proceedings before I saw Vesco or his people again. Since it would not have been appropriate for me to discuss the case with anyone at the Commission, a rule I had learned while at Commerce, I decided to ask Mitchell, recalling that Sears had said he was a friend of Mitchell.

On March 17, I saw Mitchell at his office about a number of topics, including, briefly, Vesco. I asked him whether he thought there was any reason I should not accept Vesco's contribution. He replied that he didn't know Vesco, but knew Sears well; that Sears had told him that Vesco had done nothing wrong, that no criminal charges were involved, that it was a technical matter, and that it was winding down and he expected it to be resolved satisfactorily. Under these circumstances, Mitchell said, he saw no reason why the contribution shouldn't be taken. I agreed. This was my only conversation with Mitchell about Vesco until after the election.

On April 3, Sears came to my office. He said that he and Vesco had talked over the proposed contribution and had concluded that Vesco would give only $200,000 before April 7, which would be unpublicized, and $50,000 later in the summer, which would be publicly reported. In that way it would not appear that Vesco, who was well known in New Jersey Republican circles, had failed to contribute anything, as would be the case if he gave the entire amount under right of privacy. I said I saw no objection to that, and then, before Sears left, referred to a news item in that morning's *Wall Street Journal*, which I had on my desk. It reported that ICC had divested its control of IOS.[2] Sears said he thought this

---

2. The *New York Times* headline the same day was even more specific: "Vesco Severing Links with IOS. Resigns Post at Company and Disposes of Stock."

would be the end of Vesco's problems with the SEC, and without further hesitance, I took this transaction to be the "idea" which Vesco had intimated on March 8 would settle the SEC issues. I closed my mind on any doubts about the propriety of accepting his contribution.

Sears said he would phone me when the money was in hand, and that delivery definitely would take place before the 7th. I mentioned that I had a dinner date on the night of the 6th in New York, where I would be the guest of the Interracial Council on Business Opportunity, and could arrange to receive the money at my hotel if that were more convenient. He thought it would be.

On April 6, Sears phoned early and I returned the call. The money was not yet in hand, he said, but definitely would be before the end of the day. In the afternoon we talked again. I told him that I had canceled my trip to New York because I was just too worn out after the hectic pressures of the last few days, and would have to make other arrangements to pick up the money. He replied that he expected to receive it at any minute. We talked about sending couriers, which seemed to be difficult to work out, and finally I said, in effect: "Look, we don't have the money in our possession today. Under the law, the contribution is effective before April 7th because the pledge was made earlier, and I will just accept it over the phone as of today and you can deliver it as soon as possible." That was agreeable to him, and we made a date for him to come to my office on the following Monday, April 10.

I had no hesitance in handling the payment this way, as I was working under legal advice I had received from our committee's counsel the preceding day in the Andreas case. Counsel had said that, since the law defined a contribution to include not only a payment of money but a promise to make a contribution, the transaction could be considered completed when the pledge was made, before April 7, even though the actual receipt of the funds came later. Had I foreseen that later questions would arise because the money had not been physically in our possession in Washington until a few days afterward, I would certainly have found a way to get it delivered or picked up on April 6.

On April 10 Sears and Richardson came to my office and Richardson gave me a briefcase with $200,000 in cash. We had a very casual conversation for a few minutes and, just before Richardson got up to go, he lowered his head and mumbled something that sounded to me like "Vesco hopes this will be of some help." I assumed he was referring to the campaign, but Sears got a different interpretation and hurriedly interjected:

"Now wait a minute. This is a contribution, pure and simple, and there is no consideration of any kind involved here. There is no quid pro quo." I was surprised at his sharp reaction and retorted right away: "Well, I certainly wouldn't accept it on any other basis." Richardson said he understood that, and the meeting ended.

Immediately after they left I called in the treasurer, Hugh Sloan, Jr., and gave him the briefcase. I told him to count the bills right away. He asked me whom it was from and, in a moment of supercaution, I told him "For the time being, record it under the name of John Mitchell." He was the only inside person I had discussed it with. I was concerned, as I had been all along, about leaks of the names of contributors who had given in the expectation of privacy, and it occurred to me that an amount of this size, coming during a period in which activity had dropped to nothing after the last-minute rush of April 6 to beat the privacy deadline, might be too easily the subject of office conversation that could get out. I had very much in mind the mandate given me at a meeting of campaign and White House people three weeks earlier to protect the confidentiality of our contributors. I planned to give Sloan the Vesco name later and put him in our contributor lists when the risk of unintended disclosure had diminished.

That is how the Vesco contribution came to be made. It was one of the hundreds that I received in 1972, quite a number of them equally large or larger in amount. It was not unusual to accept contributions in cash, although admittedly this one was greater than any other in that form. I did not ever see or talk to Vesco again after the first meeting on March 8, and I did not talk to Richardson again after he delivered the money on April 10. I did not see or talk to Sears again until the time of the Republican Convention in Miami Beach. None of them had any further talk with Hofgren or anyone else on the finance committee, to my knowledge. Vesco gave the other $50,000 through our New Jersey finance committee late in September and it was duly recorded and reported to the General Accounting Office, as the law required. There was no reason to suspect the trouble that ensued.

During the summer I became concerned about the small

amount of money we had collected in New Jersey for the campaign. I was told that Governor William Cahill was the only one who could stir up action in that state so I arranged for a meeting in my hotel suite in Miami Beach on August 22 with him, Sears (who by then had become New Jersey campaign chairman), and Harry Richardson[3] and Chuck Bentz of the New Jersey finance committee. This was while the Republican convention was going on. We discussed the potential sources of money in New Jersey, reviewed some of the names, and I received the assurances I wanted from Cahill that he would tell his people to gear up to do all they could to help us get contributions. As we reviewed names and came to Vesco, Sears merely said, "Bob's on board," and everyone seemed to know what that meant. I did. At about that point in the meeting, the New Jersey finance people complained that they had not received full credit against the state quota for all contributions we had received, and I promised to see that this would be checked out for them.

As the meeting broke up after half an hour or so, I got Sears aside and said that it was possible that the Vesco money had not been credited to New Jersey because the clerks in our treasurer's office who made up the reports might not yet have been informed about it. I also asked him to ride herd on the finance operation in New Jersey and see that a good job was done.

The next time I saw Sears was on December 12, when the President held a reception at the White House, followed by a dinner at Blair House, for the political leaders of his successful campaign. I was also invited. Between courses of the meal, Sears and I withdrew from our respective tables and talked for a minute before a window in the room. Two weeks earlier the SEC had filed a broadside civil suit against Vesco, charging him with looting the IOS companies of $224 million and with various other crimes. It had come as a major surprise, in view of the relaxed situation that I understood had prevailed when his contribution was made and the news stories of the termination of his control. I was concerned about having received money from a man who seemed to have gotten himself in so much trouble, even though it was clear from the SEC's complaint *that the alleged looting had not begun*

---

3. No relation to Laurence Richardson.

*until several months after the contribution had been made.* I said as much to Sears, told him we were considering returning Vesco's money, and asked for his opinion of doing so. He said he too was shocked by the Vesco disclosures, but the decision about returning the money was up to us. I said: "I think, in view of the SEC case, that it's too hot to handle." I did not see Sears again until the trial. We returned the $250,000 to Vesco late in January, after the words in the transmittal letter had been painstakingly argued over during a period of several weeks and were finally cleared by the committee's counsel and by John Dean of the White House. For some unaccountable reason, Dean had the letter on his desk for ten days before I was able to pry it loose.

That is the sum of my actions connected with Vesco's gift to the campaign. One other incident occurred, however, that formed part of the charges against me. Early in November, right after the election, I went on a two-day goose hunt in Texas at the invitation of George Cook, the campaign chairman in Nebraska and a friend since 1968. His son, Brad, who was the head of the Division of Market Regulation of the SEC, and whom I had met just twice before, was one of the eight guests. On the first day of the shoot I was stationed about fifteen yards from Brad and, during a long lull when the geese weren't flying, I walked over to his position and sat down to chat, with both of us still keeping our eyes to the sky hoping for a flight. We talked about the "bluebird" weather and the poor shooting and other generalities, and then suddenly he mentioned Vesco.

"You know, one of the interesting cases I have been working on is Vesco, Robert Vesco. He is one of your contributors. He is in pretty serious trouble and the SEC is about to file charges against him," he said. "I read recently that he gave $50,000 to your campaign. We have a trail of $250,000 that he brought into the United States in cash and then siphoned off $50,000 of it. I wonder whether that $50,000 was the money that came to you."

"Brad, I don't know," I said. "I would have assumed that the $50,000 was received in checks, because I didn't hear about it being in cash, but I really don't know. I didn't see it come in. When I get back to the office I will check it out and let you know how it arrived."

That was the conversation. Cook had asked me about the

$50,000, not the entire amount. I had not volunteered anything about receiving the other $200,000 and it troubled me a bit that I had not been more revealing. The next day I received a long-distance call in Texas from Dean, asking about the payment of some campaign bills, so I took advantage of the call to ask his advice. I told him about the conversation and asked whether I should tell Cook anything more. He replied that under such informal circumstances there was no obligation to breach the rule of privacy about contributions, but of course if the Commission formally asked for information I should give it.

Two days later I arrived back in Washington and learned from the treasurer's office that Vesco's $50,000 had been given in checks through our New Jersey committee. I called Cook and told this to him. He thanked me and said, almost incidentally: "This is an opportune time because I have before me the draft of the charge relating to the $250,000 that Vesco brought into the country and didn't account for," and he proceeded to read a few sentences and paraphrase the rest. He went on and said, "It's very poor legal work. It's very long. It is sensationalism and I don't think it ought to go into the complaint that way, so we are reworking it."

I thanked him for the information. Later in the same day, Dean and I traveled to New York together on a plane and among other items of conversation I told him about my phone call that morning with Cook. He repeated his earlier advice to the effect that I had no obligation in an informal conversation to volunteer information to Cook, or to tell him anything more than I had, especially in view of the rights of early contributors to confidentiality.

Two days later Cook called me and read the new language of the charge against Vesco relating to the $250,000. It merely said that Vesco had brought "large sums" of money into the country without accounting for them. Cook said it was better language and in fact gave the Commission broader scope in case any other similar transactions showed up. I asked him when the complaint would be filed and he replied: "In about a week or so. We are going to file the complaint and we will file transcripts of depositions at the same time."

That was the end of the conversation and the last time I talked to Cook until the following January, in 1973. We had a few phone calls then about unrelated matters, the principal one of which was from him to discuss his interest in being appointed chairman of the SEC, and then on February 1 I told him promptly about the return of the $250,000 to Vesco and gave him a copy of the transmittal letter that had gone with our check. His main comment was: "At last we know where the $250,000 went." I offered to open the finance committee's books to the SEC but nothing happened on that.

Those are the events leading up to my appearances before the grand jury in New York on March 3 and April 23, 1973, to which I agreed voluntarily and without subpoena. On May 10 Mitchell and I were indicted on ten counts each, along with Vesco and Sears for lesser numbers. Dean was named an unindicted co-conspirator, presumably on the basis of some alleged conversations between him and Mitchell, unknown to me. Richardson and Howard Cerny, another business associate of Vesco, were also named as unindicted co-conspirators.

What then were John Mitchell's actions, and how were they woven together by the prosecutors into an alleged conspiracy between us, to induce the grand jury to bring the charges?

Mitchell's account as he gave it to the jury was relatively simple. He recited in exact agreement the conversation I had had with him in March about the propriety of accepting Vesco's contribution and confirmed that we had not talked about Vesco or his SEC case at any other time or in any other context. He acknowledged that he had been a political friend of Sears for some years and that he and Sears had been in contact in 1971 and 1972 on a number of occasions.

In November 1971 Sears had asked Mitchell to inquire into the circumstances behind an arrest of Vesco in Switzerland, where he was being held without bail. Mitchell phoned the American Embassy in Switzerland and discussed the situation and reported back to Sears. Vesco was released on bail a few days later, and the charges against him were eventually ruled improper by a higher court. I knew nothing about these events until 1973 when I read about them in the press, and since they preceded any of the alleged criminal acts in the case they were really not very relevant.

Early in 1972 Sears told Mitchell that he was representing Vesco in a matter before the SEC and asked Mitchell to arrange a meeting for Sears with William Casey, the Chairman of the Commission. Sears stated that there had been so much heated controversy between the staff of the SEC and Vesco's other counsel on the case that it was not moving toward resolution, and that he believed he could help bring the parties to an agreement if he could talk to Casey. Mitchell did arrange a meeting between Sears and Casey, but unfortunately did so on the day Sears and Richardson delivered the Vesco contribution to me. It was a coincidence which certainly would have been avoided had there been a conspiracy. Sears met with Casey a month later, but nothing came of the meeting.

In the late spring Sears became campaign chairman for the Committee to Re-Elect the President in New Jersey. He and Mitchell had frequent communications thereafter, mostly over the telephone, about the campaign.

Whatever contacts Mitchell had with Sears or Casey were unknown to me. Mitchell testified he did not meet Vesco in 1972, that he never met Richardson, that he did not tell me of any of his talks or meetings with Sears or Casey, and that he never discussed Vesco with Cook.

How then did these two disparate sets of actions by two people add up to the kind of mutual crimes alleged in the indictment? What was the linkage attempted by the prosecutors to support charges of conspiracy and joint action to obstruct justice?

The government's case was described in an opening statement to the jury by one of the prosecutors in this sentence:

"This is a case about a contribution of $200,000 in cash, a briefcase full of $100 bills, to buy the political influence of John Mitchell and Maurice Stans; it is a case about fraud, about corruption and about deliberate lies under oath." On this concept the prosecution had secured the indictment against Mitchell for two counts of conspiracy to obstruct justice, two counts of obstruction of justice, and six counts of perjury before the grand jury. Against me the first four charges on conspiracy and obstruction were the same, and there were also six counts of perjury, a total of ten counts against each of us.

The conspiracy charges, in effect, were that we had worked

together to keep Vesco out of difficulties with the Securities and Exchange Commission, in return for the $200,000 contribution, and the obstruction charges were that Mitchell and I had attempted to put obstacles in the way of the SEC's investigation and action with respect to Vesco. One of the main charges of perjury against me concerned my denial that I had asked Vesco to make his contribution in cash, thereby to conceal the consideration for our actions.

My attorneys felt from the start that the conspiracy and obstruction charges were weak and unlikely to prevail, but they had a fear about the perjury issues because of the necessity of proving our word against possible conflicting testimony from others like Cook, Dean, and Richardson, who by then had strong incentives to please the prosecutors, principally the hope of leniency on other criminal matters in which they were involved.

The motivations of the prosecutors in weaving their case out of thin threads, of course, are known only to them, and I can merely report their actions. They were young, obviously ambitious, and capable. It was a time of heavy media notice and public excitement over Wategate, with which both Mitchell and I were then regularly assumed by the media to have been guiltily involved. There was no connection between the Vesco affair and Watergate, but the prosecutors were obviously convinced that, being so definitely guilty of one, we must also be guilty of the other.[4] So sure were they that they got the indictments from the grand jury on suspected circumstances and little evidence, convinced that the real proof of guilt would somehow come to light before the trial, or at least during the proceedings. Presumably they could visualize a historic trial of two Cabinet officers, and if they won on as little as one charge they might have an open field for a future in law or politics. That's how Tom Dewey got started, wasn't it?

Head of the group was John "Rusty" Wing, thirty-seven, bright, eloquent, and persuasive. Next to him was James Rayhill, thirty-six, a sharp, incisive, ferocious, and ruthless person. With

---

4. Mitchell was later indicted, tried, and found guilty in the Watergate coverup; it was eventually established that I had not in any way been involved in Watergate.

them were two still younger attorneys, around thirty, Kenneth Feinberg and John Lowe. I am certain that ambition played a large part in their attitudes in this case. The opportunity to be "giant killers" doesn't come often. I say this as a matter of fact, without resentment, because I can understand how any young prosecutor in such a circumstance would sense the challenge. At the same time I say it with conviction, because the unusually aggressive tactics which they used could have no other rational explanation.

The normal attitude for a prosecutor, I am told, is that of a professional, doing his job as best he can with the facts at hand, but without animosity toward the defendant. Wing was not that. He was emotionally involved, with a teeth-grinding determination to do everything and anything the judge would allow him to do in order to win his case. Rayhill was even worse; his specialty was confronting witnesses in advance of the trial to try to get them to concede a more damaging coloration or emphasis on their stories. A regular tactic he employed was to challenge a prospective witness in his office with the bald statement that "we have hard evidence that you're not telling the truth," leaving it to the frightened individual to wonder what it was he could have forgotten. Under such coercive conditions, often prolonged through a series of confrontations, some were brought around to "remembering" incidents or events in ways more consistent with the theories of the prosecution as to what had occurred.

Neither Wing nor Rayhill had knowledge of the workings of a political campaign. Neither was willing to accept that the hectic character of such a campaign normally leaves some minor loose ends untied or some hasty misjudgments in its wake. Their minds were clearly tainted by the stories of Watergate and the conclusion that we were involved in that escapade. It is not hard to understand from the witch-hunt atmosphere of 1972-74 how they would feel that way. Whatever the reasons, our prospects were not pleasant to contemplate once we knew what their goal was and the determination with which they were proceeding toward it.

Their forceful and sometimes ingenious tactics began well before the indictments and continued throughout the trial. Some were obvious to us and others were unknown when they took place. For example, when I was first invited to come to New York to testify before the grand jury, which I did voluntarily and blithe-ly, Wing generously offered my attorney and me the services of a car and driver who would know how to bring us to the lower level of the courthouse, thus avoiding public attention. We accepted. The driver was Carl Bogen. We learned later that Bogen was a New York City detective who had been put in charge of the investigations for the Vesco case. His presence could have had no purpose but to listen in on our conversations en route. Although this happened several times it was fruitless because we had no guilty knowledge to discuss.

At the time of my first testimony on March 5, I was accom-panied to New York by Kenneth Parkinson, who had been counsel for the campaign committee and the finance committee ever since the Watergate revelations began in June 1972, and had also advised me personally on legal matters in that period of time. After we reviewed the scope of questions that had been asked by Wing, Parkinson recommended that the time had come when I might better have my own counsel, independent of the two committees. I then retained Washington attorneys Robert Barker and Walter Bonner on April 19,[5] immediately after Wing asked me to come to New York again for another session with the grand jury. Wing refused Barker's request for the usual courtesy of allowing time to study the case and prepare for the hearing. He insisted that I testify on April 23, giving my new counsel only three days to go over the entire background, ask questions, interrogate others, and brief me on the laws. They had to work full hours over the Easter weekend to be as ready as possible.

It is common practice and proper justice for a prosecutor who has targeted a grand jury witness for likely prosecution to tell him so in advance. At no time, while we were appearing willingly, did Wing inform John Mitchell or me or our attorneys that we were targets of his investigation, and at no time did he discuss the nature of his case or the issues involved. Actually, he told Barker on April 20 that I was not a target. I understand that it is

---

5. From then on, these two highly experienced and brilliant lawyers, from different Washington law firms, guided my destiny through the nerve-wracking accumulation of civil and criminal actions, investigations, and public hearings. Barker was my general counsel, skillfully backstopped in the civil litigation by his associates Lee Knauer and John Facciola, and in the criminal matters by Bonner and his associates Ed O'Connell and John Diuguid. All did yeomen work in complete disregard of the clock.

customary to give witnesses about to be accused an opportunity to present exculpatory evidence or to clarify apparent conflicts or inaccuracies and inconsistencies in testimony. This was not done and, under pressure of time, especially on my first appearance, I testified from memory as to many dates and events, without thorough reference to calendars and other records. I was led to believe that all Wing wanted was information as to Vesco's contribution, causing me to think that his research was directed at Vesco.

My first intimation that his intention was broader was when he began to ask questions before the grand jury that had Watergate connotations. (For example, he asked me about Gordon Liddy and others, and questioned Mitchell about Howard Hunt and Donald Segretti. Their names were in the news daily in March and April 1973, associated with Watergate.) The connection was so cleverly made that one of the grand jurors is known to have stirred up the other members by shouting to them on several occasions before our indictment, "Let's get that Watergate crowd." There can be no doubt that we were targeted and set up for indictment before we appeared the second time.[6]

On May 9 Barker learned that, shortly after I testified the second time, Wing and Rayhill had demanded that Parkinson come to New York with all of his papers and notes on the matter, and he had done so. Conscious of the privilege that allows an

---

6. The whole procedure contrasts with what was at the time the practice in the Office of the Special Prosecutor in Washington, as quoted in a book by two principal staff lawyers (*Stonewall*, Ben-Veniste and Frampton, Simon & Schuster, 1977, at page 69):

"Although there is no legal or ethical obligation on the prosecutor to present exculpatory evidence to the grand jury, we made it our policy in the cover-up case to do so. We also advised subjects that we would be happy to place before the grand juries any evidence the subjects or their lawyers called to our attention that they believed to be favorable to them.

"When it came time to recommend indictment to the grand jury, the Watergate Task Force decided that each prospective defendant and his counsel would be invited to meet with the Special Prosecutor for a discussion of his case."

The New York prosecutors acted diametrically opposite—they did not tell us we were their targets, they did not present known exculpatory evidence, they did not offer to receive exculpatory data for the grand jury, they gave us no intimation of the charges to be filed, and they refused requests of our counsel for a review of any matters of suspicion. It was a rush to judgment without apparent fairness and perhaps without precedent.

attorney to keep confidential any discussions between himself and his client, Parkinson properly refused to answer questions on such talks. Rayhill challenged Parkinson's statements on other topics, such as when he first learned of the Vesco contribution, and threatened him with serious consequences for allegedly not telling the truth. In the ensuing discussions Rayhill demanded to see Parkinson's notes and records relating to contacts with other persons on my behalf, and Parkinson turned them over under what he described to me and Barker later as "duress—certainly not voluntarily."

In a recent case that had been decided in the Federal Court in New York, such data came under the legal term of "work product" and was likewise entitled to the privilege of confidentiality. The prosecutors had no right to such papers and had taken them improperly. Not only that, they used the information in questioning one or two witnesses before the grand jury immediately before asking for the indictment. There was nothing damaging to my case in these papers but there were gaps in information and inadvertencies in dates cited from recollection that required filling in, and there was no opportunity given to me to do that.

When all this became known, Barker got an affidavit from Parkinson as to these circumstances and sought to get the Department of Justice in Washington to postpone any indictment in New York until there could be an exploration of this violation of my rights. They contended that any indictment would be invalid and should not be brought. Justice refused to act, however, and the indictment was issued on May 10. Later in the proceedings, the judge held that the prosecutors had not been entitled to the Parkinson papers and directed that they be returned to him. Whatever damage had resulted from the prosecutor's use of confidential discussions by Parkinson with third persons, and of incomplete memos from me that he had shown to third persons, and whatever impressions the improper handling of that material had created for the grand jury, could not be undone. My counsel contended that the case should have ended at that point, but the judge ruled otherwise and continued it.

On the morning of May 10, before the grand jury met, the *New York Times* headlined "Mitchell and Stans to be Indicted Today." Such publicity was decidedly prejudicial since the grand jurors had not even voted on the matter and the disclosure could have come only from a leak from the District Attorney's office. Later in the day, when the indictment was voted, it was announced with unusual fanfare by the District Attorney, Whitney North Seymour, who took the unusual step of reading a summary of the charges to a news conference in a packed auditorium across the square from the Federal courthouse. Despite my growing fear as to what was to happen, I was taken by surprise at the harshness of the charges and their number. Suddenly, my entire life was on the line.

Wing added insult to injury. On the day we were arraigned in court and pleaded not guilty, he insisted that we be fingerprinted, photographed, and made to post bail. The court overruled him, holding that we were sufficiently well known and responsible persons to be released on our own recognizance.

On the day of the indictment I was with Kathleen at Walter Reed Hospital. She was confined there with her second bout of hepatitis in four months and was seriously ill and deeply jaund-iced. Groups of reporters and photographers besieged all exits from the hospital, insisting on a statement. With a heavy heart over Kathleen's condition, and a strong worry about what the news would do to her, all I could say publicly was that I was dismayed at the New York action but that "I believe in God and I believe in American justice and when all the facts are known I'm sure that I will be exonerated completely." It was a low moment in our lives, as I wondered whether she and I could withstand much longer the mounting problems we had not deserved.

In talking with her, I tried to minimize the seriousness of the predicament, and she did not doubt me because of her devoted confidence that I would not have done wrong. For my own part, I knew what a devastating blow this was to my lifelong reputation, because the publicity would be relentless to the end. I foresaw the impact on our children and grandchildren, even though I was sure that they, too, in their hearts would believe in me. All of these thoughts were shattering, and I knew that an ultimate verdict of innocence could not possibly repair the damage to my life. I had to steel myself to accept that fact, and hope that some day the public knowledge of my vindication would redeem in part at least my long pursuit of life's challenges that had brought me into the position where I had to face such a critical circumstance. This was the dominant thought for the next year: How would I muster the strength to fight this monster to the death, and how would I recover from its inevitable wounds?

This being a Federal case, the indictment was drawn in the name of "United States versus Maurice H. Stans." These words are a frightening contemplation. It was as though I stood alone against 220 million other persons, in combat, and they carried the offensive. The court was their battleground and the prosecuting attorneys would execute their front line of attack. The overwhelming thought of a nation with all its resources arrayed against one person is terrorizing and the only comfort, sometimes hard to realize, is that its courts are dedicated to fairness and that out of the outweighted battle will come a triumph of justice. David is supposed to have an even chance of winning over Goliath.[7]

The tension dragged on month by month. The case was assigned by lot to Judge Lee P. Gagliardi, who set trial for September 11. Our lawyers promptly asked for a short postponement on the ground that they needed more time to prepare this important case, and also that a delay would remove it from the effect of the prejudicial publicity of the Senate Watergate hearings. Almost all of the five months after the indictment had been spent by them and me in tending to and following the progress of the Senate hearings, and to a panoply of civil lawsuits and continuing investigations inspired by Watergate. Despite this obviously sound reason, the judge, to our consternation, insisted on going ahead and refused our petition for even a minimal additional three weeks, saying that it was a simple case that did not justify delay.

At the risk of antagonizing him, our lawyers at the last minute took the unusual course of appealing to the Circuit Court of Appeals for a writ of mandamus directing him to give us more time, challenging his "arbitrary and headlong rush to judgment."

---

7. Not everyone accepted that fact. While the *New York Times* was mercifully saying (on May 11) that "Mitchell and Stans are still innocent in the eyes of the law," the *Washington Post* could express its conclusion of guilt before trial without hesitation: "We do not share Mr. Mitchell's certainty of the outcome of the judicial proceedings. Nor do we share that of Mr. Stans, who also expressed his confidence that he would be vindicated. It [the Vesco affair] is part of that endemic sleaziness and gross insensitivity to what is important and what is right."

The appellate court gave patient consideration to their arguments on the difficulties in preparing for trial with so many diverting influences. Its decision was issued in a matter of hours, and was a strong censure of his inconsiderate refusal.

Calling it a "case without precedent in this country," the Circuit Court, because of a jurisdictional question, did not specifically direct a postponement but in strong language *advised* the judge to give us "at least the three weeks that was requested." For its reason, it said: "In a prosecution of this sort, which will receive nationwide attention, it is peculiarly important that justice not only should be done, but should seem to be done. While the high positions formerly occupied by the defendants entitle them to no more consideraton than is accorded the ordinary citizens, they deserve no less." Postponement for a few weeks, the opinion continued, "would be a small price to pay for stalling complaints, even if they were not justified, that the defendants had not been given a fair opportunity to prepare their case and to avoid an issue which will certainly continue during the trial. We cannot agree with the trial judge that a 16-count, 46-page indictment with 60 pages of bill of particulars is a simple case." With strong urging that the trial be postponed, the appellate court went on to say that "if, on further reflection, the judge should adhere to his determination, a course we hope he will not follow, defendants, if convicted, will be able to raise the issue on appeal." One of the three judges was even more forceful; he said he would have *directed* the judge to grant our request.

With this stern admonition, Judge Gagliardi then rescheduled the trial for October 23. His attitude on this matter, and his abrupt denial of almost all of a series of other motions we had filed in the case, left us greatly concerned that he might be unfriendly and that he may have formed a prejudgment of guilt, a concern that continued through most of the succeeding events until it gradually dissipated during the trial, which he handled for the greater part with fine judicial expertise. One instance of our distress at his rulings occurred in a preliminary hearing at which we had asked the court to bar John Dean from testifying because he had acted as my legal adviser through most of 1972 and any statements by him would breach the confidentiality of the lawyer-client relationship. I testified at that juncture about the many times I had received such advice and produced a file of written legal opinions and memoranda that Dean and his staff had prepared for me. Despite this, the judge ruled against us and held that Dean could testify. It was a ruling that my attorneys felt would be very prejudicial, not because of anything Dean would say, but because of the added Watergate-related notoriety and excitement his presence, as a former counsel to the President, would create at the trial.

As October 23 approached, the prosecution to our surprise asked for a postponement until they could determine whether certain White House tapes would have a bearing on their case. We had asked the court to allow us to subpoena any tapes of Presidential conversations involving Dean that related to the Vesco matter, and the prosecutors had objected. The judge ruled that Dean wouldn't be allowed to testify unless pertinent portions of any tapes were made available for our defense, whereupon the prosecution, saying that it "could not afford to risk trying the case without Dean's testimony," asked for the delay.    January 7 became the new date but this had to be deferred again because Mitchell's lawyers were engaged in a long lawsuit in Oklahoma that did not conclude until early February. Eventually, on February 20, 1974, almost a year after my first testimony to the grand jury, the judge announced the beginning of the trial.

Although there were two other named conspirator-defendants, only Mitchell and I were tried, thus focusing the entire force of the prosecution against us.    Harry Sears had been granted a separate trial, to follow ours, and Robert Vesco sat it out in Costa Rica.

Meanwhile, Vesco's own antics didn't help the climate of our situation. He fought off, successfully, efforts of the government to extradite him from the Bahamas, and again from Costa Rica. He was interviewed by reporters for the press and television, and was quoted freely and often, with the result that the case acquired an even greater notoriety in New York and across the country. None of his remarks, however, implied any guilt on our part, and some supported our positions.

Meanwhile, Wing and Rayhill worked desperately to shore up their flimsy case. There was a grapevine report in the courthouse which we did not hear until later, and of course could not confirm, that before the indictment the case had been reviewed by twelve other lawyers in the District Attorney's office, and eight of the twelve had concluded that it should not be pressed without more evidence. Whether or not this rumor was true, the prosecution acted as though it was, in their unbelievably persistent and futile nationwide search for corroboration.

There were to be four major witnesses for the government, all of them tarnished by their past records, and with motivations to testify against us. The first was John Dean, former counsel for the President, whose testimony was directed mostly against Mitchell, and who conceded that he had pleaded guilty to a number of felonious actions in the Watergate case and that he "hoped" that his testimony against us would result in a lessening of his sentence for those crimes. The second was Harry Sears, the New Jersey attorney who had been legal adviser to Vesco and his company in 1971 and 1972 and who was indicted as a co-conspirator with Mitchell and me, but had been granted a separate trial by the court upon application of the prosecutors and then was granted immunity for agreeing to testify in the case against us. Third was Laurence Richardson, former president of Vesco's company, who the SEC alleged had participated in many of the illegal acts of thievery it had charged against Vesco; when the SEC case became public knowledge and the proceedings began to tighten, Richardson had gone to the New York prosecutors and "volunteered" to provide information about Vesco and his contribution in return for overall immunity. Fourth was G. Bradford Cook, who by the time of the trial had resigned the post he had received and held for a short time as chairman of the SEC, and whose principal statements were directed against me, but who admitted on the witness stand to having perjured five times, several of them before Congressional committees, after the day on which he had promised that he was "going to tell it like it was."

After the indictment and before the trial, the prosecutors undertook a program of preparing these witnesses by bringing them in for repeated long interrogations, over and over again, until every word and phrase of testimony was satisfactory. It was no surprise that their testimony in court differed in material respects from that which they first gave to the grand jury.

In the same time-frame some of the defense witnesses told

us they were subjected to threats and intimidations by Rayhill and others to try to break down their recollection of the facts. Edward C. Nixon, the President's brother, whose pertinent knowledge was limited to one five-minute encounter with me and a short meeting he had with Vesco, was brought back from the West Coast to New York no less than ten times, and was cajoled, threatened, and accused in attempts to get him to change his testimony. Ken Talmage and Arden Chambers, two of my campaign assistants, and others confirmed that they were similarly intimidated with charges of lying and threats of prosecution; Talmage was forced to fly from the West Coast to New York six times for intensive interrogation over the same ground. Dan Hofgren was threatened with perjury if he wouldn't change his story to say that I had asked for cash in the March 8 meeting with Vesco, and was also accused of conspiring with me to mesh our stories when actually we had not talked together after the indictment. During these threatening sessions, each was told by the prosecutor, usually Rayhill, that "we have solid evidence that you are lying," when no such evidence existed. It was designed to terrorize the witness and it accomplished that. Anyone so accused was bound to be desperately scared at the implications, no matter how forthright his testimony or how clear his recollection.

Scores of our contributors across the country were telephoned and many were summoned to New York and badgered by persistent questions about their contributions, in an unsuccessful effort to find just one whose experiences would support any aspect of the prosecution's case against me. In particular, the prosecutors tried diligently, without any success, to get witnesses to say that I had urged them to give in cash, when in fact I had not.

After the trial ended, Edward C. Nixon's attorney filed with the finance committee a seventeen-page statement spelling out the inquisitions to which his client was submitted before he took the stand to testify in my defense. The simple question was whether I had asked him on March 29, 1972, in answer to his inquiry, to tell Vesco that I wanted his contribution in cash, or had said that it made no difference whether it was by check or in cash. Nixon was prepared to say that I had told him it made no difference, and that I said further that the choice was up to Vesco. This testimony would exonerate me from one charge that I had perjured in denying to the grand jury that I had asked Vesco to give in cash. These excerpts from the report of Nixon's counsel, who was a seasoned and expert trial lawyer, show how the prosecutors tried to break Nixon down:

> On June 1, 1973 "during an exhausting morning and afternoon session, E. C. Nixon laid out a clear, well-defined outline of his activities, conversations and reactions to the meeting (on March 29, 1972) with Robert Vesco . . . . The U.S. Attorney's office was not satisfied . . . but instead repeatedly asked Mr. Nixon to return to New York.
>
> "After the first session there was always the feeling on the part of this firm that a repeated interrogation in depth about the same subject matter was either to intimidate E. C. Nixon into changing his testimony or to entrap him into a statement contradicting an earlier statement.
>
> "On June 13 the interrogation 'was essentially similar to that of the 1st.'
>
> "The August 14 meeting concerned itself primarily with the matter of an alleged second meeting with Mr. Vesco which never took place."
>
> There was in the invitation for the next interview on September 6 "a subtle threat that E. C. Nixon might be accused of lying at these interviews." At the meeting, "the U.S. Attorney's office—indicated subtly that [his] response was unsatisfactory and that E. C. Nixon should 'refresh his memory' on this matter."
>
> At the September 14 meeting "the entire scope of the prior interviews was once again reviewed."
>
> "The meetings of October 2, November 13 and December 14 concerned themselves primarily with a constant refining and reviewing of the prior testimony and the cross-examination of Mr. Nixon . . . . It became apparent at this point that the prosecution . . . were completely dissatisfied with Mr. E. C. Nixon's testimony in this area."
>
> On January 16 "the entire session was devoted to the [same] questions . . . at this point, we felt that this constant cross-examination on essentially one subject . . . was nothing more or less than intimidation. "
>
> On January 26 (a Sunday), "once again the entire subject of the conversation revolved around the issue of what Mr. Stans had indicated as his desire concerning the form of the contribution. Mr. Wing indicated point blank that they thought E. C. Nixon was lying. [We] responded that he would testify to the truth as he knew

it and that he would not be intimidated."

Richardson, the Vesco aide who testified against me, had talked to me only on two brief occasions, the first on March 8 when he accompanied Vesco to my office, and the second on April 10, when he delivered the $200,000. He had never seen Mitchell. Yet the prosecutors brought him into their office forty-five times for extended questioning after the indictment was handed down. In contrast to that, Mitchell and I were hastily brought before the grand jury twice, the first without any preparation, and the second with no intimation that we were being targeted, little advance idea of the questions to be asked, and no opportunity to confront contradictory testimony by others. There was no discussion by the prosecutors with our attorneys before the indictments were presented to the grand jury. Sears was interviewed for long hours on thirty-five occasions after the indictments. It is hard to believe that the objectives of the prosecutors in these repeated talks were any different from those at the meetings with Ed Nixon, as characterized by his counsel.

# 12

## VESCO—THE LAW IN ACTION

The Federal courthouse in downtown New York is a dull gray, fortresslike stone and marble structure covering an entire city block fronting on Foley Square. Its facade is impressively but coldly lined by a row of huge Grecian pillars, their bases on an entrance level that can be reached only by walking up a flight of thirty wide steps that run across the entire front of the building. Outside and inside, it is not a place that one would go willingly, or with the aim of finding peace or happiness. It is a house of organized contention and controversy which has the task of reducing criminal and civil accusations to just judgments through a process that is formal and glacially slow. Its only visitors, other than participants in the proceedings, are the occasionally curious, a few law students, and some inveterate trial watchers, plus members of the press assigned to sift through the events of justice to find something of enough interest to be worthy of reporting to the general public.

Its Room 101 is an immense cavern, meagerly lighted and with poor acoustics. The ceiling appears to be at least forty feet up, with several massive windows twenty-five feet high on each side wall that can only be managed with difficulty by a pull-pole more than fifteen feet long. On cold days the windows sometimes get stuck and won't yield to the bailiff's efforts with the long stick, so those near the front sit directly in a chilly draft during the proceedings. The room is only a bit wider than its height, and about twice as long, its length divided by a railing to separate the spectators from the action. The judge's platform has the usual elevation of about three feet, and the witness chair, surrounded by a railing, is about a foot lower and to his left. The jury box is against the wall at the left of the judge and the witness. The walls are paneled with wainscoting to a height of about six feet, above which is plaster painted in the usual uninspiring color known as "government buff." Nothing about the appearance or atmosphere is cheerful.

In our trial, the prosecutor's shabby table, with four lawyers and masses of paper, was squarely in front of the judge. Mitchell and his lawyer were at another decrepit table behind them, and my lawyers and I were at a third off to the side opposite to and facing the jury. Centered in front of the judge and on the same level as the lawyers and defendants was the court reporter. Behind the railing separating these official actors was a spectator section that seated about two hundred people, always filled, at least a third of them members of the press, including such distant publications as the *London Times*, the *Manchester Guardian*, and *Der Spiegel*. Witnesses could not be heard in this section, and barely elsewhere, unless they spoke directly into a microphone of considerable antiquity. With cameras not permitted, five or six artists were constantly at work with big sketch pads, drawing pictures of the principals to accompany the text of the evening television news reports. Before the beginning of each session the doors were opened long enough to permit all the press and spectator seats to be filled, and then were locked to prevent the noise and confusion of departures and new entries while testimony or arguments were under way. Those who came to hear the case were given serial numbers for admission like those handed out to customers of a bakery on a busy Saturday afternoon. In this bleak, warmthless setting twelve of our peers were to decide whether John Mitchell and I would spend the rest of our days in prison, which the young prosecutors eagerly sought to accomplish.

The selection of the jury took a long time, a full eight days, because the judge used extreme care to establish that he could find eighteen impartial people to render a verdict, twelve jurors plus six alternates in case some of the jurors became incapacitated in the long trial. It was expected at the start that the case would take four or five weeks. About two hundred persons were screened to get the eighteen.

After the trial a considerable amount of publicity occurred over the contention that we had used a psychological counselor to help in the jury selection. Those stories were grossly exaggerated. What had occurred was that, well before the trial was first due to start, our attorneys had asked for its removal to a place far from New York where emotions over Watergate were less pronounced, and prospective jurors would not have been influenced by the massive publicity; to bolster the argument they had secured a professional public attitude poll of voters in the New York judicial district and in three other Federal districts in southern and midwestern states. These polls of about 600 persons in each jurisdiction showed that the prejudice against Mitchell was three times as great in New York as elsewhere. For example, 22 percent in New York believed in advance that Mitchell was guilty, whereas the proportion was 6 percent in Aberdeen, Mississippi, and 7 percent in several other cities. The report concluded that "Mitchell would be more than twice as likely to be judged guilty in New York as in Aberdeen." Because I had a less-known identity, the percentages were lower in my case but in the same proportions—16 percent in New York, 4 percent in Aberdeen, and 5 percent in the other cities.

On that knowledge, we moved for a change of venue, adding as evidence a large box containing 2,615 pages of New York press clippings and transcripts of television and radio commentators, all considered likely to prejudice any local person called upon to serve as a juror. Despite all this powerful evidence, the judge, to our disappointment, refused to grant a change in location of the trial.

When the trial was thereby destined to go ahead in New York, the data from the poll was analyzed by the poll-taker, Martin Herbst, to determine the ethnic attitudes on the case. These showed that Jews, Puerto Ricans, and readers of the *New York Times* and *New York Post* were more strongly prejudiced and would be more inclined to convict than would persons of Catholic Irish or Italian descent, or readers of the *New York Daily News*.

Blacks and Anglo-Saxons would be neutral. To some degree, our attorneys tried to take these findings into account in making the twenty peremptory challenges which the judge allowed to the defense; however, this was only partially effective since the challenges could merely be applied three at a time among the twelve prospective jurors in the jury box at a given moment; they were used mostly to eliminate the very young, or least educated, the long-haired, and the kooky-looking types; sadly, sometimes the next in line who took their places were no more appealing and had to be challenged in the following round. Although the information on potential pre-prejudice was of some help, most of the jurors were selected or rejected by our counsel on the basis of overall "gut" impressions as to which ones would be most understanding. Because the case would deal with significant sums of money and financial practices, our main disappointment was that there was not a single businessman or person of money sophistication in the twelve, and just one among the alternates. A few weeks after the trial began, however, one of the twelve jurors, a woman, became ill and was dismissed, and the businessman, a banker, moved into her place.

To insure that the jury's decisions would not be contaminated by events unfolding in Washington, the judge ordered that the eighteen be sequestered throughout the trial. They could watch television but no news programs. They could talk to family members on the phone, but with a marshal listening in so the case wouldn't be discussed. They could read newspapers, but only after all the news of the trial and of Watergate had been clipped out. All their communications were censored. They could have visitors on weekends but only under the watchful eyes and ears of the marshals.

We were doubtful from the beginning that this would work, and unknown to us a test of it came a day after the sequestration began. Mitchell was indicted in Washington in the Watergate case on March 1. After the New York trial was over we learned that the jury knew about the indictment almost at once. Some of the jurors saw the headline on a newspaper in an automobile next to the bus in which they were being loaded for transport to their hotel. It may even have been planted there for that purpose. On another occasion later in the proceedings, Walter Cronkite of CBS broadcast a long-distance telephone interview with Vesco in Costa Rica. Somehow, the jurors learned about it soon afterward. We had another fear of the sequestration process. The jurors were veritable prisoners of society and the confining effect as time went on could make them antagonists of the people whom they felt caused them to be there. One Washington lawyer, Ronald Goldfarb, was quoted as saying, "Sequestered jurors are bound to be unhappy. They can blame the defendant and say 'let's hang him and get it over with.'"

The jury consisted of two blacks, one Puerto Rican, and nine whites. There were three women and nine men. Eight were Democrats, three Republicans, and one Independent. Occupationally, there were a Western Union messenger, a bank teller, a postal clerk, a subway conductor, two life insurance clerks, a telephone installer, a yardman, a highway engineer, two supervisors, and a banker. Under the method of the draw, the bank teller, a quiet, attractive young woman, whose wedding had to be postponed because of the length of the trial, became forelady. In all, they were a good cross-section of America and our only concern as the case progressed was whether they would be taken in by the "snow job"we believed the prosecutors were attempting, or would see through all the unrelated records and testimony to the real truth. However conscientious they were, would they understand the issues, or would they find the money amount inconsistent with innocence, and would they retain the presumption of non-guilt through the weeks ahead in the face of the government's efforts?

On February 20, when Judge Gagliardi gaveled the start of the trial, Wing had his meager case prepared as well as he possibly could. He also had the backing of at least some of his associates in the United States Attorney's office. One of the witnesses being re-interviewed a few days earlier found in Wing's washroom a 10-by-20-inch, hand-made sign that screamed in huge letters, "RUSTY, GO GET THE TWO DOGS!" The opening statement, given to the jury by Rayhill, was in keeping with that attitude. At one point he insinuated that since the grand jury "of people like yourselves" had found reason to indict, the trial jury should find the defendants guilty. He knew this to be an inappropriate and prejudicial remark and that, as the judge pointed out, "the defendants start the trial with a clean slate." The judge found Rayhill's remark improper and ordered it stricken.

In presenting their case, the young prosecutors often used tactics which surprised and dismayed us and were hard to cope with. In their zeal to convict, it seemed, especially to me (unfamiliar with the ethics and procedures of criminal trials), that their conduct was sometimes extraordinarily severe and of doubtful propriety. This was especially the case with the introduction into the record of much irrelevant testimony that could have had no purpose other than to overwhelm the jurors with a false impression of the believability and thoroughness of their case:

> —Richardson was caused to testify that in July he made a number of attempts to reach me on the telephone to give me a message from Vesco asking for help. I was out of town and never got his calls. So what?
>
> —Richardson testified that through my secretary he made an appointment to see me on July 26 in New York but the meeting was never held. The prosecutors produced my date book to the jury to show the erasure of the appointment and brought an FBI photographic expert to the stand to testify as to the erased words showing the appointment. Again, so what? There were three hundred similar erasures in the same date book, merely reflecting that appointments were frequently made by my secretary, often without my knowledge, and subsequently changed or canceled.
>
> —Richardson testified that in September Vesco gave him a message to give to me at a fund-raising affair, to "get the f--king SEC off my back," but he never delivered the message. So what?
>
> —At one point the prosecutors introduced telephone records to show that ten calls had been placed in a space of a few days from Sears' office to Mitchell's office. So what? Eight of the calls were charged at minimum rate and were billed as one minute, indicating that they probably were from secretary to secretary trying to get the two on the phone at the same time.
>
> —An official of a company known as GATX Leasing and Mooring (UK) Ltd was brought to the stand all the way from London to testify that at a meeting in June 1971 Vesco had dropped the names of "Bill" Mitchell and "Murray" Stans. So what? This was long before I met Vesco, and the prosecutors knew this. The testimony was never connected to the case.
>
> —Walter Hansen, senior partner of the national accounting firm

of Peat Marwick Mitchell & Co., was put on the stand to testify that I had solicited contributions from him and his partners in March 1972, and had pointed out that contributions given before April 7 would not be made public. So what? That was not an issue in the case. Despite repeated urging by Wing, Hansen refused to say that I had *insisted* that their contributions be given before that date.

There also were introduced into the record hundreds of telephone bills, papers, and documents purported to be pertinent, and masses of immaterial detail. The judge allowed it to be received "subject to connection" but no connection with the charges was ever made on much of the government's testimony or documents. I shuddered every time I thought of the cost of reproducing the record if we had to appeal a verdict.

As is normal in a trial like this, there were some conflicts between my testimony and the others on the issues in the case, but they were minor and few:

—Richardson testified that at the end of the meeting on March 8 I set up a meeting by phone for him and Vesco to see Mitchell. Hofgren testified that I left the room briefly and came back to say, "Your next meeting is ready." No such meeting with Mitchell took place. I testified that I received a call from my secretary and announced that *my* next meeting was ready, which was a perfectly routine procedure.

—Sears testified in court that he didn't remember meeting in my office around March 1 to talk about Vesco. I recalled it clearly and he had actually described it in his earlier testimony to the grand jury.

—Richardson testified that on April 10, at the meeting when he delivered the $200,000 in cash, he told me: "I have a message for you from Vesco. He wants to know if he is going to get some help." Sears testified that what Richardson said was: "He'd like to get some help," but that he did so with his head lowered and in a timid voice not characteristic of Richardson. I did not hear Richardson clearly but thought the message was "Vesco hopes this will be of some help," which I understood as referring to the campaign.

—Richardson testified that immediately afterward I said: "Mitchell and Sears are handling that." Sears testified that I said: "That's Mitchell's department." I did not recall that statement in either form because Mitchell's name never came up at that meeting. If it had happened, it would have had to be immediately before Sears insisted that there was no quid pro quo, and I said that there couldn't be any.

—Sears testified that at the end of the meeting during the Republican Convention on August 22, I said to him: "That SEC situation has gotten too hot to handle." I testified that I had said this to Sears on December 12 after SEC charges had been filed. I was certain of the date, because I had no knowledge of any SEC developments between April, when I thought the case was resolved, and August 22, so there would have been no basis for my making such a statement at that time.

—I testified that on November 12 and 15 Dean advised me not to disclose the $250,000 Vesco contribution to Cook unless I was formally asked. Dean said that he did not recall those conversations. I remembered them vividly.

—Cook testified that on November 15, over the telephone, I asked him whether the charges that Vesco brought $250,000 into the United States needed to be spelled out in such detail. I testified that Cook originated this subject in that conversation and that he said the charge was "sensationalism" and was being rewritten.


It seemed then and seems to me now that these variances in recollection of small details almost two years after they happened were hardly so significant as to require a man to risk spending years of his life in prison, even if my accusers were to be believed on every one. The prosecutor made much of these small differences, arguing that they proved a conspiring mind on my part.

Potentially much more damaging to us in the course of the trial was the apparent failure of the prosecutor to turn certain documents over to us that recorded pretrial statements of witnesses and other persons interviewed by them regarding their knowledge of the facts. Under a principle known as the Jenks rule, the defendant at that time had the right to see any recorded accounts of interviews of persons before they were allowed to testify. Although we did receive the grand jury testimony in all instances, usually the evening before each took the stand in court, we were never given any other documents, particularly records of interviews. From several sources we received information, late in the trial, that interview memos had sometimes been prepared by the prosecution, and that some may have contained exculpatory statements. The suppression of such papers, if it occurred, could have been valuable to us in a later appeal, had that been necessary.

Weeks of the trial droned on with witness after witness called by the government, some from places far away, to identify telephone tolls, hotel bills, personal logbooks and diaries, and similar data, 99 percent of which was never used again. Things moved so slowly, in fact, that one observer said the whole proceeding was "like watching grass grow." One juror slept fitfully and others nodded at times while the government's supposed background was being laid.

Sears was the first main witness for the prosecution, and when the time came for him to take the stand, he was granted full immunity for his alleged offenses in return for his agreement to testify against us. It gave me real concern to see him on the government's side, since I couldn't imagine what he could say that would be incriminating. Would he tell the straight truth, in which case I had nothing to fear, or would he embellish and enlarge upon the facts in order to please the prosecutors, in return for his immunity, in which case Mitchell or I might be unfairly placed in serious jeopardy? Would his testimony be aimed at Mitchell or at me? Despite his deal for freedom Sears did not appear to please the prosecutors and several times they sought unsuccessfully to declare him a hostile witness, so they could cross-examine him and presumably try to break down his testimony where it was favorable to us. He said without hesitation that he had never asked anyone to fix the Vesco case with the SEC.

Richardson came on like "gang busters," well primed and eager to please the prosecution, and tried to point a heavy finger at me on several points. He overdid his testimony by volunteering inadmissible remarks such as "Stans was not pleased to see me," and his over-zeal to satisfy the prosecutors was noted by reporters and must have been evident to the jury. Much of his testimony probably had little impact, such as the accounts of his unsuccessful attempts to reach me on the telephone in July and his failure to deliver to me a message from Vesco in September. He admitted that some of his testimony had changed since he first appeared before the grand jury and said some things had just "slipped his mind" at the time. He conceded that Vesco had never mentioned anything about trying to fix the SEC case, and acknowledged that the investigation had accelerated rather than diminished after the contribution was made.

Dean was subdued and terse, and little of his direct testimony related to me. His main statement was that Mitchell had asked him in October to try to get the SEC to hold off some depositions of Vesco's business associates for about ten days until after the election. Mitchell denied this had taken place. Dean avoided one truthful answer that would have been very helpful to me—that he had advised me twice not to volunteer any information to Cook about Vesco's contribution. He said he didn't remember. He did confirm that Ed Nixon had told him early in 1973 that I had not asked that Vesco give cash.

Cook's statements were different in slight respects from those I gave later to the jury, but the only serious charge he made was that I had attempted at one point before the indictment to influence his grand jury testimony, which was not true. My attorney, Walter Bonner, was relentless in cross-examination and forced Cook to admit that he had lied on five occasions about the Vesco matter after he had told me that he was "going to tell it like it is." Several of these perjured statements were made to committees of the Senate and House of Representatives. Any inference that I had influenced Cook to do anything improper was belied by the fact that he and the SEC had pressed vigorously on with its investigation and had brought forth a strong set of charges against Vesco in November 1972. He testified that "the commission had to bring one of the most forceful and thorough cases in its history—and it did." Furthermore, when Cook resigned his position with the SEC in May 1973, he had stated publicly that the case wasn't slowed up, deterred, or its directions changed because of any political pressure on him. His admissions during the merciless cross-examination that he had perjured himself on several occasions discredited all his testimony. I felt sorry for Cook, because he is a good person and probably had been trying unnecessarily to protect everyone, which I attributed to conflicting pressures and inexperience. It was remarkable, however, how his court testimony varied from the statements he gave to my lawyers in their first interview of him prior to the indictment.

Altogether the government brought on forty-five witnesses and took almost six weeks to present its case. Day by day,

Mitchell and I had to be in court, hearing person after person give data which the prosecutors promised to weave together, some truthful, some that we knew to be false, and much that was meaningless.

One point of intense controversy arose when we proposed to introduce into the record some of the White House tapes of conversations between John Dean and the President. The prosecution objected strenuously to allowing us to even have them, but the judge ruled that they were exculpatory as far as I was concerned and we were permitted to hear them and to use them in the trial. They were the first of the White House tapes to be made public and, of course, attracted a great deal of attention. On one tape, that of March 13, 1973, Dean reported to the President that everything we had done in fund-raising was legal. On another, February 28, 1973, Dean told the President that I was an innocent victim of circumstances.[1] These excerpts were, I believe, valuable in establishing the credibility of my testimony.

Most of the remaining testimony by government witnesses had little or no relevancy as far as I was concerned, and some of it boomeranged against the prosecution. Dan Hofgren, who had been at my meeting with Vesco and Richardson on March 8, testified unequivocally that I had not asked for the contribution to be in cash, thus repudiating Richardson's testimony and confirming mine.

Wing put Rose Mary Woods on the stand to acknowledge that one early list of names supplied to her by our committee, containing the names of contributors before April 7, 1972, did not include Vesco's name, thus implying an attempt to keep his gift secret. But Wing knew that was only half the story. In cross-examination by the defense, Miss Woods canceled out his ploy by identifying a second and complete list of contributors up to the date of the election, also in her possession, which did include Vesco's name. His attempt to show a coverup failed.

There were interminable legal arguments that occupied the proceedings, usually with the jury excused from the courtroom. There were also many such questions that had to be dealt with by the judge that were argued by counsel in his chambers. We didn't

---

1. See page 258.

seem to win many of these procedural arguments, but our lawyers felt that they were important elements for appeal in the event we lost out with the jury. They also felt that these points would ultimately be helpful in resolving legal issues related to the instructions the judge would be giving to the jury at the conclusion of the evidence. There were other frequent delays and intermissions, all extending the trial and adding to the strain of its length. When we were not a part of the proceedings, Mitchell and I sat and waited in a cold, dirty, buff-walled room across the hall.

That scene gradually took on the feeling of a dungeon. The shabby walls and furniture, one long wooden table, and a half dozen rickety chairs, added to the impression. In the corner was a huge blackboard filled with figures and undecipherable sketches from a previous trial. The conversation before and after sessions was usually cheerless, full of speculation about the next witness, the prosecution tactics, the rulings of the judge, or other unfolding events. To the extent we could, Mitchell and I spent our waiting hours reading newspapers, books, and magazines, broken by a few visits from friends and relatives. Our only exercise was in walking the halls, where we would often get a friendly smile or word from a bailiff, court reporter, or the building nurse; subtly they made us feel that they were rooting for us.

There were about forty pressmen and photographers on the sidewalk at the bottom of the courthouse steps every time we arrived and departed. They rushed to meet us, thrusting microphones in our faces, asking questions and clicking pictures, walking backward as we proceeded forward, jostling each other, sometimes stumbling and falling in our path. They were looking for the casual remark that could be quoted, or the picture of windblown hair, an open mouth or body angle that could be considered unusual enough to be printed. Despite their annoying persistence, they were friendly and I felt sorry for them and the demeaning way they had to work. During the noon recess when we set out to lunch, the workers eating their sandwiches on the benches in Foley Square looked up in surprise as the cameras and microphones sometimes pursued us all the way to our restaurant, asking questions and taking shots of how we walked, talked, and ate. We finally gave up going out during the noon recess and settled for cold sandwiches and coffee brought in.

Except for the constant knowledge that our lives were at

stake, it was a horrible bore to endure. As it was, Mitchell and I managed to conceal our tension from each other until it was all over. He is a sturdy man and despite continuing family problems with his wife, Martha, and his other mounting legal problems, was stolid and emotionless throughout. The trial had barely begun when he was indicted in Washington in the Watergate case, but even that blow didn't seem to affect his equanimity.[2] I took strength from his ability to stand incredible troubles. His sense of humor and dry wit never left him.

I took copious notes as the trial progressed, noting questions to be asked of me or other witnesses, items to be pursued, records to be examined, new leads to be followed, and statements to be verified. It was the only way to survive the tedious moments. The press made special mention of my diligence, and seemed also to think it newsworthy that I wore an American flag pin in my lapel and had my favorite good luck charm, a bracelet woven of elephant-tail hair, on my wrist.

The jury's learning about a Cronkite nationwide broadcast of his live interview of Vesco during the trial may actually have been helpful. For what it was worth, Vesco said firmly that his contribution "in no way was intended to be used for the purpose of influencing the investigation." Interestingly, he also went on to volunteer without equivocation that it was Murray Chotiner, and not me, who had advised him to make his contribution in the form of cash. There was no way to get this in evidence because by this time Chotiner had died in an automobile accident. However, it did fill in a missing link and had a reasonable likelihood of being true, especially since it was learned that Chotiner had been handling some undisclosed legal matters for Vesco in this time frame.

Mitchell testified before I did. He was terse, direct, and positive in his replies, and I felt sure that his sincerity got through

---

2. Before the trial began the eastern press carried a rumor that the Watergate Special Prosecutor in Washington had offered to accept a guilty plea from Mitchell to one Watergate felony in return for dropping all other charges, including those involved in the Vesco case. I speculated momentarily at the time on the probability that such an arrangement might dispose of the Vesco trial entirely, leaving me free. Mitchell acknowledged to me later that such an offer had been made but said that in no way would he ever plead guilty to having done anything wrong.

to the jurors. Wing was ruthless in cross-examination, which lasted for more than a day, but didn't shake Mitchell's narration.

Then came my turn. I was concerned for the three preceding days because I had developed a sore throat, which the courthouse nurse twice a day swabbed with medications, without too much relief. In retrospect, I believe it was psychosomatic, because when I finally was sworn in and began to tell my story to the jury from the beginning it disappeared. That was not until I had taken into my own hands the placement of the microphone.

It had troubled me that every witness had found it hard to be heard in the courtroom without discomfiture. The microphone rested on the front railing of the jury box, too far for the witness to speak into from the chair, which was fixed to the floor and not movable. Some of them leaned backward and forward clumsily with every question and answer. Others placed the microphone on the judge's desk to their right, which meant that in answering they had to look away from the jury at their left. A few held it inconveniently in their hands. I didn't like any of these solutions, so I asked my lawyers to arrange for the court clerk to bring in a large cardboard packing box, railing high, and place it between me and the front wall of the witness stand to hold the mike. It was perfect. Without strain I could look directly at the jurors as I gave my answers, and this brought me a feeling of comfort and confidence that I'm sure improved the effect of my testimony.

My direct testimony took a full day, and my lawyers were pleased with it. The cross-examination lasted a day and a half, as Wing tried unsuccessfully to break down the facts that by that time I had well in mind. In exasperation, as he concluded, he accused me broadly of lying throughout:

"Haven't you testified falsely under oath for the last two days?" he yelled out.

I raised my voice for the only time. Deliberately, I said indignantly, "Absolutely not. That's a lie, Mr. Wing, and you know it." With that, he gave up my cross-examination.

The ordeal was coming to an end. We had a few other witnesses that corroborated some details, but the decision rested largely on Mitchell's testimony and mine. There were last-minute legal contentions on technicalities and the final phase, the closing arguments and the judge's instructions to the jury, then began.

Mitchell's attorney, Peter Fleming, spoke for four hours, summing up the case for his client, putting the issues in perspective, and belittling the conflicts of testimony.  It was a splendid job, but in my mind it was promptly excelled by the masterful, eloquent, and at times emotional appeal of my lawyer, Walter Bonner.  There were moist eyes in the courtroom as he exposed the fiction of the government's case, and pictured me as a lifelong honest and respected person who would not sell his soul for the sake of a political contribution.  He talked for four hours from the heart, almost extemporaneously, using only a bare outline of facts and dates.  He decried the "Vesco-itis" of the prosecution's case, which seemed to portray that I spent all my time for a year, at no personal advantage, doing nothing but contriving ways to help a man I had only met once in my life.  He dealt heavily with the motives and self-interests of the four major witnesses arrayed against us, pointing out that each of them expected relief from penalties for personal transgressions in return for fingering Mitchell and me.  I put my head in my hands and wept when he finished with an emotional plea to the jury to "restore to this good, decent and honorable American his good name."  Old courtroom buffs who were present, including some members of the press, said afterward that it was the best jury appeal they had ever heard.

There was one more travail to face and that was to listen to Wing's closing statement for the prosecution.  It began late in the afternoon and continued through much of the next day, a total time of five hours and thirty-seven minutes.  He was close to brilliant as he addressed the jury practically without notes, reviewing his concept of the "conspiracy" from one end to another.  His manner was calm, deliberate, unsmiling, and methodical as he tried to put the pieces of testimony together his way, emphasizing the government witnesses and belittling ours, connecting events by innuendo, and ignoring our side of the story.  It was a normal trial technique, but it shook me that our simple honest motives could be put into such a distorted light, and the night after he began I broke down in my apartment under the tension for the first time.  I did not feel confident any longer that I could expect the jury to see through the smokescreens and fantasies of the government's case, when it was so artificially but effectively pulled together. It was my only restless night. But Wing talked too long on his second day, straining to connect a lot of loose ends and isolated events into a plot that hadn't existed, and I took new hope that the jury would see through the tissue structure he was trying to build.

Throughout the trial my lawyers had been making legal points with respect to contributions, reporting, and campaign practices. When the trial was over they spent considerable time with the judge, urging instructions on the law on these technical matters which would clear up possible confusion in the minds of the jurors as to the propriety of the way the Vesco contribution had been handled. This was designed to neutralize the considerable confusion which had been injected by government witnesses and contentions. Barker told me later that he believed the obtaining of a good and balanced set of instructions to the jury on these points was among the most important legal work in the trial.

When delivered, the judge's instructions on the law were very thorough and took more than a half day for him to read. My confidence in him was restored when I heard his directions to the jury, especially those dealing with witnesses who were testifying for a consideration, and those who were admitted criminals or perjurers. On these he said, among other things:

"During the course of the trial Harry Sears, John Dean, and Laurence Richardson testified before you. Mr. Sears was named as a codefendant in this indictment. Mr. Dean and Mr. Richardson, although not named as defendants, are alleged to have been coconspirators. Thus, the Government has charged that each of these men was an accomplice.

"The testimony of an accomplice should be viewed with great caution and scrutinized carefully. In assessing the credibility of an accomplice, as with that of any witness, you may consider any interest that he may have in the outcome of the case. You may consider evidence as to any benefit the witness expects to derive or has derived from his testimony or evidence as to a motive to place responsibility on others.

"You will recall that during the course of the trial in the testimony of G. Bradford Cook, he admitted lying before a grand jury and two congressional committees.

"Now, the testimony of an admitted perjurer should be considered with caution and weighed with great care.

"You may decide, for example, that an admitted liar is unbelievable or, conversely, you may accept his testimony. The question, again as always, is did the witness testify truthfully before you, and the question of credibility is for you and you alone to decide."

These instructions went directly to the heart of the case and I took strength from them; if the jury understood and respected these words there would be no conviction, because the government's efforts to prove guilt could not be glued together.

The jury began deliberations Thursday afternoon, April 25, at 4:55, and continued until 10:35 that evening; resumed early Friday morning and carried on again until 10:00 at night; met for a long day on Saturday until recessing for dinner at 7:15; and started again on Sunday morning. It was not a comfortable time, waiting them out, while reflecting upon the fact that the rest of my life hinged on the word that would come out of their conclusions. The jury room was located next to the one in which Mitchell and I waited, and on Thursday evening for a time we could hear loud voices through the walls without knowing what was said. Friday and Saturday were quiet on that front, and we didn't know whether that was encouraging or ominous.

From time to time they would send a message to the judge asking that some testimony be reread or that a portion of the judge's charge be repeated. Each time we would try to divine the significance of the request, to guess whether it portended a favorable or unfavorable trend of thought. We took heart on Saturday when they asked the judge to repeat his instructions as to how to evaluate the testimony of a confessed perjurer or a witness being given immunity or other special consideration for testifying. The more often that was said the more helpful it would be to us, we thought.

We also believed that each hour that passed after the first evening was a good omen. It meant that the jury was getting further and further away from a quick finding of guilt, and was more likely to reach a verdict of acquittal.

There were two fears we had about the outcome from early on. One was that the jury would fail to reach agreement and we would have to go through the whole agonizing process all over again. While a split jury heavily in our favor would be encouraging, we were sure that these prosecutors would not give up without a new attempt, and that would mean another year with the same sword over our heads. I prayed that would not happen.

My own worst specter, however, was that the jury would compromise. If there were any kind of a division, they might conclude that even though we were basically innocent there must have been some measure of guilt for the government to bring the case, and resolve the dilemma by holding us guilty on one or two counts and innocent on the rest. That would be very little better than a verdict against us on all counts; while the sentence might be less, the current headlines and the historical conclusions would be the same: Stans and Mitchell guilty. I prayed with double fervor that this would not occur.

These thoughts and a myriad of others were in my mind during the dreadful hours of tension as we sweated it out. There was no sense of panic or fright; I had conditioned myself day by day as the ordeal went on that I had to steel myself for any result, and that could mean a finding of guilty and years of appeals, at frightening cost. I was determined that, come what may, I could take it, notwithstanding the knowledge of innocence and the unfairness of it all. Some of the jurors said after the verdict that we were both cool and unemotional throughout. I'm glad it came through that way, but it was a conditioned pose as far as I was concerned. I'm not sure I could have kept my resolve not to break down or rebel in some way if I had lost. Prayer and a confidence in ultimate justice can go only so far, I feared, in getting me to accept injustice.

While the trial was on, I would look from time to time at the jury and say to myself in astonishment: "Those people have my life in their hands, not only my future but everything I have done in the past. They can destroy it all." It was unreal. I would listen to a witness, knowing he was either deliberately lying or had been brainwashed, and ask myself how such things could come to pass. Yet the reality was there, and I knew it. I could tell myself it was just a horrible dream, but I could not be sure that the horror would end, or how. Under such pressures the mind works in circles, and I went from one to the other of these concerns, stopping at each to tell myself not to worry, yet going on to the next and the next until I was back over the same route. The trouble was that my own knowledge of innocence was not enough. Somehow, someway, the jury had to see it that way, to see through the haze and contradictions and persiflage and irrelevancies, to discard all the chaff and get to the heart of the whole case, to find that I was telling the truth.

One of our regular occupations each day of the trial had been jury-reading. We watched closely for a sign of understanding or sympathy as each point was made in our testimony, or for an indication of acceptance of a contrary point made by an opposing witness. We watched the varying indications of interest by the jurors, noting some who were alert throughout and others who sometimes seemed bored and barely awake. We speculated in the back room about which jurors were likely to be on our side, which ones needed convincing, which ones might give us trouble. We wondered which ones would really understand the issues, and which ones would be the leaders in the final deliberations. It was pretty much a useless exercise, and we knew it, but occasionally my lawyers found a way to appeal to perceived interests of particular jurors, and in any event it was one way of keeping our spirits up and our minds active.

I had one other means of buoying my spirits when I felt inclined to bemoan my fate or challenge the injustice of it all. Each Sunday Kathleen and I attended church services, choosing among those listed in the Saturday papers the sermons with the most reassuring titles. We went frequently to hear Norman Vincent Peale at Marble Collegiate Church, an eloquent and brilliant speaker, whose message is always on the positive side. Sometimes, we listened to Raymond Charles Barker of the Church of Religious Science, an equally uplifting speaker. Also, I carried in my pocket a dog-eared bulletin of the Church of the Truth containing a message by Dr. Ervin Seale, which I took out and read whenever I began to feel overwhelmed. It said:

> Neglect how you feel and you will feel better. The watched pot never boils it seems, but watched feelings grow more intense. The person who takes his temperature every fifteen minutes is really strengthening his fever. And the one who constantly regards his moods to note his level of cheer or gloom becomes as

busy as a weather vane.

So many of our feelings are like the wind and breezes. They come and go. Let them do so. More important than how you feel is how you do and act. Check the tendency to complain, smile, even if it hurts, do something constructive, carry on. Sooner than you think, bad feelings will not know where to find you. They will get discouraged instead of discouraging you. And you will be at peace inside.

This is how I managed to stay at peace inside while bitterness reigned outside.

At the outset we had visualized that the most difficult problem we had was to put the amount of $200,000 into a perspective that would prevent the jurors from being overwhelmed by it. To many of them that would be an immense sum of money, almost a life's earnings. How would we get them to believe that anyone, even a man of substantial wealth, would give away that much to a political campaign without a promise that something of value would come back to him? How could we impress on them the fact that in those days people did give such sums to candidates solely from patriotic motives? How could we get across to them the picture that a contribution of $200,000 from a man worth $50 million was less of a burden than $20 would be for a man worth $10,000?

We had some answers, but they might not be enough. There were twenty-two other people in the United States who had given $200,000 to our campaign, one of them $2 million and another $1 million. If we could get some of the contributors to testify as to their motives, and the absence of any favors in return, it might help. W. Clement Stone came to the courtroom prepared to testify that he contributed $2 million in 1968 and another $2 million in 1972 because it was "a once-in-a-lifetime opportunity to support a President whose philosophy he was strongly in favor of." He never requested or expected anything in return except good government. This kind of statement from him and others would have been valuable testimony for the defense because it showed that many citizens were willing to make substantial amounts available without seeking favors; it also showed that this was part of the atmosphere in which I was working as finance chairman in 1972. However, the judge refused to allow him or other givers to testify to such effect, on the ground that their motivation, whatever it was, was not relevant to Vesco's motivation.

We also brought to court as a witness the finance chairman of the 1972 Muskie Presidential campaign, who was prepared to testify that he had received and accepted cash contributions as a regular course, and that there were many bona fide reasons, including security of the donor and his family, for keeping contributions confidential. Again the judge thwarted us, by ruling that what other candidates did was not pertinent to our case.

These rulings were a severe disappointment to me and my counsel. They prevented us from showing that sizable contributions could spring from valid motives, and that cash gifts were not uncommon, two key elements in our defense. My counsel argued unsuccessfully that "before the jury it has been suggested that a $200,000 contribution is something that would buy this country, and it is important to know that substantial citizens with good intent, good motive, good purpose and a lifetime of political interest and service are willing to make substantial amounts available." Barker told me later that he felt the judge's exclusion of this line of testimony over his objection may have won considerable sympathy for us from the jury.

The judge did, however, allow me to read into the record a list of the names and amounts of the top twenty contributors, so the jury could see that Vesco did not stand alone. The prosecutor in return made much of the point that Vesco's contribution was the largest one received in cash, and this detracted somewhat from the force of our argument. We could and did explain also that Vesco's gift was a fraction of 1 percent of the $60 million that was raised, and from it made the argument that his amount was not so important in the total, or so badly needed, as to cause me to "deal" with him improperly. Despite this, the size of his contribution in relation to the normal money experience of the jurors was one of our greatest concerns.

While we were in the middle of the trial, I received an unusual but gratifying offer by letter from a man in California, addressed to me at the courthouse. In 1972 this fellow had somewhat persistently, in meetings and by mail, offered a substantial contribution if I would assure him of an ambassadorship. I told him in my office that it couldn't be done, wrote him a letter saying so, and turned down all of his money. Now that I was on trial for supposedly making a deal with Vesco, he was gracious enough to offer to come to New York with the correspondence and testify that I was a person who could not be bought. We thanked him profusely, but my counsel felt that his testimony would not be permitted as pertinent to Vesco, and they had to decline his offer. It was comforting, nevertheless, to have this voluntary affirmation of the propriety of my actions in such matters.

## 13

## VESCO—AFTERMATH

In a complex and prolonged trial, a defendant's memory is put to a severe test, and I came to observe, for the first time, how wonderfully and yet how strangely the memory functions. The brain is a marvelous electronic system, much like a computer, recording everything that is fed into it. Over one's life that can total trillions and quadrillions of bits of information. Retrieving them is the function of memory, and when put to the test of trying to recall an event one finds out how unevenly these bits are recorded. Unlike a data processing machine, in which all pieces of information fed into it are uniformly impressed and are recalled with equal weight, the mind has recorded most details lightly and they are often difficult to bring back. Some events are brilliantly etched in recollection, some do not return at all, even when the mind is refreshed with related data. Persons with very busy lives or important responsibilities have habits as they go along of choosing the kinds of things they want to remember from those which they dismiss from mind as unimportant. Throughout life the unusual and the unexpected make deeper impressions on the recording system than the usual and the repetitious. That is why, in our ordinary lives and without effort, we will remember distinctly every detail of an automobile accident or a death five years ago, but have trouble recalling what we had for dinner ten days past.

When one is forced by the circumstances of a trial to try to recall early events, he is in a quandary. His memory will go only so far and many matters the prosecutors think important may be indistinct or vague. He does his best, without success, and is made to look bad by that fact. Something that to his memory system was unimportant, perhaps by reason of the frequency of its happening, may have been unique to another person in the same transaction. Thus, it was hard for me to recall what transpired in any one out of six hundred conversations with major contributors or prospects, but each of those persons might have a clear image of what was said by everyone present.

Furthermore, concurrent outside pressures at the time of a conversation can cause a dimming of one's memory. The fact that my mind was heavily preoccupied in the later months of 1972 with Kathleen's critical illness weakened the depth of my perception of other events that occurred during that time, and in turn made the memory of them very hazy.

In any of such conditions, a defendant faces a multiple set of dangers. He can attempt to aid his recollection by adding to it what he *thinks* happened at the time, which may or may not be accurate and can lead him into further trouble. He can guess, or assume, what may have happened, with equal risk. Or he can find it hard to sort out his recollections of what did happen from what he subsequently heard or read about the incident, and sometimes fall into a trap in not drawing the line precisely.

With all these hazards in mind, I did my best to adhere to the full truth in all my testimony. With the added time available to concentrate on bringing events into focus, and to check calendars and documents, I was obviously able to be more certain at the trial on some things than I was before the grand jury. This made possible a better recollection of places, persons, conversations, and events, occasionally at some variance with the earlier recollection. I could only hope that each of the jurors had had similar difficulties with memory at one time or another in their lives and would be understanding.

There was, however, one matter which I did not tell to the jury, on the advice of my lawyers to withhold it, and for the rest of the trial I wondered whether I would second-guess that decision as long as I lived. It related to steps we had taken shortly before and during the trial to reconstruct and strengthen my memory of certain events, particularly my conversations with Brad Cook in November 1972 during and following our Texas goose hunt. That had all happened right after the election, when I was utterly exhausted from the last-minute drive for funds and the concurrent pressures of various pending civil lawsuits. It was a time when Kathleen's serious blood illness was not responding to treatment, and her sense of depression and hopelessness was traumatic for me. My doctor had urged me to take the few days off, promising to phone me if there was a change in her condition. All of these things had rested so heavily on my mind during the time I was in Texas and thereafter that I was having difficulty in recalling the events and conversations that had taken place, and it was vital that I remember more clearly just what had been done and said. One of the perjury charges alleged that I had knowingly lied about these matters.

In December 1973, two months before the trial began, I attended a series of lectures given by members of the famous Menninger Clinic. One of the psychologists had said in passing that it was possible to bring back memory of past events through professionally administered hypnosis. I told my lawyers about this and they made inquiries that brought encouraging confirmation from other specialists. It resulted in my undertaking a series of treatments through hypnosis and other methods of memory recall from Dr. Elliot Wineburg in Forest Hills that extended over about fifty hours of evening and weekend time while the trial was under way. No one else, not even Mitchell and his attorneys, knew this was going on.

The results were astounding in that, item by item, I began to visualize the details I had forgotten. My phone calls and meetings in Washington with Cook came back clearly. Then, in one two-hour session of deep hypnosis I saw and relived the precise experiences in that Texas rice field seventeen months earlier. Much of it was vivid. It gave me the exact information I needed to fill out my account of what had transpired.

The question then arose as to whether I should testify that I had gone through this procedure, and whether Dr. Wineburg should be called as a witness to confirm that he had used on me medically accepted methods of memory recall. After long deliberation my lawyers concluded that I should not mention any part of it, because the jury might think it was too "gimmicky." Notwithstanding that decision, with which I reluctantly concurred, I retained the feeling that the information I was able to recover by these treatments helped my testimony immeasurably by giving me certainty and confidence.

My relationship with my attorneys was excellent throughout and I relied on them fully, although I perhaps annoyed them sometimes by raising questions of procedure or tactics. Bob Barker is a sage and astute man who pays a great deal of attention to small details, and his advice throughout was invaluable. Walt Bonner and his associates brought to the Vesco trial a broad background as former government prosecutors, and they made a brilliant team as they and Barker parsed out every piece of the government's case and debated how to cope with it. I could not have been better represented.

Sunday, April 28, began dully. Mitchell and I sat in our dreary holding room, sipping coffee, reading the papers, and talking about desultory subjects while we waited for our fate to be decided. The place was a mess by this time, cluttered with three days of accumulation of newspapers and garbage. There had been no cleanup by the janitors on Friday night, so the one waste basket had overflowed on to the floor, papers were all over the table and in stacks under it, the remains of our lunches and wrappings and coffee cups and pop bottles were strewn about on the window sills and floor, and disorder was everywhere. Four of the lawyers who had brought us through the trial were reclining on beds in the courthouse medical unit. Under the mounting tension, and with their work on the case concluded, they had relaxed on the town on Saturday night and were now recovering from the letdown. With no expectation of an imminent verdict, they decided to take a nap and let Mitchell and me sweat things out by ourselves, while Barker, a Mormon who had not participated in the night's activities, read a law journal and made phone calls. I started to work on a crossword puzzle. There was no heat in the building on Sundays, and our room had a deep chill, so I sat in my heavy overcoat.

Suddenly, at 12:50 a court clerk burst through the door of our waiting room and said simply but electrically, "We have a verdict." The lawyers collected quickly and we paced into the courtroom expectant, fearful, and hopeful, as the final scene unfolded.

Upon returning to the table at which I had sat for so long, I raised my head to the ceiling in a silent plea of prayer as the judge and then the jury took their places. The courtroom was tense. Ten weeks of contentious trial were about to bring forth their fateful outcome. Twenty-six hours of deliberation by our peers had decided the future of our lives, and we were to learn what that was.

I don't know what caused me to notice it, but as the jury walked in I saw that the forelady of the jury, youthful Sybil Kucharski, had nothing in her hands. With eighteen counts to be decided, that could mean only one thing: All the verdicts were the same, or she would have needed a summary sheet to be sure when to say "guilty" and when to say "not guilty." But which answer was it going to be? I couldn't conceive of being found guilty on all counts, and it was still the acme of hope to expect to be acquitted on all.

Judge Gagliardi ended that reverie by asking gently, "Ladies and gentlemen of the jury, have you reached a verdict?"

"We have, your honor," replied the forelady, in quiet words.

The court clerk took over. "What do you find on Mitchell count number one?"

"Not guilty," she replied, with a slight Mona Lisa smile. As far as I was concerned it was all over. It was now incomprehensible to me that she would have different answers to the various counts, and I relaxed as the litany went on through counts two to nine for Mitchell and started with Stans count one. It was the same "not guilty," as it had to be, for I could not be guilty of a conspiracy without a coconspirator. The rest of the answers were anticlimax, all "not guilty," and the nightmare was over!

It was then that I said "I feel reborn." It was not uttered in the sense of having suddenly found a relationship with my God since I had been a religious person all my life. It meant in a more literal tenor that I had regained an opportunity to live my own life. In a longer version, I explained what I intended: "For a year I've had this sword hanging over my head. My heart stopped beating for thirty-two seconds today, and now I feel I have been reborn." And a few minutes later, recalling the agonies I had experienced in the witch-hunts of 1972 and 1973 and 1974, I said to a press conference: "Even the book of Job had a happy ending."

My final reflections are easy to recount. The trial had taken away a year of living and a year of earning power. I had survived a horrible dream. But I had no feelings of hostility or resentment toward those who had caused it. They had merely carried out their mission as they saw it, and in a way I felt sorry for them, because they had lost much more than I had. Above all, I thanked God for his justice and for American justice, on which I had relied from the beginning. And I thanked God, too, that twelve plain, ordinary people among my peers had the courage and the ability to perceive that the only issue to be decided was who was telling the truth.

Immediately after the trial, the media sought out the jurors to get the inside story of what had happened in the privacy of the jury room. The answers varied somewhat, but through all of them ran a common thread best exemplified by statements of the forewoman of the jury, Sybil Kucharski, in a television interview the next morning:

> "We felt these men were just doing their job, their everyday job. . . . We didn't feel that they were behind closed doors conspiring, each other's minds together constantly.
> "As for Mitchell, he got up there and the questions he was asked he answered them, we felt, all truthfully. He didn't appear not to be telling the truth. The same with Stans. We didn't feel they had any reason to lie. They were credible men."

She also stated, less concisely, that the jurors did not consider the government's evidence convincing, and that they did not believe some of the government testimony. They considered John Dean to be the key prosecution witness and weren't sure whether to believe him or not, since he had admitted his guilt in the Watergate matter and had acknowledged that he hoped his sentence for that would be lightened in return for his testimony against us.

The lack of credibility of the government's witnesses was named by several of the jurors as a major factor in arriving at their verdict. The Western Union messenger summed it up by noting that, "Some witnesses were too willing to help themselves." According to the *New York Times*: "Again and again the jurors, when speaking about testimony of those witnesses after the verdict was announced, used the words 'incredible' or 'unbelievable.' "

The jury had spent a whole day on the issue of whether the Vesco contribution was legal and decided that it was. As for the size of the amount, they concluded that Mitchell and Stans were substantial men who would not conspire over $200,000. Once the jurors had decided that we were credible and could be believed, and were not guilty of perjury, the rest of the charges evaporated. Ms. Kucharski said later on television: "We figured there couldn't be any conspiracy it there was no perjury."

The jury's approach to judgment hadn't started smoothly, and had some ominous overtones. The first few hours of discussion in the jury room were disorderly and very heated, with everyone trying to talk at the same time. There were some jurors at this point who had the idea that the government wouldn't bring persons to trial unless they were guilty; the forelady, Ms. Kucharski, reported later that "we didn't know how to proceed at first," so they Xeroxed the indictment and spent an hour reading it. "Some jurors thought this is what the government says, and the government brought it, so it must be so." Another juror acknowledged: "I felt at the beginning that if the government brings charges against someone, there must be something to it, but I realized after listening to the judge's instructions that I couldn't think that way."

This impression was what caused the jury to ask that his instructions regarding the presumption of innocence and of credibility to be given to tainted testimony be reread. Ms. Kucharski said: "When you have the law read to you by the judge and reread it, it becomes clear what the issues are. It was simply a case of concentrating on the facts." An early sounding seemed to show that at the outset eight jurors had believed there was guilt on some counts, but this did not mean that a majority would have found guilt on any specific one. The forelady said: "It wasn't unanimous until we looked at everything carefully, very carefully. It was an emotional thing at first. Some weren't considering the law." This was echoed by another juror who said: "A number of jurors were not clear on the law. The judge's rereading of the law helped to clear several points of confusion."

In any event, the jury had finally resolved the overall question of guilt by resolving who was telling the truth. Wing had made that challenge in his closing argument by saying: "Somebody is lying to you and your job as jurors, quite simply, is to figure it out. Who is it?" The verdict of acquittal was their answer, and they had reached it in just that way.

Interestingly, some of the jurors also gave their versions of what the Vesco situation was all about. Ms. Kucharski's opinion was that "Vesco gave the contribution hoping it would do something for him, but Mitchell and Stans didn't know what was in his mind." The letter carrier's conclusion was "I think Vesco was the real culprit of this whole thing. He may have been using these people. Sears and Vesco seemed to want to get something going. I don't think the defendants ever fell for it."

Prosecutor Wing had a simple analysis of the outcome. He told John Dean on the phone after the verdict that "we figure the jurors were impressed that Mitchell and Stans put Vesco's money in the campaign instead of their own pockets."

One phenomenon that I became acquainted with during the trial was the professional hater, an individual who apparently delights in writing poison pen letters, full of vitriol, at persons under public charges. Two or three of these had come to me when I was Secretary of Commerce, for not proceeding fast enough to solve one or other of the nation's problems, but those were caustic rather than vicious. I presume a President gets many of them. When the Vesco indictment came, I got a score or more of the real hate notes, with imprecations like "Why, you crook!" or "You have no place to hide, Bag Man," both of which were signed; or "You self-serving, greedy big time crook! thief! disgrace to your church," which was unsigned. One was more expansive: "It is difficult to believe you are for real, after all the corruption that surrounds you and your participation in this washed money associated in the Watergate crimes. I think of you as a vile person. It is too bad we cannot have an open season on persons like you and mount your head for posterity."

The first few of these, carrying the message that some persons do believe that accusation is tantamount to guilt, shook me a bit. How could people, ignorant of the facts, be so bitter? After three or four of these experiences I came to recognize them as infrequent cases of mental aberration, and concluded that the only course was to consign them to the garbage bag without giving them further thought. But there is still a surviving question: How can any person be so hateful of someone he doesn't know?

Among the promising by-products of this case were the ruminations by some of the press writers and columnists about the costs of proving innocence. My legal fees and expenses, without considering at all the loss of at least half of a year's working hours, were nearly $400,000. Mitchell's were about the same. A very large part of this was paid for us by the trustees of the surplus funds of the 1972 campaign, consistent with the accepted corporate policy of defending employees for their proper actions. But suppose the campaign had run a deficit and such finances had not been available to indemnify us? There would have been no alternative but to dig down into our own resources to pay the bills. And what kind of defense could we have presented in such a prolonged trial of complex issues if either of us had not had the financial means to be able to employ top lawyers? In its efforts to construct a case, the government prosecutors had the unlimited resources of many government agencies and their personnel, and probably spent much more than a million dollars. Is there not some principle of fairness that suggests that the government ought also to reimburse defendants for the cost of a trial on charges that prove to be unfounded?

Some of the press comments showed an enlightened view of the problem. Tom Dowling of the *Washington Star-News* said this:

> Who, after all, could afford such justice? In the case of Mitchell and Stans, the answer is [the finance committee] with its $3.4 million trust fund. . . .[1] It is difficult to think of a greater miscarriage of justice than two men plunking down three-quarters of a million dollars in order to demonstrate their innocence. This is a man saving himself through ruin.
>
> And so you do not begrudge them the helping hand of [the committee]. Surely $381,000 is too big a sum for any man to spend to stay free. . . . Yet, obviously, if it takes $381,000 to beat a government indictment, all of us but the indigent are bereft of any practical choice except to cop a plea and hope for a shorter sentence, however innocent we may be. . . . Stans and Mitchell were fortunate in their associations. They worked for an outfit that won the election with enough left over to meet its corporate obligations in the court.

---

1. Contrary to some other news reports, I did not participate when the trustees of the 1972 Liquidation Trust voted to reimburse these expenses.

Several other writers carried the subject further and suggested that the interests of justice would be served if laws were enacted to provide for reimbursement of legal costs to all persons who are put through a criminal trial and found to be not guilty. There would be less frequent occasions in which a defendant would be forced to plead guilty to avoid the expense or to rely on a public defender of uncertain skill or experience.

William F. Buckley, Jr., in a syndicated column opined:

> I find it an inexplicable outrage that men prosecuted by the government and found not guilty by the jury should be left short of the money to defend themselves.

Quoting this remark with approval, columnist Tom Wicker of the *New York Times* then wrote: "When the prosecution is blatantly unnecessary . . . why shouldn't Federal judges have some discretion to assign part or all of the defense costs to the Government?" He went on: "Everyone can judge for himself or herself whether the Mitchell-Stans trial could be so described. It seemed clearly a weak case, however. . . . Mr. Mitchell and Mr. Stans were charged with conspiring to fix the Vesco case, when that case, in fact, was not quashed or fixed."

I believe the reimbursement of costs to innocent defendants would be a good and fair law.

Another subject of some current discussion on which my experience gives me a strong viewpoint is the grand jury system. Under it, a prosecutor is allowed to present his side of the case in a secret session, and the witness is not permitted to have his lawyer in the courtroom or to give any evidence in his defense except in direct answer to the prosecutor's questions. He cannot cross-examine anyone or learn what has been said against him by others. He has no part in the selection of the jurors, runs the risk of incriminating himself by casual remarks, and may not even know he is the actual target of the inquiry. The purported reason for this imbalance is that all the grand jury is supposed to do is to determine whether there is enough evidence of guilty action by a person to justify holding him for a public trial in which both sides can give evidence as to guilt or innocence and let a trial jury decide.

The grand jury is an institution with roots in English common law and was long regarded as a citizen's bulwark against malicious prosecution. However, many critics now feel that, rather than protecting a citizen, it is often used to harass and intimidate suspects without the constitutional safeguards enjoyed by them in criminal trials. The weakness of the system is that the grand jurors must place enormous trust in the prosecutor's guidance. He tells them what the charge is, he selects the facts for them to hear, and he shapes the tone and feel of the case. When he is finished with his one-sided presentation, it is a rare grand jury that fails to bring down the indictment he wants. Most lawyers agree that the indictment process is all but automatic. Very few grand juries defy district attorneys.

Because of its failings, the grand jury system was abolished in Great Britain more than forty years ago. Learned trial lawyers are advocating a similar course in the United States, and a committee of the American Bar Association has its elimination under consideration. It is my conviction that such a result is desirable. The grand jury was misused in the Vesco case; the prosecutors invoked the Watergate crime in what was a completely unrelated matter to influence the jurors, witnesses were intimidated by the prosecutors, documents were improperly used, and neither Mitchell nor I was told that we were targets. Under such conditions, the prosecution was able to get any indictment it wanted, despite a weak circumstantial case that did not stand up.

While at it, perhaps the American Bar Association ought to set up a body to review from beginning to end the trial tactics by prosecutors in some celebrated cases, including this one, in the hope that it would lead to a curbing of extreme practices in the future by overzealous and ambitious prosecuting attorneys. There is support for this need in a book by a former Federal and State prosecutor, George V. Higgins,[2] in which he says:

> John N. Mitchell and Maurice Stans were forced to trial in the Vesco case, notwithstanding strong suspicions (harbored by people who felt little personal affection for either defendant) borne out by acquittal, that there was at least as much of Whitney North

---

2. *The Friends of Richard Nixon*, (Boston: Atlantic-Little Brown, 1975), p. 252.

Seymour's egotistical desire to leave office as United States Attorney for the Southern District of New York with a couple of big scalps up for scissoring, as there was solid evidence against the two men.

Seymour himself gave credence to this belief by his eager behavior in holding the press conference on May 10, in which he announced and read from the indictments in a manner that completely abandoned the presumption of innocence. "This is a sad day in a series of sad days for those of us who are concerned about integrity in government and in the administration of justice," he said. Such a remark, coming on top of the enormous Watergate publicity at the time, thereby convicted us on the spot before all the world, and could not fail to prejudice any prospective juror who heard of it.

In the interest of fairness, there are several steps that could be taken to reduce the number of miscarriages of justice, or the long hauls from being suspect to being acquitted. For one, the grand jury proceedings could be held before a judge or master, specially appointed for grand jury work, to keep the presentations within proper bounds. For another, the "target" should be told that he is being aimed at and his attorney should be allowed in the room to observe and possibly participate in the proceedings in a limited way. Any evidence favorable to the defendants should be presented by the prosecutors. Defendants' counsel should be allowed an informal confrontation with government counsel on the issues in the case outside the hearing of the grand jury, and an opportunity to present positive exculpatory evidence to the grand jury, if the prosecutors fail to do so. Transcripts of the remarks of the prosecutors to the jurors should be available to persons indicted. Severe penalties should be imposed for leaks to the press by jurors or prosecutors.

The number of grand jurors should be reduced more than half from the present twenty-three, and frequent absences of jurors on a case should not be permitted. And so-called investigative grand juries should not have the power of indictment; the appropriate screened evidence they collect should be presented by the prosecutors to a separate grand jury free of the coloration, impressions, and emotions of an extended investigation involving a great many witnesses over a considerable period of time called in by the prosecutors under "fishing" tactics. In other words, grand juries created for major investigations, such as organized crime or Watergate, should not be allowed to use indictments to express their accumulated prejudices, after weeks or months of listening to sordid evidence, by charging anyone remotely in sight. It would serve justice better if they were required to take the pertinent results of an investigation, and only those that are pertinent, to a new grand jury for indictment or dismissal.

Critics have charged that the grand jury is being perverted from a citizens' shield to a prosecutors' sword. Whatever the remedies, and the bar associations are much more qualified than I to propose them, the overwhelming power of prosecutors to influence grand juries is often recognized as a hazard to justice. A former Attorney General, the late Robert Jackson, once said: "A prosecutor has more control over life, liberty and reputation than any other person in America . . . . He stands a fair chance of finding at least a technical violation of some act on the part of almost anybody." Federal Judge William J. Campbell said it even more ominously: "Today, the grand jury is the total captive of the prosecutor who, if he is candid, will concede that he can indict anybody, at any time, for almost anything, before any grand jury." Picking up this theme, *Washington Post* columnist Clayton Fritchey on March 1, 1975, quoted a more recent Attorney General, Ramsey Clark, as saying, "The free-will aspect of the prosecutor should be reduced to a minimum." Fritchey concluded that "almost anything would be better than the present unrestrained freewheeling of publicity-hunting prosecutors hell-bent on advancing their political careers."

In the heat of the Washington devastation following Watergate, a still later Attorney General, Elliot Richardson, made this apt remark: "It is always easier for a prosecuting attorney to indict than not to indict."[3] Especially in periods of popular arousal and emotion it may be the line of least resistance for him to duck responsibility by passing the decision to the court system. By so doing, he can avoid the criticism that might follow if he did not take action against a well-publicized target. What Richardson did not say is what follows . . . that a vast majority of

---

3. October 20, 1973, upon his resignation as Attorney General.

the public believes an indictment connotes guilt. There is a sort of presumption that the government must be right, and that only criminals are indicted, and this is fortified each time the story of an indictment is repeated over the air or read in the press. Only exposure to the prosecutional processes of determined prosecutors and tractable grand juries makes one realize how easy it is to be indicted and how hard it is for the innocent later to remove the stigma that it creates. Winning a verdict of not guilty does not remove the mass public's lingering impression, especially in a well-publicized case, that "there must have been something to it," or that "acquittal doesn't mean innocence, it just means that there was not enough evidence to convict." The damage to reputations is irreparable, no matter how a trial comes out.

Finally, it would seem vital that steps be taken to insure the absolute sanctity of grand jury proceedings. Leaks such as occurred in 1972 and 1973 in Watergate-related matters are abhorrent to any concept of justice; the perpetrators, whether jurors or prosecutors or clerks, should be run down and brought severely to task, and the instigators who disseminate them as news should receive no mercy in the courts. The news that someone is a target of a grand jury investigation—even if he is never indicted—can be devastating to his reputation. In Federal proceedings, leaking of information is punishable by contempt of court, but the penalties are mild and rarely has anyone been punished for grand jury leaks. Since prosecutors occasionally create the leaks, a court confronted with one should be empowered to appoint special independent prosecutors to investigate them.

One element of justice that is hard to understand is the unwillingness of judges to grant changes of venue, especially when cases have had massive publicity that is bound to have a community impact deleterious to the persons charged. The added cost to the prosecution is insignificant compared to the interests of justice in having an absolutely impartial jury, and the overall inconvenience is not great, especially in a case like ours where the defendants and many witnesses are brought from considerable distances anyway. Since our trial, it has occasionally been argued in the press that our acquittal proves that justice is not likely to be impaired by the location of the trial, but I think that view is dangerous. The weight of evidence on the two sides may, in another case, be too close to prevent justice from being warped by subtle and even subconscious biases created by heavy publicity and public discussions.

The media did a complete circle on the Vesco case as it went along. From the beginning when *Washington Star-News* reporter James Polk ran across the contribution at the exact time we were drafting the language of the letter to send it back, the instant conclusion was that there had been a "fix." The charges that Vesco had looted the IOS subsidiaries of $224 million were by then highly publicized, and were automatically connected with the contribution, with practically no writers ever pointing out that the contribution had been accepted early in April 1972, months before Vesco had begun the alleged looting. This was a highly unlikely circumstance for a fix.

When our indictments were handed down in May 1973, harshly charging ten crimes against Mitchell and the same number against me, they were generally considered by the media to be tantamount to a finding of guilty. In the Watergate syndrome of that year, even though there was no connection whatever to Watergate, commentators tended to lump them together as part of a single pattern of crime, and as primary evidence of the oft-repeated accusations that we were selling favors. As the stories multiplied from day to day they sometimes dropped the legally cautious words "alleged" and "apparent" and took criminality for granted. The presumption of innocence became lost in the darkening smog.

Here are some illustations that show how certain the media were that we were unquestionably guilty, beginning right after the first disclosures of Vesco's contribution:

> —The *Daily Oregonian* on February 28, 1973, in an editorial said: "Why was [the contribution] accepted in the first place, coming from a man under indictment by an agency of the government for massive fraud?"
> —The *Washington Post* reported on the same day that "the contribution was made by Vesco, the main subject of an SEC suit charging misappropriation of $224 million."
> —The *Los Angeles Times* in a March 2 editorial was positive that "perhaps scandalously, the contribution was made at a time when

Vesco was under investigation fc    )ssible involvement in a multi-million dollar fraud."

—On April 28, the *Washington Post* said again that "at the time [of the contribution] Vesco was under investigation for allegedly looting a Geneva based corporation of $224 million."

These four comments were wrong in saying that Vesco was under investigation or under indictment for fraud at the time the contribution was made, when in fact it was received several months before the alleged fraud and looting by Vesco had begun. They set the tone for equally incorrect and unsupported conclusions in such reports as these:

—On April 28, Jack Anderson's syndicated column said: "Vesco bluntly asked [Stans], according to the testimony, how much in campaign contributions it would cost to get the SEC off his back. The figure $200,000 was suggested."

—*Newsweek* on May 7 said: "Stans reportedly wanted it [the $200,000] in 'currency,' a request confirmed by no less a figure than the President's brother, Edward Nixon . . . . These sources [close to the investigation] say that Stans, at least, repeatedly hinted that there might be help for Vesco after his money was received."

—Murray Kempton, on the CBS radio network on May 11, reported this: " . . . that summer the SEC sued Vesco for spiriting away $224 million from the overseas investors. In the interim, however, Vesco had cast about for ways to improve his excuses and he offered $200,000 to the Nixon campaign fund, and the President's finance chairman replied that he would take it so long as it was in $100 bills. That message was conveyed to Vesco by Edward Nixon, the President's brother, and delivery was duly made."

—*Newsweek*, on May 21, in a long article, said all this: "On March 8, 1972, Vesco braced Stans with a dazzling offer, allegedly as much as $500,000 to be given to CRP in return for favorable intercession with the SEC . . . . Several other well-connected persons, including the President's two brothers, are reportedly ready to corroborate specific points against the two Cabinet officers."

—*Time*, on May 21, reported that "Stans went to Cook and persuaded him to delete from the draft of the SEC complaint against Vesco any references to the money." Speaking of the case as a whole, *Time* said in the same issue, "The accusations form a sleazy story that might as well give pause to even the most hardened ward heeler."

—The *New York Post* on June 9 had reached its conclusion of guilt: "The [Vesco] investigation turned into a major Nixon administration scandal when Mitchell and Stans were indicted in May for perjury and obstruction of justice."

Reporter Polk got a Pulitzer prize for his political disclosures, particularly the Vesco affair. Yet his stories included incorrect material such as this stated as fact on April 12, 1973:

It [the Vesco $200,000 donation] became the bulk of the cash fund kept in a clandestine fund in a headquarters safe and used by Sloan for at least three secret payments to campaign aide G. Gordon Liddy, later convicted in the Watergate affair.

In reality, the Vesco money was not received by Sloan until after he had paid Liddy, under direction by campaign official Jeb Magruder, the $83,000 that was used to set up the burglary and bugging. Even more to the point, Federal Judge Hart in Washington confirmed in his findings relating to this contribution that the Vesco $200,000 was deposited in the committee's bank account on May 25. Polk's flaming statement was entirely wrong. The Vesco money had no connection whatever with the Watergate or a "clandestine fund" or "secret payments."

There were scores of similar editorials and reports that were equally unfounded and prejudicial. There were thousands more, continuing right up to the start of the trial, that, although using qualifying words of uncertainty, such as "alleged" or "reported," had a similar condemnatory result. The cumulative impact of those I read and heard was devastating.

My state of mind was shaken, too, by news statements and speculation that other indictments were ahead. As early as June 11, 1973, the *New York Post* reported that "both Mitchell and Stans face additional indictments in the Watergate case."

Just before the trial opened there was a rash of disconcerting news reports emanating from Washington that I was going to be indicted in the Watergate coverup. Between February 20 and March 1, the television commentators were especially frequent with remarks such as: "Among those expected to be named in Watergate are Ehrlichman, Colson, Mitchell, and Stans," and: "There is speculation that the two Cabinet members will be indicted in Washington." The Associated Press reported on

February 20 that "the ex-Cabinet officers are facing new indictments." When March 1 came and the Watergate indictments
were handed down, not including me, it finally became clear that
I was not one of those occupied in either the burglary or the
coverup. The media took practically no note of the omission.

After the prosecution's case began to take form, and the
government's witnesses were cross-examined, the comments
about the trial generally became neutral, guarded, and more
factual. It was comforting to read such items as these:

—On March 17, 1974, a *New York Times* article by Martin Arnold,
after Sears, Richardson, Hofgren, and Sloan had testified, concluded that "so far there has been no solid testimony that the two
former Cabinet officers did much more than seduce Mr. Vesco into
contributing $200,000."

—On March 23, the *Washington Star-News'* Richard Wilson
reported that "the trial is not proceeding precisely as desired by
the prosecution."

—*Newsweek* said on March 25 that "last week the lawyers for
Mitchell and Stans moved in and shook up the prosecution's
careful mosaic . . . . By the weekend the ambiguities seemed to
favor the defense."

—*Time* on March 25 said: "Sears sounds like a witness for the
defense," and a *Newsday* article on the same date reiterated a
similar thought: "Some observers believe the [government] team is
losing the case, that every prosecution witness who takes the
stand turns into a defense witness."

—On March 26 *Newsday* commented that "the defense was
playing rings around [the government], making prosecution witnesses sound almost like champions of the defense."

—The *Washington Star-News* of March 27 reported: "Part of the
contents of the White House tapes has been revealed for the first
time . . . and the words out of the past undercut the prosecution's
case."

—On April 1, with the prosecution's case nearly concluded,
*Time* said: "It went like that all week for the Government, just as it
has since the trial began a month ago: one step forward and
another backward."

—On April 8, *Time* then said: "When Cook was brought under
cross-examination, the strong case that he had built against Stans
began to weaken."

These reports, and others like them, reflected the progress of the trial rather well and fairly. Even so, there were some exceptions that held to the line of guilt, such as this in a *New York Post* column by Harriet Van Horne on March 29:

> How insidious, how crooked and shabby our election campaigns have become is being dramatized for us this week as the Mitchell-Stans trial unfolds in New York.

After Mitchell and I testified at length in our own defense, doubts of a conviction began to appear. *Time* said we were our "own best witnesses," as if that were a surprise. But no writer predicted we would go free.

When the case had ended, with acquittal on every one of the counts, there was the brief effort for a day by some interviewers of jury members to extract something detrimental to us in the verdict process, but these failed. A few reporters tried to disparage the results, contending that some jurors initially favoring a guilty vote were persuaded to vote for acquittal, as though that were uncommon. But generally the press and airwaves were gracious and came to agreement that the government had had a weak case from the start, and that is the impression that survived.

Peter Hamill, a columnist in the *New York Post*, said it in so many words: "The Vesco case was a weak case from the beginning, made remarkable because two Cabinet members had been indicted." William Safire, in the *New York Times*, was more blunt: "The general sadness of the day was in the way a weak indictment based on dubious evidence was used to try to catch a couple of big fish in the reign-of-terror atmosphere of Washington." That opinion prevailed across the spectrum of political views.

Conservative columnist William F. Buckley, Jr., said: "My own feeling is that the charges against Mitchell and Stans were just this side of incredible . . . . I had concluded that they were not guilty."

Liberal columnist William Raspberry conceded: "To this non-lawyer, it seems the jury was mostly right . . . the government failed, in my view, to make its case sufficiently convincing. The double acquittal may have been disappointing, but it was no travesty."

After a few days of retrospect the media dropped mention of

the case almost entirely. *Time*, in its May 6 edition, gave the trial its obituary in these equivocal words:  "There had never been anything like it in the history of American justice."

I wondered how much the public would remember, and whether the final verdict would possibly undo more than a small part of the destruction to our reputations that the daily banner headlines had provoked during the long trial.  On any scale of values, taken from beginning to end, the ratio of unfavorable to favorable publicity for Mitchell and me was at least 100 to 1.  It was hard to believe that the lasting impression of the newspaper reader or television viewer, notwithstanding our exoneration, was not governed by that ratio, although there was some comforting evidence of the public's discriminating memory in critical letters to the editors of various papers.

In the *New York Daily News*, one writer said cynically:  "How could the jury find Mitchell and Stans innocent?  After all, didn't CBS, NBC, the *Washington Post* and others tell us they were guilty?"  Another wrote that "after days and weeks of listening to TV and reading the papers about the Stans-Mitchell case, I got the idea they were guilty.  Who was right, the media or the jury?"  In the *New York Times*, a writer asked:  "Whom should the public believe?  The *New York Times*, the *Washington Post*, the *Los Angeles Times*, *Newsweek*, *Time*, network radio and TV, or the jury in the trial?  For months these men have been convicted and found guilty by the press."  And a *Newsweek* reader took that magazine to task:  "Reading your magazine, I was led to believe Stans and Mitchell were judged to be guilty long ago.  I thought the jury was just trying to decide whether to hang them or give them life.  Now I hear they are not guilty from the beginning."

Perhaps there is much more justice in the British system that prohibits press opinion on criminal cases after indictment and allows only the direct quotation of testimony while the trial is continuing.  According to Lord Widgery, Lord Chief Justice of England:  "Come the moment when there's a trial, or when a man is arrested and charged, then the reporters must calm down . . . . The rule has been that nothing must be made public pending the trial which could interfere with a fair trial.  In other words, there mustn't be publicity of a kind which might turn the jury for or against one particular side . . . . The idea of keeping out the matter which might be prejudicial goes all the way through up to conviction."

I can't help but believe that one major hazard in the path of justice in the United States would be removed if that were the practice here.

Around the corner from the Federal Court Building in Manhattan is a huge structure housing the Supreme Court of the State of New York, with a carved inscription across its entire facade proclaiming: "The True Administration of Justice is the Firmest Pillar of Good Government." No one would disagree. But perhaps we should give more attention to shoring up the pillar from time to time by improving the process. Unless we do, innocent people may be convicted the next time around, and that would be neither true justice nor good government.

# 14

## JAWORSKI ET AL.

I was allowed one day of exhilaration after the Vesco acquittal before the office of the Watergate Special Prosecutor in Washington served notice that I was being sought for campaign financing violations. What followed was another wonderland of discoveries about the processes of justice, extending over a full year.

The Office of the Watergate Special Prosecutor had been activated in May 1973, after Elliot Richardson, as a condition of his confirmation to the post of Attorney General, promised to appoint someone to investigate the Watergate and related affairs, including campaign practices and campaign financing. His designee was Archibald Cox, who built a prosecuting staff,[1] and convened three special grand juries (one of them exclusively on finances), which heard the testimony of hundreds of witnesses. Cox was discharged at Nixon's direction after about five months and was succeeded in November 1973 by Leon Jaworski, a Texas lawyer, who served a year and in turn was followed by Henry Ruth, Jr., late in October 1974. Their principal associates in the investigation of campaign funds were Tom McBride and Charles Ruff.

---

1. At its peak, the office had around fifty attorneys and about one hundred support personnel.

The person directly in charge of developing the case against me was Tom McBride, forty-four, of medium build, with sharp features, long gray hair, a quiet demeanor, and low-key voice. He had been an assistant district attorney in New York and had worked in the Organized Crime Section of the Department of Justice, for the Peace Corps, for the House Select Committee on Crime, and finally for the Law Enforcement Assistance Administration in the Department of Justice. He headed a task force which included several young, eager-beaver lawyers who soon demonstrated that they were less judicially inclined than he was.

There ensued a long series of meetings by my attorneys with McBride and his staff, sometimes attended by Jaworski, that extended over almost six months before they came to a conclusion as to how to proceed. I was ready and eager to answer any and all questions on the 1972 finances, to clear the air fully, but my attorneys insisted we fix in advance the conditions under which I would do so. After the undeserved New York experience, in which I walked casually into an ambush by testifying voluntarily to a grand jury, only to find myself the target of an unexpected indictment, my lawyers were not willing to turn me loose with the Washington prosecutors without some assurances that the same cavalier treatment would not happen again. They wanted to be sure of fair and objective consideration, after I had a full opportunity to present pertinent evidence and the legal background of our committee's actions. On the other hand, the prosecutors had a list of hundreds of transactions they wanted to investigate through me, and they were unwilling to make any concessions or promises without knowing what my testimony would be, both as to my own actions and those of others.

Our fears were accentuated by the mass of unfavorable and largely incorrect publicity about my committee and me in the months since the Watergate break-in, and the certainty that it must have had an impact, at least subconsciously, on the Special Prosecutor's staff. These fears seemed to be confirmed in early meetings by the confident statements of the prosecutors that I was "apparently guilty" of many offenses. Ruff at the outset acknowledged that he could not candidly describe himself as open-minded with regard to my innocence. An assistant, Roger Witten, said frankly that "we pay little attention to letters from companies saying Stans had no knowledge that they had made illegal contributions." These attitudes were emphasized by early remarks of Jaworski in these meetings that "everywhere we turn in the finance investigations we come across Stans' tracks."

My attorneys, in reply, argued that it was to be expected that in a national election the finance chairman's trail would extend in many directions, and the real issue was whether he had done anything wrong. When Jaworski countered with: "Well, he went around the country asking people to give in cash, didn't he?" we knew for sure that we were going to have a difficult time breaking down preconceived positions. The possibility that Stans as the man in charge of raising money might well have been all over the place without being guilty of impropriety seemed to have been lost to the multitude of accusations, rumors, and suspicions that floated in the Washington air. Whatever the source of his information, it was wrong, totally so. My counsel explained patiently to Jaworski that the allegation that I had solicited cash had been a major issue in the Vesco trial, that I had denied soliciting cash from Vesco or anyone else, and that the New York prosecutors had scoured the country without finding a single contributor who could say that I had requested that his contribution be in that form.

It became evident, too, that Jaworski had acquired the idea that I had knowingly received illegal contributions from corporations. On March 9, 1974, *Business Week* had contained the leaked statement that "the Special Prosecutor's office began a determined effort in January to develop evidence that Stans, and perhaps others, knew what they were doing when they accepted corporate money. For several days, officers of corporations under investigation were pumped intensively on just how the gifts were solicited."

McBride's predisposition toward the case came out early in the discussions my lawyers had with him. His opening remarks asserted positively and erroneously that "Stans controlled the coverup money" and "Stans caused the committee not to report the money paid to Liddy." He said there were "a hundred items on which Stans could be charged." Ruff was also hostile and very critical from the beginning.

There was no more obvious illustration of the predetermined leanings of the prosecutor's staff than in my experience with them regarding my personal files. When I had moved to

Washington in 1969 to become Secretary of Commerce I brought with me five file cabinets containing personal records concerning investments, bank accounts, insurance policies, medical data, diaries of African safaris, income tax data, paid bills, and general correspondence. When I left Commerce to join the campaign early in 1972 I took with me the same files, which had been augmented by similar personal papers collected in the three intervening years, as well as my daily diaries of meetings and telephone calls in that period. No official Commerce records and no finance committee data were included.

When the agents of the Special Prosecutor's office were fine-toothing the records of the finance committee in 1973, they came across these five files. Although the cabinets were clearly marked "Personal," they insisted on access to them, which I refused since there was nothing pertaining to the campaign among their contents. Apparently convinced that they had come across a secret cache of records that would reveal a horde of illicit transactions, McBride served a subpoena on January 9, 1974, directing the treasurer of the finance committee to turn them over at once.

Resentful of this insistence, I turned the keys to the files over to my attorneys and asked them to go through them in detail to see whether they could see anything pertaining to the campaign that should be turned over in response to the subpoena. They found nothing of that nature and so told the Special Prosecutor, providing him with a list of the contents to show their personal character.

Unconvinced, McBride secured another subpoena on February 20 for a wide assortment of material, including these personal files, and served it on February 25, when I was in New York wholly preoccupied with my defense in the Vesco case. The issue finally came up on May 17 in a formal hearing in the Federal Court in Washington. As my attorney said at the time, it was a fishing expedition beyond any limits. To bolster his case for access, McBride made the startling statement in court that I had been active in fund-raising during the three years I was Secretary of Commerce. When the skeptical judge questioned that remark, McBride insisted that "[Stans] continued to be involved, Your Honor, in political fund-raising activities . . . as an agent of political fund-raising committees" and was "fairly active" with regard to such matters during those years.

As the only evidence to support his contention, he produced Herbert Kalmbach to testify about two transactions. One was an alleged receipt by me of over a million dollars in contributed checks in 1970 from John Mulcahy of New York, which Kalmbach said I had in turn handed to him in my office. The other was an alleged directive by me to him to call on Henry Crown in Chicago in late 1971 to pick up a $25,000 contribution in cash. McBride could have learned that Kalmbach's testimony was incorrect on both matters had he checked with the principals involved instead of screaming them out in court with reckless disregard of any sense of fairness.

After listening to this surprise testimony, and after personally screening a part of the file records, the judge directed that I turn over about 2 percent of them, mostly the daily diaries of telephone calls and meetings for the years 1969 through 1972. There was nothing in them to support McBride's wild claims. Not only that; after the hearing we proved that Kalmbach's memory had been faulty on both items, but of course it was too late to undo the personal damage caused by the headlined reports of McBride's assertion that I had raised political money while a government official.

In the Mulcahy instance, we established that I was on the way to South America when Mulcahy's checks arrived at my apartment in Washington, that they had been sent to me at Mulcahy's initiative to be sure that they would be forwarded to the right channels, that I never saw or handled them, and that my secretary had found them in my mail while I was away and delivered them to Kalmbach. In the Crown instance, my attorneys contacted him, and he not only challenged the story but signed an affidavit stating that he had not talked to me at any time in 1971 and that in fact it was a Californian, Willard Keith, who had sent Kalmbach to him. Keith also gave an affidavit to that effect. McBride refused our request that he issue a public release correcting his rash statements, although he admitted in private that Kalmbach had been wrong in his recollections. Despite the excruciatingly harmful publicity when the charges were made, the public never learned the plain truth.

This whole confrontation produced absolutely nothing of significance for the prosecutors and completely supported my position that the records were personal and had no connection with the 1972 campaign, and that I had not carried on any political fund-raising while employed as an official of the government. It did evidence, however, the strong and unsupported predilection of the prosecuting staff to the belief that I was guilty of innumerable offenses and that somehow I had to be brought to task. In that sense, it was a forerunner of the treatment I received later.

On June 21, 1973, the *New York Times* reported that "well-informed sources said that Mr. McBride had accumulated allegations indicating that Republican officials (in 1972) drew up a list of corporations and officials who had problems with the government and solicited funds in late 1971 and early 1972 on that basis. One source close to the case noted that some large Republican contributors had complained privately about bringing in checks and being told to go back and get cash." On October 24, 1974, CBS and the *New York Times* said: "Stans is under investigation on five possible charges . . . including bribery, extortion, knowingly accepting illegal contributions, sale of ambassadorships, and failure to disclose contributions." These were not very consoling reports. Since they were untrue I wondered what had caused them to be created, but I never found out. Meanwhile, when some major companies pleaded guilty to making contributions in cash out of illicit funds, the judge sentencing them had wondered out loud when the recipients of the funds were going to be brought to justice. I realized then that I had an uphill road to establish conclusively that I had no knowledge of the illegal sources of any money that had been accepted, but I was positive I could do so.

I faced another hazard, too, and that was that someone guilty of a violation of the law would, in desperation induced by the climate of the time, deliberately create a story to sell me out in return for clemency or immunity. We did have outside information that one person had offered such a deal to the prosecutors, but our apprehensions relaxed when McBride one day referred to him as "a sleazy character" who could not be believed. Other than that, and the three or four cases in which officers of corporations that had made illegal gifts had been intimidated into saying that they may have been coerced to contribute by political realities, my fears turned out to be groundless. No one, to my knowledge, pointed a finger at me and, much more important, the persons with exculpatory knowledge, especially LaRue and Kalmbach, presented it freely and voluntarily in the public hearings and closed investigations.

Through my counsel, I insisted all along that I was completely innocent of wrongdoing, and therefore was not willing to engage in plea bargaining, in the sense of admitting wrong in exchange for a lesser charge or a lesser number of charges. I was sure that the evidence I would present would absolve me on all items of any willful violations of the law, and I wanted my lawyers to let me tell my story. The prosecutors in turn made it clear that if I refused to submit to their questioning under an agreement to tell all I knew, without any return commitment to me, they would get an indictment on a considerable number of transactions, leaving it to me to prove innocence in court.

After months of intermittent legal discussions in which I did not participate, an arrangement was finally worked out to break the impasse. Trustingly, I put myself at the mercy of the prosecutors. I would agree in advance to plead guilty to six misdemeanors and would cooperate by answering all their inquiries, with the understanding that after it was over they would fairly evaluate all the facts and circumstances and eliminate those of the six on which they were satisfied. I made this compact confident that I would be freed, that there was no case against me and the prosecutors would so find. By the time this agreement was reached, Jaworski had resigned as Special Prosecutor and Henry Ruth, Jr., had succeeded him.

With this understanding I submitted to questioning on twenty different days, four to five hours a day, spaced over three full months, beginning early in November 1974. On the first such occasion, I was allowed to make a general opening statement for an hour outlining and explaining the practices we had observed in fund-raising, after which the interrogations began. At once, I began to doubt the procedure I had agreed to, because the tone of the questions posed by some of the younger staff men was strongly accusatory and not in the spirit of the cooperative attitude I thought was to prevail.

After five or six hours of such questioning, McBride stopped the proceedings twice to tell my attorneys, outside my presence, that I was not giving the answers he expected and he did not believe I was telling the truth. Bewildered at the course of events,

⁷ discussed with my attorneys the desirability of terminating the agreement, but was induced to go ahead, somewhat shaken in my confidence that the outcome would be objective. Another event a month later added to my concerns. My attorneys had a scheduled meeting with McBride and some of his associates on September 9, which turned out to be the morning President Ford granted a general pardon to Nixon. When they arrived, they found the atmosphere bitter and harsh, and felt a new and distinct coldness toward their presentations. Rightly or wrongly, when this was reported to me I feared that the prosecutors' loss of a prime target like Nixon would result in a redirection of their effort to people around him, and that would certainly include me.²

On one occasion when McBride was in a testy mood and I was unable to recall seeing a letter from a contributor of which he had knowledge, he used courtroom tactics. "You destroyed it, didn't you?" he challenged in a sharp voice. I denied having done so. Upon my return to the office later in the day I at once asked a clerk to search for a letter such as he had described, and it was found within fifteen minutes in the committee files which McBride's agents had ploughed through. The next day McBride was at least gracious enough to apologize.

Altogether, I answered questions of McBride and his staff for 110 hours, covering more than 400 items, and spent at least 500 hours more searching the finance committee files for documentary evidence to support my statements and resolve their doubts. When we finished, I was sure that everything had been fully covered and resolved to their satisfaction.

I was bewildered and shattered by the final denouement of the proceedings. Ruth and McBride graciously listened while I presented a ninety-minute oral summation of the ground that had been covered and the evidence supporting my complete innocence, including for the first time an account of the many

---

2. There was later confirmation of this concern in a book by two of the senior members of the Special Prosecutor's staff describing the feeling in the organization over the pardon: "Frampton was appalled by the pardon . . . . He believed that Ford's action flew in the face of what we had been fighting for as members of the special Prosecution Force . . . . His reaction, one of anger and disgust, was shared by most of the young prosecutors within the office." Richard Ben-Veniste and George Frampton, *Stonewall* (New York: Simon & Schuster, 1977).

contributions we had rejected or returned. McBride acknowledged to Ruth that there was no evidence in conflict with what I had presented except some statements from unnamed persons whom he characterized as liars. Nevertheless, he said he believed I was shielding guilty people and had more knowledge than had been presented. "Everything Stans produced was exculpatory," he complained to my lawyers, rejecting the possibility that it all might be true. On this basis he insisted that I be held to the six counts.

My attorneys argued long and insistently that every one of the six items should be dropped, on the grounds that they could not be sustained in court and there had been no willful violations. They also contended that I was entitled to leniency in view of my extended cooperation, the precedent that such charges had never before been pressed against anyone, and the punishment I had unjustly been forced to take by going through the Vesco trial. When it was all over, Ruth agreed to drop only one of the six counts, leaving me with no other choice but to accept the remaining five or face indictment and another trial.

It was a no-win situation. I debated with myself over the next several weeks about repudiating the agreement and taking my chances in court, but that wasn't any more pleasant in prospect for several reasons. My legal fees already had amounted to $700,000, part of which had been reimbursed to me by the 1972 Campaign Liquidation Trust, and my lawyers told me that another trial might cost $250,000 more and it might take as long as a year before the whole affair ended. Our analysis of the chances of fairness in a trial in the supercharged climate of Washington at that time was not reassuring. I gave up, reluctantly, and in anguish. After a series of conferences on the dilemma, my family concurred in the decision. As Charles Bartlett, the syndicated columnist, wrote in 1974 with reference to my plea: "Stans chose this onus and a small fine over the alternative of another expensive year of legal chess."

The nature and background of the five transactions that became my "crimes" are, of course, important features in measuring the relative extent of my culpability or innocence. Only by close examination can they be seen in the minimally significant dimensions they actually had.

For example, the first charge to which I pleaded guilty was of having non-willfully received the illegal contribution of $30,000 made by the 3-M Company. The precise facts, as established for the court, were these:

On March 26, 1972, in response to my earlier solicitation, Wilbur Bennett, director of civic affairs of Minnesota Mining and Manufacturing Company (3-M), gave me $30,000 in cash, plus some employee checks, all of which I understood to be from employees of the company. It was so recorded by the committee. There being no requirement of reporting contributions at this date, the committee did not need the individual names.

In May 1973, I undertook an internal audit of everything that had gone on in connection with the 1972 finances, to assure that our records were complete and accurate. In this, I reviewed all unusual items with my new legal counsel. We had been considering for several months disclosing voluntarily all of the contributions received during the non-reporting period in 1972, to quiet insinuations as to their source, and decided as a preliminary to get the individual names from those whose contributions had come in lump sums. Accordingly, I telephoned Bennett and asked for the names of the contributors of the $30,000, whereupon he sent me by mail a list of twenty-nine names with amounts for each. Two months later, when our counsel asked for confirmation, Bennett came to Washington, accompanied by the company's general counsel. They asked that we not use the names that had been furnished, because the list had been compiled arbitrarily from the names of executives who had contributed to a political fund and the amount given us could not be specifically identified with contributors in the manner used in the list. They asked for the return of the list, but we declined, and suggested that 3-M get its CPAs to audit the fund to see if they could construct a proper accounting of the actual contributors.

On August 16, Bennett wrote me, saying that the $30,000 had actually come from corporate funds and acknowledging that it "had been designated as coming from 3-M employees." We returned the contribution.

In an affidavit dated September 23, 1974, Bennett said in part: " . . . at no time did affiant indicate to Mr. Stans or anyone connected with the finance committee that the contribution involved the use of corporate funds, inasmuch as your affiant did not, at that time, know that in fact such corporate funds were involved.

Your affiant knows of no indication that Mr. Stans or personnel of the Finance Committee to Reelect the President had any knowledge or reason to know that any part of the contribution was from corporate funds until August 1973."

For the *non-willful* receipt of these illegal funds, I was fined $1,000.

I considered this transaction in my mind dozens of times before I gave up. How could this deception by the contributor become a punishable crime on my part? What had I done wrong, even unwittingly? My attorneys went back to McBride time and again in protest. He was adamant, saying, "We have to make a lesson of this."

The second charge, of nonwillfully receiving the $40,000 contribution from Goodyear, was in almost identical circumstances:

On February 16, 1972, I solicited a contribution from Russell DeYoung, Chairman of the Board of Goodyear, following which Arden Firestone, Vice President and General Counsel of the company, delivered to me $40,000 in cash in two installments on March 9 and 14, plus some employee checks. Again, there was no requirement of public reporting of contributions and it was therefore not necessary for the committee to know all the names of the individual contributors. We understood that the money had been raised by passing the hat among the upper levels of employees, and it was accordingly recorded as having come from employees of the company.

As part of the same internal review of the committee's transactions, in preparation for any voluntary disclosures that might be desirable, I phoned Firestone in April 1973 and asked him for the names of the contributors of the $40,000. He called back and gave me over the telephone a list of eight persons who had given the money. A few months later, when our counsel wrote Goodyear asking for confirmation of the names for expected publication, the company acknowledged to us and to the Special Prosecutor that the funds had come illegally from the company and the names were fictitious. We returned the $40,000 at once.

On August 9, 1973, Fred S. Meyers, Vice President and General Counsel of Goodyear, stated in a letter to our counsel that "[Mr. Stans] was not told that the payments constituted a corporate contribution. The determination to make the contribution in cash rather than by check was made by the company."

The company's law firm, Covington and Burling, also confirmed that "at no time did Firestone tell Stans that the currency contribution constituted a contribution from corporate funds." DeYoung reiterated this in his testimony on November 15 before the Senate Watergate Committee.

For the *nonwillful* receipt of these illegal funds, I was fined $1,000.

The other three counts were for reporting violations. Although stated by the prosecution to be for failure to report, the transactions had in fact been reported, though delinquently, and the court's finding correctly termed them cases of "late reporting." They were as follows:

*Count 1*   Late reporting of a contribution of $30,000 from Ernesto Lagdameo.

On June 29, 1972, Anna Chennault, a co-chairman of the finance committee, brought to my office a Philippine national named Ernesto Lagdameo of Manila. Lagdameo tendered $30,000 in cash for the campaign and gave the names of three equal contributors, including himself. Although in 1968 we had received a legal opinion to the effect that contributions by foreigners were proper, and we had accepted some early in 1972, doubts had been raised on the point just recently by John Dean, so I took the $30,000 on the understanding that I would check to be sure before accepting the money. (Chennault confirmed this arrangement later in a signed statement presented to the Special Prosecutor.)

The committee's in-house counsel, Stanley Ebner, in answer to my query, reported to me that he thought it likely that foreign contributions were illegal. I arranged at once for $30,000 to be delivered to Chennault so it could be returned by her to Lagdameo. Her written statement acknowledged that she had received the money and that she had given it back to Lagdameo. Later I learned from an opinion of the Department of Justice that contributions such as those proffered by Lagdameo could legally have been accepted.

I was charged with a misdemeanor for failing to report these "contributions" on time. My reply was that I did not cause the committee to report the receipt or return of the money at the time because I considered that I had held it as agent, or trustee, or bailee for the contributors and it had never been received or accepted for the committee as contributions. My directive to return the $30,000 was within the reporting period in which it had been tendered, and I felt that this also nullified any obligation to report it. No purpose would have been served by reporting a transaction that was never completed.

Nonetheless, the committee did report it later in a regular public filing on June 10, 1973. The committee's outside counsel, to whom I went for advice, recommended that, even though there was no obligation to report an aborted transaction such as this, it be disclosed. The documents and evidence relating to this transaction fully established that the return of the money was an exercise of supercaution, and there was no intentional violation in the late reporting.

For the late reporting of this transaction, I was fined $1,000.

*Count 2*   Late reporting of a payment of $81,000 by the committee to Fred LaRue.

Late in June 1972, Hugh Sloan informed me that he still held $81,000 in cash as treasurer of earlier committees then inactive. For legal advice as to what to do with this money, I consulted Robert Mardian, former Assistant Attorney General of the United States, who was serving as counsel to the campaign committee. He advised that we "get the money out of the office and out of the campaign" and suggested that it be given to Fred LaRue to hold until the election was over. At that time LaRue was a senior campaign committee employee charged with the responsibility of conducting an investigation of the Watergate break-in. Sloan and I gave him the money, and LaRue confirmed in his Senate Watergate Committee testimony in 1973 that he had received it *to hold*.

Neither Sloan nor I caused the payment to be reported at the time, since it did not seem to be the kind of transaction that had to be reported. The law required the reporting of all payments made "to influence the nomination or election of a candidate for Federal office." Giving the money to LaRue to hold was not a payment for that purpose but merely a change of custodianship.

On June 10, 1973, again as part of our program of total disclosure and again on advice of counsel, we reported the $81,000 payment, together with an accounting for the funds by LaRue. He had returned the balance to the committee on May 31.

I was charged with a misdemeanor for failing to report this on time, although any responsibility to report attached to the treasurer and not to the chairman. The testimony of LaRue and Sloan relating to the transaction established that there was no intentional violation on anyone's part. Sloan, who obviously knew about the transfer, told the GAO in May 1973 that he "did not believe he was required to report these cash funds to GAO."

For the late reporting of this transaction, I was fined $1,000. Sloan was never charged.

*Count 3* Late reporting of $39,000 in contributions received through Tim Babcock.

On March 30, 1972, I solicited a contribution from Armand Hammer, Chairman and Chief Executive Officer of Occidental Petroleum Company, in the presence of Tim Babcock, an officer of the company and former Governor of Montana. The next day Babcock came to my office with $46,000 in cash from Hammer. At that time he said I could expect to receive additional funds later on.

On September 14, Babcock delivered $15,000 more, saying that this was not from Hammer but from several individuals whose names and addresses he gave me; the money was reported promptly by the committee, as required. On November 3, an associate of Babcock brought the committee $25,000, at a time when I was out of the office, without names of the contributors. Although the staff member who received the money asked for such information at the time, and he and I followed up with Babcock on numerous occasions, we did not receive the names of the contributors until much later.

On January 15, 1973, Babcock came to my office to deliver $14,000, this making a total of $100,000 raised by him. I explained to him that the committee had ample funds to pay all campaign expenses and no longer needed the money, and asked whether he and his contributors would be willing to give the $14,000 and the previous $25,000 to a non-campaign purpose being administered by Fred LaRue. I had been told that LaRue was then seeking money, at the request of the White House, for an independent fund that would be used to take over from the 1972 campaign the voter profile records and keep them up to date for White House use. Babcock was agreeable and committed the $39,000. Since this was a non-election purpose under the statute it did not need to be reported.

Again in the interest of full disclosure, this money was reported on June 10, 1973, with the several other previously unreported items. Babcock gave the committee the names of the contributors for the first time in a letter dated May 22. It was subsequently learned by the Special Prosecutor that the entire $100,000 had come from Hammer and the names given us by Babcock were fictitious. Those facts were unknown to me or anyone in the committee. To the contrary, Babcock's counsel had assured my counsel that the names had been checked and could be relied upon. Both Hammer and Babcock were fined for their actions in concealing from us the source of the funds.

The money had not been reported earlier because it had been voluntarily committed by Babcock to a purpose that didn't constitute a payment made "to influence the nomination or election of a candidate for Federal office."

For the late reporting of this transaction, I was fined $1,000.

All of my actions had been taken in good faith. The two corporate contributions had been received under circumstances in which I could see no semblance of guilt on my part. The June 10, 1973, reporting of the other three items had occurred at the first opportunity after the completion of the internal audit and the review by the committee's counsel; to insure that the full information in the report would get promptly to the Special Prosecutor, our lawyers delivered a copy personally to Cox and McBride, calling attention to the voluntary and gratuitous disclosures.

Yet I pleaded guilty to these five items in the belief that as a matter of reality I had no alternatives that made sense. My attorneys felt that these flimsy charges should not have been pursued, and that if Jaworski were still Special Prosecutor and had learned the facts he would have dropped them, even though it was clear then, as the later records show, that he was constantly being tugged by his staff toward a hard line on those accused. Ruth and McBride apparently believed they had to make an example of me by holding me to the fire, despite the fact that, as we discovered later, they had absolved Humphrey and McGovern for offenses at least as serious. Considering all the mitigating circumstances, they could with full propriety have exercised their discretion by letting me go free. They had the right to prosecute, too, and they exercised it. I don't condemn them for that, because I believe the climate of the times would have required a vast display of courage on their part to do otherwise. Later released records of the Special Prosecutor showed a keen awareness among his staff of the public's clamor for scalps.[3]

When I left the courtroom after making my plea, I read this statement to the television cameras outside the building, having taken the precaution a day earlier to see that the Special Prosecutor's office found nothing objectionable in it:

> "I pleaded guilty today in Federal Court to five misdemeanors under the election financing laws in 1972. In each of these transactions I made a good faith judgment at the time that the finance committee was complying with the law, but it now turns out that was not the case.
>
> "I have done this after long deliberation and full advice of counsel, for these reasons:
>
> "(1) This disposition, I believe, establishes once and for all that I had no guilty involvement in the Watergate burglary, the Watergate coverup, the Segretti sabotage, the ITT case, the White House plumbers affair, or the 1971 dairy industry dealings. At no time have the Special Prosecutor or the Justice Department alleged that I played any guilty part in those matters, and this action puts that conclusion on the record. This is important, in view of the many baseless public charges against me in recent years.
>
> "(2) The plea relates to three instances in which campaign receipts or disbursements were not reported on time and two instances in which I non-willfully and unknowingly took in illegal contributions, out of the hundreds of thousands of contributions and expenditures in the 1972 campaign. During the campaign I took every possible step to adhere to the law and instructed the Finance Committee's entire organization to do so, too. The violations now disclosed were not willful, and at the time they occurred were not believed to be violations.
>
> "(3) The 1972 election and its aftermath have taken three years of my life, during which time I have been heavily occupied in defense of criminal and civil actions, my income and financial resources have been seriously reduced, and my mind has been anguished over the innumerable public accusations against me that have proven to be unfounded, especially the year-long Vesco case in New York.

---

3. For example, a prosecutive memorandum dated December 13, 1975 concerning a minor reporting violation by Congressman James R. Jones named as one ground for prosecution the fact that "there has been much public discussion concerning the failure to prosecute the recipients of the much publicized corporate contributions during the 1972-74 elections."

"(4) Most importantly, the disposition of this present case will hopefully allow me to attend fully to the health of my wife, who has been hospitalized six times for a total of thirty weeks during the last thirty months, with several illnesses undoubtedly caused in part by the stresses of my situation. I want to see that she is restored to good health, and then devote part of my remaining years to interests I have been forced to neglect."

The sentencing for my plea of guilty came before Judge John Lewis Smith in May 1975.[4] It was evident that he had read the record fully, because his findings fully confirmed my position:

In the pre-Watergate era, under the Federal act, violations of the election financing laws were commonplace and an accepted practice.

It is now recognized that, although ignored in the past, such noncompliance will not in the future be accepted as the norm nor tolerated.

It is not alleged that Mr. Stans personally profited or that any money went into his own pocket.

Counts 1, 2, and 3 deal with the late reporting of three receipts or expenditures which were disclosed on advice of counsel even though deemed not to be reportable under Mr. Stans' interpretation of the Federal Election Campaign Act.

Counts 4 and 5 involve two non-willful acceptances of contributions from two corporations. Both corporations have acknowledged that the defendant did not know the corporate source of the funds. When the source of the funds were made known to Mr. Stans, each of the contributions was promptly returned.

After I pleaded guilty and before I was sentenced I went through the customary procedure of an investigation by a probation officer, including several visits to his office and a call by him at our apartment to meet with Kathleen and see how we lived. I was

---

4. Judge George T. Hart, Jr., who had handled most of the cases involving donors of illegal campaign contributions, disqualified himself from hearing my plea because his wife had on a few occasions played bridge with Kathleen. In one sense this was a relief because Hart, uninformed as to the evidence on the careful and lawful methods of solicitation we had practiced, and the way we had been deceived by phony lists of contributor names supplied by some companies, had been the one who demanded on several occasions when he sentenced illegal contributors, that the recipients also be brought to court. I feared he might have been prejudiced by his own statements.

asked to fill out questionnaires covering my life history, furnish financial statements and copies of tax returns, and provide character references. When it came to the references, he said six or eight letters would be adequate and might be all the judge would read, but my attorneys and I agreed we should do the utmost in establishing my past background, reputation, and character. I asked 140 past associates and friends who had known me well to write to the judge in my behalf if they were inclined to do so, and all but two did without urging. The letters came from people I had known in all the communities I had lived, clients and associates in the accounting profession, associates in banking and on Wall Street, members of the Eisenhower and Nixon Cabinets, ambassadors, members of the House and Senate, charitable organizations I had assisted, my black chauffeur in Washington, and many others. My son Steve voluntarily wrote on behalf of himself, his sisters and brother, testifying to family devotion; and Mamie Eisenhower sent a lovely letter from her sickbed, speaking of her husband's respect for me. Some of the key people of the finance committee staff voluntarily wrote of my insistence in following counsel's construction of the law in 1972. Every one of the letters was a touching expression of confidence and faith, and I was tearful as I read them. I knew that whatever the outcome I had not lost the respect of the people who knew me. We found that the judge did read them all, because he commented favorably in his findings on the many helpful letters received "from people in all walks of life."

In pleading guilty, I had taken the line of least resistance, but there were many factors that I weighed in the balance. I did not want my family and myself to suffer through another jury trial. I did not want to lose more time. I could not feel confident that a District of Columbia jury could set aside its political bias, especially in that year. On the other side, I knew there was no way to estimate how much my reputation would be hurt by my giving up. It was a risk I had to take, because I could not resist the inquisitions any longer without endangering my mental poise. I wanted to look forward to some good years of peace and tranquility while there was still time.

My calm, objective lawyer, Robert Barker, in answer to my plaint about such a harsh result, reflectively explained it: "The prosecutors have to satisfy the wolves," he said, "and have to satisfy their own egos." His associate counsel, aggressive Walter Bonner, agreed and said further: "If this were a civil matter, I would have said 'go ahead and fight them.'" Realistically, I feared that I would forever be listed as a member of the Watergate gang, even though these counts had no relevance to Watergate.

The financial loss from my experiences in the 1972 campaign was enormous. When I began my work as finance chairman I fully intended to be an unpaid volunteer for the year 1972, receiving only my actual out-of-pocket expenses. John Mitchell, who joined up as campaign director about the same time, was paid at the rate of $60,000 a year, which was the salary he had received as the head of a government department. When my work continued into 1973, carried along by the many lawsuits and investigations, I felt I should no longer sustain such a sacrifice in income, and the campaign's Budget Committee authorized pay to me at the same $5,000 a month, retroactive to April 7, 1972. However, when I was indicted in the Vesco case and forced to spend many hours working with the attorneys in my defense, I voluntarily cut this in half beginning with the day of the grand jury charges, May 10, 1973. When the case went to trial in February 1974, my compensation stopped until it was all over, and then pay was resumed for a few more months.

With the gradual reduction in number of lawsuits and the running out of the investigations, the finance office was finally closed on July 31, 1974, and my compensation ceased. As compared with what my earning power would have been in the business world, I calculate that the loss of income during the time of the campaign and its distressing aftermath was at least a half million dollars. The legal fees and other expenses that I had to shoulder exceeded all the compensation I received during the entire period, leaving me out-of-pocket. I'll never know what my subsequent loss of income was by reason of the continuing taint of having been associated with the campaign, but that, too, was unquestionably and provably a large amount.

It was depressing to close the books in this way on the 1972 campaign and on what will certainly be my last money-raising undertaking. While I was proud of our success in breaking all records[5]—which incidentally will never be surpassed now that

---

5. In the two Presidential campaigns and several other elections, I presided over the raising of $101 million.

the law provides government funds for Presidential candidates—any satisfaction from that was worn away by the rugged consequences of the Watergate affair.[6] The finding of the judge that my offenses were not willful was gratifying and confirmed what I had maintained all along, but it also tended to heighten my feeling that I had been victimized by circumstances, biases, and uncontrolled emotions beyond any man's power to overcome. It was ironic that, after having at last, and with massive cost in time, money, and stress, proved my innocence of Watergate, Vesco, and a host of assorted allegations and inferences, I had been forced to bow for five petty violations that, in any earlier time, would not have been considered worthy of notice. It was a turn of fate that I was held to account for five unwitting and unintended technical infractions because I had been caught in the momentary limbo between the tolerant past and the unforgiving future. I was a victim of an ex post facto shift in political morality, induced by the revelations of Watergate.

There is an array of reasons that could have influenced the prosecutors, and I find it difficult to choose among them. For one thing, I had failed to turn in any other persons for prosecution, which is often grounds for tolerance. The Special Prosecutor had a policy, not unusual in law enforcement practice, that the more a witness had to offer in the way of information that implicated others the better the deal he would get. I knew no cases of lawbreaking; I would not have condoned any. At most I acquired a few retroactive suspicions about others, in the light of the surprising disclosures that occurred, and in good faith I reviewed them with the prosecutors, but in the absence of clear evidence they did not go anywhere. There was no doubt that the prosecutors were bitterly disappointed that my testimony did not support their certainty that other persons not yet uncovered were guilty of illegalities. I not only told the truth on every inquiry, but in most instances was able to find letters or documents in the files that confirmed what I had said. This process closed out

---

6. Nixon's letter of thanks to me after the 1972 election contained this gratifying acknowledgment: "Being finance chairman with the responsibility of raising an unprecedented amount of money is difficult enough. To be bully-ragged and viciously libeled in the press over activities for which you had no responsibility at all makes your burden one that must have been almost unbearable at times."

many of the suspicions that they had been harboring. In his final report the Special Prosecutor acknowledged this cooperation.

Another possible explanation of my being singled out for prosecution is that the staff of the Special Prosecutor had such strong preconceptions of my guilt that it could not let them go entirely. This is consistent with the early remarks by Jaworski about running across my trail everywhere, and his erroneous impression that I had asked contributors to give in cash. It is consistent with the cynical attitudes and biting questions of some of the younger men on the staff after I agreed to be interviewed and to cooperate in getting the facts to resolve the open ends of their investigations. When it gradually became apparent from the evidence I presented that most of these were blind alleys, it would not have been surprising that a residual conviction on some counts became necessary in their minds to justify earlier public statements and to satisfy the built-up expectations of the media. Perhaps there had to be a victim after so many heralded allegations.

As to the two instances for which I was charged with unknowingly accepting illegal corporate contributions, the prosecutors took the position that I had acted in "reckless disregard" of the law in assuming that the money was legal. Leon Jaworski states this in his book,[7] a conclusion I wonder how he could reach since he had left the Special Prosecutor's office before I presented my evidence as to the background of the contributions and the conditions under which they were received. In both instances, the funds were stated or inferred to have come from employees when they were given to me. The 3-M official who delivered the money didn't himself even know it was from an illegal source and specifically gave it to me as coming from employees. Both Goodyear and 3-M stated in writing that I had no way of knowing the origin of the funds.

If the contention of "reckless disregard" assumes that I should have inquired as to their source, though not required by law, even that was done in early 1973, when I asked for and was given lists of contributors from these companies that I took to be correct, but which turned out later to be fictitious. The violators

---

7. Leon Jaworski, *The Right and the Power* (Reader's Digest Press, 1976).

were sophisticated companies, well aware of the law, and I believe we had the right to assume that they knew what was legal and would adhere to it. To assert that this was acting in reckless disregard is almost to imply that we should have cross-examined all of our cash contributors, or perhaps audited their books before taking their money.

As pointed out earlier, we received quite a number of other large gifts in cash that were perfectly legal;[8] there was no way we could possibly have distinguished the good from the bad. For instance, George Spater, head of American Airlines, who had previously been the company's attorney in Washington for many years, delivered $20,000 from proper sources and $55,000 from improper. If it is made to appear that a finance chairman can be safe only if he insists on an independent auditor's certificate as to the origin of a contribution, the "reckless disregard" principle becomes an absurdity.[9] My attorneys refused all along to agree to such a characterization and would not accept its mention in court when my case came up.

My attorneys also told me that, in view of the long precedent of nonprosecution of similar past offenses, and the leniency toward other violators in 1972,[10] it was within the discretion of the Special Prosecutor to waive prosecution in my case. That would have been an eminently fair disposition, and they so argued at length, especially in view of the extensive time, hardship, and expense to which I had already been put to prove my innocence in the Vesco case in New York, the extended cooperation I had given over a period of months in providing data that helped clear up the record, the unsettled complexity of the new law, the

---

8. Jaworski conceded in his book that "in many instances investigated by the office ... the contributions were from the personal funds of officers and no violation was established."

9. Ashland Oil Company's attorney told my lawyer that the path of that company's illicit money was so complex and intricate that "six certified public accountants working six months wouldn't have been able to uncover it."

10. The Special Prosecutor's final report indicates that this kind of leniency had been applied in other instances. On page 39, it says: "In a few campaign contribution cases ... potential defendants had relied on the advice of counsel or on prior explicit nonenforcement decisions by government agencies in concluding that their activities had been lawful, and the prosecutors decided not to charge them because their violations seemed to rest on honest misunderstandings of the law."

technical nature of the charges, reliance on legal advice at the time of several of the questioned transactions, my long personal history of exemplary government service, my absence of culpability in the Watergate and related illegalities, and my obvious efforts to insist on careful and proper performance, even to turning down millions of dollars of proffered money. The pleas fell on deaf ears.

There was one startling anticlimax. In his published summary report in October 1975, the Special Prosecutor acknowledged that his legal position was weak on the very principles involved in the final charges against me. Pointing out that the law fixed the responsibilities for reporting exclusively on the treasurer of a committee and none on the chairman, he recommended an amendment to make the chairman jointly accountable in the future. Noting that the law was not a full-accounting statute and required the reporting only of contributions and expenditures "for the purpose of influencing federal elections," thereby excluding nonelection items such as two of those for which I was charged, he proposed that the law be enlarged to require all transactions to be reported in the future. He conceded that there was doubt as to whether failure to report a contribution made after an election could be prosecuted. Acknowledging that the law did not define which receipts of illegal contributions could be deemed willful and which non-willful, he asked that the law be revised to provide such definitions in the future, "preferably as [the Special Prosecutor] has defined them."[11]

Whatever the reasoning, I was not allowed to go free. The unforgivable sin may have been my friendship with Richard Nixon and my association with his Administration. I had to be held up as an example, the first in fifty years for such offenses. This did not surprise me and, although my lawyers thought it was unfair and joined with me in resenting the hand-picked treatment, I could not bring myself to feel any prolonged bitterness toward my antagonists. Whatever the conscious or unconscious motivations, they were doing what their conditioning led them to

---

11. The Senate Watergate Committee in its final report recommended that in the future non-willful receipt of illegal corporate contributions should not be considered a crime but be subject only to a censure or at most a civil fine.

do, and were doing their job as they thought it should be done. It is not surprising that, considering the upset world of 1972 and its aftermath, their conclusions on the facts were different from mine.

About twenty-five years earlier a psychiatrist friend told me something that had etched itself deeply in my mind as a guideline for trying to understand controversies between individuals. "People are different," he said. "They think differently. This means that they often act differently under the same set of facts." This generalization has helped me on many occasions since to understand conflicts in opinions, and it was my reason for accepting, though not without reluctance, the unhappy fate that Special Prosecutor Ruth seemed impelled to impose on me. He may have thought he was being generous. I suppose, too, things could have been worse. If his assistant, McBride, who gave me more trouble than I thought fair, had been less objective and professional, or had I been in the hands of some of the zealous young gunners on the staff, whose attitudes were unbelievably vindictive toward me and others, I might have had no choice but to go to trial to defend myself.

The final and most heartsearing blow was from the accounting profession in which and for which I had worked thousands of hours over more than twenty-five years. At the instigation of a renegade CPA named Briloff, a bombastic professor at New York University who made unounded public assertions against me from 1973 to 1975 while knowing little of the circumstances, the Committee on Professional Ethics of the American Institute of Certified Public Accountants concluded it had to file charges against me for conduct discreditable to the profession. The specific counts before the Institute panel were that the five offenses in my plea of guilty in the Federal Court in Washington constituted discreditable actions.

I had served the Institute through the years as a member of several of its major committees, had been its vice president and then president by 1954, had received its annual award for outstanding service, had received the annual award of the American Accounting Association, an organization of teachers of accounting, and had been elected to the Accounting Hall of Fame. My private life had been exemplary and my business and government service had been beyond reproach. Yet I was forced to go through the indignity of a trial before the Institute's Trial Board.

The hearing lasted a full day and ended when the Board, after only fifteen minutes of deliberation, acquitted me by unanimous vote on all counts. It was, in a manner of speaking, a trial by my peers, and to have their evaluation of the evidence so strongly in my favor was gratifying. It fortified my recurring feeling that had I been willing to take the strain of a court trial by jury in the first instance I would have won (although I realize that a jury may have been less qualified to understand the details and reasoning which justified my actions and more likely to be influenced by the adverse publicity).[12]

It was now August 12, 1975, more than three years after the unreal world of Watergate first unfolded. The investigations were over, the grand juries had been dismissed, prosecutions were completed, and the civil litigation had come to an end save a few minor matters that would soon be tidied up. The media were busy chasing new hobgoblins. The time had come for Kathleen and me to move on from Washington and leave behind the constant reminders of our long trauma.

It was our last night in the Watergate apartment. In the morning our movers were to come with their packing boxes and crates, and collect our belongings for shipment to a destination unknown. We had decided that the best way to purge our minds of the emotions we had lived with for so long was to leave the place which had been our home for seven and a half years and be nomads for a while, traveling where we wanted and doing what we wanted. Among the things I would undertake was to write this record of experiences on the margins of history. Meanwhile, our furniture would remain in storage until we decided where to settle down.

After Kathleen had served our last meal in Washington, we

---

12. A slightly different proceeding occurred in New York, in a hearing on my right to continue to hold a license as a certified public accountant in that state. While I had no intention of further practice there, I contested the proceedings. The statute provided that any conviction of a crime constituted technical professional misconduct, and under that provision I was given the minimum punishment of a censure. More importantly, the decision affirmed the conclusion of the New York State Board of Accountancy that the actions, by themselves, to which I had pleaded guilty did not constitute unprofessional conduct.

sat in our Africana room, with the artifacts collected on our safaris, talking with the relaxed mood that comes over people who have just passed through a period of crisis and see clear skies ahead. The maelstrom was over. Its sheer revolving force would draw no more bodies and souls into the depths of its destruction, spewing out their shattered remains. Thankfully, we were among the survivors.

We talked that night of the tragedies that had befallen so many of our friends. Engulfed in the maelstrom and suctioned into a deathless humiliation were the many persons of influence and power whose guilt was established by their own admissions or by trial by a jury of their peers. We could not second-guess their fates. But beyond them was the long line of others who had been severely maligned by reason of circumstances—some who were totally innocent, or were judged so in the courts, some whose guilt was so minimal that in any other setting it would not have been dignified with attention, and some who were caught in the sudden shift between acceptable past practices and a new morality. We wondered whether they would ever get history's vindication.

Kathleen and I were probably the oldest of all those encompassed within the close orbit of Watergate and the other events of its period. We considered ourselves fortunate that we had lived full lives before it all happened, and felt distressed at the plight of so many young people whose futures were broken because of their complicity in transactions that the rules of society did not condone. However well they managed to begin anew, they could never regain the momentum of power and influence they had once held. Our sympathy extended, too, to the man who had held the highest post of authority and honor in the world, only to lose it to thoughtlessness and ineptitude, compounded by his own inability to foresee and forestall the inevitable course of affairs.[13] As his friends, we could not bring ourselves to condemn him for what we did not understand fully.

As for my own case, we reviewed our many second thoughts. Perhaps I should have met the demands of the press and ignored my counselors in 1972, perhaps I should have fought back sooner

---

13. This remark obviously needs elaboration; it is in Chapter 17.

against those who I felt were maligning me, perhaps I should have gotten independent legal advice much earlier, perhaps I should have told my story long before I did, or perhaps I should have stood my ground to the end and not capitulated on even a minor loss for the sake of expediency. These are all lost options that may look better in hindsight. One's judgment may not always be the best in the heat of battle.

There were many reasons at the time, reported in this account, why I did not do more in my defense—the press of time, respect for the advice of counsel, the mandate to protect the privacy of contributors, my dedication to the goal of fund-raising, the distractions of litigation, and preoccupation with Kathleen's illness. I suppose that by valiant efforts I might nevertheless have blunted some of the attacks and removed myself at least in small degree from the line of fire. But the Washington atmosphere of single-minded frenzy over Watergate makes that seem doubtful, even in retrospect.

I had considered for a while resigning from the campaign, as had Mitchell and Sloan. But they had reasons which did not apply to me. Had I known the depth of the morass at the time I certainly would have withdrawn, but there was nothing in the dimensions I was aware of to cause me to do so. Finally, and quite apart from the fact that resigning would have seemed an admission of guilt, it is not my nature to run from difficulty. It was up to me, as the one in charge of the campaign finances, to stay on and cooperate with the investigators, fight the civil suits, and try to protect the innocent among my workers and the contributors to the extent I could. I stuck it out, continually overwhelmed by the growing disclosures of illegal actions by others outside my orbit.

For three years our own living had been less than pleasant. While I was under charges, we had declined invitations to parties to avoid embarrassing our friends by the news accounts that would follow, and gradually the invitations ceased. I was able to talk to many old friends only through our respective lawyers. Our contacts narrowed, our circle of friends dwindled, and even those who believed in me had to exercise caution about occasions of association to avoid publicity. Fortunately, there were long-time friends who felt no inhibitions about consoling us, and many ordinary folks who wrote saying they understood the ordeal we were going through. Our relatives and our children, and all the people who knew us best, had no doubts about the eventual vindication, and their confidence had helped to buoy us up in the darkest moments.

Now that it was over, I was satisfied that my only crime was believing in and trusting others with whom I had been associated in the administration and in the campaign. Not asking more questions, failing to see straws in the wind, and appearing to be naive are all logical consequences of being too busy, working too much at the grinding wheel. To that, and only that, I could plead guilty. As to anything else, I was as John Dean told the President on a White House tape on February 28, 1973, "a victim of circumstances, of innuendo, of false charges."

Nothing in the forty-two years we had been together had prepared us for the tremors of Watergate. But we could write it off as an adventure that we had lived through and triumphed over. We had no regrets, no ill will toward anyone, and no desires but to finish our days in tranquility, in retirement but active, still taking on inviting challenges until the inevitable day when our time would run out. We were at peace with the world.

With that in our hearts, we walked out of the apartment hand in hand, turned the key in the door, and headed for a new life, our heads high. Washington was behind us.

But we were not wholly forgotten in Washington after all. In their strange ironic way, the wheels of justice continued on course. Way out in Phoenix, seven months later, I got a notice to report at once for jury duty in the Federal court in the District of Columbia. I read it slowly twice and then, exempted by distance, shredded it into little pieces while a relaxed smile coursed over my face.

# THREE

## EVALUATIONS

# 15

## THE SUPREME COURT
## HAWKS AND WRENS

The principal "public interest" organization to ride the Watergate wave was Common Cause. Looking at its tactics in retrospect, the only logical conclusion is that its leadership was more interested in membership-gaining publicity than in simple justice. During this period John W. Gardner, a former Secretary of Health, Education and Welfare and a militant liberal, was its chairman and dominating influence.[1] What is said here in criticism of Common Cause's activities is in no way intended to detract from its legitimate objectives or the proper mission of public interest groups in general.

Even if it were conceded that the Common Cause drive to get the names of persons who contributed during a period when the law protected them in the right of privacy may have had some remote legal foundation, and even if disclosure of such information may conceivably have been of value to the voters before November 7, both of which propositions are of doubtful validity, there was no public service, as the Federal court agreed, in the organization's persistent and highly publicized battle to get that information after the election was over. And there certainly was

---

1. On July 22, 1973, Gardner announced proudly that the Watergate scandal had brought Common Cause increased membership, volunteers, and money. One unverified report indicated that membership had increased from 200,000 to 300,000 during this period.

apparent political motivation in the imbalance of its demands on the Nixon organization, and the challenges to the accuracy of its reports, as compared with its attitude toward similar information from other candidates. Common Cause did not take action, for example, against Hubert Humphrey's campaign committees, whose lapses included failure to report large amounts of both receipts and expenditures.

Worst of all were its many generalities of impropriety against our committee and our contributors. On the unfounded assumption that we were guilty of Watergate, and therefore a sitting duck for any and all charges, Gardner made frequent assertions of illegality in campaign financing, accompanied by sweeping charges of overall fraud or irresponsibility. In these he was aided and abetted, and sometimes outperformed by his in-house counsel, Kenneth Guido, and the long-haired lawyer prosecuting the case, Mitchell Rogovin. Gardner's fixation was expressed in a premise stated in the Common Cause "Manual on Money and Politics" in 1972:

> As a result of this system [of campaign financing], our govern-
> ment has been up for sale . . . campaign contributions are used by
> special interests and wealthy individuals to purchase political
> power and influence.
> What a contributor may receive from his government takes many
> forms. The quid pro quo may be an appointment to high office or
> the granting of a lucrative government contract. It may mean a
> specific legislative benefit, or the reversal of a bureaucratic
> decision. We know the major campaign contributors most often
> give today in the expectation of some return on their investment.
> The individual who wants nothing but honest government for his
> money is rare.

This was an uncalled-for and unjustified reflection on the character of large numbers of American citizens. Such sweeping generalizations of a government for sale improperly undermine the confidence of its citizens. They are untrue. My own experience in several campaigns found only an infinitesimal number of persons—in 1972, perhaps 20 out of 900,000—who believed that they could buy something with a contribution. These were rebuffed and their money rejected. To assert that personal gain is the only motive for contributing is a disgraceful smear on the hundreds of thousands of patriotic Americans who view contributing, as well as voting, to be a civic duty, a step in the preservation of the principles of government they believe in.

If a man who makes a large gift to a campaign does not want a government favor, what does he want? Those who universally distrust the motivations of contributors will be surprised to know that the direct answer is that what they want is good government. Granted, "good government" is the kind that is in harmony with their ideas of what government should be and should not be. The successful businessman believes in the system of competitive enterprise and favors the candidate that he thinks will best preserve it. Some give because they fear the encroaching political power of big labor over new legislation. The wealthy individual who has worked hard for his success believes in the rewards of the system and opposes the candidate who would reduce or take away a large measure of those rewards and give them to others he believes to be less deserving, or who would deny a similar opportunity to his children and grandchildren.

These views are no more to be faulted than organized labor's selection or support of the candidate it believes will do most for its legislative program to get more for the worker and less for the business owner. Those who believe that fiscal order in the nation is essential to economic prosperity will rally to the candidate who promises balanced budgets. Those who believe individual welfare comes first support the liberal who promises more of it. Federal Judge George L. Hart, Jr., took judicial notice of the logic and propriety of such actions in an unrelated case in 1972 by saying that it was entirely legal and proper for a donor to make contributions in the hope that the legislators receiving the gifts would continue to maintain general positions agreeable to the donor. Besides those who give for ideological reasons, according to a *New York Times* article on campaign financing on January 13, 1974, there are people "who give for a sense of participation, to drop names, to get a dinner invitation to the White House, to gain business or social status."

Contributor feelings can be either positive or negative, meaning that they can represent confidence in one candidate or fear of another. A heavy preponderance of those who gave large amounts to Nixon in 1972 did so out of genuine fear: They were seriously afraid of the collapse they believed that McGovern's platform would bring to the country's economic structure if he were elected. Certainly a large proportion of those who supported Lyndon Johnson in 1964, in votes if not in money, did so out of fear that Barry Goldwater's imputed ultra-conservatism would slow the country's movement toward larger central government and decrease its protection of the unfortunate. On the issue of integrity of the contributor, there should be no difference whether the form of support is in money or in votes, or in both. Each individual does what is within his power and judgment to support his conviction. And there is no moral gap between an individual writing his own check to back a candidate whose views he likes and a labor union writing a check out of a bank account gathered from its members to back one they collectively believe in.

One wild piece of propaganda soliciting contributions for Common Cause purposes carried a two-inch banner announcing:

FOR SALE: The United States Government
All bids will be handled in secrecy

When one man puts out over two million dollars to presidential and Congressional campaigns (yes, it's a fact!), the United States Government is up for sale.
When appointments for high office, business favors, and favorable legal decisions are purchased behind the scenes by special interests (and that's a fact!), I say our system desperately needs cleaning up.

This is misstatement beyond redemption. These are not facts. Charging that corruption exists doesn't make it so, and within my experience and observation the statements are utterly false and lacking of proof. The man, for example, who gave $2 million in 1968 and again in 1972 was Clem Stone, who has already been introduced. His large contributions were made, he has said, because he sensed an opportunity to participate in the making of history. In an interview in Great Britain in 1974 he said, somewhat boastfully: "When a family is worth in these days better than $540 million, what's a million or two, particularly when you can change the course of history according to the principles for which you stand. All I wanted was good govern ment." He has told me that he believed Richard Nixon was a peacemaker who could restore harmony at home to a troubled people and help the nations of the world to new understanding.

Stone's perception or his ego may have been exalted, but in either case his goodwill scarcely deserves this kind of condemnation. He bought nothing from his government and received nothing. When the press tried to create an issue by implying that he was in line for the ambassadorship to the Court of St. James's because of the size of his contribution, he disavowed any such commitment or expectation. I know that story, because the President delegated me to have a talk with Stone when the reports appeared, to tell him that, although by all precedents he deserved a place on the team, it was unlikely that he would get one. Nixon feared the unjust public reaction that would be stirred up by narrow people like Gardner, just by reason of the circumstances and without regard to the man's qualifications. Although Stone was willing to serve his country, if asked, he expressed no disagreement with the decision that he not be appointed.

The other all-encompassing charge that appointments for high office, business favors, and favorable legal decisions are purchased behind the scenes is equally false. To the contrary, the final report of the Watergate Special Prosecutor acknowledged that, although he pursued vigorously several hundred alleged leads purporting to show such dealings, he was not able to establish a single one. As for allegations of improper influence on government action by contributors, his task force investigated over thirty such matters and concluded that "none of these inquiries developed sufficient evidence to support criminal charges." As for sales of ambassadorships and other government positions, his report concluded that, except for one instance in 1970 that occurred long before the 1972 campaign was under way, "the evidence was insufficient to support any criminal charges."

Gardner persisted in his wild swings long after the 1972 election. On October 31, 1973, he said in a radio interview that "the bulk of campaign giving is an attempt to buy influence. We know now that the administration went to corporations that were being investigated by the government. In the campaign financing thing, you see the route through which government is corrupted, elected officials are bought and sold, government is bought and sold." On March 14, 1974, in a membership ad of Common Cause in the *New York Times*, the charges continued strong:

> Would you like to have access to high government officials?
> Would you like to get special favors not available to the ordinary
> citizen? Would you really like to influence the outcome of legisla-
> tion and rulings that affect your business, your union or your tax
> return? Then invest in big campaign contributions. Not only is it
> legal, it's respectable."

Having set up that vast army of despicable straw men, Common
Cause could obviously offer to save the day by proposing to take
up single-handedly the cause of wiping them out for those who
would contribute their annual dues to its coffers.

Despite all these rash statements for his membership drives,
Gardner conceded in a *New York Times* interview reported on
September 16, 1973, that he had far overstated the case and he
couldn't produce the evidence to back his assertions:

> Although instances of a corporation's blatantly trying to buy a
> favorable decision are rare, many companies were said to believe
> that they must give generously to prevent unfavorable action
> against them.
> Ironically, many of the recent major government actions that
> have affected some of the self-admitted illegal givers seem to have
> gone against the companies," citing American Airlines (whose
> merger application was denied), Gulf Oil (hit with an antitrust suit),
> Goodyear Tire (charged in monopoly proceedings), and Phillips
> Petroleum (loser in an FTC case).

Broad generalizations without foundation seem to be the
hallmark of even the most sincerely motivated crusaders. It is the
unfortunate fault of reformers like John Gardner and movements
such as Common Cause to feel they have to create or exaggerate
their pictures of evil in order to be convincing. They ignore, as in
this case, the social damage caused by callously slandering their
fellowmen, and challenging the integrity of their government,
merely to claim later credit for eliminating imaginary ills in order
to maintain their reason for being.

While I was musing over this fact one evening during a
television show, I heard Alistair Cooke say in agreement with this
that "asininity runs through the motives of the most ardent

idealists." Or, as Supreme Court Justice Louis Brandeis once said, in a remark that eminently fits the crusading types: "The greatest dangers to liberty lurk in insidious encroachment by men of zeal, well-meaning but without understanding." But nothing so well proves my point as a quotation from John Gardner himself, made in 1968:

> One of the most corrosive of social delusions is the conviction on the part of the individual that he and his kind of people are uniquely faithful to the true American morality but that others who are morally less worthy are bringing the nation down.[2]

It was that kind of one-eyed crusading by Gardner and his associates that, in the wave of moral indignation over Watergate, induced the Congress to pass the Federal Election Campaign Act of 1974. It was an extremist piece of legislation, going far beyond the 1971 act in its restrictions and controls. It mattered not that the general and specific charges of malfeasance against our committee that were cited in support of the new law were not provable. The argued premise was that Watergate would not have happened if there had not been too much money around, a complete fallacy because at the time Watergate was financed we had raised less than one-third of what was ultimately spent. Watergate happened because some persons in authority wanted it to happen; in one way or another they would have financed it, law or no law, surplus or no surplus.

It matters not either that there was no demonstrated inadequacy in the 1971 law, which became effective on April 7, 1972. True, a few legal uncertainties developed for us and for others, over the meaning of some provisions as they applied during the brief period of transition from the previous law, but these were confusions that obviously would not recur after the transition year was over. Technical reporting infractions that happened, on both Republican and Democratic sides, could happen again under any law, and so of course could deliberate future evasions. But the two years after Watergate were a time for cries for virtue by reformers like Common Cause and public hand-washing by the

---

2. 1968 Godkin Lectures, quoted in William Safire, *Before the Fall* (Garden City, N.Y.: Doubleday & Company, 1975).

Congress, with the result that a tough new law was enacted in 1974, so tough that most Congressmen believed, and many said it was in all likelihood, unconstitutional. It was so found, in large part, by the United States Supreme Court.

The conditions of the earlier 1971 act were that an individual could contribute any amount to a candidate for Federal office, but that all contributions over $100 should be made public knowledge through regular reporting. What the 1974 amendments did was to put ceilings on the amounts which individuals could give to Federal candidates and ceilings on what the candidates could spend. They also provided for government financing of elections for President, and required that these new provisions be interpreted and enforced by a new Federal Election Commission whose members were appointed in part by the Congress and in part by the President.

As to contributions, the 1974 act provided that no person could give more than $1,000 to any candidate in an election for Federal office, or more then $25,000 to all such candidates; and it required that every contribution of $10 or more be recorded and every contribution of $100 or more be publicly reported. As to expenditures, it placed dollar limits on the amount that could be spent in an election campaign by any candidate or committee, limits on the amount which any candidate could spend from his own family funds, and limits on independent spending by any individual or group on behalf of a candidate.

Besides being of doubtful constitutionality, the new terms were unrealistic and in many respects discriminatory. Unfortunately, they were enacted on false premises amounting almost to fraud, in particular the wave of post-Watergate allegations that the finances of the Nixon campaign were rampantly corrupt. These charges were asserted in the hearings on the legislation, repeated on the floors of the House and the Senate and before the courts, and carried in the media, all with such a fury that they became accepted gospel. But they were grossly wrong, as the facts in this book must certainly make evident.

There never was a showing, either, that the violations in 1972 significantly outnumbered those of any prior year.[3] Furthermore,

---

3. In California, the principal state in which serious Federal enforcement efforts seem to have been made before 1972, 14 companies were convicted in 1968-69 for election law violations. In all, Justice prosecuted 17 companies in 1968-71 for illegal contributions.

had the data been analyzed, it could have been seen that very few violations occurred under the law of 1971 that took effect on April 7, 1972, and those that did happen were mostly the result of definitional differences and legal uncertainties during the period of shift from one law to the other.

Nevertheless, the indignation over Watergate and the alleged financing improprieties swept the public into believing that a tighter campaign financing law was needed. No one from the Nixon organization was called to testify before the Congressional committees that framed it. No one questioned seriously the extreme character of the proposals. Meager factual data were considered. Congressman John B. Anderson of Illinois worried about this on February 16, 1974, when he said that the current mood provided "an unprecedented opportunity to fashion a campaign financing system that can serve this nation well for decades to come . . . but if we proceed with too much haste or without vigorous conceptual and empirical analysis of the problems to be corrected, that tremendous opportunity may be frittered away . . . we would be well served to proceed with utmost caution and restraint."

Under insistent, almost daily, prodding by Common Cause and other reformers, the Congress yielded and enacted a law that was largely unconstitutional and unworkable. The reformers had their day of accusation without solid challenge of their premises, and the result was a statute that could not stand up under judicial scrutiny. The oversweep of the emotional response to Watergate, the far-out positions taken by the proponents of reform, the failure to question their allegations, and the self-consciousness of the Congress, resulted in a law that, even though its remnants were constitutional, was oppressive, unfair, and discriminatory.

Opponents of the bill presented many constitutional questions to be resolved by the Supreme Court. The Court held in 1975 in a long opinion, by a vote of 6 to 2, that the limitations on contributions and the requirements for reporting were constitutionally permissible, but it threw out all the limitations on expenditures as intolerable restrictions on the right of political expression guaranteed by the First Amendment to the Constitution. It also ruled that the structure of the Federal Elections

Commission was an improper trespass by the Congress on the separation of powers doctrine. These invalidations so shattered the law that Chief Justice Burger in a dissenting opinion expostulated that "what remains after today's holding leaves no more than a shadow what Congress contemplated. I question whether the residue leaves a workable program."

The Chief Justice dissented strongly and eloquently against the Court's decisions to let the limits stand on contributions, to require public disclosure of small contributions, and to provide public financing of Presidential campaigns. In his view, "the Act's disclosure scheme is impermissibly broad and violative of the First Amendment as it relates to reporting $10 and $100 contributions. The contribution limitations infringe on First Amendment liberties and suffer from the same infirmities that the Court correctly sees in the expenditure ceilings. The Act's system for public financing of Presidential campaigns is, in my judgment, an impermissible intrusion by the Government into traditionally private political process." His reasoning is so incisive that some excerpts from his dissent are worthy of historical attention:

> Disclosure is, in principle, the salutary and constitutional remedy for most of the ills Congress was seeking to alleviate. [It] is an effective means of revealing the type of political support that is sometimes coupled with expectations of special favors or rewards....
>
> Disclosure is, however, subject to First Amendment limitations which are to be defined by looking to the relevant public interests. The legitimate public interest is the elimination of the appearance and reality of corrupting influences.... The Court's theory, however, goes beyond permissible limits.... The public right to know ought not to be absolute when its exercise reveals private political convictions. Secrecy, like privacy, is not per se criminal. On the contrary, secrecy and privacy as to political preferences and connections are fundamental in a free society.... The basic point of our inquiry, however expressed, is to determine whether the Government has sought to achieve admittedly important goals by means which demonstrably curtail our liberties to an unnecessary extent. Even taking the Court at its word, particular dollar amounts fixed by the Congress that must be reported fall short of meeting the test of rationality when measured by the goals sought to be achieved. [It] seems to me that the threshold limits fixed at $10 and $100 for anonymous contributions are constitutionally impermissible on their face.... To argue that a 1976 contribution of $10 or $100 entails a

risk of corruption or its appearance is simply too extravagant to be maintained . . . Congress has used a shotgun to kill wrens as well as hawks.

. . . when it approves stringent limitations on contributions, the Court ignores the reason it finds so persuasive in the context of expenditures. For me contributions and expenditures are two sides of the same First Amendment coin . . . [Congress] imposed a flat ceiling on contributions without focusing on the actual evil attacked or the actual harm the restrictions will work . . . It is not simply speculation to think that the limitations on contributions will foreclose some candidacies. The limitations will also alter the nature of some electoral contests drastically [citing instances] . . . disclosure laws are the simple and wholly efficacious answer: They make the invisible apparent.

After stating his belief that public financing of elections is also unconstitutional, the Chief Justice went on to conclude that, in any event, "the statute as it now stands is unworkable and inequitable . . . All candidates can now spend freely; affluent candidates, after today, can spend their own money without limit; yet contributions for the ordinary candidate are severely restricted in amount—and small contributors are deterred."

There are strong realities in favor of the Chief Justice's conclusions. If there is to be free exchange of ideas in the political sphere, citizens should all be able to express whatever ideas they choose in whatever form they believe appropriate, whether it costs them money or time. Setting a limit on money contributions which Americans can give sets a maximum on their political expression. There should be no limitation on the right of an individual to use his resources of either time or money in legal pursuit of the kind of government he believes in, and no harm is done to justice by a contribution of any size so long as it is publicly known. If ambassadorships then end up going to large contributors, the Senate can refuse to confirm whenever it sees impropriety in the circumstances; the test ought to be not the size of his contribution but the capacity of the individual to perform well as an ambassador. Just as a large donation should not entitle a person to a government post, so also it ought not disqualify him if he is competent. Similarly, if there is a fear that government favors will be awarded on the basis of contributions, public disclosure is a certain inhibitor to both parties to such a contract.

It should be obvious that the contribution limit of $1,000 invites imbalances that are manifestly discriminatory. What it says in effect is that one person earning $50,000 a year may leave his job and work as an unpaid volunteer in a campaign, but his neighbor of equal earning power who must stay at his work cannot make an equivalent contribution in money. One can contribute $50,000 in services, the other can only give $1,000 in money. Or, as the Chief Justice put it in a footnote: "A lawyer's contribution of services to aid a candidate . . . is exempt, but his First Amendment activity is regulated if he falls ill and hires a replacement."

All in all, the right to give or not to give ought to be a valued aspect of political freedom, especially if it is acknowledged, as it should be, that donors do act from valid motives as part of a free and stable political process. Limitations on campaign contributions that set a ceiling on political expression make sense only to those who actually believe the lie that people invariably contribute to get direct personal advantage in return and not because they want good government.

One wonders how the Supreme Court's decision could have been so blind to these conditions, and only a careful reading of its rationale shows how the Court was misled. The decision spelled out the primary purpose of the contribution limitations as being "to limit the actuality and appearance of corruption resulting from large individual financial contributions."

Properly, it said "to the extent that large contributions are given to secure political quid pro quos from current and potential office holders, the integrity of our system of representative democracy is undermined." It acknowledged that the scope of such pernicious practices can never be reliably ascertained, but opined that "the deeply disturbing examples surfacing after the 1972 election demonstrates that the problem is not an illusory one." Its footnote at this point shows that for this conclusion the Supreme Court relied upon findings of the Court of Appeals in the same case, which it said had "discussed a number of abuses uncovered after the 1972 election."[4]

---

4. *Buckley* v. *Valeo*, 519 F 2d, 821 (April 14, 1975).

So we need to go back to that case to find out what those abuses were said to be. That opinion first offered the general conclusion that the history of abuses "recently brought to light" reflects major improprieties in campaign financing, thus presumably centering on the 1972 campaign. It posited that the new law "is a comprehensive approach to a set of conditions and abuses that have spread over the years to infest the nation's federal election campaigns." As evidence, it cited first some quotations of members of Congress that "under the present law (enacted 1971) the impression persists that a candidate can buy an election by simply spending large sums in a campaign"; that "this has increased the dependence of candidates on special interest groups and large contributors"; and that there is a "potentially corroding dependence on personal or family fortunes or the gifts of special interest backers." The Court then found that the "sheer volume of special interest group money is enormous," and proceeded to equate special interest money with large contributions, ignoring the fact that the "special interests" include laborers, teachers, miners, teamsters, doctors, senior citizens, and almost any organized groupings of the public, each having their valid causes and seeking to impress them on the candidates.

In any event, the appellate court concluded that the purpose of the new law in 1974 was to provide "remedies to achieve the objective of trammeling the pernicious influence of 'big money' campaign contributions." As evidence for its conclusions, it offered only the one specific charge that "revelations of huge contributions from the dairy industry, a number of corporations [illegally] and ambassadors and potential ambassadors, made the 1972 elections a watershed for public confidence in the electoral system." To support the "revelations," it merely cited in footnotes the unproved and unfulfilled pledge of the dairy industry in 1970 to contribute $2 million, illegal corporate gifts, "lavish" but legal contributions by the American Dental Association and H. Ross Perot (head of a company with government contracts), and the fact that thirty-one ambassadors appointed by Nixon gave a total of $1.8 million in contributions and six others "appear to have been actively seeking such appointments at the time of their contributions." It continued its assessment of the alleged corruption by saying that "larger contributions are intended to, and do, gain access to the elected official after the campaign for consideration of the contributor's particular concerns." It elaborated on this last point in a footnote stating that "Congress found and the District Court confirmed that such contributions were often made for the purpose of furthering business or private interests by facilitating access to government officials or influencing government decisions, and that, conversely, elected officials have tended to afford special treatment to large contributors." And, as a final punch, it said in another footnote that "the record before Congress was replete with specific examples of improper attempts to obtain governmental favors in return for large campaign contributions."

Since the Supreme Court's acceptance of some of the strict terms of the 1974 law expressly relied heavily on the findings of the Court of Appeals, it is worth parsing out some of these conclusions more fully. It is possible that many events of the alleged types went on in the executive branch outside my range of knowledge, but I doubt that they did. It is more likely that a "snow job" was done on the Congress and the Courts by the proponents of campaign reform. (A passing case might be made that members of the Congress are more prone to yield to pressures of contributors, considering the Bobby Baker matter, the Korean handouts, and the scattered generosity of a few oil companies, but I am inclined to believe these are exceptions rather than the rule; and there has been scant evidence of quid pro quo.)

Answers to the specific points asserted can be only part of a logical reply to the charges and innuendos. The investigations of the Watergate Special Prosecutor found no basis for criminal action on the alleged $2 million promise of the milk industry. The illegal contributions by corporations involved a tiny group of lawbreakers, twenty out of millions of corporations, acting on their own and without complicity on the part of either candidates or fund-raisers; while their actions are not to be condoned, it is not fair to tarnish all business or "big business" as corrupt because of them, or to assume that such contributions amounting in all to a mere 1.7 percent of the Nixon campaign costs in 1972 (later returned to the contributors) could have caused a distortion of the results of the election.

The few statements of corporate officials who gave illegal money that their arms were twisted by our solicitors, or that they felt they had to contribute in order to have access to government officials or to avoid being cold-shouldered by them, were merely self-serving defenses for their knowing misdeeds. Under the pressure of public attention that their confessions received, this is understandable. However, no solid evidence of undue pressures, extortion, or duress exists, and again not a single actionable case of such impropriety was found by the Watergate Special Prosecutor. Furthermore, no credible evidence exists that anyone contributed in 1968 or 1972 in consideration of promised favors in return, either through government business or government jobs.

As for ambassadorships, despite intense and unrelenting inquiries of hundreds of witnesses by investigating bodies, there is no evidence that any contributor or prospect in 1972 was offered such a post or made a contribution with a promise that he would get one. On the contrary, there is positive proof that a number of persons who proposed such an appointment as a quid pro quo were turned away. The Appellate Court's opinion does include the gracious and correct statement that "the fund raisers routinely advised that only the President could guarantee nomination." The fact that thirty-one ambassadors already in posts gave a total of $1.8 million in 1972 can be accepted by the non-cynical to mean simply that these were wealthy, non-career persons who had served their President long enough to believe with sincerity that his abilities and record, especially in the field of foreign affairs, deserved another term of office.

The essential question left, however, is whether corruption does exist in the Federal government, how much of it exists, and how much of it results from the contributor relationship. While no one would deny that some corruption does occasionally pop up, there has been no showing that it exceeds in proportion that which human frailty produces in personal and business relationships outside government.[5] Certainly there has been scant proof of corrupt favors to contributors on the part of the executive branch during the Nixon Administration. I know of no scandals touching my colleagues in the Nixon Cabinet, and if there were

---

5. The *New York Times* acknowledged on January 13, 1974, that "the manner in which we finance our political campaigns is no more dirty, cynical or unmoral than other endeavors in American life. It only appears that way because our politics are subjected to so much public scrutiny."

any that I have overlooked there were none of the Billy Sol Estes or Bobby Baker kinds that occasionally plagued earlier administrations.

I know of no decision in any Cabinet department or at the White House between 1969 and 1972 that was unduly influenced by a contributor or a contribution, past or present. If there were any, it is doubtful that they would have escaped notice by the press. I doubt that a single Cabinet officer knew who the Nixon contributors were in 1968 or 1972, because no steps were ever taken to give them that information. In my own case as Secretary of Commerce, I have already said that I seldom knew whether an individual with a complaint or a request for help was a Democrat or Republican, or a contributor or not, and I never made a decision on such a basis. If I were looking for opportunities, for example, there would have been the easy case of the American Shipbuilding Company. Its $6 million claim came before me a few weeks before I moved over to finance chairman, and I denied it in full on its merits, despite pleading calls from a half dozen Congressmen. Yet the company's chairman, George Steinbrenner, became a large contributor in 1972. If the merits had favored the company, a finding by me in that direction would certainly, in the aura of that year, have made the whole transaction seem corrupt to the suspicious. The overriding point is that no department head would dare in any case to overrule a finding of his staff, unless he could satisfy himself and them that it was incorrect, in order to favor a contributor, if he recognized one. The secret of an improper action could not be kept within the bureaucracy for a single day before leaking out.

As far as the matter of access to a government official is concerned, I always considered that to be a right of any citizen and I recognized it while in Commerce and in my earlier posts. The right to seek a redress of grievances is guaranteed by the constitution, and need not be purchased by a political gift. The right to special treatment is not assured, however, and I scrupulously avoided giving any. I believe my colleagues in the Nixon Administration were careful to do likewise. Those who contend otherwise have yet to come up with solid evidence of any wrongdoing worth talking about.

What remains is the question of whether big contributions,

then, are bad per se. The law in 1972 did not prohibit them, and both parties received more gifts of large amounts than ever before. On our side, this was neither due to special concessions nor to unusual persuasiveness by the fund-raisers. It was accounted for, very largely, by fear of the economic proposals of George McGovern and other liberal candidates in the Democratic field. The wealthy person, it seems to me, who gave generously to Nixon to insure his victory and McGovern's defeat should not be condemned more than the teacher, union leader, hippie, liberal, or revolutionary who gave time and money to his opponent out of a belief that he best bespoke for the future of the country. The wealthy person would be no less noble or patriotic in making a contribution proportionate to his own means.

In truth, what actually unfolded, after the most sweeping political investigations in history across the nation, was a surprisingly small number of finance violations brought to court. At the national level, there were only a score of corporations, large and small, that used illegal funds for contributions; and there were only about a dozen violations charged against finance committees or individuals, almost all shown to be unintentional technicalities. More crimes of greater weight are disclosed in a single New York City precinct police court on a single night. That was very little in relation to all the harsh words of attack on contributors and committees, or the severe restrictions of the 1974 law that followed. What happened was that the excitement over Watergate created an atmosphere of wrong-doing, everyone within range was brought into its orbit, everything that could be challenged by inference, innuendo, or suspicion was attacked, and the flood-tides of reform engulfed all. This meant leap-frogging the first obvious step, which would have been to enforce the existing law. Instead, the country got a new law that was an unconstitutional monstrosity, with no more justification than human cynicism. This was one of the more severe prices of Watergate.

A close look demonstrates why the $1,000 limit on contributions is unfair. It does not take into account the cost differences between Senate, House, and Presidential elections; the Supreme Court acknowledged that the amount could have been graduated for contributions just as they were for expenditures to make this distinction. Also, it discriminates against minor-party and independent candidates by making it much more difficult for them to initiate campaigns and to reach the electorate. A minor-party candidate without a widespread organization across the country may find it almost impossible to raise the qualifying funds from the required twenty states, when one altruistic wealthy supporter could provide the seed money to give him a start in that direction. That is how the campaigns of John Lindsay and Terry Sanford got off the ground in 1972; Lindsay got $269,000 of backing from one family, and Sanford received $700,000 in loans and gifts from a single contributor. They didn't succeed in mounting an impressive effort, but they were entitled to throw their hats in the ring and they might have caught on. They could not do it again under the new law. In the future, highly able candidates can be foreclosed without even such a showing because they cannot get adequate start-up money to assure momentum. In 1976, Sanford, who may have been one of his party's best candidates, could not raise the initial funds to seek exposure outside his own state and withdrew early. Would it have been an evil for society if he had received an initial $250,000, publicly disclosed, from someone with high respect for him, to get a campaign rolling?

Furthermore, the $1,000 limit adds to the advantage of an incumbent over a challenger and makes it more difficult to reinvigorate the legislative and executive branches with new faces and new approaches to national problem solving. Only a few challengers have been able in recent elections to outspend their incumbent rivals. The law's flattening of the contribution level reinforces the campaign advantages held by the officeholder in his access to government-paid mailing, travel, and use of personnel.

Similarly, there is a material inequity in the provisions requiring disclosure of every contribution amounting to more than $100. That provision is again a reflection of the fallacious Common Cause philosophy that contributions are made only to purchase favors. If that is the premise for this provision of the law, it assumes that the government of the United States can be bought for $101. If that premise is not invoked, there is no reason for such a low limit, since the burden of public knowledge can have a retarding effect on contributors, some of whom could be subject to recrimination from employers or labor unions, for example. Their right to privacy should be inviolable in the absence of a compelling reason to the contrary. The sensible and workable level above which disclosure would be required could be in the range of $3,000 to $5,000, which would permit paring published lists down to reasonable size, and would cause those giving such amounts to be more visible for public scrutiny for any evidence of government favors in return. The listing of $101 amounts and up is far broader than is justified by its ostensible purpose. The Supreme Court acknowledged that this threshold is indeed low and went on to say that "there is little in the legislative history to indicate that Congress focused carefully on the appropriate level at which to require recording and disclosure. Rather, it seems merely to have adopted the thresholds existing in similar disclosure laws since 1910."

Overbroad reporting that requires disclosure of contributions as absurdly low as $101 is certain to have a chilling effect on the political process. A rank-and-file union member may fear harassment or retaliation if he gives to a candidate disfavored by his union; a rising junior executive may risk his job if he supports candidates his employer deems unfriendly; a potential contributor may not want to take the onus involved in contributing to the opponent of a well-entrenched incumbent; an individual may not want his neighbors, friends, or lodge fellows to know his political interests. In such situations, he now has the right to a secret ballot but not to a secret manifestation of his support for a candidate if it tangibly goes beyond the act of voting. While all this applies in the case of major party candidates, it can be vastly more critical when it comes to minor party and independent candidates; hesitance of contributors in being publicly identified with a new movement may well make it impossible for the movement to burgeon and survive. The Court acknowledged that public disclosure would deter some individuals who otherwise might contribute, and conceded that "the thresholds are indeed low" and such strict requirements might well discourage participation by citizens in the political process.

There may be good reasons for government financing of Presidential elections, but they are not that contributions are invariably, often, or even occasionally used as bribes for favors granted or expected, or are sometimes extorted. Any such misuse of money or power, because of checks and balances, occurs less in the Federal government than in the normal private or business pursuits of people. Given adequate measures for protecting the opportunities of third-party and independent candidates, it would simplify electioneering. The danger is that the application of the present difficult qualifying provisions will make it impossible for a third party ever to raise its head. In 1976, Eugene McCarthy was practically X'd out from the start because the new law, which gave matching money from the government to the candidates of the two major parties, provided none for him as an independent candidate. A reasonable period of time should be allowed to elapse to see how those provisions actually work. The Supreme Court did not rule out "the possibility of concluding in some future case, upon an appropriate factual demonstration, that the public financing system invidiously discriminates against non-major parties."

The fact that the Court let stand, as constitutionally permissible, the severe limitations on individual giving and the strict requirements for reporting of contributions does not mean that they cannot be revised. The fact that such provisions are within the limits of constitutional interpretations does not mean that other means of attaining their objective would be unconstitutional. The Court made it clear that the Congress has latitude to amend these provisions to raise or remove the limit on contributions and to increase the threshold for reporting to a more sensible level. Unless these provisions are changed by the Congress, some day it will be clear to anyone that those who benefit from this needless restriction are the incumbents in office whose positions and prerogatives give them an automatic advantage over their challengers, and the organized groups like labor unions which can influence the voting of their members in the guise of political education, which is not limited. These alone will bring about imbalances of power that are not in the best interest of the people, the two-party system, or the nation.

The crusaders, in brief, went the way of extremism in forcing this legislation, ignoring the Constitution and the realities of fairness, and by overreacting missed an opportunity to perform a lasting public service. Common Cause did harm to innocent people and eroded the public's confidence in their government, by its inaccurate, unfair, and biased pronouncements. There is a place for a nonpartisan, impartial, reasonable citizens' action organization in our democratic system but in this instance Common Cause failed that mission by exaggerating the need and overreaching for the remedy.

# 16

## THE MEDIA BINGE

Senator Hugh Scott of Pennsylvania may have said it well: "The [American] media, when they are responsible, are the finest press in the world. But when they ride momentum and suddenly decide that a whisper can be turned into a charge, or a rumor into a fact, or a wrongful deed by one person into an alleged wrongful deed by another, up to that point unconnected, then the media are acting irresponsibly as well."

More recently, Donald McNaughton, chairman of Prudential Insurance Company, phrased it more starkly: "The power of the press with today's methods of mass communications has become . . . the power to destroy." It may not be unreasonable to postulate that the media reached that point during the Watergate era in its persistent drumbeat of oversimplification, antagonistic news selection, exaggerated fault-finding, and hasty conclusion-jumping.

*Time's* Thomas Griffith not long ago described the profound difference between the news process and courtroom procedure: In news reporting, he said, "The *judge* is missing—that judge who forbids misleading tactics, freely admonishes both sides, determines which evidence is valid and finally instructs the jury on how it should weigh what it has heard. In the news-gathering process, the press is both prosecutor and sole judge of its own activities—answerable in advance of publication to no one . . . free to select or disregard evidence as it pleases, free to omit counterclaims, to minimize rebuttals."[1]

The role and responsibility of the news media in our society is a subject that is being tested regularly in our courts, and perhaps will continue to be for a long time. That is as it should be. Watergate is a good topic in this context because it offers opportunity for calm and rational consideration of a situation in which many questions of this nature are clearly apparent.

One has to speak gingerly in examining publicly the actions of the media, because among some of the editorial press and electronic commentators there is a spontaneous reaction to anything that smacks of criticism. I have no desire to berate the media for performing its proper function, just because I happened to be one of its devoted topics for a time. And I realize that my public silence for months in 1972 and 1973, even though it was on advice of counsel, was intensely irritating to those who were trying to put the whole Washington story together for their readers and listeners. Digging up the facts in small pieces was obviously more time-consuming and frustrating than to have them put in hand in large doses. But I do believe there are some valid questions that can be broached on the basis of experiences during the period of the Watergate inquisitions, and that the answers might help preserve the rights, nervous systems, and reputations of innocent bystanders in the future.

There is certainly a fundamental right of the public to be informed, and I would be among the last to quarrel with that as a general proposition. The story of the Watergate burglary, who caused it and why, the attempted coverup and who participated, and all the trials into the "plumbers" and other misfeasances, were certainly worthy objects of public knowledge. It may even be that some of these involvements may never have become known had it not been for the insistent probing of investigative reporters, although I believe that conclusion is doubtful. The Justice Department investigations did not cease after the trial of the seven burglars; they continued right on until a Special Prosecutor was appointed to take over the search for culprits, and certainly he pursued the task with unremitting vigor. In all proba-

---

1. *Time*, April 17, 1978.

bility either one would have uncovered the guilty, even without the excitement of an aroused press. To believe otherwise is to believe that a host of responsible government persons, career and non-career, under oath to do their duty, would have closed their eyes to what had occurred. Even conceding that a few might succumb to baser motives, there would remain those many who insisted that the truth come out. Henry Petersen, Assistant Attorney General, complained bitterly to the Senate Watergate Committee that his organization had not been allowed to finish the job of bringing the guilty to justice.

I do believe that the press, radio, and TV should want to measure the net effects of their work against the general standard of equity to all concerned. I presume that none would contend that there are no limits to reportorial license. With that stated, the question becomes one of locating the proper limits, and these must certainly recognize the need to prevent damage to the innocent. Damage to reputations can happen when presumption, rumor, or inference are allowed to be given the facade of fact in news reports. Damage to reputations can happen when unsupported theories or conclusions are given expression under the guise of "an informed source" which can be merely the mind of the reporter himself, some flimsy rumor that he picked up, or the intentionally planted falsity of an adversary. Damage to reputations can happen, too, when the stories of suspected crimes are repeated so often that the reader accepts the frequency of repetition as connoting truth. Damage to reputations can occur, perhaps most brutally of all, when cartoonists can use the full play of their poisoned pens to indict or assassinate. Even the clever cynicism of humorists in their written columns or performances on stage can destroy. Yet few cartoonists or humorists can know the real facts; they accept what has been said before without verification.[2]

My questions come under these general heads:

How can the media conduct itself to serve the public well in informing it on criminal matters and at the same time

---

2. The media techniques of selecting, creating, building, emphasizing, exaggerating, distorting, repeating, and killing news stories are well described in *The Guns of Antenna*, Bruce Herschensohn (New Rochelle, N.Y.: Arlington House, 1976).

avoid injury to innocent persons in its reporting and editorial comments?

Should there be any limit on the right of the media to rely on undisclosed sources which their targets cannot face?

Should continued publicity in the form of rumors, reports, innuendo, or accusations be allowed after a person is indicted and before trial?

Should reporters have the right to break through the sanctity of grand jury proceedings to get raw data for news stories?

When does the right to inform the public transgress other public interests, in particular the right to privacy?

Should there be restraints on the right to report the facts of testimony or other developments in the course of trial proceedings, or to characterize such events?

What responsibility should the media have to undo the harm done to people by inaccurate news reporting or comment?

To what extent, if any, should the members of the media be held accountable for untruthful, prejudiced, or inflammatory reporting?

Some of the answers may possibly be found in this statement by John B. Oakes, senior editor of the *New York Times*:

> Newspapermen have a special obligation to retain public confidence through conscious and deliberate effort to ... pay particular attention to complaints of unfairness, bias, vindictiveness ... that is, to make ourselves voluntarily accountable.
>
> The press is not going to retain, or regain, public confidence if it is perceived to be constantly arrogant, unwilling to recognize conflicting rights, or not too concerned about maintaining the most rigid standards to protect and preserve its own integrity.

The public expects the press to function in an exemplary way. The evidence is overwhelming that it did not do so in the hysteria over Watergate. Unless it is more accountable for its actions in the future it risks restraints imposed by the society. The voluntary way would be better.

There are many lessons in Watergate, and many uncertainties that need to be answered before another Watergate occurs, so the indiscriminate destruction is minimized and the punishment is more selectively doled out. At the heart of much of the potential damage done to persons is the unresolved question of how much, if at all, the public's right to know overrides the rights of justice for those accused, guilty or innocent. Looking back, it is not easy to be calm about the many serious accusations and insinuations expressed in the media about many people, without evidence, based solely on fantasized versions and unverified leaks. The imagination of writers and commentators created ideas that went beyond current knowledge. Ideas led to suppositions, suppositions built inferences and innuendo, and these became transmitted into deliberate charges as each writer tried to be more spectacular than the last.

Anyone who is on the receiving side of such accusations cannot ignore them or dismiss them casually. Not if he respects his own good name, or his family, or what he will leave to posterity. In a sense, everything of real value in life is sundered by the vicious voice of libel. And there is so little with which to counter. Denials achieve little while the game goes on.

The finance committee's lawyers who were advising me were adamant in their insistence that I not discuss anything in public while the forces of the law were at work. Setting aside the later circumstance that some of these advisers were indicted in the Watergate affair, which I could never have anticipated, it seems certain that the Department of Justice was taking the same position, as witness its letter to Congressman Wright Patman in September 1972. As a layman, I cannot presume to know the point at which the rights of those engaged in the course of criminal justice, either as prosecutors or as persons under suspicion, override the public's right to know what is going on. It would be my judgment, however, that the persistence of the press for disclosure is not in the general public interest if it is true that disclosure could impede justice. It would seem that justice would better be served if its law-enforcement agencies and courts were allowed to do their work first and the dissemination of the news stories waited until no one's rights could be prejudiced.

Unless a solution such as that is found, what happened to bystanders in Watergate can happen to more innocents the next time around. Here is a matter in which the individual's rights to liberty and the pursuit of happiness override the gossipy values of news immediacy. The human price of Watergate was too great to be suffered again by a new coterie of victims.

Whatever the vices of Watergate may have been, therefore, it does not appear that the tactics of its investigative reporters and editorial writers can be fully justified. It is now known, in retrospect, that many of the practices inherent in these questions did occur, under the news competition of those days, to the extent of abuse of any sense of fairness. I certainly felt that much of what was directed at me was untrue and unfair. There may be others, like John Connally or "Bebe" Rebozo, whose documentation would be even more convincing than mine, but I am not the one to state their cases, especially since I cannot know all their facts or feel the depth of their anguish. I do know the day-to-day impact on me and how brutal I felt that it was.

I don't mean by this recital of press stories to imply that all were unfair or all reporters were at fault in their methods. Many writers were analytical and objective. Certainly the fact that I did not answer their questions promptly made their job more difficult and made it easy for some to jump to conclusions. Both the origin and the prolongation of many false conjectures was therefore in part my own doing. But many narratives went far overboard in assumptions, untruths, and malicious accusations. A study in detail of the media's false conceptions and conclusion-jumping in these years might provide a textbook lesson in journalism for the future, on the question of how far reporters and editorial writers should be allowed to improvise or create destructive characterizations or conclusions on the basis of hearsay or less. I cannot believe that it is right that anyone else should ever again be targeted as I was and as others were because of innocent associations with suspected wrongdoers.

Anyone who has not followed developments closely enough to know that I was wholly clear of Watergate will not see merit in this theme. Nor will anyone who believes in guilt by association, or who believes that a person must be guilty if, irrespective of other factors, he failed to answer at once to the public every insinuation or charge that is leveled against him. Nor will anyone who believes that indictment is proof of guilt.

When the truth is finally out, how does an innocent victim secure the repair of the accumulative wounds to his reputation? And what steps does the organized media take to insure that criteria are developed to prevent others from suffering in the same manner thereafter? In the case of a single erroneous news story, a correction or "amplification" is sometimes made, albeit always on an inside page and with negligible attention, often leaving much of the damage unrepaired. When the incorrect charges or insinuations extend over a period of months and years, how is a whole reputation to be restored?

Instances of inaccurate and unfounded news reporting given in this volume are enough to document the desirability of fair answers to these questions, although more examples could be cited, enough to fill a separate book. A few more specifics may help to show how difficult, almost impossible, it is to get a remedial treatment when an inaccuracy is called to the attention of a publication.

After I pleaded guilty in court on March 12, 1975, to five misdemeanors, *Time* magazine's report of the proceedings contained the remarks that "Stans insisted that his criminal violations of the campaign-funding laws were not willful," but after listening to the prosecutor "Federal Judge John Lewis Smith observed that this sounded much like willfulness to him." The judge had said no such thing, and my secretary, Arden Chambers, on her own initiative wrote to *Time* in protest. The answer came back insisting that the report was correct. My attorney then wrote to *Time*, pointing out that the court transcript, taken by a professional reporter stationed much closer to the proceedings than *Time*'s observer, contained no such statement, and asking for a retraction. *Time* refused, but said with ill grace that it would place the correspondence in its files so the remark wouldn't be repeated. After the proceedings two months later, when the judge's words specifically upheld my statement in court that the actions were not willful, *Time* never even mentioned the outcome of the case. Its readers were left with the last reported account, wholly wrong, saying that the judge believed my actions to be willful.

On March 13, the *Miami Herald* published an unbelievably irresponsible editorial about my plea, obviously written from biased recollections, containing a dozen wrong assertions as facts, including these:

[Stans] turns out to be the greatest living political con artist. [He] raised $58 million. That is $43 million more than had been publicly acknowledged by the reelection committee in January 1973, before the Watergate scandal and coverup became unraveled.

... now the country knows how Mr. Stans worked the boardrooms of some of the country's largest corporations, putting the arm on executives for illegal contributions.

Mr. Stans says he pleaded guilty to five misdemeanor charges ... because this action clears him once and for all of any involvement in the Watergate burglary and the Nixon coverup. That has to be a laugh.

Public financing of elections would be a bargain, compared with the ripoff by Mr. Stans and his political agents.

Any informed person could not have brought himself to make such statements; nor could anyone who had done a modicum of research before putting his hate on paper. It was so blatantly bitter and erroneous that my attorney pointed out the correct facts and insisted on a retraction of equal length in the same editorial space. The paper refused to apologize but, after a long controversy, finally agreed, under threat of a suit for libel which I certainly would have pursued, to publish on its editorial page a reply from my counsel responding at equal length to the editorial.

Columnist Jack Anderson, never one to miss the fun when human blood might be drawn, joined in at frequent intervals. On July 13, 1973, his column heartlessly complained that Kathleen had been allowed to use the facilities of the Army's Walter Reed Hospital in Washington after I had ceased to be Secretary of Commerce, even though a hospital spokesman had told him that it was a continuation of treatment begun when I held that post and she was paying the regular hospital charges. On April 13, 1974, he reported that Nixon contributors had been appointed to the National Defense Executive Reserve, consisting of 3,600 corporate executives "who would step into top jobs in Federal agencies if war broke out." The Reserve had been in existence for years and no contributors had been appointed or were members except by coincidence; the list of members was never used for solicitation and appointments were never made from contributor lists, so far as I know. On April 30, he alleged that I had maneuvered tax breaks for the movie industry. On August 21, he printed a report that I had used the Presidential yacht, *Sequoia* and its Navy crew in 1972 "to entertain GOP contributors." These last two stories were wholly false, also, as he might easily have found had he checked them out with responsible persons. I had nothing to do with tax benefits for the movie people. I was not on the *Sequoia* in 1972. Our demands for retractions were ignored.

Here are some more press accounts:

—*Newsweek* on May 21, 1973, employed cleverly contradicting words in using Vesco's contribution to indict our committee, by saying that " . . . . *in fact* this $200,000 *allegedly* went into Stans' wall safe to help pay for the CRP's campaign-espionage operations." As fact and as allegation the statement was wrong, since Judge Hart later found that the $200,000 received from Vesco had been deposited intact in the FCRP bank account on May 25, 1972.

—UPI on May 22, 1973, in a report by Mike Feinsilber, announced that "in addition to their involvement in the Watergate case, they were involved in an attempt by the SEC to block the merger between the $2 billion Hartford Fire Insurance Co. and ITT," naming as alleged culprits Mitchell, Stans, Colson, and Ehrlichman. The reference was wrong.

—On June 4, 1973, *Newsweek* printed a report I had gone to corporate officers demanding 1 percent of their company's profits as campaign contributions. When my attorney challenged this as completely false, *Newsweek* countered by saying it had merely repeated a report it had received, and acknowledged that no evidence had accompanied it.

—*Newsweek* on July 2, 1973, said bluntly, ". . . and even Maurice Stans has yet to account for $55,000 in personal expense money." Not a scintilla of fact existed to support that statement. I had accounted for every cent of expense money. By then we had concluded that it was futile to reply.

—On December 2, 1973, the *New York Times* printed a full-page advertisement of an organization identified as the "League of Friends of Thomas Jefferson," in which I was accused of "impeachable crimes" for having been indicted in the Vesco case, and also alleging that we "used extortion against American companies for millions of dollars and caused them to commit illegal acts." There was no effective way to answer those obviously false statements.

—*Time* on February 8, 1974, printed an unverified story that Ken Jamieson, board chairman of Exxon, had "abruptly dismissed GOP fund raiser Maurice H. Stans from his office," thereby keeping

Exxon free from scandal. If *Time* had checked with Jamieson or me it would have found that I was never in his office and never talked to him about a contribution. When these facts were communicated to *Time* its editors refused the request of my attorney that it print a correction.

—The Washington *Star—News* on November 3, 1975, carried on its front page this banner: "Mystery Trip of Stans, Hunt to Nicaragua," asserting that it had discovered that we had mysteriously traveled there in 1972, presumably together. It was copied in a number of other papers across the country. After my attorney twice protested that I was not in Nicaragua in 1972 and didn't know Hunt, the *Star—News* withdrew the story on an inside page and some of the other papers issued similar retractions.

—*Time* as late as May 3, 1976, said without qualification that "the White House tried to use the Occupational Safety and Health Administration to raise money from employers during Nixon's 1972 reelection campaign." Nothing in the record of any public hearing or court proceeding supports that conclusion, and I never heard of such an effort during the 1972 campaign or later.

When I pleaded guilty in March 1975 to the five technical financing infractions and said they were not intentional, some of the press saw it differently. They reached their judgments at once, without the burden of waiting for the evidence or the mitigating circumstances that the judge would have to deal with when he came to sentencing. The *New York Times* said: "Now that they have been exposed, the skilled operators in this political money game such as Mr. Stans protest their essential innocence and admit to only technical violations of the law. But these self-serving declarations carry little weight." The *Washington Post* editorialized in this manner:

The case of Maurice Stans illustrated the gap between what was illegal and what was wrong. Mr. Stans has just pleaded guilty to five misdemeanor counts for accepting unlawful corporate gifts and failing to make adequate reports. Everything else he did in the course of raising $60 million for the Nixon reelection effort may have been legal at the time. But his operations were so heavy-handed, so shameless and so secretive that they became the outstanding example of the need for systematic reform."

And the *Christian Science Monitor*, forswearing all its Christianity in an especially unkind appraisal, concluded that " . . . . Stans sought to excuse them as not being 'willful' or not believed to be violations at the time. Clearly a man in his position should have known what the law was. But beyond this, a sensitivity to the substance as well as the appearance of propriety should have steered him away from the acceptance of illegal corporate contributions and the other misdemeanors he has now admitted."

There were hundreds more, some quoted earlier in this book. Because of all the other pressures of those days, we could not undertake to answer more than a few of the published slanders or incorrect statements. When we did, usually the best we could hope for was non-repetition. The laws of libel being what they are, we had no practical weapon with which to compel a publication to retract even the grossest and vilest attacks. The Supreme Court of the United States, in the famous Sullivan case, has concluded that, in the interest of "full and robust debate," it is impossible for a public figure to recover damages for anything that is said about him unless he can prove that it was done with malice. Libel suits can be filed, but in the absence of a change of heart by the Supreme Court in this insensitive result, there is little hope that the makers of irresponsible charges can be made to pay for damages done to reputations.

The fact remains that it is agonizing to see or hear stories in the media, knowing them to be wrong and realizing that they have reached millions of people who cannot know that. And there is not much difference in impact between an attributed source or an unidentified source; the effect is the same on the reader and the pain is as great for the person wronged.

Not everyone ignored the concept of fairness so blatantly. After all the facts were known and my innocence from Watergate was established, and the massive allegations of campaign improprieties had been reduced by the processes of law to the few minor, unintentional violations never previously considered by the government to be deserving of punishment, one or two writers made note of the result for their readers. National columnist Charles Bartlett wrote a column in July 1975 analyzing my situation in these terms:

The ordeal of Maurice Stans should serve as an intimidating

lesson [to other fund-raisers] .... Stans is leaving Washington, jaunty once again after being pursued for almost three years by feverish hounds of suspicion. No campaign treasurer has ever raised as much as Stans' $60 million or been investigated as ruthlessly.

Stans survived this inquiry, accepting guilt in the end on five technical, non-willful violations. No political fund-raiser has ever been convicted for offenses hinged to a mere neglect to report contributions that were sent back to the donors. But Stans chose this onus and a small fine over the alternative of another expensive year of legal chess.

But the media have not, in Stans' case, been as responsive to the facts as the courts. The broad presumption of his implicity in the blazing scandal, which produced about $95 million in lawsuits against him, was reported far more enthusiastically than the failure to find him guilty of any significant venality.

This failure did not reflect a lack of effort. Stans was grilled for 125 hours on 400 subjects by agents of the special prosecutor. He became the affair's most heavily investigated figure next to Richard Nixon. He had to persuade his interrogators that his office financed the break-in without any knowledge of it or the subsequent efforts to cover it up.

The prosecutors proceeded on a premise that no one could raise so much political money and stay completely honest. They tried to link Stans to the ITT convention donation, the milk money, the dirty tricks, the sale of ambassadorships in 1968 and 1972, and extortion from companies involved with the government. They searched hard for contributors from whom he had solicited cash and instances in which he had sought contributions as Secretary of Commerce ....

The prosecutors failed for two reasons. One is that Stans is a straightforward man, an ex-accountant with no taste for the guile of politics. The other is that Republicans had no need to strain for huge sums of money in 1972. The big checks poured in when Stans pointed to the populist inclinations of George McGovern. He was able to turn down $1 million from Michele Sindona without blinking.

This column was printed by the *Houston Chronicle* under the perceptive heading: "Where Are Apologies to Stans?" It was used by all of Bartlett's news outlets except the *Washington Star—News*, which for some reason thought it unfit to print for its readers. *The Columbia Record* (South Carolina), in an editorial emanating from the Bartlett column, reasoned therefrom:

> . . . . the genteel, almost-scholarly accountant has decidedly and emphatically earned the right to his "good name," which should be forthwith restored to him by the American people.
>
> The problem is that in the mish-mash of truth, half-truth and innuendo that constitute the unwholesome affair in our body politic called "Watergate," the public is likely to stir together the guilty and the guiltless.
>
> Stans was never guilty of any significant venality.
>
> In the current climate, the public should understand that Maurice Stans is an honest and direct individual, cleared of all the nasty accusations. Give him back his good name.

On September 16, Senator Howard Baker of Tennessee, the ranking Republican on the Senate Watergate Committee, who had heard all the testimony on the case, inserted these two pieces in the Congressional Record, stating, "I feel that the contents are significant, and in the spirit of fair play, I bring [them] to the attention of the Senate."

So far as I know, that was all. No fair summing up by the *Washington Post* or Walter Cronkite.   No corrections by Woodward and Bernstein.  No "amplifications" by the *New York Times*.   No retractions by Jack Anderson or Daniel Schorr or Nicholas von Hoffman or Herblock the cartoonist or Harriet Van Horne, or all the other columnists and reporters who so eagerly played follow the leader with the hatchet.  No filling in of the record by *Time* magazine or *Newsweek* and, incidentally, no apology from Senator Frank Moss for his mouthing of exorbitant criminal charges on the floor of the United States Senate, merely because he was asked to do so by his party's campaign machinery, to the effect that I was guilty of felonious conduct.  No "regrets" by Larry O'Brien or George McGovern for their intemperate political accusations.

Without doubt, investigative journalism accomplished some worthy objectives in the Watergate affair, but it also trampled over many blameless people in the rush to accusation, and never went back after it was over to help them on to their feet.

There is a permanence about published stories, true or untrue, that stems from the fact that press "morgues" are long-lived.

A subject can be pinioned forever by one inaccurate account, repeated each time he makes the news, because it is almost impossible to purge a morgue of misinformation. A lie can be permanent.

Nothing mars the integrity of the press more than its unwillingness to acknowledge its errors, even when confronted with convincing evidence. Retractions are a one-in-a-million event, and even if a person is persuasive or persistent enough to get one, it never reaches more than a tiny part of the readers who saw the mistake. And, even if it could reach the original audience, that audience would by then have passed the mistake along to a second audience, which would be altogether unreachable. The chances of a correction being made are even less in radio and television. Once a "fact" has been broadcast in print or on the air it can move back and forth and in many directions, and no force in the world can dictate where it will stop. And no force can repair the damage that inaccuracy can bring.

No one has attempted to catalog all the published untruths and mistruths of the Watergate era. I have quoted a number—just a small portion—of those in the realm of Nixon campaign finances. The news research for this book did not go far beyond that topic. Nixon summarizes some in the non-finance area in his memoirs.[3] A few writers have mentioned others on a sampling basis.[4] A full retrospective review of the Eastern papers, the news weeklies, the wire services, and the network scripts of the Watergate epoch, if it were ever made, and it ought to be, would reveal the greatest aggregation of fantasy ever concocted. Historians who do their homework from these source records will be overwhelmed at the way sadistic instincts took over the news business, and the incredible number of stories which were told that bore no relation to accuracy. Anyone who challenges this conclusion need only go back and take a good look with benefit of hindsight. One certainly has the right to ask whether much of this reporting was the proper function of the media.

---

3. *RN: The Memoirs of Richard Nixon*, (New York: Grosset & Dunlap, 1978).

4. Herschenson, *Guns of Antenna*; Raymond Price, *With Nixon*, (New York: Viking Press, 1977).

No less a person than Charles Ruff, who was the fourth and last in the sequence of Watergate Special Prosecutors, acknowledged the extent to which Watergate had spread its poisons and shifted the presumption of innocence to guilt. In a court proceeding in 1977, in which he sought to keep certain information in the Prosecutor's files from public dissemination, he said:

> "The aura of Watergate is such that any connection of an individual to a Watergate investigation carries with it an implication of criminality and political corruption which is inescapable and which places these individuals in a position of having to defend their conduct even though not charged with any offense."

Thus the poison of Watergate still persists.

Irresponsible journalism, and unwillingness to correct error, continued as late as 1978, almost six years after Watergate. I happened to be in Las Vegas on February 27 on business and, to my astonishment, read in the *Las Vegas Review-Journal* (it presumably also appeared in other papers of the syndicate) a column by two lesser journalists, Martha Angle and Robert Walters of Newspaper Enterprise Association, Inc., containing statements long since discredited by evidence in the public domain. They accused me of "venal and rapacious" fund-raising tactics in 1972, of coercion, of soliciting illegal corporate gifts, of soliciting contributions in 1971 while I was in government, of selling influence in the Administration, and the same old false list of alleged crimes.

The information they relied on was in early records of the Special Prosecutor that had been dislodged by a public interest group under the Freedom of Information Act. It had all been overtaken by sequent disclosures proving that such things didn't exist.

My lawyer demanded a retraction, which was refused. The syndicate proposed that we write our own reply, which we did, but they wouldn't print that. The slow minuet of their stalling went on for six months until we finally gave up.

This is not one man's problem and its measure does not rest on one man's experiences. To document the similar experiences of others would fill volumes. The bottom line is that many sophisticated persons on the scene identified the events in terms no less characteristic of a witch-hunt than I have. Price summed up the situation well in one sentence: "The accusations, the innuendos, the predictions of charges to come, all followed one another so rapidly and in such profusion that in the public mind there was soon no line of demarcation between true and false."[5] And he nailed it down in this quote from Philip L. Guyelin, editorial page editor of the *Washington Post*, who conceded as much in saying: "There is, in truth, an ugly atmosphere in Washington and around the nation today—a prosecutorial impulse, a tension and an emotional pitch which makes it difficult to judge the guilt or innocence, the integrity or the motives, of public officials caught up anywhere near the eye of the Watergate storm . . . ."

Price's summary of concerns about the influence and power of the media includes these most pertinent to the Watergate era:

> "They have acquired a power out of proportion to their accountability, and out of proportion to the ability—or inclination—they have yet shown to use that power responsibly; . . . they pretend to far greater accuracy than they deliver, to far greater authority than their reports really have, and to a high-minded pursuit of truth even when they are maneuvering to keep the facts from getting in the way of a good story; . . . they display too much bias, and bias too unbalanced on one side; . . . they are too self-righteous, and regularly exempt themselves from the moral standards they impose on everyone else, piously condemning the sins of others while practicing the same sins themselves; . . . competitive pressure to get the story first translates into a pattern of scrambling to report the news before it happens, and as a result reporting it wrong, often grossly distorting it; . . . they display an excessively defensive, even paranoiac, reaction to criticism; . . . and like surgeons, newsmen bury their mistakes."

His is a strong indictment, but every word of it is borne out by the events of 1972 to 1975.

Reporters Woodward and Bernstein of the *Washington Post*, who became wealthy for their revelations, used a range of des-

---

5. Price, *With Nixon*.

picable tactics in compiling their news accounts. Worst of these were illegal attempts to breach the wall of grand jury secrecy by aproaching jurors "in an attempt to get information." They surreptitiously took off the names of the jurors from the courthouse records, then sorted out those whose occupations (such as government employment) led them to believe it would be risky to contact. In this conspiracy, according to their own book,[6] they were aided and abetted by no less than Benjamin Bradlee, executive editor, Howard Simons, managing editor, Harry M. Rosenfeld, metropolitan editor, and Barry Sussman, city editor. Bernstein approached "a half dozen" members of the jury and asked questions but contends that he was rebuffed and learned nothing. Judge Sirica was purportedly very agitated when he got wind of this, but all he did was to lecture in the courtroom about such tactics without naming the culprits.

To cover up the sometimes contemptible ways by which they extracted stories, they attributed many of their writings to information secured from a character named "Deep Throat" in nighttime clandestine meetings. It is possible that such a person existed, in which case it would most likely have had to be someone high in the FBI, or in the U.S. Attorney's office in Washington, who had access to FBI full field investigation reports. More likely, they used "Deep Throat" as a cover for a number of sources, including their imagination, and to disguise facts improperly secured. That is my belief, in which case they might as well have called their character "Qwerty Uiop," because he was merely a product of their typewriter.

Jack Anderson actually secured grand jury transcripts which he used as the basis for several columns, and displayed them boastingly to other reporters. When Judge Sirica took note of this illegality, Anderson agreed to return the transcripts to the court, and did so, but was never punished for what was a serious offense.

Throughout this time, Washington was awash with news

---

6. *All the President's Men*, in which they congratulated themselves for having escaped punishment from the court.

leaks, sometimes inspired by the sources to make points of their own, often wheedled by persistent reporters out of staffers of investigating and prosecuting forces, sometimes planted to see what replies they stimulated. Usually they originated in middle levels but occasionally they came from top officials. It was Special Prosecutor Cox himself, just after being fired, who indiscreetly told Senators Hart and Kennedy that Attorney General Kleindienst was a target of investigation, and from there to the printed page was a matter of hours. In April 1974, the IRS organization leaked numerous stories about its probe of Rebozo and related matters. The GAO investigators were most talkative of all; Woodward and Bernstein got many leads from them, some of which turned out to be so biased that they did not stand up.

Most news developments, in fact, began as leaks. The New York prosecutors in the Vesco trial leaked their coming indictments; the Watergate Special Prosecutor's staff dribbled out daily confidential stories about what was going to happen next. The Senate Watergate Committee staff members vied with each other to see who would be first to tell a media contact about a new discovery.

Many were mere hints that sometimes got badly garbled when repeated for the public. Typical of thousands of such leaks is this one by Daniel Schorr of CBS on September 11, 1973: "Staff investigators [of the Senate Watergate Committee] say they have indications that apart from direct contributions, $200,000 of which appears on a secret White House list to be released soon, Howard Hughes interests made cash payments totaling about $100,000 through Gordon Liddy and Howard Hunt." At the same time UPI reported that "the Senate Watergate Committee is investigating the possibility that $100,000 given by billionaire Howard Hughes was used to help pay for President Nixon's San Clemente home, a committee source said." There was not a germ of truth in either of these versions, and neither deserved publication.

Leaks were often premature, usually composed of sketchy and unfair tidbits, frequently inaccurate, and of course they seldom stated both sides of the story. Geared to sensationalism, the media repeated them at once with gusto, usually identified as certain facts, and the poor victim had little chance to counter. If the leak turned out to be incorrect in whole or in part, there was no later correction. Leaking was one of the most insidious and harmful aspects of the Watergate-era journalism.

On the heels of the daily and weekly news emissions came a wave of books. The media stories were analyzed, supplemented, and interpreted by a flood of volumes, as fast as the authors could get into print. The early ones relied entirely on the news reports, with no independent research, so they carried all the errors of the daily agglomerations of leaks, rumors, and inferences, and because of that were brutally unfair.

Among the worst of the lot were Richard Ney's junky *Wall Street Jungle*, containing libelous wild charges against Kleindienst, Mitchell, and me (all untrue); *They Could Not Trust the King*, by Stanley Tretick and William V. Shannon (" ... the Administration raised an unprecedentedly huge fund, partly by putting corrupt pressure on business corporations having tax, regulatory, contractual, or other difficulties with the government"—wholly untrue); *The Breaking of a President*, by Marvin Miller ("Under direct examination Judge Sirica elicits from Sloan that Mitchell and Stans approved a $199,000 payment to Liddy"—untrue); *The Watergate Hearings*, by the *New York Times* staff (" ... CRP officials cannot account for $900,000 in cash contributions"—untrue); *Washington Journal*, by Elizabeth Drew ("The cash contributed by Vesco went into the secret fund in Maurice Stans' safe. The fund financed the espionage-and-sabotage activities against the Democrats"—untrue); *The Great Cover-Up*, by Barry Sussman ("The first great problem with the money was that an investigation of it would not only eventually lead to Liddy but before it did it would link Maurice Stans and other reelection chieftains to the Watergate burglars"—untrue); and *Watergate*, by the London *Sunday Times* team (frequently inaccurate and careless).

Even such a usually objective and careful source as Congressional Quarterly in *Chronology of a Crisis* could misquote about a "payment of $30,000 in cash from the Philippine sugar industry to help pay for the Watergate cover-up"—untrue. An otherwise realistic author like George V. Higgins in *The Friends of Richard Nixon*[7] could let himself get so far off base as to say:

---

7. Boston: Little Brown, Atlantic Monthly Press, 1975.

"Stans had been scuttering around the country shaking down, among others, airlines which had new route requests pending before the Civil Aeronautics Board, government-regulated industries, and government contractors"—wholly untrue in its only possible meaning.

Examples of the deliberate bias that was so damnable appears throughout the book *All the President's Men* by the two *Washington Post* reporters, Carl Bernstein and Bob Woodward, published in May 1974. It is a boastful account of their work in smoking out the Watergate facts in 1972 and early 1973 and it mentions my name on at least thirty pages with all of the implications of guilt, even though they well knew by then that I had played no culpable part in the Watergate incident or the coverup. Nowhere in the book is there even a footnote exonerating me. To the contrary, there are frequent references to "the cash in Stans' safe" and regular assertions that it was that cash which financed both the bugging and the coverup. In this and other respects, the book merely repeats the largely erroneous assumptions that the authors evolved day by day and published in the early months of the Watergate investigations, and disregards entirely the subsequent disclosures that greatly altered the facts behind those assumptions.

It says that a $200,000 contribution received in cash from Robert Vesco "had been added to the cash fund in Stans' safe, and had helped to finance the Watergate operation and other undercover activities." This in the face of a finding of Judge Hart in the Federal Court for the District of Columbia that the $200,000 was part of a bank deposit made by the finance committee on May 25, 1972. The Vesco money had no identification with Watergate.

The book contains a racy account of how I allegedly assured contributors of anonymity by "moving their contributions through a Mexican middleman whose bank records were not subject to subpoena by U.S. investigators," and how this protection would allow the finance committee to receive illegal contributions from corporations, and contributions from businessmen and labor leaders having trouble with government agencies, and from "special-interest groups and such underground sources of income as the big Las Vegas gambling casinos and mob-dominated unions." All this would be done, they said, by taking contributed checks or securities across the border to

Mexico, converting them to cash and bringing the proceeds back to Washington. Not less than $750,000 had moved in this way, it was said. This fanciful tale was credited by the authors to a talkative "swashbuckling" attorney in Houston and an irresponsible investigator in the office of the Miami state's attorney.

"If a guy pleaded broke," the attorney was quoted, "Maury would get him to turn over stock in his company or some other stock. He was talking 10 percent . . . ."

All of this was plain crap, and the authors knew it. No such things had ever happened or been suggested, by me or by anyone connected with my committee. Because the story was so unbelievable, Woodward and Bernstein said, they were "wary" and did not publish it at the time they heard it, but they nonetheless took several pages of their book to spell out the weird lies in detail.

I checked with their named source, the Houston lawyer. He said that Bernstein had quoted the story to him as having come from the state's attorney's office in Miami, and that he in turn had denied it to Bernstein. He offered to support me with his testimony if I decided to sue.

One of the most scurrilous and careless messes to follow it was a product of columnist-author Jimmy Breslin.[8] He attributes absurd remarks to Congressman Tip O'Neill that by then both would have known were totally without foundation. It was clearly one more book written from discredited newspaper clippings.

These books were all in the spirit of the times. Accuracy gave way to sensationalism, with no concern about where the chips might fall and who they might hit. And how does the victim correct the falsities in a book?

The long-range solution of press fairness is to be found, hopefully, in the creation of a really effective nationwide voluntary mechanism for self-discipline by the media with participation by qualified members of the public. Just as the professions of law and accounting and medicine have their uniform codes of ethics, which they themselves police and enforce, so should the press and the electronic news communicators. These could provide, in answer to the questions asked earlier, that:

---

8. Jimmy Breslin, *How the Good Guys Finally Won* (New York: Viking Press, 1975).

—The media, under its own code of ethics and enforcement procedures, with full publicity of its actions, should insure that in serving the public it does not impair the rights of accused or suspected persons, intrude upon the processes of justice, or damage unfairly the reputation of individuals who are innocent of the subject matter discussed.

—News stories affecting persons should be solidly based on verified data or direct quotes, and should not be allowed to contain inferences or allegations based on hypothetical assumptions, or on rumor or hearsay, even though so identified. Unverified leaks should not be published.[9]

—Similar to the British system, continued publicity about a case after indictment should be restricted to factual statements of events or testimony, without elaboration or interpretation.

—The media should insist that its reporters respect the confidentiality of grand jury proceedings, and not seek or publish raw data from them.

—The right of the public to know should be undisputed, but that right should be subordinate in timing to the procedures of law in order to protect legal proceedings and the rights of individuals.

—Complaints by persons about inaccurate or unfair news accounts, editorials, or comments should be given immediate and objective review by the media involved and, if found to be justified, should be recognized by full and honest correction forthwith in equivalent space or time. When a criminal matter, public hearing, or similar event is ended, it should be the responsibility of the media outlet, upon request of any party, to assess the accuracy of its published material and similarly retract any unfair or unjustified statements.

—The standards of reporting thus established should be enforced by a professional body, half of whose numbers shall be

9. Historian Daniel J. Boorstin has made one proposal, somewhat impractical, for dealing with the networks: " ... it would be a public service if, as a self-denying ordinance, the networks would agree not to publish news until a week after it is reported. Give them a chance to sort it out ... the basic problem that electronic media have brought to news reporting is 'Too much too soon.' "

chosen from the general public, with powers of punishment. For example, the penalty for damaging use of untruthful, prejudicial, or inflammatory material, or for refusal to retract, should range from public censure to banishment from the profession, the latter in case of willful or reckless offenses.

—Prior restraint should be imposed on the media by a court when and if the court finds that premature disclosure or discussion is likely to impair an individual's right to a fair and impartial trial or the prosecution of another case.

—Additionally, the Supreme Court ought to take judicial notice of the inequity of its Sullivan case edict, and open the courts to persons with reputations to lose, whether they are in public life or not, to allow them to sue for libel when they are improperly and incorrectly maligned by the media. While there need be no prior legal restraint, immunity from liability should not follow.

Perhaps the most important of these is a fairness doctrine that would require after-the-fact reappraisals, upon request of a person claiming to be injured, with prompt follow-up articles that remedy, in a meaningful way, the damages done by inaccurate reporting or unsupported editorial comment. The Federal Trade Commission seems to have the power to require a company to run retractions of unsupported statements in past business advertising. It would be sound if a responsible press found fairness in news reporting to be a sufficiently worthy goal to do the same willingly, by its own code of ethics, and to require a retraction when appropriate, in the same space and format as the erroneous report. Such rules for "truth in reporting" would not only represent equity to the individuals involved by balancing early accounts with the later truth, thus preventing irremediable damage, but would give the media a credibility they do not now have.

Despite the encomiums some of its members have heaped on themselves for Watergate reporting, it was not the media's finest hour.

# 17

## THE PRESIDENT WHO
## TRIED TOO HARD?

What place will history give to Richard Nixon?

For decades to come, historians will be probing his deeds, drawing from them their evaluations of the Presidency that ended so disastrously. Not until that process has gone its course will the people have a true measure of the man and his contributions, positive and negative, to his country and the world.

Meanwhile, the most frequent picture today is that of a man standing alone in the fiery ruins of the Watergate holocaust, the central guilty figure in the nation's worst political tragedy. No other impression is possible to Americans who lived through the hour-by-hour, blow-by-blow hammerings of the news media, in print and over the air, and the caustic carpings by political foes, in the months following mid-1972. Granted, he contributed to that result by various actions: his silence, his denial of the coverup, and his misstatements and untruths. Yet many perceptions of this man are obscured and lost and the nation has been left with the impression of a person predominantly dishonest.

Even now, where in the literature that accumulates to make history is any accounting made of the redeeming values of Richard Nixon? Surely there must be some. Where is the balancing of good and bad that comprises any person's worth to his society, especially for this man of paradox so brutally condemned in his own country while still revered as a major statesman in a large part of the world? Did he deserve his fate, or was he the victim of a political coup? Was he an evil quasi-dictator or an able, far-sighted leader who, when his zealous subordinates got into careless trouble, too generously tried to cover up their sins at his own peril?

Perhaps enough time has elapsed since Watergate to begin looking beneath the accumulated realities and artificialities for a balanced judgment of his overall worth to the nation over a lifetime of public service. To do otherwise is to condemn Richard Nixon to the brutal destiny described by Shakespeare:

> The evil that men do lives after them;
> The good is oft interred with their bones.

It seems fair that one should ask whether, after three hundred years of the sharpening of our sciences of communications and of human motivation since that was written, a better judgment is not possible. In short, where is the truth and how should history rate Nixon?

As one who had been a friend for more than fifteen years before Watergate, and an associate in government and in election endeavors for more than half of that, I have tried often to reconcile in my mind the Watergate image of Richard Nixon with the Nixon I knew. In that process, I had to sort out my own feelings toward him, avoiding the easy consequence of becoming spiteful or bitter because I had become seared with some of the heat aimed in his direction and had my own career tarnished because of the association.

My emotions during and after these experiences could have led me up a number of paths, most of them ending in anger and resentment. As time went on, public disclosures began to fill in my perception of what had gone on. I could see how I had been deceived by the guilty, kept in the dark throughout, and even used at times to fit their purposes. Most notable was the White House tape of February 28, 1973, in which Nixon approved John Dean's plan to have me nominated for an ambassadorship so that at my confirmation hearing before the Senate I would take the brunt of the Watergate questioning and thus defuse the spirit and news value of the Ervin Committee's efforts. There were numerous

other deceptions, too. But as the entire Watergate picture unfolded and I could measure and comprehend what had taken
place behind the scenes without my knowing, a more reasoned
judgment led me to the conclusions in this chapter.

After a time the principal emotion which survived my own
experiences was one of distress at the shattering of the man
whose star I had chosen to follow. By his own actions, Richard
Nixon had abdicated the high place in history to which his record
before Watergate entitled him, and to which another four years in
office could have added luster. Why?

He has given me no direct personal reason to feel anything
but friendly toward him. There has been no indication in any of
his published records and tapes that he ever said anything critical
or caustic about me. While I could feel offended by his willingness in 1973 to allow his White House subordinates to use me as a
shock troop in a Senate confirmation proceeding, I could also
consider his approval of that ploy as an expression of high confidence. He appointed me Secretary of Commerce and gave me
good support even when I was under criticism for doing or failing
to do some things; I think he believes I performed well there. He
has told me and others that I did a superlative job as his finance
chairman in three different elections. It was certainly not his
direct doing that caused me to be victimized by Watergate. I do
not blame him for my being drawn as a bystander into that
maelstrom. So as a friend I cannot walk away from Richard Nixon
solely because he became the first President of the United States
who was forced to resign and certainly not without considering
in great depth what his motivations may have been.

One's feelings on a matter like this, however, are infinitely
more complex than that simple statement might imply. When a
friend is privately or publicly accused of wrongdoing, it is in-
stinctive to disbelieve the charges against him; one does not easily
believe ill of those he trusts and admires. When a friend is
publicly condemned by his peers after a formal public proceeding, one's mind shifts from doubting the event to wondering how
and why it happened and what it meant.

It may have been inevitable that in the early fury of retribution the public lost sight of anything good about Richard Nixon.
Yet there were many things in his life on the plus side that need to
be brought back into the equation of judgment. His meteoric rise

from a modest background. His perseverance in unveiling the treachery of Alger Hiss. His excellent and unflawed record as Vice President for eight years under Eisenhower. His courage and perspicacity in fighting back from two election defeats. Above all, his leadership as an international peacemaker, which succeeded in opening long-closed barriers to understanding among the world's peoples and may in the long run have saved millions of lives from the devastations of confrontation and war.

It was in pursuing his goals for the country and the world with singlemindedness that Richard Nixon slipped. In trying to surmount obstacles he built a regime that centralized power in a close circle, to more easily overcome opposition and force events his way. In his zeal for accomplishment, he allowed those around him, many young and inexperienced in government and politics, to be over-zealous. In their eagerness to help attain his objectives they misdirected the nuts-and-bolts efforts into a ruthlessness that slighted the rights of others. When the revelations of these actions began to unfold, he and they committed the only meaningful sin of Watergate, the covering up of what were misdeeds in order to maintain the momentum toward the objectives he so earnestly wanted to achieve.

His performance in the duties of office in other respects was outstanding. His foreign policy was imaginative and successful, and his work for world peace was historic. He ended the twenty-year-old cold war by his personal initiatives. His breaking down of the curtains between the United States and the Communist nations of China and the Soviet Union set the stage for detente that could last far longer than the generation of peace he sought. He may have done more for the peace of the world than any President in this century.

His mark on the domestic scene was a less spectacular one, but nonetheless worthy and notable in many ways. His first five years restored quiet to our cities, and to our campuses, after a decade of violence and turmoil. On the economic front he had only limited and uncertain accomplishments in his first term, and he found no way to cope with the worldwide inflation that followed the unprecedented rise in the prices of international commodities, especially oil, in his last year in office. He did succeed in many other domestic initiatives, and he achieved progress in reducing racial bias and improving the nation's health and stability. History, if it is to be fair, must balance this accounting against the sad negative of Watergate.

This terse appraisal of his efforts and achievements as President is not mine alone. When his record was submitted to the American people, at the end of four years, they not only reelected him but did so by a vote so one-sided, giving him 61 percent of the vote and forty-nine states, that it must be deemed a landslide of endorsement, even if it is discounted for the fact that some persons chose him out of fear of George McGovern. It was the most overwhelming vote of confidence given to a candidate for President since George Washington. Despite the intimations of Watergate improprieties before the election, the public clearly wanted him to carry on his programs for the nation. They liked what he had done and approved what he proposed to do. Yet he fell soon afterward because of the clumsy handling of a small incident in his campaign for reelection.

I do not seek to be a self-appointed apologist for Richard Nixon, nor am I qualified to speak for his state of mind when he dealt with Watergate as he did. As one who worked with him for years, however, it is not possible for me to come around to accepting the oft-tendered picture of Richard Nixon as a master criminal out to advance his own interests regardless of cost to the nation. At no time in my relationship with him did I ever have reason to believe he was other than an honest and ethical public servant dedicated to giving his best to the advancement of his country's interests. Nevertheless, he was named as an unindicted co-conspirator in the Watergate coverup by a grand jury, and was charged by the House Judiciary Committee with three counts of "high crimes and misdemeanors" in impeachment hearings. I know now about the evidence that came to public light in those proceedings, and it would serve no purpose to resift all that, or to attempt to question the motives of any of his accusers. Since neither matter ever brought him to trial, only he can say what his defenses or explanations are, and what he did willfully cause to happen, and only he can justify his actions before the court of history. That is not a task I can undertake, but as a friend and close associate I owe it to him to at least try to understand.

The White House tapes are keenly distressing, not because of their profanity or deleted expletives, which are not unusual for persons under the pressure of Presidential frustrations, but because his actions shown by them sometimes conflict with the brilliance I would have expected from him under the circumstances. Nevertheless, I have come to believe that I can reconcile that conflict, acknowledging that I give him the benefit of the most favorable view I can compose, in the face of reasons to doubt.

It seems most common in analzying a public personality to conclude that he is a very complex person, torn by conflicting emotions, and acting according to various tugs and pulls concealed in his character. One author has described Richard Nixon as a cake of eight different layers.[1] I don't see any reason to strain so intensely to account for him. He was not always consistent, but what normal person is? Several other authors[2] have pointed out that Nixon had a "dark side" to his nature, although acknowledging that it was far outweighed by the qualities of his good side. There is no reason why this should be considered surprising or unusual. Probably no one ever lived, including Jesus of Nazareth, who did not yield at times to frustration, anger, doubt, or gloom. The responsibilities and stresses of the Presidency are so heavy, and the legitimate political forces so strong, as to distort anyone's efforts to behave wholly consistently in that job or to maintain an even keel at all times. Evidence is lacking that until Watergate reached its explosive stages Nixon was in any important way un-normal in his Presidential actions.

True, there were people much closer to him than I, some in government and a few in his personal life, who had better opportunities to observe his private and Presidential actions. Many of my contacts with him in government were on ceremonial occasions like formal White House dinners, or at official events like a Cabinet meeting or public dedication; these do not lead to either intimate acquaintanceship or to relaxed interchange. Notwithstanding, there ran through our association a frequency of dealings that reflected, I believe, a strong mutual respect and a cordiality that was much more than casual, and gave me a good measure of the man. His failure to mention my name on two

1. William Safire, *Before the Fall* (Garden City, N.Y.: Doubleday & Company, 1975).
2. H. R. Haldeman, *The Ends of Power* (New York: New York Times Books, 1978). Raymond Price, *With Nixon* (New York: Viking Press, 1977).

celebrated public occasions, the first when he introduced his Cabinet in December 1968 and the second a month later when I was sworn in as Secretary of Commerce, was amusing and likely due to oversight, certainly not to inability to remember who I was.

There was at the same time a stiffness in our relationship that somehow held back close communications. I was not one of those associates he took into intimate confidence, as he did John Mitchell, George Shultz, and John Connally, for example. For my part, my respect for his intellectual capacity often caused me to hesitate before expressing myself to him until I was sure I had something new to say. Even then, I sometimes did not get across to him very well. I remember one 1969 Cabinet colloquy when the topic of the government's finances came up. I could see clearly the consequences that certain pending proposals would bring to the budget and I said so quite tersely: "Mr. President, a big deficit is inevitable if you follow these policies." It was a statement of certain fact, but he took it as a criticism and turned away cooly without response.[3]

In matters of official business while I was in his Cabinet, I tried to bother him as little as possible out of respect for his tremendous workload. I took it that my responsibility was to handle my duties as best I could and go to him only when in serious doubt or in need of his help, which was seldom. In the course of the scheduled meetings I had with him every few months to review matters in Commerce, he was always observant and helpful. Beyond those routine occasions, I recall only once that I asked for a special hearing and that was to appeal a decision by Budget Director George Shultz to reduce my request in 1971 for $100 million for a minority enterprise program. Nixon listened to my plea, and complimented me on the activity, but stuck to Shultz's lesser amount.

My main impression of Richard Nixon is his towering intellect, enhanced by an astoundingly capable power of organizing thoughts and expressing them. He was one of the most adept

---

3. It is sometimes said that Nixon did not react well to criticism, and there is some truth to the statement. Like most strong-minded men, confident of goals, he perceived most criticism of his actions or proposals to reflect ignorance of his long-term aims and unreasoning distrust of his motives. Other Presidents before him reacted similarly. Yet I observed that when differences of opinion were more softly phrased as suggestions, he was quite willing to listen.

public speakers of his day. I had no doubt from the first few times I heard and saw him in action in about 1958 that he was qualified to be President of the United States, and that conviction grew with each new association. In 1972 I worked for him to be re-elected with a total dedication based on the belief that he would be our greatest President in the twentieth century. He could have been, had Watergate not intervened. Presidents, despite the aura surrounding them, are not supermen. They are mortals blessed with just a little more acumen, sense of timing, creativity, dedication, and persuasiveness than the average. He had enough of these qualities to be outstanding.

I do not believe any man could have been more determined to do the best possible job as President than Richard Nixon. Trained for it through many years of service in the House of Representatives, in the Senate, and as Vice President, he won his second attempt to gain the White House by a close margin in 1968 without carrying either wing of the Congress for his party. Thus he was destined at the outset to be a minority President, with all the difficulties which that can mean under our constitutional system of the separation of powers between the legislative and executive branches.

Nixon's dedication made him probably the most disciplined man ever to head the government of the United States. He drank sparingly, didn't smoke, exercised daily, displayed no interest in extramarital sex, and stuck to a strict diet to control his weight. Above all, he managed his workload; he regulated the monstrous demands on his time, so that he could keep his head above the grindstone and still be able to find quiet to contemplate and develop major initiatives of national and international policy. Nixon did not want merely to respond to events; he wanted to anticipate them, to influence their direction and outcome, and in the process to create measures that would reduce future problems. He was more constructively creative than any President since Franklin Roosevelt.

One of my friends said facetiously in 1970 that "anyone who rates his job highly enough to eat cottage cheese and catsup to keep in shape can't be all bad." I felt that a person with such a regulated and orderly control of his life, and with the intelligence of Nixon, had a high probability of being a superior President. Senator Everett Dirksen, I believe, once described politics as the art of the possible, and Nixon had both the experience and the pragmatism to make the most of it.

He had some drawbacks. No person limited by human capabilities could be perfect and Nixon had obvious imperfections. His early political struggles had given him an image of ruthlessness, he sometimes appeared ill at ease in formal situations, and because of that or perhaps because of an inherent social diffidence was considered a cold personality. President John Kennedy referred critically to his stodgy, graceless exterior. To me, he was an introvert doing his best to act like an extrovert, which was what his career demanded. I did not hold these against him as flaws, but many people did.

He had another disadvantage. Without doubt, his long history of contentious relations with the press contributed to the venom with which some attacked him. Liberals among them still resented his cornering of Alger Hiss. His 1962 "last press conference" had never been forgiven, because to the media it represented his inner feelings of disdain for their function. But most of all there was a carry-over of negative feelings from the trying period of the Vietnam war—of distrust originating with Lyndon Johnson's Presidency that carried over into Nixon's, and of antagonism in direct response to the hammering speeches of Nixon's Vice President, Spiro T. Agnew. In retrospect, it is likely that at no time in his career did Nixon really trust the media, and they knew it. All of this came back with a vengeance when he allowed himself to get off base in Watergate, and it pursued him relentlessly to the end. His failure to find the formula for an amicable working relationship sometime in his political life may have made impossible any hope of balanced reporting when he was finally caught in retreat. And certainly a considerable part of the frenzy inflicted on me, John Mitchell, and others mentioned in earlier chapters was the harvest of the years of distrust of Nixon and his doings.

In short, the personal Richard Nixon I knew before Watergate was a man of ambition, energy, ability, and dedication. His Presidency was an intense one, hard-working, determined, wide-ranging, organized, and creative. He was a man of action, knowing what he wanted to do in his job, certain he could override the obstacles he knew he had to face. At the same time, he gave me the impression of being a modest man, somewhat awed by the circumstances of position and power he had achieved. This may account for the care and attention he generally gave to avoiding mistakes in judgment, as exemplified by the thoroughness of his consideration of new ideas before he adopted them. He wanted to know in writing, fully thought out by those knowledgeable, the various options on a new proposal, and the pros and cons of each option, and he studied them carefully. He took volumes of such papers on almost every trip to Camp David, so he could solve his problems by thinking them through, often sending them back for more work on weak points.

Like many brilliant minds, Nixon did not have much tolerance for mediocrity. He was not demanding in an unreasonable way, but he did expect quality performance from those around him. He could be caustic about those who did not deliver. Like Eisenhower, he did not often praise people face to face, but he often remarked to others on a man's good performance, and he searched out opportunities to increase the responsibilities and recognition of those he thought capable. He put a high value on loyalty, and responded in kind to those who demonstrated loyalty to him.

Like Presidents before him, he was irate about leaks that inhibited careful management of the government by premature disclosure of matters under consideration or under correction, or that disclosed information that he believed best served the nation by being kept confidential. The leaks that came out were accountable for his distrust of the bureaucracy, which he once said was "96 percent against us." He wanted interdepartmental differences of opinion worked out quietly, not in the press. And many times he expressed the belief that the press was strongly antagonistic to him and his administration. At times, his words evidenced a kind of underdog mentality, a sketch of a man fighting to do the right thing against odds unreasonably imposed to impede his progress.

Behind the scenes, I was several times surprised to find him critical about businessmen in general, more than I thought justified, and I went out of my way to try to convince him otherwise. His complaint was that business people did not work hard enough to support his initiatives, even those that were soundly in the interest of the national economy, and that they were sometimes petty or selfish in asking for laws or regulations in their own interest. Nevertheless, he was a strong advocate of the free enterprise system and disdainful of those who reviled or downgraded it.

He had an unlimited capacity for hard work, and was all business at all times, with an average work day of probably sixteen hours, if all the protocol events are counted. He was competitive to a high degree, taking the challenges of the Congress or the media as calls to battle, demanding strategy that planned the game many moves ahead.

Despite his all-business attitude, Nixon could be mild-mannered and considerate of others. He spent time on phone calls and messages to friends on occasions of their birthdays and weddings, or in greetings at times of illness or hospitalization. He was generous in dividing his perquisites with Cabinet officers and others associated closely with him in the administration, allowing them to use the Presidential facilities at Camp David, the *Sequoia* on the Potomac, the Western White House, or his box seats at Kennedy Center when he was not in attendance. When it came to subordinates who did not perform to his standards, he was chickenhearted. He disliked firing anyone, as was demonstrated on several occasions, notably his confrontation with Interior Secretary Walter J. Hickel.

He was, I believe, at heart a religious man, although no acknowledgment of that seems to have been made by anyone since his withdrawal. There is no other way to account for his active associations with top churchmen like Norman Vincent Peale and Billy Graham, or for his instituting and continuing Sunday religious services in the East Room of the White House when he was in Washington. Each service was conducted by a clergyman of high reputation, from many different religions, accompanied by a choir of special skill selected from churches around the country. Kathleen and I were regularly among the 250 invitees and were stirred by the ecumenical range of the programs and the inspiring voices of the singers. It would be hard for us to believe that Nixon had any motive other than spiritual in presiding over these events, and certainly it would stretch the imagination to believe he was hypocritical in actually presenting them for any other purpose, considering the demands on his time.

I saw no motivation in him but a desire to be a superlative

President. He seemed to want power only to accomplish that goal. He had never shown an ambitious longing for wealth, and certainly could have enriched himself in a multitude of ways, if he had sought to do so. There is no evidence that, except for his eight years of private life between 1961 and 1969 which he spent in the private practice of law, he accumulated any private means. His long government service, as is usually the case, was little more than a break-even, financially.

The American public tends to have an all-or-nothing way of evaluating its public personalities. One manifestation of this syndrome appears after an election. Everything the winner did in his campaign was right; everything the loser did was wrong. Thus Kennedy didn't make a mistake in 1960; Nixon did everything wrong. Had a few hundred thousand votes been reversed, the opposite would have been said—Nixon did everything right, Kennedy did everything wrong. The winner wins all the way, the loser loses all the way.

That is how heroes and bums are made. Kennedy, who died a hero, was so revered that his Presidential fiascos are still over-looked, and his philanderings cause little surprise. Truman, whose courage in a few tough decisions made him look good in retrospect, emerges as a great President and his sins of medio-crity are forgiven. Johnson, who ended in disgrace over foreign policy, did so poorly on Vietnam that he is not thought to have done anything else right. So goes the way of politics.

That is why Richard Nixon after Watergate is often pictured as a Hitlerian character without conscience, merit, or virtue because Watergate gave his haters and detractors the "proof" they had long been looking for.

Herbert Hoover left office in 1933 amid condemnation for the nation's economic suffering, condemnation that took decades to evaporate before there was uncovered the perspective that he was a victim of economic circumstances long abuilding. Will Nixon's black cloud some day be lifted and reveal a President who stumbled over a molehill while trying to build mountainous deeds of progress for a nation and a world? Surely not now, but perhaps the historians, who need thirty years or more to do their chores, will see him in a much more favorable light than is possible while those who cheered so heartily at his downfall are still alive and vocal.

I once had a partner who gave me a memorable lesson. As we all sometimes do, I made disparaging remarks in a conclusive way about a person who had been derelict in some of his work. My ⌐ssociate took me to task, at the same time pointing out the man's good traits. He then said simply: "Every man ought to be judged on his net. There is some good in every bad person, and some bad in every good person, and the one should be subtracted from the other in reaching a judgment." His use of an accounting term in this context was apt, and I have tried to follow it since. History will best serve us if it finds a way to judge Richard Nixon on his net. There is no practical way to quantify the performance of a President in office, as there is for the head of a corporation, who can be measured by the bottom line on the profit statement. But it is possible to enumerate some of the things Nixon did while in the White House, to be considered in the scale of his value to the country. Even his most damning critics are forced to concede that some of his programs for the United States were worthy and that he had some notable successes with them. The extent of such approval varies over the spectrum from believer to cynic, supporter to opponent.

I was fortunate to have been able to observe some of his projects at close range and to see the results of others. The greatest accolades have come to him in the field of foreign policy where his moves toward "a generation of peace" could, over-shadowing all his troubles, award him high credit. The ending of the American presence in Vietnam, the return of the prisoners of war, and the slow rebuilding of negotiations toward peace in the Middle East are tangible, but their significance may prove to be less valuable for history than his "opening of the door" to China and his creation of detente with the Soviet Union. The Nixon Doctrine delimited the aims and responsibilities of the United States in other world situations. Except for Presidents like Wilson, Roosevelt, and Truman, who were forced to define a defensive reaction for our country under conditions of military aggression in the world, none in my lifetime had shown as driving and constructive a desire to relieve mankind from the antago-nisms of man as did Nixon. To a degree, the worth of his work in foreign policy will be appraised over the years according to the period it survives, which may not be a fair evaluation at all. The failure of South Vietnam to maintain itself after our departure, or the possible failure of the Middle East to hold the peace, should not detract from the practical idealism he applied to try to prevent such things from happening. He must be graded high on foreign policy.

On the domestic scene, the rating is more difficult, partly because some of his ideas scarcely got off the ground in his first term. Had he served normally for eight years they may have fared better. Government reorganization, from the standpoint of reducing the burdens on the occupant of the White House by reducing the number of persons reporting to him, has merit; his plans may not have been the best conceivable, but they offered a change that would have been worth trying. Reducing the size of the Federal establishment and localizing government decisions is another desideratum which he urged, and it got only a token start through partial adoption of his revenue-sharing proposals. It is inevitable that these subjects will revive under other Presidents and Nixon's ground-breaking path should help them then.

Others of his innovations did get momentum. Among those in the Department of Commerce, where I presided, were the rebuilding of the American merchant fleet and modernizing of shipyards, the creation of a National Oceanic and Atmospheric Administration to centralize management of the oceans, tidelands, and atmosphere, and the organization and stimulation of the country's first meaningful program to help blacks and other minorities to enter the world of business. Elsewhere, in human relationships, which perhaps should count the most, his notable effort was on behalf of a "family assistance plan" that would make long-range sense out of a host of overlapping and confusing welfare programs. The Congress did not adopt it; much of the opposition contended that it was too generous.

There were many other initiatives for which he should receive credit in the scaling of his performance. His proposals ended the military draft in favor of a voluntary force, increased the proportion of the budget going for human resources, removed the Post Office from political control, gave support to Federal mass transit financing, instituted a drive against organized crime, sponsored a tax reform bill that was enacted in 1969 with most of the provisions he advocated, induced Congress to protect senior citizens against inflation by providing for automatic increases in social security benefits, extended unemployment insurance coverage, got Congress to enact a new Manpower Training Act, provided greatly enlarged funding for control of air pollution and water pollution, sponsored a new foreign trade act to improve trade conditions and reduce damage to American industry from low-labor-cost imports, made many proposals for consumer protection and occupational safety, and created an Environmental Protection Agency. Not all of these were enacted exactly as he proposed, and not all turned out to be as successful as he intended, but the range of his initiatives is clearly evident. A *Fortune* editorial as early as September 1970 conceded that "Nixon has already presided over a massive reordering of national priorities." It had been, *Fortune* said, "a vigorous political leadership of which the President and the public have a right to be proud."

Despite all this, and because of Watergate, it is common for people to speak about Nixon in terms of disillusionment, but that is not the noun that comes to my mind as most fitting. True, my dreams of his eminence are shattered by his fall from grace. He failed to be the peerless leader I thought he would become. The picture of him as a man of careful analysis, poring over pros and cons, making monumental decisions on fine logic, is shaken by the tapes of Watergate. My illusion is gone, true, but that is not the main loss.

The word that best describes my state of mind is sorrow. Sorrow that Richard Nixon didn't perceive the inevitable consequences when Watergate first came to his attention; and even more astonishingly, that he did not pounce on a better alternative than allowing a coverup. Sorrow that he did not immediately stop the course of action that ultimately led so many of his top associates into disgrace, and cost him his Presidency. Sorrow over the disastrous consequences to the world, the country, the party, his family, and his deserved place in history. Sorrow that his actions deprived the nation of the constructive judgment and action he could have brought to bear on its problems for another three years. Sorrow above all over a historic opportunity lost for a single man to be the peacemaker of his generation. The list of sorrows could be as endless as my mental processes could envision what might have been. Sorrow is my word for Richard Nixon, with a lingering hope that a kinder generation may find a new scale to measure his value, put the pluses in his life into juxtaposition with the minuses, and thereby find a "net" that is a fairer judgment for history than is possible now.

How, then, do I account for his Watergate?  Here is my meditative analysis:

Richard Nixon came from a humble family of limited means. He was a shy person, and even in his greatest moments never overcame that inherent shyness.  With those attributes, it is entirely usual that he would have been determined from youth on to "make a mark in life." This picture of a young man struggling all the way to the Presidency of the United States is an uncomplex one and does not require him to be characterized as a blending of many different personalities.  He was an ambitious, capable American living the great dream, working hard all the way.

Once President, he wanted to be the best President the country ever had.  In short, Nixon's overwhelming characteristic was ambition, and his ambition to succeed caused him to try too hard, and that caused his eventual downfall.  On that basis I can understand him and empathize with him.

When Nixon ran for the Presidency in 1968 he was probably the best trained man the country had ever found for the job.  He had been Vice President for two full terms, even a sort of Acting President during a severe illness of Dwight Eisenhower.  He had been in the tough world of business for eight years, with an opportunity realized by few high-level politicians and only a few previous Presidents to see at first hand how the nation's productive wheels turn.

There can be no doubt that in all these experiences a man of his analytical capacity would be accumulating ideas as to what the country needed for its long-term future, and what the world of nations needed.  These ideas could easily be translated into what he would do if he were President—perhaps not as a program in numbered paragraphs but as a partly conscious, partly subconscious catalog of plans that could be drawn upon. There is no doubt in my mind that on January 20, 1969, as he took the oath of office, Richard Nixon had such a concept of his forthcoming job, and that he wanted through the powers of his office to improve life in the country and in the world.

He knew it would be difficult.  His Republican party was in the minority in both houses of the Congress, which meant that he could expect an item-by-item struggle to get legislation enacted. That is exactly what occurred. Some of his proposals were badly abused, some not enacted at all, some twisted into shapes he could not accept. It was a running fight, and he geared up to cope with it as best he could. Meanwhile, he was confronted from the outset with the bane of Presidents, unauthorized news leaks; his plans were often telegraphed ahead to the opposition and even the minor performance gaps of his administration were public property, bitingly criticized.

He reacted in several ways. He took major policy responsibilities away from his department heads and moved them into the White House. That insured closer uniformity of objectives for his team, and eliminated some public family bickering. I did not believe at the time that this was a desirable move and felt that it reduced Cabinet members to mere administrators with an insufficient voice in matters of policy. Even so, it would have worked better if the White House staff had provided a suitable means of direct confrontation between departments on issues involving more than one of them. As early as March 7, 1969, I had addressed a memorandum to Counselor Arthur Burns and Chief of Staff Haldeman proposing a better process in the White House to resolve interagency differences in terms of the President's program, citing the effectiveness of the Eisenhower procedure whereby heads of agencies sat around a table with Presidential aide Sherman Adams, who listened to all sides and then hammered out an agreement that met the administration's overall objectives. My proposal was not warmly received, however, and Presidential aides continued to exercise their own judgment of his desires on complex issues, with the agencies often feeling that they had an inadequate opportunity to be heard. Nevertheless, it is ridiculous to assert, as some writers have, that this difference in style had anything to do with the happenings of Watergate.

Nixon tried to cope with the leaks, first through a series of national security wiretaps, and then by allowing his staff to set up a so-called "plumbers" group. The theft and release to the press of the Pentagon papers in 1971 by Daniel Ellsberg sent his blood pressure to the ceiling, and caused him to demand that somehow, some way, something be done to punish Ellsberg and set an example. His aides took it from there and performed disastrously.

Digging hard to locate leaks of information that ought to be privileged, if done within the proprieties of the law, is one thing and is understandable; using governmental power in illegal actions that abort due process is another and cannot be condoned. The nocturnal invasion of the office of Ellsberg's psychiatrist did more than result in Ellsberg going free for an offense for which he probably should have been convicted; when it became known, it disturbed a large body of public opinion because it showed a disregard for the orderly institutional and legal ways of the country. More than anything these actions of his subordinates hurt Nixon severely when they came to light.

Frustrated by some of the developments of his first few years in the White House, including the defeat of his proposals for welfare reform, government reorganization, and "blocked grants" for welfare and education, it was inevitable that he contemplated the new election coming up in 1972 with some hope of relief. His entire organization caught the mood of the necessity of winning big, so big that he would have a mandate for his next four years that the Congress could not ignore. With a smashing victory would come also more Republicans in both houses of the Congress, to give power to his plans. It was not a question of just winning, it had to be a matter of winning by the biggest margin in history. The goal was to corral every conceivable vote, every conceivable percentage point, and that is the way the election campaign of 1972 was run. I saw it in the overkill and overlap of repeated television, radio, direct mail, telephone, and person-to-person appeals. As finance chairman, I protested the cost, but was brushed aside. No expense was considered by his aides to be too great under the circumstances, and even if the incremental return from spending another million dollars was only 100,000 unneeded votes, it was spent. That is why the 1972 campaign cost $56 million, despite all my objections.

Within this environment, one of the "plumbers" group, Gordon Liddy, apparently proposed to a campaign official, Jeb Magruder, that some benefit might be gained if the moves of the political opposition could be anticipated, perhaps by bugging their phones or reading their files or putting informers into their organization. Or possibly it was the other way, Magruder to

Liddy. Equivalent tactics had been used before, by both parties.[4] That was presumably the genesis of Watergate. That is how a plot as absurd and as petty and as fruitless as the Watergate burglary came to happen.

Nixon was not a party to the Watergate break-in. That has been established, especially by the White House tapes beginning in June 1972, which showed his initial consternation at learning about it. Why then did he apparently allow himself to be involved, first passively and then actively, in the coverup? Why did he not insist on immediate full disclosure in June 1972? Was his knee-jerk approval of the coverup a case of his being instinctively evil or instinctively protective?

Only Richard Nixon can answer those questions and it is possible that even he, in retrospect, may not be sure of the answers, since some of the early decisions were so lightly considered. Writers will speculate about them endlessly, as they have, with little or no authority for their conclusions about what went on in the man's mind. The preponderance of present judgment among Americans seems to be that, since he is evil, given to profanity and some obscenity, his motivation was deliberately criminal. With no less right to conjecture, it is possible to believe that his motivation was wholly patriotic, and within that goal little thought was given to alternatives or eventualities. Nixon wanted to protect his close aides from the consequences of their escapades; he wanted to protect his campaign from being harmed; he wanted to protect his administration from repeated censure; and above all he wanted to protect his opportunity to pursue his goals for the nation.

I cannot be sure how calculatingly he made that decision; it may have been wholly casual, or it may have been made with benefit of some deliberation. But I think a case can be made for his believing that, in preventing the facts of Watergate from being known, and with it the "plumbers" operation, he was doing a necessary service to his country. He may have been trying to insure that his positive programs for the nation would have the greatest possible chance for success, which would not be likely if the mandate he hoped to obtain and did obtain on November 7

---

4. Victor Lasky, *It Didn't Start with Watergate* (New York: The Dial Press, 1977).

was severely marred, or even lost, by disclosures of impropriety in his organization. In this manner he could reason that, since he was not covering acts of his own, the national benefits of the coverup far outweighed the normal objections of conscience.

Just as some of his top associates thought in the case of the "plumbers" that a little bit of illegality was permissible to counter the potential damage to national security caused by persistent and sometimes illegal leaks, so could he have concluded that some drastic action was necessary to prevent his objectives for the nation from being undermined. That line of thought would not be unlikely in a man so totally dedicated to his mission and so sure of his course. He grabbed at the straws offered by his key subordinates, trusted them, cussed out all concerned, and returned to his desk.

Then when the propped-up structure began to collapse, as McCord, Dean, and the other culprits one by one began to walk out from under, the frustration at the top was unbearable. The wild thrashing around for something to grab onto for survival generated brusque profanity and light obscenity on the inside, and mistruths and equivocation on the outside. The oppressive struggle with a problem that wouldn't be solved drove him to desperation and his greatest mistakes, because then he lost touch with reality and no longer could cope. Suddenly it was a hopeless coverup that stumbled on erratically until it eventually fell apart in all directions. Desperate firings and hirings, speeches, press conferences, and counter-posed leaks served little purpose to stem the tide once the dam had broken. The President had no choice but to abdicate. He had lost everything.

None of this excuses the actions, but it does rationalize them. However one divides the unfulfilled responsibility among those in the play, there still remains the necessity to balance out the failings of Richard Nixon in this one series of events against his worthy deeds as a lifetime public servant.

What about the tapes which so harshly seem to indict him in his own words? The expletives, I believe, should be dismissed, not because they are in any sense proper, but because they can be condoned under the pressures of the office. Dwight Eisenhower could be as caustically profane as Richard Nixon; I heard him many times. Lyndon Johnson was noted for vulgar expressions. I doubt that Harry Truman or John Kennedy were much more pious under the stress of tough decisions or unnerving frustrations.

Only a tiny fraction of the tapes has been made public. Who knows what genius or generosity by Nixon may be contained in those not revealed? Again, time and events may bring about a more favorable balance of evidence.

Why was there a taping system at all? On this I have no difficulty in accepting his own reply. He wanted the tapes to preserve a record of history in the making. Being distrustful of the daily media and their impact on the writing of history, he wanted incontrovertible first-hand evidence to back his own accounts of how events were handled in his administration. He was not the first President to use this device for that purpose, but he did it on a larger scale. Ironically, their worst parts turned the public against him, without anyone knowing what the best parts might have recorded.

New developments of recent years are making some of Nixon's actions less discreditable than they were once made to appear. In the House Judiciary hearings in 1974 there was strong contention that he had misused the forces of government agencies for political purposes, by getting them to spy on and punish enemies of his regime, and this became one of the counts of impeachment. It was not publicly known then, but subsequent revelations have established, that Presidential use of the FBI, the CIA, the IRS, and the Postal Service to exercise surveillance over radical and revolutionary groups dangerous to the nation extended at least as far back as Franklin D. Roosevelt. Employing these agencies to target political adversaries was no less common, and in some instances much more frequent and intensive.[5] As author M. Stanton Evans has written, "In the light of these disclosures it is plain that Nixon, whatever his sins, was hopelessly outclassed in public infamy by the likes of Franklin Roosevelt, John Kennedy, and Lyndon Johnson. Yet it was Nixon who caught and continues to catch the brickbats, while these Democratic heroes have

---

5. This case is fully documented in Lasky's book *It Didn't Start with Watergate*.

somehow avoided media censure."[6,7]

Granted that the civil rights of our citizens are inviolable, it would seem that subversive actions that deliberately violate the nation's security, or the property, security, and lives of individuals, would bring into question the rights of the perpetrators to unhindered reliance on the full protection of the laws. There is precedent over the years for Presidential actions that assume some degree of latitude in meeting emergencies. If a President does not act in such instances he may be surrendering the lives of innocent people in exchange for those of terrorists and extremists.

In some democratic nations there are ample tools, such as the British Official Secrets Act, that provide authority for executive action to protect the sovereignty of the nation. In the absence of specific statutes along such lines, I believe the American citizenry would still expect the Chief Executive to cope with such forces by exercising his inherent powers in order to "insure domestic tranquility and provide for the common defense." The alternative of default is unthinkable.

It is easy now to forget the political and social climate which Nixon inherited and which he ultimately turned around in his first term. The unpopular Vietnam war, which had accelerated during the Johnson Administration to a point at which more than a half million men were endangered in that small, distant country, with deaths of more than 300 a week and thousands injured, had produced widespread disaffection. The youth of the country were, understandably, in revolt against the whole adventure. Political differences were wide—between a Goldwater calling for all-out victory and a McGovern demanding

---

6. *National Review*, May 27, 1977, p. 626.

7. Renata Adler, a member of the staff of the House Judiciary Committee in the impeachment inquiry, in a retrospective article in *Atlantic Monthly* in November 1976, confirmed this: " ... with every document published by the Senate Select Committee with Respect to Intelligence Activities (the Church Committee), it was becoming more clear that the case for the impeachment of Richard Nixon, in 1974, had fallen apart .... In view of the Church Committee's account of the conduct of previous administrations, including violations of law and abuses of power since at least 1936, the first two Articles [of impeachment] seemed to dissolve; as to [the third Article], there had been disagreement about it from the start .... The problem with all three Articles, and with their accompanying Summary of Information and Final Report, and with the thirty-odd volumes of Statements of Information ... is that ... all those volumes never quite made their case or any case."

instant withdrawal. To many, the nation's pride rode on the outcome. To others, a social revolution required abandonment of many traditional values, including patriotism. Flags were burned in protest; draft cards were publicly torn up. Violence begot violence, and public attention exalted leaders of violence. It was a distressing time in the nation's life—one of great tension and polarization, of angry demonstration and vicious name calling, and of talk about overthrowing the government. Worse, it was a period in which judges and policemen were being murdered, ordinary citizens kidnapped and highjacked, and life was insecure; when public buildings, even the United States Capitol, were being bombed, and riots were gutting parts of our cities. It was age of revolution, guerrillas, and terrorism.

This was a time to try the soul and the capacity of any President, and it was Nixon's misfortune that when he took office he had to walk directly into the limelight with the task of extricating the nation, with some semblance of honor, from the Vietnam conflict and quiet the strident forces in the nation. It is understandable that, in the course of that mission, he would think it necessary to use strong tactics against those he considered to be the leaders of the subversion and the contributors to its force.

There is much less to be said for such things as investigating the tax returns of Larry O'Brien or bugging the phones of Martin Luther King, but there is merit in the idea that, after all, the beneficiaries of such special attentions need to fear for their actions only if they have something illegal, improper, or immoral to hide. But this rationalization does not justify invading the privacy of persons to fish for improprieties that might be politically useful to the discoverer.

It seems true now that Nixon did no worse than two or three of his predecessors in using this kind of power to protect the country, safeguard his administration, or harass his enemies. However, precedent does not justify wrongdoing. While the precedents set by others in office before him may not excuse some of Nixon's apparent misuse of investigative agencies, they certainly do make his actions easier to comprehend, and they do raise the question of whether he was not grossly over-maligned and over-punished for them. In my heart, I cannot seriously fault Nixon on this count.

One of the regrettable effects of Nixon's downfall is the damage it did to the Republican party. The coalition he had put together in 1972 ending in a landslide might well have been preserved to keep the party in power for another twenty-five years especially with him in the continuing role of respected elder statesman. The impression that Republican principles were more responsible and that liberal Democratic concepts, exemplified by McGovern, were irresponsible was widely current. The election had reversed the strengths of the two parties much as Roosevelt had reversed them in 1932.

The public reacted strongly to Watergate in the Congressional elections of 1974, turning out Republican Senators, Representatives, Governors, and state legislators. Once again, as it did after 1964, the question of the continued viability of the party began to surface among the commentators. Goldwater had gone down because he was viewed as too extreme. Nixon had fallen because he was viewed as corrupt. Both were personal issues, not defaults by the part as a whole. For the same reason that I did not expect the demise of the party after Goldwater's disastrous defeat, I did not see it as inevitable after Nixon's departure under pressure.

The advantage of the two-party system is its offering of alternative choices to the electorate. As a minority party, temporarily wounded, the Republicans may face a dry spell before they regain important political power, but that need not be long. Voters vote against candidates as much as or more than they vote for them, and a combination of an unsatisfying Democratic administration and a new leadership of the Republicans is probably all that is necessary for the two to be restored to an oscillating parity. Nixon's acts did hurt the Republican party, seriously but not fatally.

It has become commonplace for observers to write off the whole web of Watergate as proof of Lord Acton's famed maxim that "power tends to corrupt, and absolute power corrupts absolutely." Anyone who challenges this application of the rule may be in the minority, but I do not see it as appropriate here. Watergate happened at the center because Richard Nixon was an ambitious man who wanted power not to accumulate personal gain but to be able to serve his country better. It happened in the concentric circles near him because those persons were loyal to his mission, and in their eagerness to help attain it went too far. It happened to people in the outer fringes because they trusted implicitly those in the inner reaches. No one sought to gain wealth for himself . . . not a Magruder, or a Mitchell, or a Kalmbach, or any of the others. They were evincing their dedication to a cause, and the intensity of that dedication led them astray. It had happened in earlier administrations, too, sometimes with similar motives, and sometimes with more mercenary objectives, but then the standards of integrity were less strictly enforced and the powers of the media were less developed. Nixon was a generation too late; in an earlier decade he would have escaped his fate.

In short, I cannot dismiss or alter Nixon's part in the Watergate affair, or the other actions that forced his resignation, but I can comprehend how they may have happened. My hope is that, for those who prefer to believe in the inherent goodness of every man, some of his tarnish will be removed when the cruel glare of past publicity dissolves under the more kindly light of reason and the settling passage of time. It would seem appropriate that Richard Nixon, the President who dedicated his life to public service, who believed it was his destiny to find world peace, but who faltered and fell over a minor obstacle in his desperate desire to be a great President, be remembered as a man who tried too hard to reach his goals.

In fairness to his motives, and with a degree of charity that forgives some of his methods, would not the following make a proper epitaph to his career:

Richard Nixon
The President Who Tried Too Hard

# POSTSCRIPT

Nothing in this book is intended to be taken as challenging equitable and even-handed justice. Nor is any of it intended to be taken as a justification for wrongdoing. The laws must be enforced.

Nothing that is said should be deemed to question the right of government investigators to search out information by legitimate means; of prosecutors to take to court persons they believe to be guilty of criminal acts; of public interest organizations to crusade for causes on the basis of uninflated reasons; of news hawks and their outlets to report honestly presented factual news; of Congressional committees to seek information in an orderly way to improve the laws; or of politicians to campaign forcefully on the issues of the day.

The theses herein, wholly consistent with these premises, are: that repetitive investigations of the same subject matter can constitute harassment, and that public revelation of the subjects and targets of investigation is unduly damaging; that prosecutions on flimsy charges are inappropriate and the use of underhand tactics, threats, and concealment by prosecutors are unconscionable; that violation of the privacy of individuals is not a proper function of journalism; that speculation and premature disclosure are unsuitable tactics of reporting, and that mistakes should be fully and publicly corrected; that Congressional hearings involving public policy should not be blatant political forums or trial courts; that public interest organizations should be held accountable for distortions and untruths; and that politicians should not play games with the truth in order to destroy their opposition.

Most important of all, that each of these groups of our society recognize that the individuals they sometimes grind to earth by their ambitious, heartless tactics are living, breathing human beings.

Watergate demonstrates the necessity of drawing a line somewhere between what is proper and what is improper in these activities. The problem is to decide where fairness ends. What is the line between fair and unfair enforcement? What is the line between fair and unfair journalism? What is the line between fair and unfair public advocacy? What is the line between fair and unfair political action? It seems clear that a need has been demonstrated for society to address itself to these questions, thereby to determine what is in its interest and what is not, what is reasonable action and what is unwarranted license. This ought to be resolved before much more mischief is done.

Watergate exacted many prices. It is not very material to learn whether the actual expenditures of the government in running down its ramifications was a probable $25 million or a possible $50 million. And there is no accounting for the direct time of members of the Congress, the Judiciary, the Department of Justice and other executive departments, and the White House, and the divided attention to duties during the period of high drama. How much better the nation might have been managed without the pursuit of Watergate to distract its servants is wholly in the realm of conjecture.

The real cost of Watergate, because there were no lines of demarcation between fairness and unfairness in the pertinent disciplines, must be assessed in human terms—what happened to the individuals, their families, their careers, their reputations, their health, their lives. This is the best measure of the quality of justice, and in Watergate it was unjustifiably high because its sweep was unreasonably wide.

No one can condone Watergate. It was a criminal disgrace,

unaccountably stupid from the first meeting in the office of the Attorney General to talk about covert tactics, through the crassness of the cover-up and the unrealistic belief that a crime known to so many people could be indefinitely concealed, to the demeaning act of a vindictive Congress in denying to a resigned President the money to answer his mail.

Historians with a duty, psychologists with curiosity, politicians with speeches to make, and writers with space to fill will probe, analyze, and relive Watergate at stylish intervals long beyond the end of this century. No one can know with certainty all the motives of the guilty persons or the extent of ultimate damage done to the nation and the world. For those who are guilty, however, it can only be hoped that the eventual appraisal of history will fairly balance their good with their bad, something that could not happen in the electrified atmosphere of 1972 to 1975. For those innocents who were trampled in the rush to judgment by the media, the politicians, and a scandalized public, it is essential in the interest of justice that their reputations not be left permanently clouded and sullied in newspaper morgues, but that somehow they be given the public vindication to which they are entitled.

There is work to be done.

# INDEX

Abourezk, James, 28, 39
Abplanalp, Robert, 70, 132
Accounting, social responsibility of, 92-94
Accounting Hall of Fame, 109
Acton, Lord, 458
Adams, Sherman, 451
Adler, Polly, 227
Adler, Renata, 456n
Advance men, expenditures of, 138, 144
Agnew, Spiro, 32, 49, 144, 172, 260-261, 265, 443
Akeley, Carl, 86
Albright, Joseph P., 56n
Alexander, Herbert E., 43n, 164n, 168n, 283
Alexander Grant & Company, 88-89, 91, 94, 96
Alger, Horatio, 85, 86, 87
*All the President's Men* (book), 65n, 224, 428n, 431-32
*All the President's Men* (film) 216n
Allen, Richard, 184n
Allen, Robert, 55, 187, 211, 212, 215, 277
Allott, Gordon, 224
Ambassadorships
    appellate court on contributions and, 403, 404
    to contributors, 141
    Kalmbach and sale of, 21n, 180n
    rejected offers for, 187, 188, 337-38
    supposed sale of, 14, 20-21, 55, 180-81, 263, 395, 405
American Accounting Association, 92
American Airlines, 24-27, 381, 396
American Bar Association, 349
"American Business in 1990" (White House conference), 150
American Civil Liberties Union, 205
American Dental Association, 405
American Institute of Certified Public Accountants (*formerly* American Institute of Accountants), 89, 92
    author's trial before, 383-84
American Shipbuilding Company, 24-26, 43, 406
American Telephone & Telegraph, 130

AMPI, *see* Milk industry
Anderson, Jack, 219, 243, 250, 263, 354, 419-20
    grand jury transcripts secured by, 428
Anderson, John B., 399
Anderson, Robert B., 133
Andreas, Dwayne O., 51, 207-10, 215, 217n, 219, 222, 243, 277, 297
Andrews, Roy Chapman, 86
Angle, Martha, 426
AP (Associated Press), 253-54, 262, 291, 355
Arab contributions, alleged, 183-84
Arctic research, 177
Arizona, Republican offices fire-bombed in, 16
Arnold, Martin, 356
Ashbrook, John, 203
Ashland Oil, Inc., 24-27, 36-37, 41, 272-73, 381n
Ashland Petroleum Gabon, 24
Associated Milk Producers, Inc., *see* Milk industry
Association of State Democratic Chairmen, 81, 248, 251
Atkins, Orin, 273-74

Babcock, Tim, 29, 373-74
Bahamas, FCRP alleged to have transferred funds through, 182, 184, 264
Baker, Bobby, 285, 404, 406
Baker, Howard, 266n, 270, 271n, 272, 279, 424
Baker, Russell, 263
Barker, Bernard L., 12, 15
    Mexican bank checks in account of, 207-13, 216-19, 222, 231-35, 237-47, 252, 275
    notarization case against, 218-20
Barker, Raymond Charles, 335
Barker, Robert, 267, 271, 275, 282, 306, 308, 337, 342, 377
Barnes, Walter T., 32
Barrick, Paul, 63, 156, 174, 191, 221, 276
Barth, Roger, 51
Bartlett, Charles, 368, 422-24